𝕹𝖊𝖜 𝖆𝖓𝖉 𝕴𝖒𝖕𝖗𝖔𝖛𝖊𝖉 𝕰𝖉𝖎𝖙𝖎𝖔𝖓.

A

LEXICON

OF

FREEMASONRY:

CONTAINING

A DEFINITION OF ALL ITS COMMUNICABLE TERMS,
NOTICES OF ITS HISTORY, TRADITIONS,
AND ANTIQUITIES,

AND AN ACCOUNT OF ALL THE RITES AND MYSTERIES OF THE
ANCIENT WORLD.

BY

ALBERT G. MACKEY, M.D.

AUTHOR OF THE "MYSTIC TIE,"

*Grand Secretary and Grand Lecturer of the Grand Lodge of South Carolina; Secretary General
of the Supreme Council, Thirty-third Degree, for the Southern Jurisdiction of the
United States; G∴H∴P∴ of the Grand Chapter of South Carolina, etc.*

Φθέγξομαι οἶς θέμις ἐστὶ, θύρας δ' ἐπίθεσθε βεβήλοις.—ΟΡΦ.
"I will reveal to those to whom it is lawful,
But close the door against the uninitiated."
ORPHIC HYMN.

1860.

A Lexicon of Freemasonry
by Albert G. Mackey
foreword by Michael R. Poll

A Cornerstone Book
Published by Cornerstone Book Publishers
Copyright © 2014 & 2020 by Cornerstone Book Publishers

Cornerstone Book Publishers
Hot Springs Village, AR

First Cornerstone Edition – 2014
Second Cornerstone Edition - 2020

www.cornerstonepublishers.com

ISBN: 9781613423554

TO

Brother Albert Pike,

OF ARKANSAS,

GRAND HIGH PRIEST, S∴P∴R∴S∴ Etc.

My Dear Sir and Brother:

The second edition of this work was dedicated to a learned and venerable brother, the Hon. Thomas Douglas, of Florida, as a slight tribute to his many virtues. In offering a third edition to the public, I gladly avail myself of the opportunity to inscribe your name upon its pages, as a memorial of our friendship and a token of my high appreciation of your character as a learned and indefatigable student of masonic literature.

I am, as ever, yours fraternally,

ALBERT G. MACKEY, M. D.

PREFACE TO THE FIRST EDITION.

THE title-page of this work will sufficiently explain the nature of its contents. It is intended to furnish the inquirer, by an easy mode of reference, with a definition of all the terms peculiar to our order—an explanation of the symbols with which it abounds—a record of its numerous histories and traditions—and an illustration of the various points of difficulty which are continually embarrassing the progress of the Masonic student.

The time has passed when a Mason could expect to obtain the reputation of a skilful workman by a mere hackneyed knowledge of the ritual of our order. Something more than this, the Master who desires to perform his duties faithfully and well, must bring to the pedestal. The intelligent brother will expect from him who sits in the place of wisdom, not only an ability to explain the ceremonies which distinguish our institution, but a capacity to trace them to their primitive source, and a knowledge of the history and antiquities of the order.

The numerous instructive works, that have lately issued from the press on the *science* of Freemasonry, render it now inexcusable that the Mason should be without some portion of that knowledge which is hereafter to be demanded as the test of a skilful workman. To give to every brother an opportunity of obtaining the necessary information, by placing before him, in a compendious form, the matter scattered through many volumes, some of which are, in this country, rare and generally inaccessible, is the object of the Lexicon now presented to the public.

A work of this kind has, hitherto, I believe, been unknown in our language. Glossaries of all the arts and sciences abound, but Freemasonry is without its appropriate Dictionary. How I have supplied this defect is not for me, but for my readers, to judge.

The difficulties, however, of arranging the materials of an extensive subject in alphabetical order, for the first time, and without any preceding guide, are such, that it has been found impossible to avoid the omission, in their proper places, of a few articles. These have been added in a *Supplement*, to which the inspector is referred for any word which he shall fail to find in the body of the work.

This work, though the labour of years, is still, I know, imperfect. Yet, " with all its imperfections on its head," I present it to my brethren, because I know that I am not asking more than I shall receive, when I crave—for its excellencies, their candid consideration—for its errors, their fraternal indulgence.

A. G. MACKEY.

CHARLESTON, S. C., *March* 12, 1845.

Foreword to the Cornerstone Edition

Someone once told me that people born in a city are far more suspicious than country folk. I grew up in a city, but on a military base (my father was an Army Colonel), so I was never really sure as to how my thinking was defined. But I do know that when I joined Freemasonry, my thinking on pretty much everything changed. Right out of the gate, I was put in the charge of someone who I had no choice but to trust. I knew full well that, if he wanted to, he could make a tremendous fool out of me. But he didn't. I could tell by the tone of his voice and his actions that he knew what he was doing. He was worthy of my trust. I was told later on that everything that happened was designed to teach (among other things) a lesson of trust. I was told that we can, and should, trust our Brothers because they *are* our Brothers. That brought back a flood of memories of my Grandfather who died when I was only 12. He was the reason that I wanted to become a Mason. One of the things I remember of him was something that he said about Freemasonry and trust. He said that he would trust a Mason he did not know alone in his home with all of his valuables. A few years ago, I asked a Mason I knew if he would do the same. He laughed and said that he is not crazy and that he would trust *no one* he did not know alone in his home with his valuables. How interesting.

My father was a WWII veteran. I remember him talking about trust and those who he served with in combat. He said that trust in those around you during that time was absolutely necessary. He said that in order to survive you had to be completely sure that the guy next to you had your back and was going to be there when needed. He said that when the fighting started, their training kicked in and everything that they did was a result of their training. He trusted them because he knew how they were trained (educated) and that they were worthy of trust. I thought a lot about what he said.

A buddy of mine served in Vietnam. He told a different story than my Dad. He said that towards the end of the conflict, when new troops came in, they were immediately sent to the front. None of the ones who had been around a while wanted to be anywhere near them. When I asked him why, he said that it was because they were dangerous. Towards the end of the conflict, basic training was minimal. The ones who had been around a while knew that the training of the new guys was so lacking that not only would they likely get themselves killed but all those around them. I found that as interesting as what my father had told me.

I've been a Mason now for going on 45 years. Just like I have changed in that time, so has Freemasonry changed. Some changes are for the good and some not so good. One of the "not so good" changes was our fear of declining membership some years back. Lodges were losing members and not getting new ones to replace the ones lost. We started taking in some who we may not have taken at one time. We also started moving those who joined into leadership positions before they even knew the difference between a Landmark and a pancake breakfast. We traded education for fellowship. While we may not have seen it, we started becoming something else — something other than Freemasonry. To make it worse, it came on so slowly that most of us did not even notice the change.

Make no mistake, Freemasonry has serious problems. The "lack of training" of too many of our members has resulted in them viewing Freemasonry as only another club. Too many do not understand who or what we are and allow ego combined with bad judgement to crcate seriously damaging situations. Our choice is to deal with the problems or watch our foundation crumble.

Recently, I read of a young girl who was attacked by an alligator. While being bitten, this child had the presence of mind to shove both of her thumbs into the alligator's nostrils. She remembered that this is what she was told to do if she was ever attacked. The alligator could not breath, opened its mouth, and that allowed her to free herself so that she could get away. We need the same calm, presence of mind. We need the balance of both competent Masonic education and the backbone to reduce the unruly to order — to do what is needed. Weakness in either area can result in our failure.

The reason my father trusted those around him in WWII was because he knew that they had received proper training. The reason my friend *did not* trust those around him in the later part of the Vietnam War was because he questioned their training. Far too often, even the Masters of Lodges are completely unable to answer the most basic questions on the history, philosophy, laws, or customs of Freemasonry. It is very reasonable to question their training, their Masonic education and knowledge of Freemasonry. Is it any wonder that trust is lacking in Masonry? If we are unable to trust our Brothers or have reasonable doubt in their abilities, then we tear at the fabric of who we claim to be. We want to trust our Brothers, we need to trust our Brothers, and if we can't, it damages us at our core.

As with most everything, Freemasonry has a choice. We can act or we can sit back and do nothing. I believe that to do nothing seals an extremely bad fate for us. But I also believe that to do the wrong thing will bring equally undesirable results. I believe that the ability to know right from wrong comes from our training, our teachings. It's not enough that we say that we are Freemasons, we need to *be* Freemasons. We need to know who and what we are, and live it. We are seriously sick, and we need to take a very bitter pill. We need proper Masonic education. We need to make sure that all of our members (especially those who lead us) understand our unique laws, customs, words, phrases, and philosophy. We need to be firm about this education. Without education or "training," we cannot trust our Brothers. As difficult as it may seem, those who cannot or do not wish to learn, cannot lead us in any manner. We simply cannot trust an untrained Mason. The choice as to what we do about our current situation is ours.

Albert Mackey's *A Lexicon of Freemasonry* is proven and sound Masonic education. It provides a foundation for any serious Freemason. Of course, it will provide nothing if you place it into a bookshelf and leave it there unread. But, if you study this book, talk about it with your Brothers, and make the serious attempt to learn from the education provide, you will help turn us around. But don't stop with this one book. Develop a hunger for Masonic education and devour as many like book as possible. Be the proverbial "life-long EA," the ones who makes it his life mission to grow each day of this life. With this, you will be the Mason you can be.

Michael R. Poll
Cornerstone Book Publishers

LEXICON OF FREEMASONRY.

A

ABBREVIATIONS. Abbreviations are much more in use among French than among English or American Masons. An alphabetical list, however, of those principally employed, is appended for the benefit of such as may be engaged in the examination of masonic writings. It must be observed, that a masonic abbreviation is generally distinguished by three points in a triangular form (thus, ∴) following the letter: various attempts have been made to explain the origin of these dots, but if they have any allusion at all, we presume it to be to the three lesser lights placed in a triangular form around the altar, or, as they were first introduced by our French brethren, they may refer to the situation of the three principal officers of the lodge in the French rite, where the Master sits in the east and the two Wardens in the west. Ragon says that the three points were first used on the 12th of August, 1774, by the Grand Orient of France in an address to its subordinates.

A∴ Dep∴ *Anno Depositionis.* In the year of the deposit. The date used by Royal and Select Masters.

A∴ Inv∴ *Anno Inventionis.* In the year of the discovery. The date used in Royal Arch Masonry.

A∴ L∴ *Anno Lucis.* In the year of light. The date used in Ancient Craft Masonry.

A∴ L∴ G∴ D∴ G∴ A∴ D∴ L∴ U∴ *A la Gloire du Grand Architecte de l' Univers.* To the glory of the Grand Architect of the Universe. The caption of all French Masonic writings.

A∴ L'O∴ A l'Orient, or at the East. The seat of the lodge. (*French.*)

A∴ M∴ Anno Mundi, or in the year of the world. The date used in the Ancient and Accepted or Scotch rite.

A∴ O∴ Anno Ordinis, or in the year of the Order. The date used by Knights Templars.

B∴ A∴ Buisson Ardente, or Burning Bush. (*French.*)

B∴ B∴ Burning Bush. These two abbreviations are found in the caption of documents of the Ancient and Accepted rite.

C∴ C∴ Celestial Canopy. Another abbreviation found in the same documents.

E∴ A∴ Entered Apprentice.

F∴ Frère, or Brother. (*French.*)

F∴ C∴ Fellow Craft.

FF∴ Frères, or Brethren. (*French.*)

G∴ Grand.

G∴ L∴ Grand Lodge.

G∴ M∴ Grand Master.

I∴ T∴ N∴ O∴ T∴ G∴ A∴ O∴ T∴ U∴ In the name of the Grand Architect of the Universe. Sometimes found at the head of English diplomas.

J∴ W∴ Junior Warden.

M∴ M∴ Mois Maçonnique, or masonic month. (*French.*) March is the first masonic month among French Masons.

M∴ M∴ Master Mason.

M∴ W∴ Most Worshipful.

R∴ A∴ Royal Arch.

R∴ +∴ Rose Croix. The mark attached to their signature, by those who are in possession of the degree of Prince of Rose Croix.

R∴ ☐ Respectable loge, or Worshipful lodge. (*French.*)

R∴ W∴ Right Worshipful.

S∴ P∴ R∴ S∴ Sublime Prince of the Royal Secret.

S∴ S∴ S∴ Trois fois salut, or thrice greeting. The caption of French masonic writings.

S.·. W.·. Senior Warden.

T.·. G.·. A.·. O.·. T.·. U.·. The Grand Architect of the Universe.

V.·. Vénérable, or Worshipful. (*French.*)

V.·. L.·. Vraie lumière, or true light. (*French.*)

V.·. W.·. Very Worshipful.

W.·. M.·. Worshipful Master.

☐. An oblong square is the sign adopted for the word "lodge."

🗗. Two squares indicate the plural, or "lodges."

ABIF. A Hebrew word אביו, signifying "his father." The word *ab*, or *father*, was a title of honour "often used," says Adam Clarke, "in Hebrew, to signify a master, inventor, or chief operator." In this sense it is used in II Chronicles, ch. iv. v. 16, where it is said, "the pots also, and the shovels, and the flesh hooks, and all their instruments, did Huram his father, (*Huram abif*,) make to King Solomon." The Greek, Latin, French, and English versions, translate the Hebrew words literally as "Hiram his father," but Luther in his German version has preserved the spirit of the original by writing "mochte Huram Abif," looking upon this latter word as a title of honour bestowed by Solomon on his chief builder. See *Hiram the Builder*.

ABLUTION. A purification by water, whereby, in some of the higher degrees of masonry, the candidate is supposed, as in the religious systems of antiquity, to be cleansed from the taint of an inferior and less pure condition, so as to be prepared for initiation into a higher and purer degree. See *Lustration*

ABRAXAS. In the MS. found by Mr. Locke in the Bodleian library, the original of which is said to have been in the hand-writing of King Henry VI., it is asserted that Masons conceal, among other secret arts in their possession, "the facultye of

2

Abrao." This is an evident allusion to the word Abraxas, which was the name applied by the arch-heretic Basilides to the Supreme Deity, from whom all other deities were emanations, being seven in number, with 365 virtues, which were typified by the numerical value in Greek of the word, as is shown below. It, like the incommunicable name of God among the Jews, was supposed to be possessed of magical virtues. Abraxas was also the name of small statues, on which were inscribed figures of the Egyptian gods, combined with Hebrew and Zoroasteric symbols, and characters in a variety of languages. According to Beausobre and Lardner, these stones were mostly of Egyptian origin. The deity Abraxas is said to be identical with Mithras or the sun. The letters of both names, taken according to their numerical value in the Greek language, amount exactly to 365, thus :

a	=	1	μ	=	40
β	=	2	ϵ	=	5
ρ	=	100	ι	=	10
a	=	1	θ	=	9
ξ	=	60	ρ	=	100
a	=	1	a	=	1
ς	=	200—365	ς	=	200—365

The word Abraxas is of uncertain origin. Saumaise says that it is purely Egyptian, and should properly be pronounced Abrasax. Beausobre, in his History of Manicheism, enters into a long etymological disquisition to prove that it is derived from two Greek words Ἀβρος Σαω, and signifies "the magnificent Saviour, he who heals and preserves." Ἀβρος is also an epithet of the sun, and hence we again come to the conclusion that Mithras and Abraxas are identical.

It was therefore typical of the annual course of the earth around the sun, constituting the solar year, and was a part of the sun worship of the first seceders from pure Freemasonry.

It is a singular coincidence, that Belenus, the deity of the Gauls, and who is supposed from his form and ornaments to be identical with Mithras, was also equivalent, in the numerical value of the letters of his name in Greek, to 365, thus:—

β	η	λ	ε	ν	ο	ς
2,	8,	30,	5,	50,	70,	200—365.

ABSENCE. It is contrary to the principles of Freemasonry, to inflict pecuniary fines for non-attendance. The obligations and duties inculcated by the order are of such a nature, as to compel the attendance of its members who are without reasonable excuse. It would, therefore, be a descent in the grade of punishment, and manifestly tend to weaken the solemn nature of those obligations which every member and officer contracts, were the lodge to attempt the imposition of any trifling pecuniary penalty for inexcusable absence. The regular attendance of each brother, at his lodge, is strictly insisted on in the ancient charges, which prescribed as a rule, " that no Master or Fellow could be absent from the lodge, especially when warned to appear at it, without incurring a severe censure, until it appeared to the Master and Wardens that pure necessity hindered him." This regulation has been perpetuated by the modern constitutions.

ACACIA. The ancient name of a plant, most of whose species are evergreen, and six of which, at least, are natives of the East. The acacia of Freemasonry is the Mimosa Nilotica of Linnæus, a shrub which grew in great abundance in the neighbourhood of Jerusalem. According to the Jewish law, no interments were permitted within the walls of the city, and as it was unlawful for the cohens or priests to pass over a grave, it became necessary to place marks wherever a dead body had been interred, to enable them to avoid it. For this purpose, the acacia was used. Much of the masonic history of the acacia is incommunicable, but it may be permitted to say, that its evergreen nature, united to other circumstances, is intended to remind us of the immortality of the soul. The Greek work αχαχια signifies "innocence or freedom from sin;" and Hutchinson, who

fancifully supposes the Master's to be a Christian degree, exemplifying the rise of the Christian dispensation after the destruction of the Mosaic, alluding to this Greek meaning of acacia,
says that it implies "that the sins and corruptions of the old
law, and devotees of the Jewish altar, had hid religion from
those who sought her, and she was only to be found where *innocence* survived, and under the banner of the divine lamb." (Spirit
of Masonry, p. 99.) Without adopting this heresy, we shall
find abundant reason for admiring the propriety of the Greek
meaning, as applied to him whose history is, in our order, most
closely connected with the acacia. Coincident with the acacia,
were the palm of the Egyptian mysteries, the myrtle of the
Grecian, and the mistletoe of the Druids.

ACACIAN. A term derived from *αχαχια*, "innocence," and
signifying a Mason, who, by living in strict obedience to the
obligations and precepts of the fraternity, is free from sin. First
used, I believe, by Hutchinson.

ACCEPTED. A title which, as applied to Freemasons, is
equivalent to the term "initiated." It alludes to the acceptance
into their society, by operative Masons, of those who were not
operatives. An Accepted Mason is one who has been adopted
into the order, and received the freedom of the society, as is the
case with other companies in Europe. This is evident from the
regulations made on St. John's day, 1663, under the Grand
Mastership of the Earl of St. Albans, where the word is repeatedly used in this sense. Thus: "No person hereafter, who
shall be *accepted* a Freemason, shall be admitted into any lodge
or assembly, until he has brought a certificate of the time and
place of his *acceptation*, from the lodge that *accepted* him, unte
the Master of that limit or division where such lodge is kept."
And again: "No person shall be *made* or *accepted* a Freemason,
unless," etc.

ACCLAMATION. A certain form of words used in connexion with the battery. In the Scotch rite it is *huzza;* in French, *vivat;* and, in the rite of Misraim, *hallelujah.* In the York, it is *so mote it be.*

ACHAD. Hebrew אחד. One of the masonic names of God, signifying *the one.* It is derived from the passage in Deuteronomy vi. 4: "Hear, O Israel: the Lord our God is (*achad*) one."

ACHISHAR. He is mentioned in 1 Kings iv. 6, under the name of *Ahishar,* as being "over the household." He was the steward, or, as Adam Clarke says, the chamberlain of Solomon. The masonic spelling of the name, *Achishar,* is more consonant with the Hebrew than that adopted by the English translators of the Bible. He is one of the persons referred to in the degree of Select Master.

ACKNOWLEDGED. Candidates who are invested with the Most Excellent Master's degree, are said to be "received and acknowledged" as such; because, as the possession of that degree supposes a more intimate knowledge of the science of masonry, the word *acknowledged* is used to intimate that such a character is conceded to its possessors. The word *received* conveys an allusion to the original reception of the first M. E. Masters by King Solomon.

ACTING GRAND MASTER. By the constitutions of England, whenever a prince of the blood royal accepts the office of Grand Master, he is empowered to appoint a peer of the realm as Acting Grand Master.

ADMISSION. The requisites for admission into our order are somewhat peculiar. The candidate must be free born, under no bondage, of at least twenty-one years of age, in the possession of sound senses, free from any physical defect or dismember-

2*

ment, and of irreproachable manners, or, as it is technically
termed, "under the tongue of good report." No atheist, eunuch,
or woman can be admitted. The requisites as to age, sex, and
soundness of body, have reference to the operative character
of the institution. We can only expect able workmen in able-
bodied men. The mental and religious qualifications refer to the
duties and obligations which a Freemason contracts. An idiot
could not understand them, and an atheist would not respect them.
Even those who possess all these necessary qualifications can be
admitted only under certain regulations. Not more than five
candidates can be received at one time except in urgent cases,
when a dispensation may be granted by the Grand Master, and
no applicant can receive more than two degrees on the same day.
To the last rule there can be no exception.

ADONIRAM. The principal receiver of King Solomon's tribute, and the chief overseer of the 30,000 brethren who were
sent to cut the timber for the temple in the forests of Lebanon.
He is introduced in the degrees of Secret and Perfect Master,
and Intendant of the Building, in the Scotch rite, and in the
degree of Royal Master. He is said to have married a sister of
Hiram the Builder.

ADONIRAMITE MASONRY. *Maçonnerie Adonhiramite.*
This rite was established in France at the close of the eighteenth
century. It consists of twelve degrees, namely: 1, Entered
Apprentice; 2, Fellow Craft; 3, Master Mason; 4, Perfect Master; 5, Elect of Nine; 6, Elect of Perignan; 7, Minor Architect,
or Scotch Apprentice; 8, Grand Architect, or Scotch Fellow
Craft; 9, Scotch Master; 10, Knight of the East; 11, Knight
of Rose Croix; 12, Prussian Knight.

Of these degrees, the 6th, 7th, 8th, and 9th are peculiar to
Adoniramite Masonry; the others do not much differ from the
corresponding degrees in the ancient Scotch rite. The title of
the order is derived from Adoniram, who took charge of the

works after the loss of the principal conductor, and to the time of whose superintendence the legends of the most important degrees refer.

ADONIS, MYSTERIES OF. The mysteries which, in Egypt, the cradle of all the Pagan rites, had been consecrated to Osiris, in passing over into Phenicia were dedicated to Adonis.* According to the legend, Venus, having beheld Adonis when a child, became so enamoured of him, that she seized him, and concealing him from sight, exhibited him to Proserpine alone. But she, becoming equally enamoured of his beauty, sought to obtain possession of him. The dispute between the goddesses was reconciled by Jupiter, who decided that Adonis should dwell six months of the year with Venus, and the remaining six months with Proserpine. This decree was executed; but Adonis, who was a great hunter, was afterward killed on Mount Libanus by a wild boar, who thrust his tusk into his groin. Venus, inconsolable for his death, inundated his body with her tears, until Proserpine, in pity, restored him to life. Macrobius explains the allegory thus : "Philosophers have given the name of Venus to the superior hemisphere of which we occupy a part, and that of Proserpine to the inferior.† Hence Venus, among the Assyrians and Phenicians, is in tears, when the Sun, in his annual course through the twelve signs of the Zodiac, passes over to our antipodes. For of these twelve signs, six are said to be superior, and six inferior. When the Sun is in the inferior signs, and the days are consequently short, the goddess is supposed to weep the temporary death and privation of the Sun, detained by Proserpine, whom we regard as the divinity of the southern or

---

* *Adonis*, in the Phenician language, like *Adon* in the cognate Hebrew, signifies lord or master. The idol Tammuz, mentioned in the 8th chapter of Ezekiel, was considered by Jerome, and after him by Parkhurst, as identical with Adonis.

† By superior hemisphere, he means the Northern, and by inferior the Southern.

antipodal regions. And Adonis is said to be restored to Venus, when the Sun, having traversed the six inferior signs, enters those of our hemisphere, bringing with it an increase of light and lengthened days. The boar which is supposed to have killed Adonis is an emblem of winter; for this animal, covered with rough bristles, delights in cold, wet, and miry situations, and his favourite food is the acorn, a fruit peculiar to winter. The Sun is said, too, to be wounded by the winter, since, at that season, we lose its light and heat; effects which death produces upon animated beings. Venus is represented on Mount Libanus in an attitude of grief; her head, bent and covered with a veil, is sustained by her left hand near her breast, and her countenance is bathed with tears. This figure represents the earth in winter, when, veiled in clouds and deprived of the Sun, its powers have become torpid. The fountains, like the eyes of Venus, are overflowing, and the fields, deprived of their floral ornaments, present a joyless appearance. But when the Sun, emerging from the southern regions of the earth, passes the vernal equinox, Venus is once more rejoiced, the fields are again embellished with flowers, the grass springs up in the meadows, and the trees recover their foliage."

The cultivation of the mysteries of Adonis was propagated from Phenicia into Assyria, Babylonia, Persia, Greece, and Sicily. The celebration began in Phenicia at the period when the waters of the river Adonis, which descend from Mount Libanus, are tinged with a reddish hue derived from the colour of the soil peculiar to the mountain. The Phenician women believed that the wound of Adonis was annually renewed, and that it was his blood which coloured the stream. The phenomenon was the signal for the commencement of the rites. Every one assumed the appearance of profound grief. At Alexandria, the queen bore the statue of Adonis, accompanied by the noblest females of the city, carrying baskets of cakes, bottles of perfumes, flowers, branches of trees, and pomegranates. The procession was closed by women bearing two beds splendidly embroidered in gold and silver, one for Venus and the other for Adonis. At Athens they placed in various parts of the city the figure of a dead youth. These figures were afterward taken away by women clad in the habiliments of mourning, who celebrated their funeral rites. On the second day of the mysteries, sorrow was converted into joy, and they commemorated the resurrection of Adonis. The mysteries of Adonis were, at one time, introduced into Judea, where the Hebrew women were accustomed to hold an annual lamentation for him, under the name of Tammuz, of which Ezekiel speaks, viii. 14: "Behold there sat women weeping for Tammuz." According to Calmet and Faber, Adonis was also identical with Baal-peor, the idol of the Moabites, mentioned in the twenty-fifth chapter of Numbers.

Our knowledge of the ceremonies which accompanied the Adonisian initiation is but scanty. "The objects represented," says Duncan, "were the grief of Venus and the death and resurrection of Adonis. An entire week was consumed in these ceremonies: all the houses were covered with crape or black linen: funeral processions traversed the streets, while the devotees scourged themselves, uttering frantic cries. The orgies were then commenced, in which the mystery of the death of Adonis was depicted. During the next twenty-four hours, all the people fasted, at the expiration of which time the priests announced the resurrection of the god. Joy now prevailed, and music and dancing concluded the festivals."[*]

Julius Fermicius, a Christian writer of the fourth century, thus describes a portion of the Adonisian ceremonies :[†]

"On a certain night an image is laid out upon a bed, and bewailed in mournful strains. At length, when they are satiated

---

[*] Religions of Profane Antiquity; their Mythology, Fables, Hieroglyphics, and Doctrines. Founded on Astronomical Principles. By Jonathan Duncan, B. A. p. 350.

[†] In an oration inscribed to the Emperors Constans and Constantius. The classical reader may compare the original language of Fermicius, which I here insert: Nocte quadam simulacrum in lectica supinum ponitur, et per numeros

with their fictitious lamentation, light is introduced, and the priest, having first anointed the mouths of all those who had been weeping, whispers with a gentle murmur: *Trust ye, initiates*, for the god being saved, out of pains salvation shall arise to us."

Hence the ceremonies were a representation of the death and resurrection of Adonis in the person of the aspirant.

ADOPTIVE MASONRY. By the immutable laws of our institution, no woman can be made a Freemason. It follows, therefore, as a matter of course, that lodges which admit females to membership, can never legally exist in the order. Our French brethren, however, with that gallantry for which the nation is proverbial, have sought, by the establishment of societies, which have, indeed, but a faint resemblance to the peculiar organization of Freemasonry, to enable females to unite themselves in some sort with the masonic institution, and thus to enlist the sympathies and friendship of the gentler sex in behalf of the fraternity.

To the organizations thus established for the initiation of females, the French have given the name of "Adoptive Masonry," *maçonnerie d'adoption*, and the lodges are called *loges d'adoption*, or "adoptive lodges," because, as will hereafter be seen, every lodge of females was finally obliged to be adopted by, and under the guardianship of some regular masonic lodge.

In the beginning of the eighteenth century, several secret associations sprang up in France, which, in their external characters and mysterious rites, attempted an imitation of Freemasonry, differing, however, from that institution, of which they were, perhaps, the rivals for public favour, by their admission of female members. The ladies very naturally extolled the gallantry

---

digestis fletibus plangitur. Deinde cum se ficta lamentatione satiaverint, lumen infertur. Tunc a sacerdote omnium qui flebant, fauces unguntur quibus perunctis, sacerdos lento murmure susurrat:

Θαρρειτε μυσται του θεου σεσωσμενου
Εσται γαρ ημιν εκ πονων σωτηρια.

of these mushroom institutions, and inveighed with increased hostility against the exclusiveness of masonry. The Royal Art was becoming unpopular, and the fraternity believed themselves compelled to use strategy, and to wield in their own defence the weapons of their opponents.

At length, the Grand Orient of France, finding that these mystic societies were becoming so popular and so numerous as to endanger the permanency of the masonic institution, a new rite was established in 1774, called the "Rite of Adoption," which was placed under the control of the Grand Orient. Rules and regulations were thenceforth provided for the government of these lodges of adoption, one of which was that no men should be permitted to attend them except regular Freemasons, and that each lodge should be placed under the charge, and held under the sanction and warrant of some regularly constituted masonic lodge, whose Master, or, in his absence, his deputy, should be the presiding officer, assisted by a female President or Mistress. Under these regulations a Lodge of Adoption was opened in Paris in 1775, under the patronage of the lodge of St. Anthony, and in which the Duchess of Bourbon presided, and was installed as Grand Mistress of the Adoptive rite.

The rite of Adoption consists of four degrees, as follow:

1. Apprentice.
2. Companion.
3. Mistress.
4. Perfect Mistress.

The first, or Apprentices' degree, is simply introductory in its character, and is intended to prepare the candidate by its initiatory ceremony for the emblematic lessons which are contained in the remaining degrees.

In the second degree, or Companion, the scene of the temptation in Eden is emblematically represented, by the ceremonial of initiation, and the candidate is reminded in the course of the lecture, (for there is a lecture or catechism to each degree,) of all the unhappy results of the first sin of woman, until they terminated in the universal deluge.

The building of the Tower of Babel, and the consequent dispersion of the human race, constitute the legend of the third degree, or that of Mistress. Jacob's ladder is also introduced into the ceremonies of this degree, and the candidate is informed that it symbolically denotes the various virtues which a Mason should possess, while the Tower of Babel is an emblem of a badly regulated lodge, in which disorder and confusion are substituted for the concord and obedience which should always exist in such a place.

In the fourth degree, or that of Perfect Mistress, the officers represent Moses, Aaron, their wives, and the sons of Aaron, and the ceremonies and instructions refer to the passage of the Israelites through the wilderness, as a symbol of the passage of man and woman through this, to another and a better world.

It will be seen, from this brief sketch, that the rite of Adoption professes, in some measure, to imitate the symbolic character and design of true Freemasonry. It cannot be denied that the idea has been very ingeniously and successfully carried out.

The officers of a lodge of Adoption consist of a Grand Master and Grand Mistress, an Orator, an Inspector and an Inspectress, a Depositor and a Depositrix, a Conductor and a Conductress.* They wear a blue sash or collar, with a gold trowel suspended thereto. The Grand Master uses a mallet, with which he governs the lodge, and the same implement is placed in the hands of the Grand Mistress, the Inspector and Inspectress, and Depositor and Depositrix. Every member wears a plain white apron and white gloves.

The brethren, in addition to the insignia of their rank, wear swords and a gold ladder with five rounds, which is the proper jewel of Adoptive masonry.

---

* The Inspectress, assisted by the Inspector, acts as Senior Warden, and the Depositrix, assisted by the Depositor, as Junior Warden. The Conductress and the Conductor are the Deacons.

The business of the lodge is conducted by the sisterhood, the brethren only acting as their assistants.

The Grand Mistress, however, has very little to say or do, she being only an honorary companion to the Grand Master, which mark of distinction is conferred on her as a token of respect for her character and virtues.

The lodge-room is elegantly and tastefully decorated with emblems, which, of course, vary in each degree. In the degree of Apprentice, for instance, the room is separated by curtains into four apartments or divisions, representing the four quarters of the world, Europe, Asia, Africa, and America. The division at the entrance of the lodge represents Europe, in the middle on the right is Africa, on the left America, and at the extreme east is Asia, where are erected two splendid thrones, decorated with gold fringe, for the Grand Master and Grand Mistress. Before them is placed an altar, and on both sides, to the right and left, are eight statues, representing Wisdom, Prudence, Strength, Temperance, Honour, Charity, Justice, and Truth. The members sit on each side in straight lines, the sisters in front, and the brothers behind them, the latter having swords in their hands. There cannot, in fact, be a more beautiful and attractive sight, than a lodge of Adoptive Masons properly organized and well attended.

Looking to the mixed sexual character of these lodges, it is not surprising that every thing is followed by a banquet, and on many occasions by a ball. These, says Clavel, are inseparable from a lodge of Adoption, and are, in fact, the real design of its organization, the initiatory ceremonies being but a pretext.

In the banquets of the regular lodges of the French rite, the members always use a symbolic language, by which they designate the various implements and articles of food and drink upon the table. In imitation of this custom, the ladies, in the banquets of the Adoptive lodges, have also established a symbolic language, to be used only at the table. Thus the lodge-room is called "Eden;" the doors "barriers;" the minutes "a ladder;"

3

a glass is called "a lamp;" water is styled "white oil," and wine
"red oil." To fill your glass is "trim your lamp," with many
other equally eccentric expressions.

Such is the organization of French Female Masonry, as it was
established and recognized by the masonic authorities of that
kingdom. It is still practised as a peculiar rite, although its resemblance to true Freemasonry is only in name. Under these
regulations, the lodge "La Candeur" was opened in Paris on the
11th of March, 1785, a Marquis being in the chair, and a
Duchess acting as Deputy or Grand Mistress. In the same year
the Duchess of Bourbon was installed with great pomp as Grand
Mistress. The revolution checked their progress, but they were
revived in 1805, when the Empress Josephine presided over the
"Lodge Imperiale d'Adoption des Francs Chevaliers," at Strasburg. The adoptive lodges were at first rapidly diffused throughout all the countries of Europe, except the British Empire,
where they were rejected with contempt, but they soon declined,
and are at present confined to the place of their origin.

ADVANCED. When a candidate is invested with the Mark
Master's degree, he is said to be "advanced." The term is very
appropriately used to designate that the Master Mason is now
promoted one step beyond the degrees of Ancient Craft Masonry
on the way to the Royal Arch.

AFFILIATED. A mason who is a member of a lodge is
said to be "an affiliated mason," in contra-distinction to a de-
mitted or non-affiliated one, who is not a member of any lodge.

AFFILIATION. The act by which a lodge receives a Mason
among its members. A profane is *initiated*, but a Mason is
affiliated. The general rule is, that a candidate must be initiated
in the lodge nearest to his residence, but after a Mason has been
made, he may unite himself with any lodge that he chooses, and
which is willing to receive him.

AFRICAN ARCHITECTS. In the year 1767, one Bau-cherren instituted in Prussia, with the concurrence of Frederick II., a society which he called "the Order of African Architects." The object of the institution was historical research, but it contained a ritual which partook of Masonry, Christianity, Alchemy, and Chivalry. It was divided into two temples, and was composed of eleven degrees. In the first temple were the degrees of— 1, Apprentice; 2, Fellow Craft; and 3, Master. In the second temple were the degrees of—4, Apprentice of Egyptian Secrets; 5, Initiate in the Egyptian Secrets; 6, Cosmopolitan brother; 7, Christian philosopher; 8, Master of Egyptian Secrets; 9, Esquire; 10, Soldier; and 11, Knight. The society constructed a vast building intended as a Grand Chapter of the order, and which contained an excellent library, a museum of natural history, and a chemical laboratory. For a long time the African Architects decreed annually a gold medal worth fifty ducats to the author of the best memoir on the history of masonry.

Ragon, who seldom speaks well of any other rite than his own, has, however, in his "Orthodoxie Maçonnique," paid the following tribute to the African Architects :—

"Their intercourse was modest and dignified. They did not esteem decorations, aprons, collars, jewels, &c., but were rather fond of luxury, and delighted in sententious apothegms whose meaning was sublime but concealed. In their assemblies they read essays and communicated the results of their researches. At their simple and decorous banquets instructive and scientific discourses were delivered. While their initiations were gratuitous, they gave liberal assistance to such zealous brethren as were in needy circumstances. They published in Germany many important documents on the subject of Freemasonry."

AGE. In the French, Scotch, and some other rites, each degree has an emblematic age; that of the E∴ A∴ is three years, because, in the system of mystical numbers, three is the number of generation, which comprises three terms, the agent, the recipient, and the product. Five is the age of the F∴ C∴, five being emblematic of active life, characterized by the five senses. And seven is the age of the M∴ M∴, it being the perfect number, in allusion to the seven primitive planets which completed the astronomic system.

AHIMAN REZON. This is the name of the Book of Constitutions, which was used by the Ancient Division of Freemasons, which separated in 1739 from the Grand Lodge of England. The "True Ahiman Rezon" was compiled in 1772 for the government of the Ancient Masons, by Laurence Dermott, at that time Deputy Grand Master of that body. The title is derived from three Hebrew words, *ahim*, brothers, *manah*, to choose or appoint,* and *ratzon*, the will or law, so that it literally signifies "the law of chosen brothers." The Book of Constitutions of the Grand Lodge of South Carolina, and that of Pennsylvania, is also called the Ahiman Rezon. See *Book of Constitutions*.

AHOLIAB. A skilful architect, appointed with Bezaleel to construct the tabernacle. Moses, Aholiab, and Bezaleel, the builders of the tabernacle, are in the Royal Arch degree appropriately placed in juxtaposition with Shem, Ham, and Japheth, who constructed the ark of safety, and with Joshua, Zerubbabel, and Haggai, who built the second temple.

ALARM. The signal of the approach of a person demanding admission to the lodge is thus called in masonic language.

ALL-SEEING EYE. An emblem of the Master's degree. It reminds us of that superintending Providence who knows the

---

* *Manah* means to choose, appoint, or distribute into a peculiar class out of a generality, and is hence really equivalent to "accept"—Dalcho's signification, *to prepare*, is incorrect.

most secret thoughts of our hearts, and rewards us according to our merits.*

This emblem was also found in the ancient mysteries,† and was there, as in masonry, preserved as a testimony of the unity of that omniscient and omnipresent Deity, the teaching of whose existence, in contradistinction to the popular mythology, was the aim and object of all these institutions.

ALPHA AND OMEGA. The first and last letters of the Greek alphabet, equivalent therefore to the beginning and ending of any thing, or to the whole of it in its completeness. The Jews used the first and last letters of their alphabet, *Aleph* and *Tau*, to express proverbially the whole compass of things; as when they said that "Adam transgressed the whole law, from Aleph to Tau."‡ St. John substituted the Greek for the Hebrew letters, as being more familiar to his readers.

ALPHABET OF ANGELS. The Jews speak of a celestial and mystical alphabet, which they say was communicated by the angels to the patriarchs. Kircher gives a copy of it in his Œdipus Egyptiacus, tom. ii. p. 105. This alphabet is several times alluded to in the ritual of the Scotch rite.

ALTAR. The place where the sacred offerings were presented to God. After the erection of the Tabernacle, altars were of two kinds, altars of sacrifice and altars of incense. The altar of masonry may be considered as the representative of both these forms. From thence the grateful incense of Brotherly Love, Relief, and Truth, is ever rising to the Great I AM; while on it,

---

* *Deus totus visus,*—God is all eyes, says Pliny.

† Among the Egyptians the Eye was the symbol of Osiris, and signified Providence. Hence they consecrated, in their temples, eyes made of precious materials.

‡ Adam Clarke, Commentary on Rev. i. 8.

3*

the unruly passions and the worldly appetites of the brethren
are laid, as a fitting sacrifice to the genius of our order.

The proper form of a masonic altar is that of a cube, about
three feet high, with four horns, one at each corner, and having
spread open upon it the Holy Bible, square, and compasses, while
around it are placed in a triangular form and proper position the
three lesser lights.

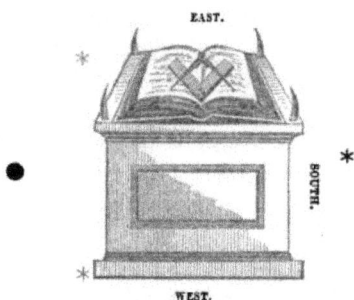

This diagram will ex-
hibit the correct position
in which the lights should
be placed around the al-
tar, the stars designating
the places of the lights in
the East, West, and South,
and the black dot the va-
cancy in the North where
there is no light.

Placing the lights all in the east at the head of the altar is a
common error, but a great one, as it does not meet the require-
ments of the ritual, which not only places them in a different
position, but says that they surround the altar.

AMERICAN MYSTERIES. Among the many evidences of
a former state of civilization among the aborigines of this country
which seem to prove their origin from the races that inhabit the
Eastern hemisphere, not the least remarkable is the existence of
fraternities bound by mystic ties, and claiming, like the Freemasons, to possess an esoteric knowledge which they carefully
conceal from all but the initiated. De Witt Clinton, once the
General Grand High Priest of the United States, relates, on the
authority of a respectable native minister, who had received the
signs, the existence of such a society among the Iroquois. The
number of the members was limited to fifteen, of whom six were

to be of the Seneca tribe, five of the Oneidas, two of the Cayugas, and two of the St. Regis. They claim that their institution has existed from the era of the creation. The times of their meeting they keep secret, and throw much mystery over all their proceedings.

The mysteries of the Mexican tribes were characterized by cruelty and bloodshed. In the celebration of these shocking rites, the aspirant was previously subjected to long and painful fastings, and compelled to undergo, in even a heightened form, all the terrors and sufferings which distinguished the mysteries of the Eastern continent. He was scourged with cords, wounded with knives, and cauterized with red-hot cinders. So cruel were these probations, that many perished under their infliction; and yet he who recoiled from the trial, or suffered an involuntary groan to escape his lips, was dismissed with contempt, and considered thenceforth as unworthy to mingle in the society of his equals. It was in the temple of Vitzliputzli that the Mexican mysteries were celebrated on the grandest scale. The candidate, being first anointed with a narcotic unguent, descended into the gloomy caverns of initiation, which were excavated beneath the temple. The ceremonies were intended to represent the wanderings of the god, and the caverns through which the aspirant was to pass were called the *path of the dead.*

He is conducted through these caverns amid shrieks of anguish and groans of despair, which seem to rise from every side, phantoms of death flit past his eyes, and while trembling for his safety, he reaches the body of a slain victim whose heart has been ripped from his breast, and whose limbs are still quivering with departing life; suddenly he finds himself in a spacious vault, through which an artificial sun is darting his rays, and in the roof of which is an orifice through which the body of the sacrificed victim had been precipitated. He is now immediately under the high altar. Finally, after encountering many other horrors, he reaches a narrow fissure which terminates the suit of subterranean apartments, and being protruded through it by his guide, he finds himself in open air, and in the midst of a vast multitude, who receive him with shouts as a person regenerated or born again.*

This was the first degree of the Mexican mysteries. There was a higher grade attainable only by the priests, in which the instruction was of a symbolic character, and referred to the deluge and the subsequent settlement of their ancestors on the lake of Mexico. The details of this legend bear a remarkable similarity to the scriptural account of the wanderings and final settlement of the Israelites. The tribe was led by the god Vitzliputzli, who was seated in a *square ark*, and held in his hand a *rod formed like a serpent*. The ark was called the throne of God, and its four corners were surmounted by serpents' heads. During their marches and encampments, Vitzliputzli revealed to them a mode of worship and a code of laws to govern them after they had taken possession of the promised land. In the midst of their encampment, they erected a tabernacle with an altar, on which was placed the sacred ark. After a tedious expedition, they finally arrived at an island in the middle of a lake, where they built the city of Mexico, and furnished it with a pyramidal temple.

The mysteries of the Peruvians were more simple and humane, and consisted principally of a lustration, performed annually on the first day of the September moon.

AMPLE FORM. When the Grand Lodge is opened by the Grand Master in person, it is said to be opened in "ample form;" when by the Deputy Grand Master, it is in "due form;" and when by any other officer, it is said to be simply "in form."

ANCIENT AND ACCEPTED RITE. See *Scotch Rite.*

ANCIENT CRAFT MASONRY. The degrees of Entered Apprentice, Fellow-Craft, and Master Mason, are thus called,

---

* It may as well be remarked in this place, that this regeneration, or raising from death to a second life, constituted the great end of all the pagan rites.

because they were the only degrees which were anciently practised by the craft.

ANCIENT MASONS. See *Modern Masons.*

ANCIENT REFORMED RITE. A rite differing very
slightly from the French rite. It is practised in Belgium and
Holland.

ANDERSON. James Anderson, D. D., the compiler of the
English Book of Constitutions, was a native of Scotland, but, for
many years of his life, a resident of England and the minister
of the Scotch Presbyterian church in Swallow street, Picadilly,
London. Besides the Book of Constitutions, to which he is
principally indebted for his reputation, he was also the author of
an extensive and singular work entitled "Royal Genealogies."
Chambers, in his "Scottish Biography," describes him as "a
learned but imprudent man, who lost a considerable part of his
property in deep dabbling in the South Sea Scheme." The precise dates of his birth and death are not known.

ANDROGYNOUS MASONRY. Degrees imitative of ma-
sonry, which have been instituted for the initiation of males and
females, so called from two Greek words signifying *man* and *woman*. They were first established in France in the year 1730,
under the name of "lodges of adoption." In America there are
several androgynous degrees, such as the Good Samaritan, the
Heroine of Jericho, and the Mason's Daughter. See *Adoptive
Masonry.*

ANGLE. See *Right Angle.*

ANNIVERSARY. The two anniversaries of Symbolic Masonry are, the festivals of St. John the Baptist, and St. John the
Evangelist, 24th of June and 27th of December. See in this
work the title *Dedication*. The anniversary of the Princes of
Rose Croix is Shrove Tuesday.

ANNO LUCIS. *In the Year of Light.* Used in masonic dates, and usually abbreviated A. ·. L. ·. See *Year of Life.*

ANTIQUITY OF MASONRY. Freemasonry is in its principles undoubtedly coeval with the creation, but in its organization as a peculiar institution, such as it now exists, we dare not trace it further back than to the building of King Solomon's temple. It was, however, in its origin closely connected with the Ancient Mysteries, and the curious inquirer will find some gratification in tracing this connection.

When man was first created, he had, of course, a perfect knowledge of the true name and nature of the Being who created him. But when, by his own folly, he fell "from his high estate," he lost, with his purity, that knowledge of God which in his primeval condition formed the noblest endowment of his mind. And at length the whole human race having increased in wickedness until every thought and act was evil, God determined, by a flood, to purge the earth of this excess of sin. To Noah, however, he was merciful, and to this patriarch and his posterity was to be intrusted the knowledge of the true God. But on the plains of Shinar man again rebelled, and as a punishment of his rebellion, at *the lofty tower of Babel, language was confounded, and masonry lost,* for masonry then, as now, consisted in a knowledge of these great truths, that there is one God, and that the soul is immortal. The patriarchs, however, were saved from the general moral desolation, and still preserved true masonry, or the knowledge of these dogmas, in the patriarchal line. The Gentile nations, on the contrary, fell rapidly from one error into another, and, losing sight of the one great I AM, substituted in his place the names of heroes and distinguished men, whom, by a ready apotheosis, they converted into the thousand deities who occupied the calendar of their religious worship.

The philosophers and sages, however, still retained, or discovered by the dim light of nature, some traces of these great doctrines of masonry, the unity of God, and the immortality of the soul. But these doctrines they dared not teach in public, for history records what would have been the fate of such temerity, when it informs us that Socrates paid the forfeit of his life for his boldness in proclaiming these truths to the Athenian youth.

They therefore taught in secret what they were afraid to inculcate in public, and established for this purpose the Ancient Mysteries, those truly masonic institutions, which, by a series of solemn and imposing ceremonies, prepared the mind of the initiate for the reception of those unpopular dogmas, while, by the caution exercised in the selection of candidates, and the obligations of secrecy imposed upon them, the teachers were secured from all danger of popular bigotry and fanaticism. A full description of these Mysteries will be found in this work under the appropriate title. Their members went through a secret ceremony of initiation, by which they became entitled to a full participation in the esoteric knowledge of the order, and were in possession of certain modes of recognition known only to themselves. In all of them, there was, in addition to the instructions in relation to the existence of a Supreme Deity, a legend in which, by the dramatic representation of the violent death and subsequent restoration to life of some distinguished personage, the doctrines of the resurrection and the soul's immortality were emblematically illustrated.

Among these religious institutions was that of the Dionysian Mysteries, which were celebrated throughout Greece and Asia Minor, and in which the peculiar legend was the murder of Bacchus, or, as the Greeks called him, Dionysus, by the Titans, and his subsequent restoration to life. The priests of Dionysus, having devoted themselves to architectural pursuits, established, about one thousand years before the Christian era, a society of builders in Asia Minor, who are styled by the ancient writers "The Fraternity of Dionysian Architects," and to this society was exclusively confined the privilege of erecting temples and other public buildings.

The fraternity of Dionysian Architects were linked together
by the secret ties of the Dionysian Mysteries, into which they
had all been initiated.   Thus constituted, the fraternity was distinguished by many peculiarities that strikingly assimilate it to
our order.   In the exercise of charity, the "more opulent were
sacredly bound to provide for the exigencies of the poorer brethren."   For the facilities of labour and government, they were
divided into lodges, each of which was governed by a Master and
Wardens.   They employed in their ceremonial observances many
of the implements which are still to be found among Freemasons,
and used like them, a universal language, by which one brother
could distinguish another in the dark as well as in the light, and
which served to unite the members scattered over India, Persia,
and Syria, into one common brotherhood.   The existence of this
order in Tyre, at the time of the building of the Temple, is universally admitted; and Hiram, the widow's son, to whom Solomon intrusted the superintendence of the workmen, as an inhabitant of Tyre, and as a skilful architect and cunning and
curious workman, was doubtless one of its members.   Hence we
are scarcely claiming too much for our order, when we suppose
that the Dionysians were sent by Hiram, King of Tyre, to assist
King Solomon in the construction of the house he was about to
dedicate to Jehovah, and that they communicated to their Jewish
fellow-labourers a knowledge of the advantages of their fraternity,
and invited them to a participation in its mysteries and privileges.
In this union, however, the apocryphal legend of the Dionysians
gave way to the true legend of the Masons, which was unhappily
furnished by a melancholy incident that occurred at the time.

Upon the completion of the Temple, the workmen who had
been engaged in its construction necessarily dispersed, to extend
their knowledge and to renew their labours in other lands.   But
we do not lose sight of the order.   We find it still existing in
Judea, under the name of the ESSENIAN FRATERNITY.   This
was rather a society of philosophers than of architects, and in
this respect it approached still nearer to the character of modern

speculative masonry. The Essenians were, however, undoubtedly connected with the Temple, as their origin is derived by the learned Scaliger, with every appearance of truth, from the KASSI-DEANS, a fraternity of Jewish devotees, who, in the language of Lawrie, had associated together as "Knights of the Temple of Jerusalem, to adorn the porches of that magnificent structure, and to preserve it from injury and decay." The Essenians were peculiarly strict in scrutinizing the characters of all those who applied for admission into their fraternity. The successful candidate, at the termination of his probationary novitiate, was presented by the Elders of the society with a white garment, as an emblem of the purity of life to which he was to aspire, and which, like the unsullied apron, the first gift that we bestow upon an Entered Apprentice, was esteemed more honourable than aught that any earthly prince could give. An oath was administered to him, by which he bound himself not to divulge the secrets with which he should be intrusted, and not to make any innovations upon the settled usages of the society. He was then made acquainted with certain modes of recognition, and was instructed in the traditionary knowledge of the order. They admitted no women into their fraternity; abolished all distinctions of rank; and devoted themselves to the acquisition of knowledge and the dispensation of charity.

From the Essenians, Pythagoras derived much if not all of the knowledge and the ceremonies with which he clothed the esoteric school of his philosophy; and while this identity of doctrines and ceremonies is universally admitted by profane historians, many of the most competent of our own writers have attributed the propagation of masonry into Europe to the efforts of the Grecian sage. It is certain that such an opinion was prevalent not less than four centuries ago; for in the ancient manuscript, now well known to Masons, which was discovered by the celebrated Locke among the papers of the Bodleian Library, and which is said to be a copy of an original in the handwriting of King Henry the Sixth, himself a Mason, it is expressly said that Pythagoras

4

brought masonry from Egypt and Syria into Greece, from whence, in process of time, it passed into England.

I shall not vouch for the truth of this assumption; for notwithstanding the celebrity of Pythagoras even at this day among our fraternity, and the adoption into our lodges of his well-known problem, I am rather inclined to attribute the extension of masonry into Europe to the frequent and continued communications with Palestine, in the earlier ages of the Christian dispensation. About this period we shall find that associations of travelling architects existed in all the countries of the continent; that they journeyed from city to city, and were actively engaged in the construction of religious edifices and regal palaces.* The government of these fraternities of Freemasons—for they had already begun to assume that distinctive appellation—was even then extremely regular. They lived in huts or *lodges,* (a name which our places of meeting still retain,) temporarily erected for their accommodation, near the building on which they were employed. Every tenth man received the title of Warden, and was occupied in superintending the labours of those placed under him, while the direction and supervision of the whole was intrusted to a Master chosen by the fraternity.

Freemasons continued for a long time to receive the protection and enjoy the patronage of the church and the nobility, until the former, becoming alarmed at the increase of their numbers and the extension of their privileges, began to persecute them with an unrelenting rigour, which eventually led to their suspension on the continent. Many lodges, however, had already been established in Great Britain, and these, shielded by the comparative mildness and justice of the British laws, continued to propagate the doctrines of the order throughout England and Scotland, and to preserve unimpaired its ancient landmarks. From the royal city of York in England, and the village and abbey of Kilwinning, the cradle of masonry in Scotland, our order continued to be

---

* See the article *Travelling Freemasons,* in this work.

disseminated and to flourish, throughout the two kingdoms, with undiminished lustre, long after the lodges of their less fortunate brethren had been dissolved by the persecutions on the continent. From this period, the institutions of masonry began to be extended with rapidity, and to be established with permanency. The dignity of the order was elevated, as the beauty of its principles became known. Nobles sought with avidity the honour of initiation into our sacred rites, and the gavel of the Grand Master has been more than once wielded by the hand of a king.

APHANISM. It is stated in the preceding article that in the Ancient Mysteries there always was a legend of the death and subsequent resurrection, or finding, of the body of some distinguished personage. That part of the ceremonies which represented the concealing of the body was called the *aphanism*, from the Greek work αφανιζω, to conceal.

APPEAL. The Master is supreme in his lodge, so far as the lodge is concerned. He is amenable for his conduct in the government of the lodge, not to its members, but to the Grand Lodge alone. In deciding points of order, as well as graver matters, no appeal can be taken from that decision to the lodge. If an appeal were proposed, it would be his duty, for the preservation of discipline, to refuse to put the question. If a member is aggrieved with the conduct or the decision of the Master, he has his redress by an appeal to the Grand Lodge, which will, of course, see that the Master does not rule his lodge "in an unjust or arbitrary manner." But such a thing as an appeal from the Master to the lodge, is unknown in masonry. See *Master of a Lodge*.

The General Grand Chapter of the United States has determined that there can be no appeal from the decision of a High Priest to his Chapter.

A similar decision has been made by the Hon. W. B. Hubbard, the General Grand Master of the Knights Templar, in relation to appeals from Grand Commanders to their Encampments, and his decision appears to have been sustained by the General Grand Encampment.

APPRENTICE. The Entered Apprentice is the first degree in masonry, and though it supplies no historical knowledge, it is replete with information on the internal structure of the order. It is remarkable, too, for the beauty of the morality which it inculcates. As an Entered Apprentice, a lesson of humility, and contempt of worldly riches and earthly grandeur, is impressed upon the mind by symbolic ceremonies, too important in their character ever to be forgotten. The beauty and holiness of charity are depicted in emblematic modes, stronger and more lasting than mere language can express; and the neophyte is directed to lay a corner-stone of virtue and purity, upon which he is charged to erect a superstructure, alike honourable to himself, and to the fraternity of which he is hereafter to compose a part.

This degree is considered as "the weakest part of masonry," and hence, although an Entered Apprentice is allowed to sit in a lodge of his degree, he is not permitted to speak or vote on the proceedings.

When a candidate is initiated into this degree, he is techically said to be "entered," that is, he has been permitted to enter the ground-floor of the temple, for a reason well known to Masons.

APRON. The lambskin or white leather apron, is the badge of a Mason, and the first gift bestowed by the Master upon the newly initiated Apprentice. The apron is worn by operative Masons, to preserve their garments from spot or stain. But we, as speculative Masons, use it for a more noble purpose. By the whiteness of its colour, and the innocence of the animal from which it is obtained, we are admonished to preserve that blameless purity of life and conduct, which will alone enable us hereafter to present ourselves before the Grand Master of the Universe, unstained with sin and unsullied with vice.

Investiture constituted an important part of the Ancient Mysteries; and as the white apron is the investiture of masonry, we find something resembling it in all the pagan rites. The Essenians clothed their candidate with a white robe, reaching to the ground, and bordered with a fringe of blue riband, as an emblem of holiness. In the mysteries of Greece the garment of initiation was also white; because, says Cicero, white is a colour most acceptable to the gods. This robe was considered sacred, and never taken off by the possessor, until worn to rags. In Persia, in the mysteries of Mithras, the robes of investiture were the Girdle, on which were depicted the signs of the Zodiac; the Tiara; The White Apron; and the Purple Tunic. In the mysteries of Hindostan, the aspirant was presented with a consecrated Sash, consisting of a cord of *nine* threads, which was worn from the left shoulder to the right side. An apron, composed of the three masonic colours, blue, purple, and scarlet, was worn by the Jewish priesthood; and the prophets, on all occasions when about to perform any solemn duty, invested themselves with a girdle or apron. Lastly, all the ancient statues of the heathen gods, which have been discovered in Greece, Asia, or America, are decorated with superb aprons. We hence deduce the antiquity and honour of this important part of a Freemason's vestments, and substantiate the correctness of our claim, that it is " more ancient than the Golden Fleece or Roman Eagle, and more honourable than the Star and Garter."

The masonic apron is a pure white lambskin, from fourteen to sixteen inches wide, and from twelve to fourteen deep, with a fall about three to four inches deep; square at the bottom, without ornament, and bound in the symbolic degrees with blue, and in the Royal Arch with scarlet. In this country the construction of the apron is the same in each of the symbolic degrees, which are only distinguished by the mode in which the

4*

apron is worn. But in England the apron varies in each of the degrees.*

The E∴ A∴ has a plain apron without ornament.

The F∴ C∴ has an addition of two sky blue rosettes at the bottom.

The M∴ M∴ has an additional rosette on the fall, and has sky-blue lining and edging, and silver tassels.

W∴ Masters and Past Masters, in lieu of rosettes, wear perpendicular lines on horizontal ones, like a ⊥ reversed, forming three sets of two right angles.

The silk or satin apron is a French innovation, wholly unmasonic, incompatible with the emblematic instruction of the investiture, and should never be tolerated in a lodge of York Masons.

ARCH, ANCIENT. The "Ancient Arch" is the 13th degree of the Ancient Scotch rite. It is more commonly called "*Knights of the Ninth Arch*," to which title the reader is referred.

ARCH, ANTIQUITY OF THE. Writers on architecture have, until within a few years, been accustomed to suppose that the invention of the Arch and Keystone was not anterior to the era of Augustus. But the researches of modern antiquaries have traced the existence of the Arch as far back as 460 years before the building of King Solomon's temple, and thus completely reconciled masonic tradition with the truth of history. See *Keystone.*

ARCH OF HEAVEN. Job xxvi. 11, compares heaven to an arch supported by pillars. "The pillars of heaven tremble and are astonished at his reproof." Dr. Cutbush, on this passage, remarks—"The arch in this instance is allegorical, not only

---

* A similar system is adopted in Germany.

of the arch of heaven, but of the higher degree of masonry, commonly called the Holy Royal Arch. The pillars which support the arch are emblematical of Wisdom and Strength; the former denoting the wisdom of the Supreme Architect, and the latter the stability of the Universe."—*Am. Ed. Brewster's Encyc.*

ARCH OF STEEL. The Grand honours are conferred, in the French rite, by two ranks of brethren elevating and crossing their drawn swords. They call it *voute d'acier.*

ARCH, ROYAL. See *Royal Arch.*

ARCHITECTURE. The art of constructing dwellings, as a shelter from the heat of summer and the cold of winter, must have been resorted to from the very first moment in which man became subjected to the power of the elements. Architecture is, therefore, not only one of the most important, but one of the most ancient of sciences. Rude and imperfect must, however, have been the first efforts of the human race, resulting in the erection of huts clumsy in their appearance, and ages must have elapsed ere wisdom of design combined strength of material with beauty of execution.

As Geometry is the science on which masonry is founded, Architecture is the art from which it borrows the language of its symbolic instruction. In the earlier ages of the order, every Mason was either an operative mechanic or a superintending architect. And something more than a superficial knowledge of the principles of architecture is absolutely essential to the Mason, who would either understand the former history of the institution or appreciate its present objects.

There are five orders of Architecture, the Doric, the Ionic, the Corinthian, the Tuscan, and the Composite. The first three are the original orders, and were invented in Greece; the last two are of later formation, and owe their existence to Italy

Each of these orders, as well as the other terms of Architecture, so far as they are connected with Freemasonry, will be found under their appropriate heads throughout this work.

ARITHMETIC. That science which is engaged in considering the properties and powers of numbers, and which, from its manifest necessity in all the operations of weighing, numbering, and measuring, must have had its origin in the remotest ages of the world.

In the lecture of the degree of "Grand Master Architect," the application of this science to Freemasonry is made to consist in its reminding the Mason that he is continually to *add* to his knowledge, never to *substract* any thing from the character of his neighbour, to *multiply* his benevolence to his fellow-creatures, and to *divide* his means with a suffering brother.

ARK. The Ark of the Covenant or of the Testimony was a chest originally constructed by Moses at God's command, (Exod. xxv. 16,) in which were kept the two tables of stone, on which were engraved the ten commandments. It contained, likewise, a golden pot filled with manna, Aaron's rod, and the tables of the covenant. It was at first deposited in the most sacred place of the tabernacle, and afterward placed by Solomon in the Sanctum Sanctorum of the Temple, and was lost upon the destruction of that building by the Chaldeans. The masonic traditions on the subject of its future history are exceedingly interesting to Royal Arch Masons.

The ark was made of shittim wood, overlaid, within and without, with pure gold. It was about three feet nine inches long, two feet three inches wide, and of the same extent in depth. It had on the side two rings of gold, through which were placed staves of shittim wood, by which, when necessary, it was borne by the Levites. Its covering was of pure gold, over which were placed two figures called Cherubim, with expanded wings. The covering of the ark was called *kaphiret*, from *kaphar*, to forgive sin, and hence its English name of "mercy-seat," as being the place where the intercession for sin was made.

ARK AND ANCHOR. Emblems of a well-grounded hope and a well-spent life, used in the Master's degree. They are emblematical of that divine *ark* which safely wafts us over this tempestuous sea of troubles, and that *anchor* which shall securely moor us in a peaceful harbour, where the wicked cease from troubling and the weary shall find rest.

There is no symbol more common than the ark to the spurious masonry of the Ancient Mysteries, and the true or speculative Freemasonry. In the due celebration of their kindred mysteries, says Faber, a certain holy ark was equally used by the Greeks, the Italians, the Celts, the Goths, the Phenicians, the Egyptians, the Babylonians, the Hindoos, the Mexicans, the Northern Americans, and the Islanders of the Pacific Ocean.* Historically this ark referred to the ark of Noah, but symbolically it was used as a coffin to receive the body of the candidate, and was an emblem of regeneration or resurrection. With this view the explanation we have given above from the masonic ritual accurately accords, and hence the ark and anchor have been appropriately adopted as symbols of the third degree, or that in which the doctrine of the resurrection is emphatically taught.

ARK AND DOVE. An illustrative degree, preparatory to the Royal Arch, and usually conferred, when conferred at all, immediately before the solemn ceremony of exaltation. The name of Noachite, sometimes given to it, is incorrect, as this belongs to a degree in the ancient Scotch rite. It is very probable that the degree, which now, however, has lost much of its significance, was derived from a much older one called the *Royal Ark Mariners,* to which the reader is referred. The previous article shows that the ark and dove formed an important part of the spurious Freemasonry of the ancients.

---

* Origin of Pagan Idolatry, vol. iii. p. 121.

ARMS OF FREEMASONRY. "The Masons," says Bailey, "were incorporated about the years 1419, having been called the Freemasons. Their armorial ensigns are, *azure* on a cheveron between three castles *argent;* a pair of compasses somewhat extended, of the first. Crest a castle of the second."

The arms of the Grand Lodge, according to Dermot, are the same as those now adopted by Royal Arch Masonry in this country, which may be blazoned as follows:

Party per cross *vert* voided *or;* in the first quarter, *azure,* a lion rampant, *or,* for the tribe of Judah; in the second, *or,* an ox passant, *sable* for Ephraim; in the third, *or,* a man erect, *proper,* for Reuben; in the fourth, *azure,* a spread eagle, *or,* for Dan. Crest an ark of the covenant; and supporters, two cherubim, all *proper.* Motto, "Holiness to the Lord."

The impossibility of blazoning a coat, except in the terms of heraldry, will, I trust, be my excuse for the technical nature of this description, which, I know, must be unintelligible to all who are unacquainted with the principles of heraldry. The plate of this coat of arms may, however, be seen in Cross's Chart.

These arms are derived from the "tetrarchical" (as Sir Thos. Browne calls them) or general banners of the four principal tribes: for it is said that the twelve tribes, during their passage through the wilderness, were encamped in a hollow square, three on each side, as follows: Judah, Zebulon, and Issachar, in the east, under the general banner of Judah; Dan, Asher, and Naphtali, in the north, under the banner of Dan; Ephraim, Manasseh, and Benjamin, in the west, under the banner of Ephraim; and Reuben, Simeon, and Gad, in the south, under Reuben. See *Banners.*

ARTS, LIBERAL. The seven liberal arts and sciences are illustrated in the Fellow Craft's degree. They are Grammar, Rhetoric, Logic, Arithmetic, Geometry, Music, and Astronomy. Grammar is the science which teaches us to express our ideas in appropriate words, which we may afterward beautify and adorn by means of Rhetoric, while Logic instructs us how to think and reason with propriety, and to make language subordinate to thought. Arithmetic, which is the science of computing by numbers, is absolutely essential, not only to a thorough knowledge of all mathematical science, but also to a proper pursuit of our daily avocations. Geometry, or the application of Arithmetic to sensible quantities, is of all sciences the most important, since by it we are enabled to measure and survey the globe that we inhabit. Its principles extend to other spheres; and, occupied in the contemplation and measurement of the sun, moon, and heavenly bodies, constitute the science of Astronomy; and lastly, when our minds are filled, and our thoughts enlarged, by the contemplation of all the wonders which these sciences open to our view, Music comes forward, to soften our hearts and cultivate our affections by its soothing influences.

The preservation of these arts as a part of the ritual of the Fellow Craft's degree, is another evidence of the antiquity of Freemasonry. These "seven liberal arts," as they were then for the first time called, constituted in the eighth century the whole circle of the sciences. The first three were distinguished by the title of *trivium*, and the last four by that of *quadrivium*, and to their acquisition the labours and studies of scholars were directed, while beyond them they never attempted to soar.

Mosheim, speaking of the state of literature in the eleventh century, uses the following language : "The seven liberal arts, as they were now styled, were taught in the greatest part of the schools, that were erected in this century for the education of youth. The first stage of these sciences was grammar, which was followed successively by rhetoric and logic. When the disciple, having learned these branches, which were generally known by the name of *trivium*, extended his ambition further, and was desirous of new improvement in the sciences, he was conducted slowly through the quadrivium (arithmetic, music, geometry, and astronomy), to the very summit of literary fame."[*]

---

[*] Hist. Ecclesiast., Cent. xi., p. ii., c. 1, § 5.

ASHLAR. "Free stone as it comes out of the quarry."—
Bailey. In speculative masonry we adopt the Ashlar in two different states, as symbols in the Apprentice's degree. The Rough
Ashlar, or stone in its rude and unpolished condition, is emblematic of man in his natural state—ignorant, uncultivated, and
vicious. But when education has exerted its wholesome influence
in expanding his intellect, restraining his passions, and purifying
his life, he then is represented by the Perfect Ashlar, which, under the skilful hands of the workmen, has been smoothed, and
squared, and fitted for its place in the building.

Oliver says that the Perfect Ashlar should be "a stone of a
true die square, which can only be tried by the square and compasses."* But he admits that some brethren do not consider this
form as essential. In American lodges it certainly is not.

ASSEMBLY. The annual meetings of the craft, previous to
the organization of Grand Lodges in their present form, were
called "General Assemblies." Thus, under the Grand Mastership of the Earl of St. Albans, we read of the "Regulations made
in General Assembly, Dec. 27, 1663."

Anderson says,† that it is written in the Old Constitutions, that
"Prince Edwin purchased a free charter of King Athelstane, his
brother, for the Freemasons to have among themselves a correc-
tion, or a power and freedom to regulate themselves, to amend
what might happen to be amiss, and to hold a yearly communication in a General Assembly." This charter was granted A. D.
926, and in that year the first General Assembly in England was
held at the city of York, where due regulations for the government of the craft were adopted. These regulations of the Assembly at York have ever since remained unaltered, and it is from
our submitting to their authority that we derive the name we bear
of "Ancient York Masons."

---

* Landmarks, vol. i., p. 146.   † Constitutions, p. 84.

ASTRONOMY. The science which instructs us in the laws that govern the heavenly bodies. Its origin is lost in the abyss of antiquity; for the earliest inhabitants of the earth must have been attracted by the splendour of the glorious firmament above them, and would have sought in the motions of its luminaries for the readiest and most certain method of measuring time. With Astronomy the system of Freemasonry is intimately connected. From that science many of our most significant emblems are borrowed. The lodge itself is a representation of the world; it is adorned with the images of the sun and moon, whose regularity and precision furnish a lesson of wisdom and prudence; its pilars of strength and establishment have been compared to the two columns which the ancients placed at the equinoctial points as supporters of the arch of heaven; the blazing star which was among the Egyptians a symbol of Anubis or the dog-star, whose rising foretold the overflowing of the Nile, shines in the east; while the clouded canopy is decorated with the beautiful Pleiades. The connection between our order and astronomy is still more manifest in the spurious Freemasonry of antiquity, where, the pure principles of our system being lost, the symbolic instruction of the heavenly bodies gave place to the corrupt Sabean worship of the sun, and moon, and stars—a worship whose influences are seen in all the mysteries of Paganism.

ASYLUM. During the session of an Encampment of Knights Templars, a part of the room is called the *asylum*; the word has hence been adopted, by the figure synecdoche, to signify the place of meeting of an Encampment.

ATELIER. (*French.*) A lodge.

ATHEIST. One who does not believe in the existence of God. Such a creed can only arise from the ignorance of stupidity or a corruption of principle, since the whole universe is filled with the moral and physical proofs of a Creator. He who does

5

not look to a superior and superintending power as his maker and his judge, is without that coercive principle of salutary fear which should prompt him to do good and to eschew evil, and his oath can, of necessity, be no stronger than his word. Masons, looking to the dangerous tendency of such a tenet, have wisely discouraged it, by declaring that no atheist can be admitted to participate in their fraternity; and the better to carry this law into effect, every candidate, before passing through any of the ceremonies of initiation, is required, publicly and solemnly, to declare his trust in God.

ATHOL MASONS. The Masons who, in 1739, seceded from the authority of the Grand Lodge of England, and established themselves as an irregular body under the name of "Ancient Masons," having succeeded in obtaining the countenance of the Duke of Athol, elected that nobleman, in 1776, their Grand Master, an office which he uninterruptedly held until 1813, when the union of the two Grand Lodges took place. In consequence of this long administration of thirty-seven years, the "Ancient Masons" are sometimes called "Athol Masons."

ATTOUCHEMENT. (*French.*) A grip.

AUGUST. A title bestowed upon the Royal Arch degree, in consequence of the imposing nature of its ceremonies, and the important mysteries it contains.

AUM, AUN, OR ON. The Hindoo and Egyptian chief deity. See more on this subject in *Jehovah.*

AXE. See *Knight of the Royal Axe.*

B.

BABEL. This word, which in Hebrew means *confusion*, was the name of that celebrated tower attempted to be built on the plains of Shinar, A. M. 1775, about one hundred and forty years after the deluge, and which, Holy Writ informs us, was destroyed by a special interposition of the Almighty. The Noachite Masons date the commencement of their order from this destruction, (see "*Noachites*,") and much traditionary information on this subject is preserved in the ineffable degree of "Patriarch Noachite," to which title the reader is referred.

At Babel, what has been called Spurious Freemasonry took its origin. That is to say, the people there abandoned the worship of the true God, and by their dispersion lost all knowledge of his existence, and of the principles of truth upon which masonry is founded. Hence it is that our traditionary ceremonies speak of the lofty tower of Babel as the place where language was confounded and masonry lost.*

BABYLON. The ancient capital of Chaldea, situated on both sides of the Euphrates, and once the most magnificent city of the ancient world. It was here, that upon the destruction of Solomon's Temple by Nebuchadnezzar in the year of the world 3394, the Jews of the tribes of Judah and Benjamin, who were the inhabitants of Jerusalem, were conveyed and detained in captivity for seventy-two years, until Cyrus, King of Persia, issued a decree for restoring them, and permitted them to rebuild their temple under the superintendence of Zerubbabel, the Governor of Judea, and with the assistance of Joshua the High Priest, and Haggai the Scribe.

* For more on this subject, see *Ornan*.

BADGE OF A MASON.   This is the lambskin or white leather apron, which must be worn in all lodges during the hours of labour.   See *Apron*.

BAHRDT'S RITE.   This was a rite founded by a masonic charlatan of the name of Bahrdt, about the close of the eighteenth century.   He opened a lodge at Halle, in Germany, under the name of the "German Union," and succeeded in securing the protection of the Prince of Anhaldt-Bernburg, and the co-operation of twenty-one persons of rank and character.   This rite had six degrees, viz: 1, The Youth; 2, The Man; 3, The Old Man; 4, The Mesopolyte; 5, The Diocesan; 6, The Superior.   The Grand Lodge, however, dissolved the fraternity on the ground of their working without a charter, and Bahrdt himself was shortly after imprisoned for writing a corrupt work.

BALLOT.   In the election of candidates, lodges have recourse to a ballot of white and black balls.   Unanimity of choice, in this case, is always desired and demanded; one black ball only, if it be accompanied with good reasons, of the sufficiency of which the lodge shall judge, being generally required to reject a candidate, and two having this effect without the assignment of any reasons whatever.   This is an inherent privilege not subject to dispensation or interference of the Grand Lodge, because, as the ancient constitutions say, "the members of a particular lodge are the best judges of it; and because, if a turbulent member should be imposed upon them, it might spoil their harmony or hinder the freedom of their communications, or even break and disperse the lodge, which ought to be avoided by all true and faithful."   Many Grand Lodges in this country insist on unanimity.*

In balloting for a candidate for initiation, every member is expected to vote.   No one can be excused from sharing the

---

* See the word *Unanimity*.

responsibility of admission or rejection, except by the unanimous
consent of the lodge. Where a member has himself no personal
or acquired knowledge of the qualifications of the candidate, he
is bound to give implicit faith to the recommendation of his brethren of the reporting committee, who, he has no right to suppose,
would make a favourable report on the petition of an unworthy
applicant.

With these prefatory remarks, I proceed to a description of the
general, and what is believed, to be the most correct usage, in balloting for candidates.

The committee of investigation having reported favourably, the
Master of the lodge directs the Senior Deacon to prepare the ballot-box.* The mode in which this is accomplished is as follows:
The Senior Deacon takes the ballot-box, and opening it, places
all the white and black balls indiscriminately in one compartment,
leaving the other entirely empty. He then proceeds with the box
to the Junior and Senior Wardens, who satisfy themselves by an
inspection that no ball has been left in the compartment in which
the votes are to be deposited. The box in this and the other
instance to be referred to hereafter, is presented to the inferior
officer first, and then to his superior, that the examination and
decision of the former may be substantiated and confirmed by the
higher authority of the latter. Let it, indeed, be remembered,
that in all such cases the usage of masonic *circumambulation* is
to be observed, and that, therefore, we must first pass the Junior's
station before we can get to that of the Senior Warden.

These officers having thus satisfied themselves that the box is
in a proper condition for the reception of the ballots, it is then
placed upon the altar by the Senior Deacon, who retires to his
seat. The Master then directs the Secretary to call the roll,

---

* There is no necessity for the Master to inquire if it is the pleasure of the
lodge to proceed to the election. The by-laws of all lodges requiring that an
election should follow the favourable report of the committee, the ballot-box is
ordered to be prepared as a matter of course, and in accordance with the constitutional rule.

which is done by commencing with the Worshipful Master, and proceeding through all the officers down to the youngest member. As a matter of convenience, the Secretary generally votes the last of those in the room, and then, if the Tiler is a member of the lodge, he is called in, while the Junior Deacon tiles for him, and the name of the applicant having been told him, he is directed to deposit his ballot, which he does and then retires.

As the name of each officer and member is called, he approaches the altar, and having made the proper masonic salutation to the Chair, he deposits his ballot and retires to his seat. The roll should be called slowly, so that at no time should there be more than one person present at the box, for the great object of the ballot being secrecy, no brother should be permitted so near the member voting as to distinguish the colour of the ball he deposits.

The box is placed on the altar, and the ballot is deposited with the solemnity of a masonic salutation, that the voters may be duly impressed with the sacred and responsible nature of the duty they are called on to discharge. The system of voting thus described, is, therefore, far better on this account than that sometimes adopted in lodges, of handing round the box for the members to deposit their ballots from their seats.

The master having inquired of the Wardens if all have voted, then orders the Senior Deacon to "take charge of the ballot-box." That officer accordingly repairs to the altar, and taking possession of the box, carries it, as before, to the Junior Warden, who examines the ballot, and reports, if all the balls are white, that "the box is clear in the South," or, if there is one or more black balls, that "the box is foul in the South." The Deacon then carries it to the Senior Warden, and afterward to the Master, who, of course, make the same report, according to the circumstance, with the necessary verbal variations of "West" and "East."

If the box is *clear*—that is, if all the ballots are white—the Master then announces that the applicant has been duly elected, and the Secretary makes a record of the fact. But if the box is *foul*, the subsequent proceedings will depend upon the number of balls, and upon the peculiar by-laws of the lodge in which the ballot has been taken.

The box having been declared to be *foul*, the Master inspects the number of black balls; if he finds only one, he so states the fact to the lodge, and orders the Senior Deacon again to prepare the ballot-box. Here the same ceremonies are passed through that have already been described. The balls are removed into one compartment, the box is submitted to the inspection of the Wardens, it is placed upon the altar, the roll is called, the members advance and deposit their votes, the box is scrutinized, and the result declared by the Wardens and Master. If again but one black ball be found, the fact is announced by the Master, who orders the election to lie over until the next regular meeting,* and requests the brother who deposited the black ball to call upon him and state his reasons. If, however, on this ballot two black balls are found, or if there were two or more on the first ballot, the Master announces that the petition of the applicant has been rejected, and directs the usual record to be made by the Secretary and the notification to be given to the Grand Lodge.

BALUSTRE. All documents issued by the Sovereign Inspectors or Supreme Councils of the 33d degree, Ancient Scotch rite, are called "Balustres."

BANNERS. In symbolic masonry, six banners are generally borne in processions, the material of which is white satin or silk, bordered with a blue fringe, and on each of which is inscribed one of the following words: Faith, Hope, Charity, Wisdom, Strength, Beauty.

In the Royal Arch Chapter, there are four officers who carry banners. The Royal Arch Captain carries a white banner, as an

---

* Unless the by-laws require unanimity.

emblem of that purity of heart and rectitude of conduct which
ought to actuate all those who pass the white veil of the sanctuary.
The Master of the Third Veil carries a scarlet banner, emblematical of that fervency and zeal which should characterize the possessors of the Royal Arch degree of which it is the appropriate colour.
The Master of the Second Veil carries a purple banner, which is
emblematic of union, because it is produced by a due mixture of
scarlet and blue, the former the colour of Royal Arch and the latter of symbolic masonry, and inculcates harmony betwen these
divisions of the craft. The Master of the First Veil carries a blue
banner, which is emblematic of universal friendship and benevolence, and is the appropriate colour of the first three degrees.

On the tracing board of the Royal Arch degree, as practised in
the Chapters of England, are found the banners of the twelve tribes
of Israel, which were as follow :

Judah, scarlet, a lion couchant.
Issachar, blue, an ass crouching beneath its burden.
Zebulon, purple, a ship.
Reuben, red, a man.
Simeon, yellow, a sword.
Gad, white, a troop of horsemen.
Ephraim, green, an ox.
Manasseh, flesh-coloured, a vine by the side of a wall.
Benjamin, green, a wolf.
Dan, green, an eagle.
Asher, purple, a cup.
Naphtali, blue, a hind.

We come now to what may be called the General Standard of
Freemasonry. This is a banner belonging peculiarly to the order,
as the beauseant did to the Templars, and which may be borne in
all processions of the craft, to distinguish them from any other
association of men. Its device is nothing but the coat of arms
of the order of speculative Freemasons as it was long since adopted, and as it is described by Dermott, in his Ahiman Rezon. In
this country this banner has, by some, been improperly supposed

to belong exclusively to the Royal Arch, in consequence of Cross having placed the representation of its device in his chart, among the plates which are illustrative of that degree. But it is, in fact, the common property of the order, and may be carried in the processions of a Master's lodge, as well as in those of a Chapter. I refer, for an exemplification of it, to the fortieth in the series of plates given in the Chart of Jeremy Cross. The escutcheon, or shield on the banner, is divided into four compartments or quarters by a green cross, over which a narrower one of the same length of limb, and of a yellow colour, is placed, forming what the heralds call "a cross *vert*, voided *or ;*" each of the compartments formed by the limbs of the cross, is occupied by a different device. In the first quarter is placed a golden lion on a field of blue, to represent the standard of the tribe of Judah; in the second, a black ox on a field of gold, to represent Ephraim; in the third, a man on a field of gold to represent Reuben; and, in the fourth, a golden eagle on a blue ground, to represent Dan. Over all is placed, as the crest, an ark of the convenant, and the motto is, "Holiness to the Lord."

These were the banners of the four principal tribes, for "when the Israelites marched through the wilderness," says Dr. Ashe, "we find that the twelve tribes had between them four principal banners or standards, every one of which had its particular motto; and each standard also had a distinct sign described upon it. They encamped round about the tabernacle, and on the east side were three tribes under the standard of Judah; on the west, were three tribes under the standard of Ephraim; on the south, were three tribes under the standard of Reuben; and, on the north, were three tribes under the standard of Dan; and the standard of Judah was a lion, that of Ephraim an ox, that of Reuben, a man, and that of Dan, an eagle—whence were framed the hieroglyphics of cherubim and seraphim to represent the people of Israel."

As the standard or banner of Freemasonry in thus made up of and derived from these banners of the four leading tribes of Israel,

it may be interesting to learn what was the symbolic meaning
given by the Hebrews to these ensigns. Vatablus quotes a Jewish
writer, as saying that the man in the banner of Reuben, signified
religion and reason; the lion, in that of·Judah, denoted power;
the ox, in that of Ephraim, represented patience and toilsome labour; and the eagle, in that of Dan, betokened wisdom, agility,
and sublimity. But although such may have been the emblematic
meaning of these devices among the Israelites, the combination of
them in the masonic banner is only intended to indicate the Jewish
origin of our institution from Solomon, who was the last king of
Israel under whom the twelve tribes were united.

BANQUET. The Banquets in English and American masonry
do not differ from the convivial meetings of other societies, with the
exception, perhaps, that the rule prohibiting the introduction of
debates on religious and political subjects, is more rigidly enforced.
But in the French lodges, the Banquets are regulated by a particular system of rules, and the introduction of ceremonies which
distinguish them from all other social assemblies. The room is
closely tiled, and no attendants, except those who are of the fraternity, are permitted to be present.

BAREFOOT. See *Discalceation.*

BEADLE. An officer in a council of Knights of the Holy
Sepulchre, corresponding to the Junior Deacon of a symbolic
lodge.

BEAUSEANT. The banner composed of a black and a white
horizontal stripe, which was peculiar to the ancient Templars.

BEAUTY. One of the three principal supports of masonry,
the other two being WISDOM and STRENGTH. It is represented
by the Corinthian column and the J∴ W∴, because the Corinthian is the most beautiful and highly finished of the orders, and

because the situation of the J∴ W∴ in the S∴ enables him the better to observe that bright luminary which, at its meridian height, is the beauty and glory of the day. H∴ A∴ is also considered as the representative of the column of Beauty which supported the Temple.

BEEHIVE. An emblem of industry appropriated to the third degree. This is a virtue ever held in high esteem among the craft, for our old charges tell us that "all Masons shall work honestly on working days, that they may live creditably on holidays." There seems, however, to be a more recondite meaning connected with this symbol. The ark has already been shown to have been an emblem common to Freemasonry and the ancient mysteries, as a symbol of regeneration—of the second birth from death to life. Now in the mysteries a hive was a type of the ark. "Hence," says Faber, "both the diluvian priestesses and the regenerated souls were called bees; hence bees were feigned to be produced from the carcase of a cow, which also symbolized the ark; and hence, as the great father was esteemed an infernal god, honey was much used both in funeral rites and in the mysteries."*

BEL. Bel, Baal, or Bul, is the name of God as worshipped among the Chaldeans and Phenicians. See *Jehovah*.

BENAC. A corrupted form of a Hebrew word signifying "the builder."

BENEFIT FUND. In 1798, a society was established in London, under the patronage of the Prince of Wales, the Earl of Moira, and all the other acting officers of the Grand Lodge, whose object was "the relief of sick, aged, and imprisoned brethren, and the protection of their widows, children, and orphans." The payment of one guinea per annum entitled every member,

* Orig. of Pag. Idol., vol ii. 133.

when sick or destitute, or his widow and orphans in case of his death, to a fixed contribution.

Benefit funds of this kind have, until very lately, been unknown to the Masons of America, but within a few years several lodges have established a fund for the purpose. The lodge of Strict Observance in the city of New York, and others in Troy, Ballston, Schenectady, etc., have adopted Benefit Funds. In 1844, several members of the lodges in Louisville, Kentucky, organized a society under the title of the "Friendly Sons of St. John." It is constructed after the model of the English society already mentioned. No member is received after 45 years of age, or who is not a contributing member of a lodge; the per diem allowance to sick members is seventy-five cents; fifty dollars is appropriated to pay the funeral expenses of a deceased member, and twenty-five for those of a member's wife; on the death of a member a gratuity is given to his family; ten per cent. of all fees and dues is appropriated to an orphan fund; and it is contemplated, if the funds will justify, to pension the widows of deceased members, if their circumstances require it.

Further reflection and a more careful investigation of the principles of our order, since the first edition of this work, have convinced me that the establishment in lodges of such benefit funds as are described in the last paragraph, are in opposition to the pure system of masonic charity. They have, therefore, been very properly discouraged by several Grand Lodges.

BIBLE. Emphatically is the Bible called a greater light of masonry, for from the centre of the lodge, it pours forth upon the East, the West, and the South, its refulgent rays of Divine truth. The Bible is used among Masons as the symbol of the will of God, however it may be expressed. See *Furniture*.

BLACK. This colour is a symbol of grief and mourning. In the degree of Knight Templar it refers to the execution of James de Molay; in the elu degrees of the Scotch and other rites to the death of the chief builder at the temple; and in the Rose Croix to the crucifixion.

BLAZING STAR. The blazing star constitutes one of the ornaments of the lodge. Formerly it was said to be "commemorative of the star which appeared to guide the wise men of the East to the place of our Saviour's nativity." But as this allusion, however beautiful, interferes with the universal character of masonry, it is now generally omitted, and the blazing star is said to be an emblem of Divine Providence. In the English ritual it is emblematic of Prudence. Dr. Hemming, quoted by Oliver, says that it refers to the sun "which enlightens the earth with its refulgent rays, dispensing its blessings to mankind at large, and giving light and life to all things here below."

BLUE. The appropriate colour of the first three degrees or ancient craft masonry, and has been explained as emblematic of universal friendship and benevolence, instructing us, that in the mind of a Mason those virtues should be as extensive as the blue arch of heaven itself.

BLUE MASONRY. The degrees of Entered Apprentice, Fellow Craft, and Master Mason, are called Blue Masonry, and lodges in which they are conferred are called Blue Lodges, because the decorations of these degrees are of this colour.

BOAZ. The name of the left hand pillar that stood at the porch of King Solomon's temple. It is derived from the Hebrew ‎בַ‎, b "in," and ‎עֹז‎, oaz, "strength," and signifies "in strength." See *Pillars*.

BONE. This word which is now corruptly pronounced in one syllable is the Hebrew word *boneh*, ‎בּוֹנֶה‎, "builder," from the verb *banah*, ‎בָּנָה‎, "to build." It was peculiarly applied, as an

6

epithet, to Hiram Abif, who superintended the construction of the temple as its chief builder.

BOOK OF CONSTITUTIONS. The Book of Constitutions is that work in which is contained the rules and regulations of the order, an exposition of the duties of officers, the rights of members, the detail of ceremonies to be used on various occasions, such as consecrations, installations, funerals, etc.; and, in fine, a summary of all the fundamental principles of masonry. To this book, reference is to be made in all cases, where the bye-laws of the Grand Lodge are silent or not sufficiently explicit.

The earliest notice that we have of any such Constitutions is in a record, written in the reign of Edward IV., which states that Prince Edwin, having assembled the Masons at York, in 926, then framed the English constitutions of masonry from the writings brought there in various languages. These Constitutions continued for a long time to govern the English craft under the name of the "Gothic Constitutions;" but as they were found, at the revival of masonry in the beginning of the eighteenth century; to be very erroneous and defective—probably from carelessness or ignorance in their frequent transcription—in September, 1721, the Duke of Montagu, who was then Grand Master, ordered Brother James Anderson to digest them "in a new and better method."

Anderson having accordingly accomplished the important task that had been assigned him, in December of the same year, a committee consisting of fourteen learned brethren, was appointed to examine the book, and they, in the March communication of the subsequent year, having reported their approbation of it, it was, after some amendments, adopted by the Grand Lodge, and published in 1723, under the title of "the Book of Constitutions of the Freemasons, containing the History, Charges, Regulations, etc., of the Most Ancient and Right Worshipful Fraternity. For the use of the lodges."

In 1735, a second edition was published, under the superintendence of a committee of Grand officers. This was the last edition issued during the life-time of Dr. Anderson; but, in the year 1754, it was resolved "that the Book of Constitutions should be revised, and the necessary alterations and additions made, consistent with the laws and rules of masonry." Again, in 1766, a similar revision took place, under the care of the Grand officers and twenty-one Masters of lodges; and the amendments having been unanimously approved by the Grand Lodge, in January, 1767, the fourth edition was published.

This book is carried in all processions before the Grand Master, on a velvet cushion, and the right of so carrying it is vested in the Master of the oldest lodge—a privilege which arose from the following circumstances. During the reign of Queen Anne, Freemasonry was in a languishing condition, in consequence of the age and infirmities of the Grand Master, Sir Christopher Wren. On his death, and the accession of George the First to the throne, the four old lodges then existing in London, determined to revive the Grand Lodge, which had for some years been dormant, and to renew the quarterly communications and the annual feast. This measure they accomplished, and resolved, among other things, that no lodge thereafter should be permitted to act, (the four old lodges excepted,) unless by authority of a charter granted by the Grand Master, with the approbation and consent of the Grand Lodge. In consequence of this, the old Masons in the metropolis vested all their inherent privileges as individuals in the four old lodges, in trust, that they would never suffer the ancient landmarks to be infringed; while, on their part, these bodies consented to extend their patronage to every lodge which should thereafter be regularly constituted, and to admit their Masters and Wardens to share with them all the privileges of the Grand Lodge, that of precedence only excepted. The extension of the order, however, beginning to give to the new lodges a numerical superiority in the Grand Lodge, it was feared they would at length be able, by a majority, to subvert the privileges of the original Masons of England, which had been centred in the four old lodges. On this account, a code of articles was drawn up with the consent of all the brethren, for the future government of the society. To this was annexed a regulation, binding the Grand Master and his successors, and the Master of every newly constituted lodge, to preserve these regulations inviolable; and declaring that no new regulation could be proposed, except at the third quarterly communication, and requiring it to be publicly read at the annual feast to every brother, even to the youngest Apprentice, when the approbation of at least two-thirds of those present should be requisite to render it obligatory. To commemorate this circumstance, it has been customary for the Master of the oldest lodge to attend every grand installation, and taking precedence of all present, the Grand Master excepted, to deliver the Book of Constitutions to the newly installed Grand Master, on his promising obedience to the ancient charges and general regulations.

This book, guarded by the Tyler's sword, constitutes an emblem in the Master's degree, intended to admonish the Mason that he should be guarded in all his words and actions, preserving unsullied the masonic virtues of silence and circumspection which are inculcated in that book.

BOOK OF THE LAW. The Holy Bible, which is always open in a lodge, as a symbol that its light should be diffused among the brethren. The passages on which it is opened differ in the different degrees. In this country these passages are as follows: in the first degree, at Psalm cxxxiii; in the second, at Amos vii. 7, 8; in the third, at Ecclesiastes xii. 1–7.

BREAST PLATE. A piece of embroidery about ten inches square, worn by the Jewish High Priest on his breast, and attached by its upper corners to the shoulders, and by its lower to the girdle of the Ephod. It was made of the same rich embroidered stuff of which the Ephod was. The front of it was set with twelve precious stones, on each of which was engraved the name of one of the twelve tribes. These stones were divided from each other by golden partitions, and set in four rows according to the following order. It must be remembered that they are to be read according to the Jewish system of writing, from right to left, commencing with the Sardius in the right hand upper corner.

CARBUNCLE,	TOPAZ,	SARDIUS,
*	*	*
LEVI.	SIMEON.	REUBEN.
DIAMOND,	SAPPHIRE,	EMERALD,
*	*	*
ZEBULUN.	ISSACHAR.	JUDAH.
AMETHYST,	AGATE,	LIGURE,
*	*	*
GAD.	NAPHTALI.	DAN.
JASPER,	ONYX,	BERYL,
*	*	*
BENJAMIN.	JOSEPH.	ASHER.

The colours of these stones have been described by Biblical naturalists as follows:

1. The *Sardius*, or ruby, was of a red colour, with an admixture of purple. 2. The *Topaz*, or modern chrysolite, was pale green, with an admixture of yellow. 3. The *Carbuncle* was a fiery red. 4. The *Emerald* was of a beautiful and pure green. 5. The *Sapphire*, or modern lapis lazuli, was a deep blue, veined with white and spotted with small golden stars. 6. The *Diamond* is perfectly white. 7. The *Ligure*, or hyacinth, was of dull red, much mixed with yellow. 8. The *Agate* was of a grey horny ground, spotted with different colours, chiefly of a dusky hue. 9. The *Amethyst* was of a purple colour, composed of strong blue and deep red. 10. The *Beryl*, or modern aqua marina, was a pellucid gem of a bluish green. 11. The *Onyx* was of a bluish white colour, resembling the tint of the human nail. 12. The *Jasper* was of a beautiful green, sometimes clouded with white, red, or yellow.

The following are the Hebraic characters in which the names of the twelve tribes were engraved on these stones, in the same order in which they are arranged in the preceding diagram.

לוי	שמעון	ראובן
זבלון	יששכר	יהודה
גד	נפתלי	דן
בנימן	יוסף	אשר

The breast-plate was never to be separated from the priestly garments, and was called the "memorial," because it was designed to remind the High Priest how dear the tribes whose names it bore should be to his heart. This ornament forms a a part of the vestments of the High Priest in a Royal Arch Chapter.*

BRIGHT. A mason is said to be "bright" who is well acquainted with the ritual, the forms of opening and closing, and the ceremonies of initiation. This expression does not, however, in its technical sense, appear to include the superior knowledge of the history and science of the institution, and many bright masons are therefore not necessarily learned masons, and on the contrary some learned masons are not well versed in the exact phraseology of the ritual. The one knowledge depends on a retentive memory, the other is derived from deep research.

---

* The judges in ancient Egypt wore breast-plates. For more on this subject, see *Urim* and *Thummim*.

BROKEN COLUMN. Among the Hebrews, columns were used metaphorically, to signify princes or nobles, as if they were the pillars of a state. Thus, in Psalms xi. 3, the passage, reading in our translation, "if the foundations be destroyed, what can the righteous do?" is in the original, "when the columns are over-thrown," i. e. when the firm supporters of what is right and good have perished. So the passage in Isaiah xix. 10, should read, "her (Egypt's) columns are broken down," that is, the nobles of her state. In Freemasonry, the broken column is, as Master Masons well know, the emblem of the fall of one of the chief supporters of the craft.

BROTHER. The term which Freemasons apply to each other. Freemasons are brethren, not only by common participation of the human nature, but as professing the same faith, as being jointly engaged in the same labours, and as being united by a mutual covenant or tie, whence they are also emphatically called "Brethren of the Mystic Tie."

BROTHERLY LOVE, RELIEF AND TRUTH. These words constitute the motto of our order, and the characteristics of our profession. They need no explanation, but they prove that a society which could adopt them, can be founded only on the principles of virtue. One of the ancient charges calls brotherly love "the foundation and cape stone, the cement and glory of this ancient fraternity."

BURNING BUSH. The burning bush, out of the midst of which the angel of the Lord appeared unto Moses at Mount Horeb, is referred to in the ceremonies of Royal Arch Masonry, because it was there that the Tetragrammaton was delivered to the Jewish lawgiver. This was, therefore, the great source of true masonic light, and hence Supreme Councils of the 33d degree date their protocols "near the B∴ B∴" or "Burning Bush,"

to intimate that they are in their own rite the exclusive source
of all masonic instruction.

BY-LAWS. Every subordinate lodge is permitted to make
its own by-laws, provided they do not conflict with the regulations of the Grand Lodge, nor with the ancient usages of the fraternity   But of this, the Grand Lodge is the only judge, and
therefore the original by-laws of every lodge, as well as all subsequent alterations of them, must be submitted to the Grand Lodge
for approval and confirmation before they can become valid.

C.

CABBALA. The Cabbala is that peculiar science or philosophy of the Jews which is occupied in the mystical interpretation
of the Scriptures, and in metaphysical speculations concerning
the Deity and the spiritual world. As much use is made of these
cabbalistic speculations in the higher philosophical degrees of
masonry, a brief description of the system will not perhaps be
considered irrelevant to the objects of this work.

The Cabbala is of two kinds: *theoretical* and *practical.* With
the practical Cabbala, which is engaged in the construction of
talismans and amulets, we have nothing to do. The theoretical
is divided into the *literal* and *dogmatic.* The dogmatic Cabbala
is nothing more than the summary of the metaphysical doctrines
taught by the Cabbalistic doctors. It is, in other words, the
system of Jewish philosophy. The literal is a mystical mode of
explaining sacred things by a peculiar use of the letters of words,
and is the one which is connected with philosophical and ineffable
masonry.

There are three principal branches of the literal Cabbala, which
are denominated *Gematria, Notaricon,* and *Temura.*

1. Gematria is a mode of contemplating words according to the value of the letters of which they are composed. The Hebrews, like other ancient nations, having no figures in their language, made use of the letters of their alphabet instead of numbers, each letter having a particular numerical value according to the following table:

Aleph	א	1	Yod	י	10	Koph	ק	100
Beth	ב	2	Caph	כ	20	Resh	ר	200
Gimel	ג	3	Lamed	ל	30	Shin	ש	300
Daleth	ד	4	Mem	מ	40	Tau	ת	400
He	ה	5	Nun	נ	50	Final Caph	ך	500
Vau	ו	6	Samech	ס	60	Final Mem	ם	600
Zain	ז	7	Ain	ע	70	Final Nun	ן	700
Cheth	ח	8	Pe	פ	80	Final Pe	ף	800
Teth	ט	9	Tsaddi	צ	90	Final Tsaddi	ץ	900

Any two words, the letters of which have the same numerical value, are mutually convertible, and each is supposed to contain the latent signification of the other. Thus the words in Genesis xlix. 10, "Shiloh shall come," are supposed to contain a prophecy of the Messiah, because the letters of "Shiloh shall come," יבא שילה and of "Messiah," משיח, both have the numerical value of 358, according to the above table. It was by Gematria, applied to the Greek language, that we found in the article *Abraxas* in this work, the identity of Abraxas and Mithras. This is by far the most common mode of applying the Cabbala.

2. Notaricon is a mode of constructing one word out of the initials or finals of many, or a sentence out of the letters of a word, each letter being used as the initial of another word. Thus of the sentence in Deuteronomy xxx. 12, "Who shall go up for us to heaven?" in Hebrew מי יעלה לנו השמימה the initial letters of each word are taken to form the word מילה, "circumcision," and the finals to form יהוה "Jehovah;" hence it is concluded that Jehovah hath shown circumcision to be the way to heaven. Again: the six letters of the first word in Genesis

בְּרֵאשִׁית "in the beginning," are made use of to form the initials of six words which constitute a sentence signifying that
"In the beginning God saw that Israel would accept the law,"

בראשית ראה אלהים שיקבלו ישראל תורה

3. Temura is Cabbala by permutation of letters. Sometimes
the letters of a word are transposed to form another word, making
what is familiarly known as an anagram, or the letters of a word
are changed for others according to certain fixed rules of alphabetical permutation, the 1st letter being placed for the 22d, the
2d for the 21st, the 3d for the 20th, and so on. It is in this
way that Babel, בבל is made out of Sheshach שׁשׁך, and hence
the Cabbalists say that when Jeremiah used the word Sheshach
(xxv. 26) he referred to Babel.

A very interesting account of the Cabbala will be found in
Allen's "Modern Judaism," from which work, indeed, I have
principally condensed the present synopsis.

CABIRI, MYSTERIES OF THE. The Cabiri were originally Syrian or Phenician gods, and all that we know about them
is to be found in a fragment of Sanconiathon, quoted by Euse-
bius, which tells us that they were the children of Sydyk, (whom
Faber* and some other authors suppose to be Noah,) and that
they were the inventors of ship-building. In the time of Chronos
(or Saturn) their descendants, while navigating the sea, ran
aground on Mount Casius and there erected a temple.

The worship of the Cabiri was first established in the island of
Samothrace, where it may be supposed that these navigators first
landed on passing from the continent. Here they founded the
mysteries of the Cabiri, which were subsequently celebrated at
Thebes and Lemnos, but more especially at Samothrace, whence
they were sometimes called the Samothracian rites. The name

---

* Dissert. on the Mysteries of the Cabiri. Bishop Cumberland thinks Sydyk
identical with Shem, a just man, in Hebrew, *Sadek*.

of the Cabiri was derived originally from Phenicia, and the word signifies in that language *powerful*.* There were four of these gods, Axieros, Axiokersos, Axiokersa, and Cadmillus.† The last had been slain by the three others, and his murder was commemorated in the secret rites. The aspirant presented himself crowned with an olive branch, and girded about the loins with a purple riband or apron. He was placed upon a throne, around which the priests and initiated performed sacred dances. Funeral rites were then enacted, in which the candidate represented Cadmillus. The hierophants declared that the object of the mysteries was, to make men just and virtuous. Candidates who had been guilty of any crime, were compelled to confess to a priest, who purified them.

Many persons annually resorted to Samothrace to be initiated into the celebrated mysteries, among whom are mentioned Cadmus, Orpheus, Hercules, and Ulysses. Jamblichus says, in his life of Pythagoras, that from those of Lemnos that sage derived much of his wisdom. The mysteries of the Cabiri were much respected among the common people, and great care was taken in their concealment. The priests were called Corybantes, and made use of a language peculiar to the rites.‡

There is much perplexity connected with this subject, but it is generally supposed that the mysteries were instituted in honour of Atys, the son of Cybele. According to Macrobius, Atys was one of the names of the sun; in confirmation of this, we know that the mysteries were celebrated at the vernal equinox. They

---

* Compare the cognate Hebrew, *kabir*, "to be greater."

† Some authors suppose that these four gods refer to Noah and his three sons, saved in the ark, and thus they connect the Samothracian rites with the Arkite worship. See Drummond's Origines, vol. ii. p. 130. The Scholiast on Apoll. Rhod. says their names were Ceres, Proserpine, and Bacchus.

‡ Larcher says that those who had been admitted to these mysteries, were highly esteemed, as they were supposed to have nothing to apprehend from tempests; and Plutarch tells us, that they who learned the names of the Cabiri, pronounced them slowly, as an amulet to avert calamity.

lasted three days, during which they represented in the person
of Atys, the enigmatical death of the sun in winter, and his regeneration in the spring. In all probability, in the initiation,
the candidate passed through a drama, the subject of which was
the violent death of Atys. Candidates on their admission, underwent an examination respecting their previous life, and after
being purified and initiated were presented with a purple girdle,
which was worn like an *apron* around their bodies, as an amulet
to preserve them against all dangers.

The mysteries were in existence at Samothrace as late as the
eighteenth year of the Christian era, at which time the Emperor
Germanicus embarked for that island, to be initiated, but was
prevented from accomplishing his purpose by adverse winds.

CABLE TOW. A properly constructed tracing board of the
Entered Apprentice is always enclosed within a cord or cable tow,
having four tassels placed at the four angles, referring to the four
cardinal virtues and their illustrated points, while the cable tow
is emblematic of the cord or band of affection which should unite
the whole fraternity, as in Hosea xi. 4, "I drew them with cords
of a man, with bands of love." But there is another and not
figurative use of this implement, with which Masons are well acquainted.

CAGLIOSTRO. Joseph Balsamo, Marquis of Pelligrini, more
commonly known by the title which he assumed at Paris, of
Count Cagliostro, was one of the most ingenious imposters that
ever lived. He was the author of a work entitled "Maçonnerie
Egyptienne," and the founder of a pseudo-masonic system, which
he called the rite of Egyptian masonry. He established this rite,
(the idea of which he had obtained from some manuscripts accidentally purchased at London,) at first, in Courland, in the year
1779,.whence he afterward introduced it into Germany, France,
and England. For the purpose more speedily of captivating the
credulous and the imaginative, he united with this form of ma-

sonry, the visionary schemes of Alchemy, declaring that one of the objects of initiation was the possession of the philosopher's stone and the elixir of immortality.

Both men and women were admitted into the lodges of the Egyptian rite, though the ceremonies for each sex were slightly different, and the lodges for their reception were entirely distinct. The system was called a hierarchy, and was divided into three degrees, Egyptian Apprentice, Egyptian Fellow-craft, and Egyptian Master.

Cagliostro, after having been banished from France by the government, and compelled to fly from England by his creditors, was finally arrested at Rome by the Inquisition, in 1789, on a charge of practising the rites of Freemasonry, and condemned to perpetual imprisonment. He was never afterwards heard of, and is supposed to have died, or to have been put to death, during his incarceration.

CALENDAR, MASONIC. Freemasons, in affixing dates to their official documents, never make use of the common calendar or vulgar era, but have one peculiar to themselves, which, however, varies in the different rites.

Masons of the York and French rites, that is to say, the Masons of England, Scotland, Ireland, France, Germany, and America, date from the creation of the world, calling it "Anno Lucis," which they abbreviate A∴ L∴, signifying *in the year of light.* Thus with them the year 1850 is A∴ L∴ 5850. This they do, not because they believe Freemasonry to be coeval with the creation, but with a symbolic reference to the light of masonry.

In the Scotch rite, the era also begins from the date of the creation, but Masons of that rite, using the Jewish chronology, would call the year 1850 A∴ M∴ or Anno Mundi (in the year of the world) 5610. They sometimes use the initials A∴ H∴, signifying Anno Hebraico, or, *in the Hebrew year.* They have also adopted the Hebrew months, and the year therefore ends with them on the 16th of September, the new year beginning on the 17th of the same month, which is the first of Tisri.

The Masons of the rite of Mizraim, which is practised in France, adopt the chronology of Archbishop Usher, and adding four years to the usual computation of the age of the world, would make the year 1850 A.·. L.·. 5854.

Masons of the York rite begin the year on the first of January, but in the French rite it commences on the first of March, and instead of the months receiving their usual names, they are designated numerically, as first, second, third, &c. Thus the 1st January, 1850, would be styled in a French masonic document, the "1st day of the 11th masonic month, Anno Lucis, 5850." The French sometimes, instead of the initials A.·. L.·., use *L'an de la V.·. L.·.*, or, *Vraie Lumiere*, that is, "Year of True Light."

Royal Arch Masons commence their era with the year in which Zerubbabel began to build the second temple, which was 530 years before Christ. Their style for the year 1850 is, therefore, A.·. Inv.·., that is, *Anno Inventionis*, or, in the Year of the Discovery, 2380.

Royal and Select Masters very often make use of the common masonic date, *Anno Lucis*, but properly they should date from the year in which Solomon's Temple was completed, and their style would then be, *Anno Depositionis*, or *in the Year of the Deposite*, and they would date the year 1850 as 2850.

Knights Templars use the era of the organization of their order in 1118. Their style for the year 1850 is A.·. O.·., *Anno Ordinis*, or, *in the Year of the Order*, 732.

I subjoin, for the convenience of reference, the rules for discovering these different dates.

1. *To find the Ancient Craft date.* Add 4000 to the vulgar era. Thus 1850 and 4000 are 5850.

2. *To find the date of the Scotch rite.* Add 3760 to the vulgar era. Thus 1850 and 3760 are 5610. After September add one year more.

3. *To find the date of Royal Arch Masonry.* Add 530 to the vulgar era. Thus 530 and 1850 are 2380.

4. *To find the Royal and Select Masters' date.* Add 1000 to the vulgar era. Thus 1000 and 1850 are 2850.

5. *To find the Knights Templar's date.* Subtract 1118 from the vulgar era. Thus 1118 from 1850 is 732.

The following will show, in one view, the date of the year 1850 in all the branches of the order:

Year of the Lord, A. D. 1850—Vulgar era.

Year of the Light, A∴ L∴ 5850—Ancient Craft Masonry.

Year of the World, A∴ M∴ 5610—Scotch rite.

Year of the Discovery, A∴ I∴ 2380—Royal Arch Masonry.

Year of the Deposite, A∴ Dep∴ 2850—Royal and Select Masters.

Year of the Order, A∴ O∴ 732—Knights Templars.

CANDIDATE. In ancient Rome, he who sought office from the people wore a white shining robe of a peculiar construction, flowing open in front, so as to exhibit the wounds he had received in his breast. From the colour of his robe or *toga candida,* he was called *candidatus,* whence our English word *candidate.* The derivation will serve to remind our brethren of the purity of conduct and character which should distinguish all those who are candidates for admission into our order. For the constitutional qualification of masonic candidates, see *Admission.*

CAPE STONE. Properly *Cope Stone,* which see.

CAPTAIN GENERAL. The third officer in an Encampment of Knights Templars. He presides over the Encampment in the absence of his superiors, and is one of its representatives in the Grand Encampment. His duties are to see that the council chamber and asylum are duly prepared for the business of the meetings, and to communicate all orders issued by the Grand Council. His station is on the left of the Grand Commander, and his jewel is a level surmounted by a cock, the emblem of courage.

CAPTIVITY. Solomon having erected and dedicated a temple to Jehovah, died in the year of the world 3029. His dominions did not long retain their integrity, for during the reign of his son and successor, Rehoboam, ten of the tribes revolted against his authority; and thus the separate kingdoms of Judah and Israel were established, the temple remaining in the possession of the former. After a series of events unnecessary to be narrated here, the city of Jerusalem was attacked by Nebuchadnezzar, and after a year's siege, was surrendered at midnight, in the eleventh year of the reign of Zedekiah, to Nebuzaradan, the captain of Nebuchadnezzar's guards. Nebuzaradan, having rifled the temple of its sacred vessels and its two pillars at the entrance of the porch, set it and the city on fire, on the tenth day of the fifth month, corresponding to the latter part of July; and conveyed those of the people who had escaped the sword, as captives to Babylon. Here they remained in servitude, until they were released by Cyrus, king of Persia, who, in the first year of his reign, published that famous decree which liberated the Hebrew captives, and permitted them to rebuild "the city and house of the Lord."* Many interesting circumstances in relation to this captivity, and its termination, are interspersed through some of the higher degrees, such as the Royal Arch, the Red Cross Knight, Knight of the East, and to parts of Jerusalem.

CARDINAL VIRTUES. These are Prudence, Fortitude, Temperance, and Justice. They are dilated on in the first degree; and the practice of them urged upon the candidate, by certain striking allusions Prince of the ceremonies of initiation.

---

* Lightfoot says that the seventy years of the captivity began in the third year of Jehoiakim and terminated in the first year of Cyrus, which he dates Anno Mundi 3470. *Harmony of the Four Evang. Proleg. ⅔ vii.*

CARPET. A painting or diagram, containing the emblems of a particular degree. The same as flooring or tracing board. It is called a carpet, because the larger ones used in a lodge are generally laid upon the ground for the purposes of instruction.

CASSIA. Sometimes improperly used for *Acacia.*

CATENARIAN ARCH. If a rope be suspended loosely by its two ends, the curve into which it falls is called a catenarian curve, and this inverted forms the catenarian arch, which is said to be strongest of all arches. As the form of a symbolic lodge is an oblong square, that of a Royal Arch Chapter, according to the English ritual is a catenarian arch.

CAUTION. It was formerly the custom to bestow upon an Entered Apprentice, on his initiation, a new name which was "caution." The custom is now very generally discontinued, although the principle which it inculcated should never be forgotten.

CENTRE, OPENING ON THE. In the ritual of the English lodges, it is usual for the W∴ M∴ when he has opened a lodge in the third degree, to declare it duly "opened on the centre." This practice is thus explained : "None but Masters' Lodges are so opened. Apprentice and Craft Lodges are mixed lodges,—the first including brethren of the three degrees—some higher and some lower in masonry than others, consequently there is not a masonic equality among them. The Master Mason is under a stronger obligation to his brother of an equal degree, than to one of an inferior degree. On the contrary, in a lodge of Masters, all are equal, all stand upon the same level, all are equally near and equally distant to each other—*as the central point of the circle is equally near and equally distant to its circumference.* Hence, we say a Master's lodge is opened on the centre."—Moore's Mag. v. iii. p. 356. An attempt has been made in the "Trestle Board," published under the sanction of the late Baltimore Masonic Convention, to introduce the custom into the American lodges. It has, however, been rejected in South Carolina.

CEPHAS. A Syriac word signifying a rock or stone. In the degree of Royal Master, it is used in reference to the cubical stone of masonry.

CERTIFICATE. A diploma issued by a Grand Lodge, or by a subordinate lodge under its authority, testifying that the holder thereof is a true and trusty brother, and recommending him to the hospitality of the fraternity abroad. The character of this instrument has sometimes been much misunderstoood. It is by no means intended to act as a *voucher* for the bearer, nor can it be allowed to supersede the necessity of a *strict examination*. A stranger, however, having been tried and proved by a more unerring standard, his certificate then properly comes in as an auxiliary testimonial, and will be permitted to afford good evidence of his correct standing in his lodge at home; for no body of Masons, true to the principles of their order, would grant such an instrument to an unworthy brother, or to one who, they feared, might make an improper use of it. But though the presence of a Grand Lodge's certificate be in general required as collateral evidence of worthiness to visit, or receive aid, its accidental absence, which may arise in various ways, as from fire, captivity, or shipwreck, should not debar a strange brother from the rights guaranteed to him by our institution, provided he can offer other evidence of his good character. The Grand Lodge of New York has, upon this subject, taken the proper stand in the following regulation :—"That no Mason be admitted to any subordinate lodge, under the jurisdiction of this Grand Lodge, or receive the charities of any lodge, unless he shall, on such application, exhibit a Grand Lodge Certificate, duly attested by tho proper authorities, *except he is known to the lodge to be a worthy brother.*"*

Since the publication of the first edition of this work, the Certificate system has been warmly discussed by the Grand Lodges of the United States, and considerable opposition to it has been made by some of them on the ground that it is an innovation. If it is an innovation, it certainly is not one of the present day, as we may learn from the Regulations made in General Assembly of the Masons of England, on St. John the Evangelist's day, 1663, during the Grand Mastership of the Earl of St. Albans, one of which reads as follows:

"That no person hereafter who shall be accepted a Free-mason shall be admitted into any lodge or assembly, until he has brought a certificate of the time and place of his acceptation from the lodge that accepted him, unto the Master of that limit or division where such lodge is kept."

CHAIN, MYSTIC. To form the mystic chain is for the brethren to make a circle, holding each other by the hands, as in surrounding a grave, &c. Each brother crosses his arms in front of his body, so as to give his right hand to his left hand neighbour, and his left hand to his right hand neighbour. The French call it *chaine d'union.*

CHALK, CHARCOAL AND CLAY. By these three substances, are beautifully symbolized the three qualifications for the servitude of an Entered Apprentice.

CHAMBER OF REFLECTION. In the French and Scotch rites, a small room adjoining the lodge, in which, preparatory to initiation, the candidate is enclosed for the purpose of indulging in those serious meditations which its sombre appearance, and the gloomy emblems with which it is furnished, are calculated to pro-

* Order of the Grand Lodge of New York, June 8, 1843.

duce. It is also used in the degree of Knight Templar for a similar purpose.

CHANCELLOR. An officer in a Council of Knights of the Red Cross, corresponding in some respects to the Senior Warden of a symbolic lodge.

CHAPITER. An ornamental finish to the top of a pillar.

CHAPLAIN. The office of chaplain of a lodge is one which is not recognized in the ritual of this country, although often conferred by courtesy.

CHAPTER. A convocation of Royal Arch Masons is called a Chapter. In Britain, Royal Arch Masonry is connected with and under the government of the Grand Lodge; but in America, the jurisdictions are separate.* Here, a Chapter of Royal Arch Masons is empowered to give the preparatory degrees of Mark, Past, and Most Excellent Master; although, of course, the Chapter, when meeting in either of these degrees, is called a lodge. In some Chapters, the degrees of Royal and Select Master are also given as preparatory degrees; but in most of the States, the control of these is conferred upon separate bodies, called "Councils of Royal and Select Masters." The presiding officers of a Chapter are the High Priest, King, and Scribe, who are, respectively, representatives of Joshua, Zerubbabel, and Haggai. In the English Chapters, these officers are generally styled either by the founders' names as above, or as 1st, 2d, and 3d Principals. Chapters of Royal Arch Masons in this country, are primarily under the jurisdiction of State Grand Chapters as lodges are under Grand Lodges; and secondly, under the General Grand Chapter of the United States, whose meetings are held triennially,

---

* Formerly in this country, Chapters were chartered by and under the control of Grand Lodges.

and which exercises a general supervision over this branch of the
the order, throughout the Union. The convocations of several of
the ineffable degrees are also called Chapters. See *Royal Arch*.

CHAPTER, GRAND. A Grand Chapter consists of the
High Priests, Kings, and Scribes, for the time being, of the seve-
ral Chapters under its jurisdiction, and of the Past Grand and
Deputy Grand High Priests, Kings, and Scribes of the said
Grand Chapter. Its organization differs from that of a Grand
Lodge : Past High Priests not being eligible to a seat, after the
expiration of their time of service, as Past Masters are in the
Grand Lodge; unless they shall have served as Grand and
Deputy Grand High Priests, Kings or Scribes. Grand Chapters
have the sole government and superintendence, (under the Gene-
ral Grand Chapter,) of the several Royal Arch Chapters, and
Lodges of Most Excellent, Past and Mark Masters, within their
several jurisdictions.

Until the year 1797, there was no organization of Grand
Chapters in the United States. Chapters were held under the
authority of a Master's warrent, although the consent of a neighbouring Chapter was generally deemed expedient. But in 1797,
delegates from several of the Chapters in the Northern States
assembled at Boston, for the purpose of deliberating on the expediency of organizing a Grand Chapter, for the government and
regulation of the several Chapters within the said States. This
Convention prepared an address to the Chapters in New York
and New England, disclaiming the power of any Grand Lodge to
exercise authority over Royal Arch Masons, and declaring it expedient to establish a Grand Chapter. In consequence of this
address, delegates from most of the States above mentioned, met
at Hartford, in January, 1798, and organized a Grand Chapter,
formed and adopted a constitution, and elected and installed their
officers. This example was quickly followed by other parts of
the Union; and Grand Chapters now exist in nearly all the
States.

CHAPTER, GENERAL GRAND. The General Grand
Chapter of the United States was organized in 1806, and meets tri-
ennially; it consists of the Grand and Deputy Grand High Priests,
Kings, and Scribes, for the time being, of the several State Grand
Chapters, and of the Past General Grand High Priests, Deputy
General Grand High Priests, Kings, and Scribes of the said
General Grand Chapter.* It exercises a general supervisory
authority over the State Grand Chapters, and immediate juris-
diction in all States or Territories where a State Grand Chapter
has not been established.

CHARGES. The fraternity had long been in possession of
many records, containing the ancient regulations of the order;
when, in 1722, the Duke of Montague being Grand Master of
England, the Grand Lodge finding fault with their antiquated
arrangement, it was directed that they should be collected, and
after being properly digested, be annexed to the Book of Constitutions, then in course of publication under the superintendence
of Brother James Anderson. This was accordingly done, and
the document now to be found in all the Abiman Rezons, under
the title of "The old Charges of the Free and Accepted Masons,"
constitutes, by universal consent, a part of the fundamental law
of our order. The charges are divided into six general heads of
duty, as follows: 1. Concerning God and religion. 2. Of the
civil magistrate, supreme and subordinate. 3. Of lodges. 4. Of
Masters, Wardens, Fellows, and Apprentices. 5. Of the man-
agement of the Craft in working. 6. Of behaviour under different circumstances, and in various conditions. These charges
contain succinct directions for the proper discharge of a Mason's
duties, in whatever position he may be placed; and from them
have been abridged, or by them suggested, all those well known
directions found in our Monitors, which Masters are accustomed

---

* By an amendment to the Constitution adopted in 1853, Past General
Grand Officers are no longer ex officio members.

to read to candidates, on their reception into the different degrees, and which have, therefore, also been denominated charges.
The word, however, in strictness and to avoid confusion, ought
to have been confined to the *Old Charges* above alluded to.*

CHARITY. "Though I speak with the tongues of men and
of angels, and have not charity, I become as sounding brass, or
a tinkling cymbal. And though I have the gift of prophecy and
understand all mysteries and knowledge, and have all faith so
that I could remove mountains, and have not charity, I am nothing." (1 Corinth. xiii. 1, 2.) Such was the language of an
eminent apostle of the Christian church, and such is the sentiment that constitutes the cementing bond of Freemasonry.
Charity is the chief corner-stone of our temple, and upon it is to
be erected a superstructure of all the other virtues, which make
the good man and the good Mason. The charity, however, of
which our order boasts, is not alone that sentiment of commisera-
tion, which leads us to assist the poor with pecuniary donations.
Like the virtue described by the apostle, already quoted, its application is more noble and more extensive. "It suffereth long
and is kind." The true Mason will be slow to anger and easy to
forgive. He will stay his falling brother by gentle admonition,
and warn him with kindness, of approaching danger. He will
not open his ear to his slanderers, and will close his lips against
all reproach. His faults and his follies will be locked in his
breast, and the prayer for mercy will ascend to Jehovah for his
brother's sins. Nor will these sentiments of benevolence be confined to those who are bound to him, by ties of kindred or worldly
friendship alone; but extending them throughout the globe, he
will love and cherish all who sit beneath the broad canopy of our
universal lodge. For it is the boast of our institution, that a

---

* I have omitted the republication of these charges in the present edition,
since they have now become accessible to every Mason, by their insertion in
several modern works on Freemasonry.

Mason, destitute and worthy, may find in every clime a brother, and in every land a home.

CHARLES XII., ORDER OF. An order of knighthood instituted in 1811 by Charles XII., King of Sweden, and which was to be conferred only on the principal dignitaries of the masonic institution in his dominions. In the manifesto establishing the order, the king says:—"To give to this society, (the masonic) a proof of our gracious sentiments toward it, we will and ordain that its first dignitaries to the number which we may determine, shall in future be decorated with the most intimate proof of our confidence, and which shall be for them a distinctive mark of the highest dignity." The number of knights are 27, all masons, and the King of Sweden is the perpetual Grand Master.

CHERUBIM. The second order of the angelic hierarchy, the first being the seraphim. The two cherubim that overtopped the mercy-seat or covering of the ark, in the holy of holies, were placed there by Moses, in obedience to the orders of God : "And thou shalt make two cherubim of gold, of beaten work shalt thou make them, in the two ends of the mercy-seat. And the cherubim shall stretch forth their wings on high, covering the mercy-seat with their wings, and their faces shall look one to another; toward the mercy-seat shall the faces of the cherubim be." (Exod. xxv., 17, 19.) It was between these cherubim, that the shekinah or divine presence rested, and from which issued the Bathkol or voice of God. Of the form of these cherubim, we are ignorant; Josephus says, that they resembled no known creature, but that Moses made them in the form in which he saw them about the throne of God; others, deriving their ideas from what is said of them by Ezekiel, Isaiah, and St. John, describe them as having the face and breast of a man, the wings of an eagle, the belly of a lion, and the legs and feet of an ox, which three animals, with man, are the symbols of strength and wisdom.

CHIEF OF THE TABERNACLE. The twenty-third degree in the Ancient Scotch Rite. It commemorates the institution of the order of the priesthood in Aaron and his sons Eleazar and Ithamar. Its officers are three, a Sovereign Sacrificer and two High Priests, and the members of the "Hierarchy," as the lodge is styled, are called Levites. The apron is white, lined with deep scarlet and bordered with red, blue and purple riband. A gold chandelier of seven branches is painted on the centre, and a violet-coloured myrtle on the flap. The jewel, which is a thurible, is worn from a broad yellow, purple, blue and scarlet sash, from the left shoulder to the right hip.

CHISEL. One of the working tools of a Mark Master, and emblematic of the effects of education on the human mind. For, as the artist, by the aid of this instrument, gives form and regularity to the shapeless mass of stone, so education, by cultivating the ideas and by polishing the rude thoughts, transforms the ignorant savage into the civilized being. The chisel is speculatively to the Mark Master what the Ashlar is to the Entered Apprentice.

In the English ritual, the chisel is one of the working tools of the Entered Apprentice, with the same emblematic signification as we give to it in the Mark Master's degree.

CHIVALRY. Although Freemasonry and the institution of Chivalry are not identical, yet we are permitted, from a variety of considerations, to infer that the latter was a branch of the former. And even if we should not come to this conclusion, the close connection which, at the present day, exists between some of the orders of chivalry and the order of Freemasonry, will authorize us in devoting a few words to a brief examination of this venerable institution.

The origin of chivalry is involved in very great obscurity Almost every author who has written on this subject, has adopted an hypothesis of his own. Some derive the institution from the

equestrian order of ancient Rome, while others trace it to the
tribes who, under the name of Northmen, about the ninth century, invaded the southern parts of Europe. Warburton ascribes
the origin of chivalry to the Arabians; Pinkerton, Mallet and
Percy, to the Scandinavians. Clavel derives it from the secret
societies of the Persians, which were the remains of the mysteries
of Mithras.

Chivalry, like Freemasonry, was a ceremonial institution, and
its ceremonies were highly symbolical in their character. It was
divided into three degrees: that of *Page*, which might answer to
our Apprentice; of *Esquire*, similar to our Fellow Craft; and of
Knight, which was equivalent to our Master. The education of
the page was conducted with the greatest care. He was confided
to the charge of some noble dame, who inculcated an unlimited
deference to the female sex, and taught him to appreciate the
duties and honours of the profession in which he was about to
embark. When arrived at a proper age, which was generally
that of fourteen, he was presented at the altar, where the priest,
having consecrated a sword, suspended it from his shoulder, by
which simple ceremony, he was advanced to the second degree
of chivalry, and became an Esquire. From this time, he was
attached to the person of a knight, and becoming the sharer of
his toils and dangers, was still further instructed in his duties.
Having served a probationary term in these subordinate degrees,
he was, at length, if found worthy, promoted to the honour of
knighthood, which was the third degree, and the one in which
the knowledge of the mysteries was conferred. The day before
the ceremony of installation, was passed by the novice in fasting,
and the night in a church, prostrated at the foot of the altar, and
in the midst of profound darkness. The next day he knelt before the knight, who was to receive him, and took, between his
hands, the solemn obligation, always to fly to the assistance of
the oppressed, and to sacrifice himself for the honour and defence
of the mysteries of chivalry. The knight then girded the candidate with a sword, struck him on the neck with his own, which

act was called the accolade, kissed his cheeks and forehead, and gave him, with the open palm of his hand, a gentle slap, the last he was ever to receive without resentment. He then arose, and was clothed with the various pieces of his armour, the emblematic sense of which was explained to him.

The formulary of this part of the reception has been preserved,* and furnishes abundant evidence of the symbolic character of the institution. The sword which he received was called "the arms of mercy," and he was told to conquer his enemies by mercy rather than by force of arms. Its blade was two-edged, to remind him that he must maintain chivalry and justice, and contend only for the support of these *two chief pillars of the temple of honour.* The lance represented Truth, because truth, like the lance, is straight. The coat of mail was the symbol of a fortress erected against vice, for, as castles are surrounded by walls and ditches, the coat of mail is closed in all its parts, and defends the knight against treason, disloyalty, pride, and every other evil passion. The rowels of the spur were given to urge the possessor on to deeds of honour and virtue. The shield, which he places betwixt himself and his enemy, was to remind him that the knight is as a shield interposed between the prince and the people, to preserve peace and tranquility.

After the reception, the knight was exhibited with great pomp before the people. A banquet, followed by the bestowal of largesses and alms, concluded the ceremonies. The knights were in possession of signs of recognition known only to themselves,† and were also united by a system of mysteries, allusions to which will often be found in the allegories that we meet with in the romances of chivalry. The greater part of the stories of Turpin and the other old romancers is filled with astronomical allusions applied to Charlemagne, and indeed this prince and his twelve paladins ought, says Clavel, to be considered in these legends, as

---

* La Roque, Traité de la Noblesse.

† Clavel Hist. Pitt. de la Franc-Maçon, p. 354.

the sun and the twelve genii or signs of the twelve palaces of the zodiac.

CHRIST, ORDER OF. When the Knights Templars were overthrown throughout Europe, they were protected in Portugal, and converted by the sovereign into a new order, called the Order of Christ, and the secret part of the ritual was abolished. A masonic order of the same name was at one time established in Paris by a Portuguese.

CIRCLE. See *Point within a Circle.*

CIRCUMAMBULATION. Circumambulation, or a procession around the altar, always formed a part of the ancient religious ceremonies. In Greece, the priests and the people walked thrice round the altar during the sacrifice, and sung a sacred hymn. On these occasions, the procession moved according to the course of the sun, and a hymn is still preserved in the writings of Callimachus, which was chanted by the priests of Apollo, at Delos, and the substance of which was, "we imitate the example of the sun and follow his benevolent course." The Druids used the same ceremonies, and always made three turns round the altar, accompanied by all the worshippers. In some parts of Britain, this practice continued to be observed for ages after the destruction of the Druidical religion, and Martin, in his Description of the Western Islands, written not a century ago, tells us that "in the Scottish isles the people never come to the ancient sacrificing and fire-hallowing cairns, but they walk three times round them, from east to west, according to the course of the sun. This sanctified tour, or *round by the south,* is called Deiseal, from Deas or Deis, the right hand, and Soil or Sul, the sun ; *the right hand being ever next the heap or cairn.*"

Oliver says that in levelling the foot-stone of the temple, King Solomon and the twelve tribes circumambulated Mount Moriah three times in jubilee procession.

CIRCUMSPECTION. A necessary watchfulness is recommended to every man, but in a Mason it becomes a positive duty, and the neglect of it constitutes a heinous crime. On this subject, the Old Charges are explicit. "You shall be cautious in your words and carriage, that the most penetrating stranger shall not be able to discover or find out what is not proper to be imitated; and sometimes you shall divert a discourse and manage it prudently for the honour of the Worshipful Fraternity."—*Old Charges, VI.* 4.

CLANDESTINE. Not legal. A body of Masons uniting in a lodge without the consent of a Grand Lodge, or although originally legally constituted, continuing to work after its charter has been revoked, is styled a "Clandestine Lodge," and its members are called "Clandestine Masons." With clandestine lodges or Masons, regular Masons are forbidden to associate, or converse on masonic subjects.

CLAY GROUND. In the clay ground between Succoth and Zeredatha, Hiram Abif cast all the sacred vessels of the temple, as well as the pillars of the porch. This spot was about 35 miles in a north-east direction from Jerusalem, and it is supposed that Hiram selected it for his foundry, because the clay which abounded there was, by its great tenacity, peculiarly fitted for making moulds. The masonic tradition on this subject is sustained by the authority of Scripture. See 1 Kings vii. 42, and 2 Chron. iv. 17.

CLEFTS OF THE ROCKS. The whole of Palestine is very mountainous, and these mountains abound in deep clefts or caves, which were anciently places of refuge to the inhabitants in time of war, and were often used as lurking places for robbers. It is, therefore, strictly in accordance with geographical truth that the statement, in relation to the concealment of certain persons in the clefts of the rocks, is made in the third degree.

8*

CLOSING. The duty of closing the lodge is as imperative and the ceremony as solemn as that of opening, nor should it ever be omitted through negligence, nor hurried over with haste, but every thing should be performed with order and precision, so that no brother shall go away dissatisfied. From the very nature of our constitution, a lodge cannot properly be adjourned. It must either be closed in due form, or the brethren called off to refreshment. But an adjournment on motion, as in other societies, is unknown to our order. The Master can, alone, dismiss the brethren, and that dismission must take place after a settled usage. In Grand Lodges, which meet for several days successively, the session is generally continued from day to day, by calling to refreshment at the termination of each day's sitting.

CLOTHED. A Mason is said to be properly clothed when he wears white leather gloves, a white apron, and the jewel of his masonic rank. The gloves are now often, but improperly dispensed with, except on public occasions. This costume is of ancient date, for, in an indenture of covenants made in the reign of Henry the Sixth, of England, "between the church wardens of a parish in Suffolk and a company of Freemasons, the latter stipulate that each man should be provided with a pair of white gloves and a white apron, and that a lodge, properly tyled, should be erected at the expense of the parish, in which they were to carry on their works."—See *Quarterly Review, Vol. XXIV. p.* 146.

CLOUDED CANOPY. See *Covering.*

COCK. The ancients made the cock a symbol of courage, and consecrated him to Mars, Pallas and Bellona, deities of war. As an emblem of this quality, he is used in the jewel of the Captain General of an Encampment of Knights Templars.

Rhigelline, however, gives a different explanation of this symbol. He says that the cock was the emblem of the sun and of life, and that as the ancient Christians allegorically deplored the death of the solar orb in Christ, the cock recalled its life and resurrection.* The cock, we know, was a symbol among the early Christians, and is repeatedly to be found on the tombs in the catacombs of Rome. Hence, I am, on further reflection, induced to believe that we should give a Christian interpretation to the jewel of a Knight Templar as symbolic of the resurrection.

COERCION. Among the imperative requisites of a candidate for Freemasonry, is one that he should come of his free will and accord. Masons cannot, therefore, be too cautious how they act or speak before uninitiated persons who have expressed any desire of entering the order, lest this perfect freedom of their will be infringed. Coercion is entirely out of the question. Mercenary or interested motives should be strenuously discouraged, and no other inducement used than that silent persuasion which arises from a candid exposition of the beauties and moral excellences of our institution.

COFFIN. In the ancient mysteries, the aspirant could not claim a participation in the highest secrets until he had been placed in the Pastos, Bed or Coffin. The placing him in the coffin was called the symbolical death of the mysteries, and his deliverance was termed a raising from the dead. Hence arose a peculiarity in the Greek verb *teleutao*, which, in the active voice, signified "I die," and in the middle voice, "I am initiated." "The mind," says an ancient writer, quoted by Stobæus, "is affected in *death* just as it is in the *initiation* into the mysteries. And word answers to word, as well as thing to thing; for τελευταν is *to die*, and τελεισθαι *to be initiated*." The coffin in masonry is an emblem of the Master's degree, but its explication is here incommunicable.

---

* Maçonnerie considerée comme le resultat des religions Egyptienne, Juive et Chretienne, tom. ii. p. 67.

COLLAR. An ornament worn around the neck by the officers of lodges, to which is suspended a jewel indicative of the wearer's rank. The colour of the collar varies in the different grades of masonry. That of a symbolic lodge is blue; of a Past Master, purple; of a Royal Arch Mason, scarlet; of a Secret Master, white bordered with black; of a Perfect Master, green, &c. These colours are not arbitrary, but are each accompanied with an emblematic meaning.

COLOURS. Each grade of masonry is furnished with its emblematic colour. Colours have always been invested with mystic meanings. Thus, they are used as the distinguishing mark of different nations, as well as of different professions. White has been considered as emblematic of joy, and is hence selected as the appropriate dress for bridal occasions. On the contrary, the sombre appearance of black has confined its use to seasons of grief and mourning. The heralds have adopted colours as a part of their highly symbolic science, and among them, every colour is the symbol of a particular virtue and quality of the mind. The three symbolic colours of the ancient Druids, appropriated to their three degrees, were Green, emblematic of Hope; Blue, of Truth; and White, of Light. The colours of Ancient York Masonry are blue, purple and scarlet. Besides these, the different degrees of chivalry, and of Scotch masonry, have their appropriate colours. The reader is referred to these colours under their appropriate names.

COLUMN. A round pillar made to support as well as to adorn a building, whose construction varies in the different orders of architecture. See *Broken Column.*

COMMANDER, GRAND. The Grand Commander is the presiding officer in an encampment of Knights Templars. His style is Most Eminent, and the jewel of his office is a cross, from which issue rays of light.

COMMITTEE. The well-known regulation which forbids private committees in the lodge, that is, select conversations between two or more members, in which the other members are not permitted to join, is derived from the Old Charges: "You are not permitted to hold private committees or separate conversation, without leave from the Master, nor to talk of any thing impertinent or unseemly, nor to interrupt the Master or Wardens, or any brother speaking to the Master."—*Old Charges*, § VI. 1.

COMMON GAVEL. See *Gavel.*

COMMUNICATE. When the peculiar mysteries of a degree are bestowed upon a candidate by mere verbal description of the bestower, without his being made to pass through the constituted ceremonies, the degree is technically said to be *communicated*. This mode is, however, entirely confined to the Scotch rite. In York Masonry it is never permitted.

COMMUNICATIONS. The meetings of Lodges are called Communications, and of Grand Lodges, Grand Communications.

COMPANION. A title bestowed by Royal Arch Masons upon each other, and equivalent to the word brother in symbolic lodges. It refers, most probably, to the companionship in exile and captivity of the ancient Jews, from the destruction of the Temple by Nebuchadnezzar, to its restoration by Zerubbabbel, under the auspices of Cyrus.

COMPASSES. As in operative masonry, the compasses are used for the admeasurement of the architect's plans, and to enable him to give those just proportions which will insure beauty as well as stability to his work; so, in speculative masonry, is this important implement symbolic of that even tenor of deportment, that true standard of rectitude which alone can bestow happiness here and felicity hereafter. Hence are the compasses the most prominent emblem of virtue,* the true and only measure of a Mason's life and conduct. As the *Bible* gives us *light* ou our duties to God, and the *square* illustrates our duties to our neighbour and brother, so the *compasses* give that additional *light* which is to instruct us in the duty we owe to ourselves—the great imperative duty of circumscribing our passions, and keeping our desires within due bounds. "It is ordained," says the philo- sophic Burke, "in the eternal constitution of things, that men of intemperate passions cannot be free; their passions forge their fetters."

COMPOSITE. One of the five orders of architecture intro- duced by the Romans, and compounded of the other four, whence it derives its name. Although it combines strength with beauty, yet, as it is a comparatively modern invention, it is held in little esteem among Freemasons.

CONSECRATION. When a new lodge is formed, it is ne- cessary that it should be hallowed or consecrated to the purposes of masonry. The ceremonies on this occasion vary in different countries. They are detailed in all the Monitors.

CONSECRATION, ELEMENTS OF. The masonic elements of consecration are *corn, wine,* and *oil,* which are called the corn of nourishment, the wine of refreshment, and the oil of joy. They are emblematic of health, plenty, and peace. See *Corn.*

CONSISTORY. The meetings of members of the 32d de-

---

* Those brethren who delight to trace our emblems to an astronomical origin, find, in the compasses, a symbol of the Sun, the circular pivot repre- senting the body of the luminary, and the diverging legs his rays.

gree, or Sublime Princes of the Royal Secret, are called Consistories. Its officers are, a Thrice Illustrious Grand Commander, two Thrice Illustrious Lieutenant Grand Commanders, Grand Orator, Grand Chancellor, Grand Treasurer, Grand Secretary, Grand Master Architect, Physician General, Keeper of the Seals, Grand Master of Ceremonies, Captain of the Guards, and Tyler.

CONSTITUTION OF A LODGE. Any number of Master Masons, not less than seven, being desirous of forming a new lodge, must apply by petition, to the Grand Lodge of the State in which they reside, praying for a Charter or Warrant of Constitution to enable them to assemble as a regular lodge. Their petition being favourably received, a warrant is immediately granted, and the Grand Master appoints a day for its consecration and for the installation of its officers. In this consecration and installation consists the constitution of a lodge, and when thus consecrated, and its officers installed by the authority of the Grand Lodge, it is said to be *legally constituted*.

CONSTITUTIONS. See *Book of Constitutions*.

CONVOCATION. The meetings of Chapters of Royal Arch Masons are styled Convocations; those of Grand Chapters are Grand Convocations.

COPESTONE.* The topmost stone in a building; the last laid, as the foundation stone is the first. "To celebrate the copestone," is to celebrate the completion of the edifice, a custom still observed by operative Masons.

CORINTHIAN ORDER. This is the lightest and most

---

* In masonic language this word is usually but incorrectly pronounced *copestone*. Its derivation is from the Saxon *cop*, the head.

ornamental of the pure orders, and possesses the highest degree
of richness and detail that architecture attained under the Greeks.
Its capital is its great distinction, and is richly adorned with
leaves of acanthus, olive, &c., and other ornaments. The column
of Beauty which supports the lodge, is of the Corinthian order,
and its appropriate situation and symbolic officer are in the S.·.

CORN. Corn, wine, and oil are the masonic elements of consecration. The adoption of these symbols is supported by the
highest antiquity. Corn, wine, and oil were the most important
productions of Eastern countries; they constituted the wealth of
the people, and were esteemed as the supports of life and the
means of refreshment. David enumerates them among the
greatest blessings that we enjoy, and speaks of them as "*wine*
that maketh glad the heart of man, and *oil* to make his face
shine, and *bread* which strengtheneth man's heart." Ps. civ. 14.
In devoting any thing to religious purposes, the anointing with
oil was considered as a necessary part of the ceremony, a rite
which has descended to Christian nations. The tabernacle in
the wilderness, and all its holy vessels, were, by God's express
command, anointed with oil; Aaron and his two sons were set
apart for the priesthood with the same ceremony; and the prophets and kings of Israel were consecrated to their offices by the
same rite. Hence, Freemasons' lodges, which are but temples to
the Most High, are consecrated to the sacred purposes for which
they were built, by strewing corn, wine, and oil upon the "*lodge*,"
the emblem of the Holy Ark. Thus does this mystic ceremony
instruct us to be nourished with the hidden manna of righteousness, to be refreshed with the Word of the Lord, and to rejoice
with *joy* unspeakable in the riches of divine grace. "Wherefore, my brethren," says the venerable Harris, "wherefore do
you carry *corn*, *wine*, and *oil*, in your processions, but to remind
you, that in the pilgrimage of human life, you are to impart a
portion of your *bread* to feed the hungry, to send a cup of your

wine to cheer the sorrowful, and to pour the healing *oil* of your consolation into the wounds which sickness hath made in the bodies, or affliction rent in the hearts of your fellow-travellers?" —*Discourses*, IV. 81.

In processions, the corn alone is carried in a golden pitcher, the wine and oil are placed in silver vessels, and this is to remind us that the first, as a necessity and the "staff of life," is of more importance and more worthy of honour than the others, which are but comforts.

CORNER-STONE. The first stone, in the foundation of every magnificent building, is called the corner-stone, and is laid in the north-east, generally with solemn and appropriate ceremonies. To this stone, formerly, some secret influence was attributed. In Alet's Ritual, it is directed to be "solid, angular, of about a foot square, and laid in the north-east." Its position, as Oliver justly remarks, "accounts in a rational manner, for the general disposition of a newly initiated candidate, when enlightened but uninstructed, he is accounted to be in the most superficial part of masonry."—*Signs and Symbols*, p. 225.

CORNUCOPIA. The horn of plenty. It is a symbol of abundance, and as such has been adopted as the jewel of the Stewards of a lodge, to remind them that it is their duty to see that the tables are properly furnished at refreshment, and that every brother is suitably provided for.

CORYBANTES, MYSTERIES OF THE. Rites instituted in Phrygia, in honour of Atys, the lover of Cybele. The goddess was supposed first to bewail the death of her lover, and afterwards to rejoice for his restoration to life. The ceremonies were a scenical representation of this alternate lamentation and rejoicing, and of the sufferings of Atys, who was placed in an ark or coffin during the mournful part of the orgies.

COTYTTO, MYSTERIES OF. These mysteries were instituted in Thrace, and passed over into Greece and Rome, where
they were known as the rites of the Bona Dea. They were celebrated by females alone, and were conducted with so much
secrecy that their ceremonies are entirely unknown.

COUNCIL. In several of the higher degrees of masonry, the
meetings are styled councils—as a council of Knights of the
Red Cross, and of Princes of Jerusalem. A portion of the room
in which a chapter of Royal Arch Masons or Knights of the
Red Cross meets, is emphatically designated as the Grand
Council.

COUNCIL OF ROYAL AND SELECT MASTERS. Bodies
in which the degrees of Royal and Select Masters are given.
The names and number of the officers vary slightly in different
councils. They are perhaps most properly, a Thrice Illustrious
Grand Master, Illustrious Hiram of Tyre, Principal Conductor of
the Works, Recorder, Master of the Exchequer, Captain of the
Guards and Steward. Some of the monitors add a Conductor
of the Council, but I am not aware that such an officer is necessary according to the true ritual.

COUNCIL OF THE TRINITY. An independent masonic
jurisdiction, in which are conferred the degrees of Knight of the
Christian Mark, and Guard of the Conclave, Knight of the Holy
Sepulchre, and the Holy and Thrice Illustrious Order of the
Cross. They are conferred after the Encampment degrees. They
are Christian degrees, and refer to the crucifixion.

COVERING OF THE LODGE. Our ancient brethren met
beneath no other covering than the cloudy canopy of heaven.
The innumerable stars that decked its concave surface, were as
living witnesses of the power and wisdom of Him, at whose

sacred name they were taught to bow; and were nightly winning
from the virtuous Mason, by their bright effulgence, the prayer
of hope, and the hymn of praise. Our lodges still claim this
noble roof, emblematically, as their only covering, which admonishes them with a "sic itur ad astra," to aspire from earth to
heaven, and to seek there the rest from labour, and the reward
of toil.

COWAN. One of the profane. This purely masonic term is
derived from the Greek *kuon*, a dog. In the early ages of the
church, when the mysteries of religion were communicated only
to initiates under the veil of secrecy, the infidels and unbaptized
profane were called "dogs," a term probably suggested by such
passages of Scripture as Matt. vii. 6, "Give not that which is
holy to dogs," and Philip. iii. 2, "Beware of dogs, beware of
evil workers, beware of the concision." Hence, as *kuon*, or dog,
meant among the early fathers one who had not been initiated into
the Christian mysteries, the term was borrowed by the Freemasons, and in time corrupted into *cowan*. The attempt made by
some anti-masonic writers to derive the word from the *chouans*
of the French Revolution is absurd. The word was in use long
before the French Revolution was even meditated. I have in
my possession a copy of the edition of Anderson's Constitutions,
printed in 1769, which contains at p. 97, this word: "Working
Masons ever will have their own wages * * * let *cowans* do as
they please."

CRAFT. The ordinary acceptation is a trade or mechanical
art, and collectively, the persons practising it. Hence, "the
Craft," in speculative masonry, signifies the whole body of Freemasons, wherever dispersed.

CRAFTED. A word sometimes colloquially used, instead of
the lodge term "passed," to designate the advancement of a candidate to the second degree.

CRAFTSMAN. A Fellow Craft.

CREATED. Knights of the Red Cross, Knights of Malta, and Knights Templars, when advanced to those degrees, are said to be "dubbed and created."

CREED OF A MASON. The creed of a Mason is brief, unentangled with scholastic subtleties, or with theological difficulties. It is a creed which demands and receives the universal consent of all men, which admits of no doubt, and defies schism. It is the belief in GOD, the supreme architect of heaven and earth; the dispenser of all good gifts, and the judge of the quick and the dead.

CROSS. The cross was an important emblem in the Pagan mysteries, and was used as an hieroglyphic of life. It is retained in one of its modifications, the triple tau, as an emblem of the R.·. A.·. degree, according to the English ritual, and is to be found plentifully dispersed through the symbols of the ineffable and philosophical degrees. As an emblem in the degrees of chivalry, it bears a strictly Christian allusion. But I do not recognize it as appertaining to symbolic masonry. See *Triple Tau.*

CROSS-LEGGED. It was an invariable custom in the Middle Ages, in laying out the body of a Knight Templar after death, to cross one leg over the other; and in all the monuments of these knights now remaining in the various churches of Europe, there will always be found an image of the person buried, sculptured on the stone, lying on a bier in this cross-legged position. Templars of the present day will readily connect this posture with an appropriate portion of the degree as now conferred.

When, in the 16th century, a portion of the Knights Templars of Scotland united themselves with a masonic lodge at Sterling, they were commonly known by the name of the "cross-legged Masons." Oliver relates the fact, but assigns no plausible reason for the appellation. It was, I presume, given in allusion to this funeral posture of the Templars, and a "cross-legged Mason" would, therefore, be synonymous with a masonic Knight Templar.

CROW. An iron implement to raise weights. It is one of the working tools of a Royal Arch Mason. For its symbolic meaning, see *Pickaxe*.

CROWN, PRINCESSES OF THE. *Princesses de la couronne.* A species of androgynous masonry, established at Saxony, in 1770.—*Clavel, Hist. de la Franc-Maçon.*

CRUSADES. A few masonic writers have endeavoured to trace the introduction of masonry into Europe, to these wars. Those who entertain this opinion, suppose that the order was unknown in Christendom until it was brought there by the knights who had visited the Holy Land, and who, they contend, were instructed in its mysteries by the Jews of Palestine. But this theory is wholly untenable; for the first crusade commenced in 1065; and we have the best evidence that a convention of Masons assembled at York, on the summons of Prince Edwin, as early as 926, or 139 years before a single knight had entered Asia.

CRUX ANSATA. The crux ansata or cross, surmounted by a circle, thus, was, in the Egyptian mysteries, a symbol of eternal life.

CUBE. The cube is defined to be a regular solid body, consisting of six square and equal faces or sides, and the angles all right angles. In the double cube, four of the faces are oblong squares. The cube, from its perfect form, constitutes an important geometrical figure among Masons. The perfect Ashlar, it is supposed by some, should be of this figure, and the form of the

9*

lodge, taken in its height and depth, as well as its length and breadth, is a double cube, though in its superfices it constitutes only an oblong square.

CUBICAL STONE. The cubical stone forms an important part of the ritual of the Royal Arch and Rose Croix, as well as some other of the high degrees. We have a masonic legend respecting a cubical stone, on which the sacred name was inscribed in a mystical diagram. On this stone, Adam made his offerings to God. This stone is called "the masonic stone of foundation," and our traditions very minutely trace its history. When Jacob fled from Esau to his uncle Laban, in Mesopotamia, he carried this stone with him, and used it as his pillow on the occasion of his memorable dream, the foot of the ladder appearing to rest on the stone. It was subsequently taken by him into Egypt, and when the Israelites departed from that country, Moses conveyed away with his followers the stone of foundation, as a talisman, by which they were to be conducted into the promised land. In the battle with the Amalekites, he seated himself on this stone. Afterward this stone was deposited in a secret crypt of the temple, in a manner well known to Select Masters, and there remained hidden until, at the rebuilding of the temple by Zerubbabel, it was discovered by three zealous sojourners, and made the corner-stone of the second temple.*

CUBIT. A measure of length, originally denoting the distance from the elbow to the extremity of the middle finger, or the fourth part of a well proportioned man's stature. The Hebrew cubit, according to Bishop Cumberland, was twenty-one inches; but only eighteen according to other authorities. There

---

* The stone pillar, anointed with oil, was a common patriarchal hieroglyphic, connected with the worship of the Supreme Being; and, as Faber remarks, a rude stone, anointed in the same way, was among the heathens one of the most ancient symbols of the Great Father. The cubical stone is, indeed, an important link, connecting the spurious and the true Freemasonry.

were two kinds of cubits, the sacred and profane—the former equal to thirty-six, and the latter to eighteen inches. It is by the common cubit that the dimensions of the various parts of the temple are to be computed.

CYRUS. Cyrus king of Persia, was a great conqueror, and after having reduced nearly all Asia, he crossed the Euphrates, and laid siege to Babylon, which he took by diverting the course of the river which ran through it. The Jews, who had been carried away by Nebuchadnezzar, on the destruction of the temple, were then remaining as captives in Babylon. These Cyrus released A. M. 3466, or, B. C. 538, and sent them back to Jerusalem to rebuild the house of God, under the care of Joshua, Zerubbabel and Haggai.

D.

DARKNESS. Darkness among Freemasons is emblematical of ignorance; for, as our science has technically been called "Lux," or light, the absence of light must be the absence of knowledge. Hence the rule, that the eye should not see, until the heart has conceived the true nature of those beauties which constitute the mysteries of our order. In the spurious Freemasonry of the ancient mysteries, the aspirant was always shrouded in darkness, as a preparatory step to the reception of the full light of knowledge. The time of this confinement in darkness and solitude, varied in the different mysteries. Among the Druids of Britain, the period was nine days and nights; in the Grecian mysteries, it was three times nine days; while among the Persians, according to Porphyry, it was extended to the almost incredible period of fifty days of darkness, solitude and fasting.

In the beginning, LIGHT was esteemed above darkness, and

the primitive Egyptians worshipped *On*, as their chief deity, under the character of eternal Light. But, as the learned Oliver observes, "this worship was soon debased by superstitious practices." Darkness was then adored as the first born, as the progenitor of day, and the state of existence before creation. The apostrophe of Young to Night, embodies the feelings which gave origin to this debasing worship of darkness:

> "O majestic night !
> Nature's great ancestor ! day's elder born !
> And fated to survive the transient sun !
> By mortals and immortals seen with awe !"

Freemasonry has restored Darkness to its proper place, as a state of preparation; the symbol of that antemundane chaos from whence light issued at the divine command; of the state of nonentity before birth, and of ignorance before the reception of knowledge. Hence, in the ancient mysteries, the release of the aspirant from solitude and darkness was called the act of regeneration, and he was said to be born again, or to be raised from the dead. And in masonry, the darkness which envelopes the mind of the uninitiated, being removed by the bright effulgence of masonic light, Masons are appropriately called "the sons of light."

DATES. See *Calendar, Masonic.*

DEACON. In every well regulated symbolic lodge, the two lowest of the internal officers are the Senior and Junior Deacons. The former is appointed by the Master, and the latter by the Senior Warden. It is to the Deacons that the introduction of visitors should be properly entrusted. Their duties comprehend also, a general surveillance over the security of the lodge, and they are the proxies of the officers by whom they are appointed. Hence their jewel, in allusion to the necessity of circumspection and justice, is a square and compasses. In the centre, the Senior

Deacon wears a sun, and the Junior Deacon a moon, which serve to distinguish their respective ranks. In the rite of Misraim, the deacons are called acolytes.

The office of Deacons in Masonry appear to have been derived from the usages of the primitive church. In the Greek church, the deacons were always the πυλωροι, pylori or doorkeepers, and in the Apostolical Constitutions the deacon was ordered to stand at the men's door, and the sub-deacon at the women's, to see that none came in or went out during the oblation.*

DECLARATION OF CANDIDATES. See *Questions to Candidates.*

DEDICATION. When a masonic hall has been erected, it is dedicated, with certain well known and impressive ceremonies, to *Masonry, Virtue,* and *Universal Benevolence.*

Lodges, however, are differently dedicated. Anciently, they were dedicated to King Solomon, as the founder of ancient craft masonry, and the first Most Excellent Grand Master. Christian lodges are generally dedicated to St. John the Baptist, and St. John the Evangelist; and in every well regulated lodge, there is exhibited a certain point within a circle, embordered by two perpendicular lines, called the "lines parallel," which represent these two saints. In those English lodges which have adopted the union system of work, the dedication is to "God and his service," and the lines parallel represent Moses and Solomon. This change was adopted by the Grand Lodge of England, in 1813, to obviate the charge of sectarianism. I have, however, in another work, endeavoured to prove that to this charge we by no means render ourselves amenable by this dedication to the above saints, since it is made to them, not as Christians, but as eminent Masons; not as saints, but as pious and good men; not as teach-

* Const. Apost., lib. viii., Cap. ii.

ers of a religious sect, but as bright exemplars of all those virtues which Masons are taught to reverence and practice.*

With respect to the original cause of this dedication, the English lodges have preserved a tradition, which, as a matter of curiosity, may find a place in this work. I am indebted for it to Brother Moore's excellent Magazine, vol. ii., p. 263.

"From the building of the first temple at Jerusalem, to the Babylonish captivity, Freemasons' lodges were dedicated to King Solomon; from thence to the coming of the Messiah, they were dedicated to Zerubbabel, the builder of the second temple; and from that time to the final destruction of the temple by Titus, in the reign of Vespasian, they were dedicated to St. John the Baptist; but owing to the many massacres and disorders which attended that memorable event, Freemasonry sunk very much into decay; many lodges were entirely broken up, and but few could meet in sufficient numbers to constitute their legality, and at a general meeting of the craft, held in the city of Benjamin, it was observed that the principal reason for the decline of masonry was the want of a Grand Master to patronize it; they, therefore, deputed seven of their most eminent members to wait upon St. John the Evangelist, who was at that time Bishop of Ephesus, requesting him to take the office of Grand Master. He returned for answer, that though well stricken in years, (being upwards of ninety,) yet having been in the early part of his life initiated into masonry, he would take upon himself that office; he thereby completed by his learning, what the other St. John had completed by his zeal, and thus drew what Freemasons term a line parallel; ever since which Freemasons' lodges in all Christian countries have been dedicated both to St. John the Baptist, and St. John the Evangelist."

But the task is not difficult to trace more philosophically, and, I believe, more correctly, the real origin of this custom. In the

---

* See an article by the author on this subject, in Moore's Freemasons' Mag., v. iii. p. 6.

spurious masonry, so well known as the mysteries of Pagan nations, we may find the most plausible reasons for the celebration of our festivals in June and December, and for the dedication of our lodges to St. John the Baptist, and St. John the Evangelist.

The post-diluvians, according to the testimony of the Jewish writer, Maimoindes, the Magians of Persia, until their ritual was improved and purified by Zoroaster, and most probably the ancient Druids, introduced into their rites a great respect for, and even an adoration of the Sun, as the source of light and life, and fruition, and the visible representative of the invisible creative and preservative principle of nature. To such sects, the period when the sun reached his greatest northern and southern declination, by entering the zodiacal signs, Cancer and Capricorn, marked, as it would be, by the most evident effects on the seasons, and on the length of the days and nights, could not have passed unobserved; but, on the contrary, must have occupied a distinguished place in their ritual. Now these important days fall respectively on the 21st of June and the 22d of December.

In the spurious masonry of the ancients these days were, doubtless, celebrated as returning eras in the existence of the great source of light, and object of their worship. Our ancient brethren adopted the custom, abandoning, however, in deference to their own purer doctrines, the idolatrous principles which were connected with these dates, and confining their celebration exclu-sively to their astronomical importance. But time passed on. Christianity came to mingle its rays with the light of masonry, and our Christian ancestors, finding that the church had appropriated two days near these solstitial periods to the memory of two eminent saints, it was easy to incorporate these festivals, by the lapse of a few days, into the masonic calendar, and to adopt these worthies as patrons of our order. To this change, the earlier Christian Masons were doubtless the more persuaded by the peculiar character of these saints. St. John the Baptist, by announcing the approach of Christ, and by the mystic ablution to which he subjected his proselytes, and which was afterward

adopted in the ceremony of initiation into Christianity, might well
be considered as the *Grand Hierophant* of the church, while the
mysterious and emblematic nature of the Apocalypse assimilated
the mode of teaching adopted by St. John the Evangelist to that
practised by the fraternity.

It is thus that I trace the present system of dedication, through
these saints, to the heliacal worship of the ancients.

Royal Arch Chapters are dedicated to Zerubbabel, Prince or
Governor of Judah, and Encampments of Knights Templars to
St. John the Almoner. Mark lodges should be dedicated to
Hiram the Builder; Past Masters' to the Sts. John, and Most
Excellent Masters' to King Solomon.

DEDICATION OF THE TEMPLE. The temple having
been completed, Solomon dedicated it to Jehovah in the month
Tizri, 2999 years after the creation, and 1005 before the advent
of Christ. Masonic tradition tells us that he assembled the nine
Deputy Grand Masters in the holy place from which all natural
light had been carefully excluded, and which only received the
artificial light which emanated from the east, west, and south,
and there made the necessary arrangements,* after which he
stood before the altar of the Lord, and offered up that beautiful
invocation and prayer which is to be found in the 8th chapter of
the 1st Book of Kings.

DEGREES. Ancient Craft Masonry, or as it is called by the
Grand Lodge of Scotland, "St. John's Masonry," consists of but
three degrees, Entered Apprentice, Fellow Craft, and Master
Mason. The degrees in all the rites vary in number and character, inasmuch as they are comparatively modern; but they all
commence with the three degrees of Ancient Craft Masonry.

In all the Pagan mysteries, there were progressive degrees of
initiation. In the mysteries of Hindostan, there were four de-

---

* Oliver, Landmarks, i. 580.

grees; three in those of Greece; the same number among the Druids; and two among the Mexicans. The object of these steps of probation was to test the character of the aspirant, and at the same time to prepare him by gradual revelations, for the important knowledge he was to receive at the final moment of his adoption.

DELTA. A triangle. The name of a piece of furniture in an Encampment of Knights Templars, which, being of a triangular form, derives its name from the Greek letter Δ, delta. It is also the title given, in the French and Scotch rites, to the luminous triangle which encloses the ineffable name.

DEMIT. A Mason is said to demit from the order when he withdraws from all connection with it. It relieves the individual from all pecuniary contributions, and debars him from pecuniary relief, but it does not cancel his masonic obligations, nor exempt him from that wholesome control which the order exercises over the moral conduct of its members. In this respect the maxim is, *once a Mason and always a Mason.*

DEPUTY GRAND MASTER. The assistant, and in his absence, the representative of the Grand Master. He was formerly appointed by his superior, but is now elected by the craft. While the Grand Master is present, the D.·. G.·. M.·. has neither duties nor powers; these are exercised only in the absence of the presiding officer.

DERMOTT, LAURENCE. He was at first the Grand Secretary and afterwards the Deputy Grand Master of that body of masons, who, in 1739, seceded from the Grand Lodge of England and called themselves "Ancient York Masons," stigmatizing the regular masons as "moderns." In 1764, Dermott published the Book of Constitutions of his Grand Lodge under the title of "Ahiman Rezon; or a help to all that are or would be Free and

Accepted Masons, containing the quintessence of all that has been published on the subject of Freemasonry." This work passed through several editions, the last of which was edited, in 1813, by Thomas Harper the Deputy Grand Master of the Ancient Masons, under the title of "The Constitutions of Freemasonry, or Ahiman Rezon." It is not, however, considered as any authority for masonic law.

DESAGULIERS. John Theophilus Desaguliers, LL.D., F.R.S., and a distinguished writer and lecturer on experimental philosophy, was the second Grand Master after the reorganization of Freemasonry in 1717. In 1720, he compiled, with Dr. Anderson, the earliest form of masonic lectures that are now extant, although the use of them has long since been abandoned for more modern and complete ones. He was born at Rochelle, in France, on the 12th March, 1683, and died at London in 1749.

DEUS MEUMQUE JUS. God and my right. The motto of the 33d degree, Ancient and Accepted rite.

DIONYSIAN ARCHITECTS. The priests of Bacchus, or, as the Greeks called him, Dionysus, having devoted themselves to architectural pursuits, established about 1000 years before the Christian era, a society or fraternity of builders in Asia Minor, which is styled by the ancient writers the Fraternity of Dionysian Architects. An account of this institution is given under the head of *"Antiquities of Freemasonry."*

DIONYSIAN MYSTERIES. These mysteries were celebrated throughout Greece and Asia Minor, but principally at Athens, where the years were numbered by them. They were instituted in honour of Bacchus, and were introduced into Greece from Egypt, which, as we shall have abundant occasion to see in the course of this work, was the parent of all the ancient rites. In these mysteries, the murder of Bacchus by the Titans was commemorated, in which legend he is evidently identified with the Egyptian Osiris, who was slain by his brother, Typhon. The aspirant in the ceremonies through which he passed, represented the murder of the god, and his restoration to life.

The commencement of the mysteries, or what we might masonically call the opening of the lodge, was signalized by the consecration of an egg, in allusion to the mundane egg from which all things were supposed to have sprung. The candidate having been first purified by water, and crowned with a myrtle branch, was introduced into the vestibule, and there clothed in the sacred habilaments. He was then delivered to the conductor, who, after the mystic warning, εχας, εχας, εστε βεβηλοι, "Depart hence, all ye profane!" exhorted the candidate to exert all his fortitude and courage in the dangers and trials through which he was about to pass. He was then led through a series of dark caverns, a part of the ceremonies which Stobæus calls "a rude and fearful march through night and darkness." During this passage he is terrified by the howling of wild beasts, and other fearful noises; artificial thunder reverberates through the subterranean apartments, and transient flashes of lightning reveal monstrous apparitions to his sight. In this state of darkness and terror he is kept for three days and nights, after which he commences the aphanism or mystical death of Bacchus. He is now placed on the pastos or couch, that is, he is confined in a solitary cell, where he is at liberty to reflect seriously on the nature of the undertaking in which he is engaged. During this time, he is alarmed with the sudden crash of waters, which is intended to represent the deluge. Typhon, searching for Osiris, or Bacchus, for they are here identical, discovers the ark in which he had been secreted, and tearing it violently asunder, scatters the limbs of his victim upon the waters. The aspirant now hears the lamentations which are instituted for the death of the god. Then commences the search of Rhea for the remains of Bacchus. The apartments are filled with shrieks and groans; the initiated mingle with their howlings of despair, the frantic dances of the Corybantes; every thing is

a scene of distraction and lewdness; until, at a signal from the
hierophant, the whole drama changes; the mourning is turned
to joy; the mangled body is found; and the aspirant is released
from his confinement, amid the shouts of Ευρηχαμεν, Ευγχαιρομεν,
"we have found it, let us rejoice together." The candidate is
now made to descend into the infernal regions, where he sees the
torments of the wicked, and the rewards of the virtuous. It
was now that he received the lecture explanatory of the rites,
and was invested with the tokens which served the initiated as a
means of recognition. He then underwent a lustration, after
which he was introduced into the holy place, where he received
the name of Epopt, and was fully instructed in the doctrine of
the mysteries, which consisted in a belief in the existence of one
God, and a future state of rewards and punishments. These
doctrines were inculcated by a variety of significant symbols.
After the performance of these ceremonies, the aspirant was dismissed, and the rites concluded with the pronunciation of the
mystic words *Konx Ompax*, an attempted explanation of which
will be found under the head of Eleusinian mysteries.

DISCALCEATION. The ceremony of taking off the shoes,
as a token of respect, whenever we are on or about to approach
holy ground. It is referred to in Exodus, (iii. 5,) where the
angel of the Lord, at the burning bush, exclaims to Moses:
"Draw not nigh hither; put off thy shoes from off thy feet, for
the place whereon thou standest is holy ground." It is again
mentioned in Joshua, (v. 15) in the following words: "And the
captain of the Lord's host said unto Joshua, Loose thy shoe
from off thy foot; for the place whereon thou standest is holy."
And lastly, it is alluded to in the injunction given in Ecclesiastes,
(v. 1) "Keep thy foot when thou goest to the house of God."
The rite, in fact, always was, and still is, used among the Jews
and other Oriental nations, when entering their temples and
other sacred edifices. It does not seem to have been derived
from the command given to Moses; but rather to have existed as

a religious custom from time immemorial, and to have been borrowed, as Mede supposes, by the Gentiles, through tradition, from the patriarchs.

The direction of Pythagoras to his disciples, was in these words: Ἀνυπόδητος Θύε καὶ πρὸσκυνει—that is, "Offer sacrifice and worship with thy shoes off."

Justin Martyr says that those who came to worship in the sanctuaries and temples of the Gentiles, were commanded by their priests to put off their shoes.

Drusius, in his Notes on the Book of Joshua, says that among most of the Eastern nations it was a pious duty to tread the pavement of the temple with unshod feet.*

Maimonides, the great expounder of the Jewish law, asserts that "it was not lawful for a man to come into the mountain of God's house with his shoes on his feet, or with his staff, or in his working garments, or with dust on his feet."†

Rabbi Solomon, commenting on the command in Leviticus xix. 30, "Ye shall reverence my sanctuary," makes the same remark in relation to this custom. On this subject Dr. Oliver observes: "Now the act of going with naked feet was always considered a token of humility and reverence; and the priests, in temple worship, always officiated with feet uncovered, although it was frequently injurious to their health."‡

Mede quotes Zago Zaba, an Ethiopean Bishop, who was ambassador from David, King of Abyssinia, to John III., of Portugal, as saying: "We are not permitted to enter the church, except barefooted."§

The Mahommedans, when about to perform their devotions, always leave their slippers at the door of the mosque. The Druids practised the same custom whenever they celebrated their

---

* Quod etiam nunc apud plerasque orientis nationes piaculum sit, calceato pede templorum pavimenta calcasse.

† Beth Habbechirah, c. 7.

‡ Historical Landmarks, vol. ii. p. 481.

§ Non datur nobis potestas adeundi templum nisi nudibus pedibus.

sacred rites; and the ancient Peruvians are said always to have left their shoes at the porch, when they entered the magnificent temple consecrated to the worship of the Sun.

Adam Clarke thinks that the custom of worshipping the Deity barefooted, was so general among all nations of antiquity, that he assigns it as one of his thirteen proofs that the whole human race have been derived from one family.

Finally, Bishop Patrick, speaking of the origin of this rite, says in his commentaries: "Moses did not give the first beginning to this rite, but it was derived from the patriarchs before him, and transmitted to future times from that ancient, general tradition; for we find no command in the law of Moses for the priests performing the service of the temple without shoes, but it is certain they did so from immemorial custom; and so do the Mohammedans and other nations at this day."

DISCOVERY. "Anno inventionis," or "in the year of the discovery," is the style assumed by Royal Arch Masons, in commemoration of an event which took place soon after the commencement of the rebuilding of the Temple by Zerubbabel. See *Calendar, Masonic.*

DISPENSATION. A permission to do that which, without such permission, is forbidden by the constitutions and usages of the order. The power of granting Dispensations is confided to the Grand Master, or his representative, but should not be exercised except on extraordinary occasions, or for excellent reasons. The dispensing power is confined to only four circumstances. 1. A lodge cannot be opened and held, unless a Warrant of Constitution be first granted by the Grand Lodge; but the Grand Master may issue his Dispensation, empowering a constitutional number of brethren to open and hold a lodge until the next communication of the Grand Lodge. At this communication, the Dispensation of the Grand Master is either revoked or confirmed. A lodge under Dispensation, is not permitted to be represented, nor to vote in the Grand Lodge. 2. Not more than five candidates can be made at the same communication of a lodge; but the Grand Master, on the showing of sufficient cause, may extend to a lodge the privilege of making as many more as he may think proper. 3. No brother can at the same time belong to two lodges, within three miles of each other. But the Grand Master may dispense with this regulation also. 4. Every lodge must elect and install its officers on the constitutional night, which, in most masonic jurisdictions, precedes the anniversary of St. John the Evangelist. Should it, however, neglect this duty, or should any officer die, or be expelled, or remove permanently, no subsequent election or installation can take place, except under dispensation of the Grand Master.

DISTRICT DEPUTY GRAND MASTER. An officer appointed to inspect old lodges, consecrate new ones, install their officers, and exercise a general supervision over the fraternity in districts where, from the extent of the jurisdiction, the Grand Master or his Deputy cannot conveniently attend in person. He is considered as a Grand Officer, and as the representative of the Grand Lodge in the district in which he resides. In the English Grand Lodge, officers of this description are called Provincial Grand Masters.

DORIC ORDER. The oldest and most original of the three Grecian orders. It is remarkable for robust solidity in the column, for massive grandeur in the entablature, and for harmonious simplicity in its construction. The distinguishing characteristic of this order, is the want of a base. The flutings are few, large, and very little concave. The capital has no astragal, but only one or more fillets, which separate the flutings from the torus.* The column of strength which supports the lodge, is of the Doric order, and its appropriate situation and symbolic officer are in the W. .

---

* Stuart, Dict. of Architecture.

DOVE, KNIGHTS AND LADIES OF THE. *Chevaliers et Chevalières de la Colombe*. A secret society framed on the model of Freemasonry, to which women were admitted; it was instituted at Versailles, in 1784, but it is now extinct.

DRESS OF A MASON. Oliver says* that "the ancient symbolical dress of a Master Mason was a yellow jacket and blue breeches, alluding to the brass compasses with steel points, which were assigned to the Master, or Grand Master, as governor of the craft. But the real dress was a plain black coat and breeches, with white waistcoat, stockings, aprons and gloves." In this country the masonic costume is a full suit of black, with white stockings where shoes are worn, and white leather aprons and gloves. Knights Templars have their gloves and aprons also black.

DRUIDS. The Druidical rites were practised in Britain and Gaul, though they were brought to a much greater state of perfection in the former country, where the isle of Anglesea was considered as their chief seat. The word Druid has been supposed to be derived from the Greek Δρυς, or rather the Celtic *Derw*, an oak, which tree was peculiarly sacred among them; but I am inclined to seek its etymology in the Gaelic word *Druidh*, which signifies a wise man or a magician. The druidical ceremonies of initiation, according to Oliver, "bore an undoubted reference to the salvation of Noah and his seven companions in the ark." Indeed, all the ancient mysteries appear to have been arkite in their general character. Their places of initiation were of various forms; circular, because a circle was an emblem of the universe; or oval, in allusion to the mundane egg, from which, according to the Egyptians, our first parents issued; or serpentine, because a serpent was the symbol of Hu, the druidical Noah; or winged, to represent the motion of the Divine Spirit; or cru-

* Landmarks, vol. i. p. 160.

ciform, because a cross was the emblem of regeneration.* Their
only covering was the *clouded canopy*, because they deemed it
absurd to confine the Omnipotent beneath a roof,† and they were
constructed of embankments of earth, and of unhewn stones,
unpolluted with a metal tool. No one was permitted to enter
their sacred retreats, unless *he bore a chain.* The chief priest or
hierophant, was called the Archdruid. Their grand periods of
initiation were quarterly, taking place on the days when the sun
reached his equinoctial and solstitial points, which at that remote
period were the 13th of February, the 1st of May, the 19th of
August, and the 1st of November. The principal of these was
the 1st of May, (which, according to Mr. Higgins,‡ was the festival of the Sun entering into Taurus,) and the May-day celebration which still exists among us, is a remnant of the druidical
rites. It was not lawful to commit their ceremonies or doctrines
to writing, as we learn from Cæsar;§ and hence the ancient
Greek and Roman writers have been enabled to give us but little
information on this subject.

The institution was divided into three degrees or classes, the
lowest being the *Bards;* the second the *Faids,* or *Vates,* and
the highest the Druids.|| Much mental preparation and physical
purification were used previously to admission into the first degree. The aspirant was clothed with the three sacred colours,

---

* The cross, as an emblem of regeneration, was first adopted by the Egyptians, who expressed the several increases of the Nile, (by whose fertilizing in-
undations their soil was regenerated,) by a column marked with several crosses.
They hung it as a talisman around the necks of their children and sick peo-
people. It was sometimes represented in an abridged form, by the letter T.—
Pluche, Historie du Ciel.

† It was an article in the druidical creed, that it was unlawful to build temples to the gods; or to worship them within walls or under roofs."—*Dr. Henry's Hist. Eng.*

‡ Higgins' Celtic Druids, p. 149. The astronomic relations of this day
have been altered by the procession of the equinox.

§ "Neque fas esse existimant, ea literis mandare."—*Bell. Gall.* vi. 13.

|| See Strabo, lib. iv, and Ammian. Marcellinus, lib. xv.

white, blue, and green; white as the symbol of Light, blue of
Truth, and green of Hope. When the rites of initiation were
passed, the tri-coloured robe was changed for one of green; in
the second degree, the candidate was clothed in blue, and having
surmounted all the dangers of the third, and arrived at the summit of perfection, he received the red tiara and flowing mantle
of purest white. The ceremonies were numerous, the physical
proofs painful, and the mental trials appalling. They commenced
in the first degree, with placing the aspirant in the pastos, bed,
or coffin, where his symbolical death was represented, and they
terminated in the third, by his regeneration or restoration to life
from the womb of the giantess Ceridwin, and the committal of the
body of the *newly born* to the waves in a small boat, symbolical
of the ark. The result was, generally, that he succeeded in
reaching the safe landing-place that represented Mount Ararat,
but if his arm was weak, or his heart failed, death was the almost
inevitable consequence. If he refused the trial, through timidity,
he was contemptuously rejected, and declared forever ineligible to
participate in the sacred rites. But if he undertook it and succeeded, he was joyously invested with all the privileges of druidism.

The doctrines of the Druids were the same as those entertained
by Pythagoras. They taught the existence of one Supreme Being;
a future state of rewards and punishments; the immortality of the
soul, and a metempsychosis;* and the object of their mystic rites
was to communicate these doctrines in symbolic language.

With respect to the origin of the Druids, the most plausible
theory seems to be that of Mr. Higgins, that the Celts, who practised the rites of Druidism, "first came from the east of the
Caspian sea, bringing with them their seventeen letters, their
festivals, and their gods." Without such a theory as this, we
shall be unable to account for the analogy which existed between
the rites of druidism and those of the other pagan mysteries, the

---

* Cæsar says of them: "In primis hoc volunt persuadere, non interire ani-
mos, sed ab aliis post mortem ad alios transire putant."—*Bell. Gall.,* l. vi.

latter of whom undoubtedly derived their origin from the mysteries of ancient India through those of Egypt.

DUE FORM. See *Ample Form.*

DUE GUARD. We are by this ceremony strongly reminded of the time and manner of taking our solemn vows of duty, and hence are *duly guarded* against any violation of our sacred promises as initiated members of a great moral and social institution.

E.

EAGLE, DOUBLE HEADED. The double headed eagle is the ensign of the kingdom of Prussia, and as Frederick II. was the founder and chief of the 33d or ultimate degree of the Scotch or Ancient and Accepted rite, as it is now called, the double headed eagle has been adopted as the emblem or jewel of that degree, to denote its Prussian origin.

EAR OF CORN. This was, among all the ancients, an emblem of plenty. Ceres, who was universally worshipped as the goddess of abundance, and even called by the Greeks, *Demeter*, a manifest corruption of *Gemeter*, or *mother earth*, was symbolically represented with a garland on her head composed of ears of corn, a lighted torch in one hand, and a cluster of poppies and ears of corn in the other. And in the Hebrew, the most significant of all languages, the two words which signify an ear of corn, are both derived from roots which give the idea of abundance. For *shibboleth*, which is applicable both to an ear of corn and a flood of water, has its root in *shabal*, to increase or to flow abundantly; and the other name of corn, *dagan*, is de-

rived from the verb, *dagah*, signifying to multiply or to be increased.

EAST. The East has always been considered peculiarly sacred.
This was, without exception, the case in all the ancient mysteries.
In the Egyptian rites, especially, and those of Adonis, which were
among the earliest, and from which the others derived their existence, the Sun was the object of adoration, and his revolutions
through the various seasons were fictitiously represented. The
spot, therefore, where this luminary made his appearance at the
commencement of day, and where his worshippers were wont,
anxiously, to look for the first darting of his prolific rays, was
esteemed as the figurative birthplace of their god, and honoured
with an appropriate degree of reverence. And even among those
nations where Sun-worship gave place to more enlightened doctrines, the respect for the place of Sun-rising continued to exist.
Our Jewish brethren retained it, and handed it down to their
Christian successors. The camp of Judah was placed by Moses
in the East as a mark of distinction; the tabernacle in the wilderness was placed due East and West; and the practice was continued in the erection of Christian churches. Hence, too, the
primitive Christians always turned towards the East in their
public prayers, which custom St. Augustine accounts for, "because the East is the most honourable part of the world, being
the region of light whence the glorious sun arises."* And hence
all masonic lodges, like their great prototype, the Temple of Jerusalem, are built, or supposed to be built, due East and West,
and as the North is esteemed a place of darkness, the East, on
the contrary, is considered a place of light.†

---

* St. August. de Serm. Dom. in Monte, c. 5.

† In the primitive Christian Church, according to St. Ambrose, in the ceremonies accompanying the baptism of a catechumen, "he turned towards the
West, the image of darkness, to abjure the world, and towards the East, the
emblem of light, to denote his alliance with Jesus Christ." See *Chateau-
briand, Beauties of Christianity, Book I., ch. 6.*

EAVESDROPPER. A listener. The name is derived from the punishment which according to Oliver, was directed, in the lectures, at the revival of masonry in 1717, to be inflicted on a detected cowan, and which was—" To be placed under the eaves of the house in rainy weather, till the water runs in at his shoulders and out at his heels."

ECLECTIC MASONRY. This was an order or rite established at Frankfort, in Germany, in the year 1783, by Baron de Knigge, for the purpose, if possible, of abolishing the "hautes grades," or philosophical degrees which had, at that period, increased to an excessive number. This "Eclectic masonry" acknowledged the three symbolic degrees only, as the true ritual, but permitted each lodge to select at its option any of the higher degrees, provided they did not interfere with the uniformity of the first three. The founder of the rite hoped by this system of diffusion to weaken the importance and at length totally to destroy the existence of these high degrees. But he failed in this expectation, and while these high degrees are still flourishing, there are not a dozen lodges of the Eclectic rite now in operation in Europe. Into this country it has never penetrated.

ECOSSAIS. The fifth degree in the French rite. It is occupied in the detail of those precautions made use of just before the completion of the Temple, for the preservation of important secrets, and is very similar in the character of its legend to the American degree of Select Master. See *Scotch Mason.*

ECOSSAISM. By this word I mean those numerous Scotch degrees which find their prototypes in the degree established by the Chevalier Ramsay, and which he called Ecossais, or Scotch Mason, because he asserted that the system came originally from Scotland. From the one primitive degree of Ramsay an hundred others have sprung up, sometimes under the name of Ecossais, and sometimes under other titles, but still retaining one uniform

11

character,—that of detailing the mode in which the great secret was preserved. This system of Ecossaism is to be found in all the rites. In the French it bears the name of Ecossais, and is described in the preceding article. In the ancient Scotch rite it is divided into three degrees, and consists of the Grand Master Architect, Knight of the Ninth Arch Elect, Perfect and Sublime Mason. Even in the appendages to the York rite we find an Ecossais under the name of the Select Master.

Some idea of the extent to which these degrees have been multiplied, may be formed from the fact that Oliver has a list of eighty of them. Baron de Tschoudy enumerates twenty-seven of them, which he does not consider legitimate, leaving a far greater number to whose purity he does not object.

EGYPTIAN MYSTERIES. Egypt was the cradle of all the mysteries of paganism. At one time in possession of all the learning and religion that was to be found in the world, it extended into other nations the influence of its sacred rites and its secret doctrines. The importance, therefore, of the Egyptian mysteries, will entitle them to a more diffusive explanation than has been awarded to the examination of the other rites of spurious Freemasonry.

The priesthood of Egypt constituted a sacred caste, in whom the sacerdotal functions were hereditary. They exercised also an important part in the government of the state, and the kings of Egypt were but the first subjects of its priests.* They had originally organized, and continued to control the ceremonies of initiation. Their doctrines were of two kinds, exoteric or public, which were communicated to the multitude, and esoteric or secret, which were revealed only to a chosen few; and to obtain them, it was necessary to pass through an initiation, which, as we shall see, was characterized by the severest trials of courage and fortitude.

---

* In the Royal Arch degree, the King is an officer inferior to the High Priest.

The principal seat of the mysteries was at Memphis, in the neighbourhood of the great Pyramid. They were of two kinds, the greater and the less; the former being the mysteries of Osiris and Serapis; the latter those of Isis. The mysteries of Osiris were celebrated at the autumnal equinox: those of Serapis, at the summer solstice; and those of Isis at the vernal equinox.

The candidate was required to exhibit proofs of a blameless life. For some days previous to the commencement of the ceremonies of initiation, he abstained from all unchaste acts, confined himself to an exceedingly light diet, from which animal food was rigorously excluded, and purified himself by repeated ablutions. Being thus prepared, the candidate, conducted by a guide, proceeded in the middle of the night, to the mouth of a low gallery, situated in one of the sides of the pyramid. Having crawled, for some distance, on his hands and knees, he at length came to the orifice of a wide and apparently unfathomable well, which the guide directed him to descend. Perhaps he hesitates and refuses to encounter the seeming danger; if so, he, of course, renounces the enterprise, and is reconducted to the world, never again to become a candidate for initiation; but if he is animated by courage, he determines to descend; whereupon the conductor points him to an iron ladder, which makes the descent perfectly safe. At the sixtieth step, the candidate reached the entrance to a winding gallery through a brazen door, which opened noiselessly and almost spontaneously, but which shut behind him with a heavy clang, that reverberated through the hollow passages. In front of this door was an iron grate, through the bars of which the aspirant beheld an extensive gallery, whose roof was supported on each side, by a long row of majestic columns, and enlightened by a multitude of brilliant lamps. The voices of the priests and priestesses of Isis, chanting funeral hymns, were mingled with the sound of melodious instruments, whose melancholy tones could not fail to affect the aspirant with the most solemn feelings. His guide now demanded of him, if he was still firm in his purpose of passing through the trials and dangers that awaited him, or whether, overcome by what he had already experienced, he was desirous of returning to the surface and abandoning the enterprise. If he still persisted, they both entered a narrow gallery, on the walls of which were inscribed the following significant words: "The mortal who shall travel over this road, without hesitating or looking behind, shall be purified by fire, by water and by air, and if he can surmount the fear of death, he shall emerge from the bosom of the earth; he shall revisit the light, and claim the right of preparing his soul for the reception of the mysteries of the great goddess Isis." The conductor now abandoned the aspirant to himself, warning him of the dangers that surrounded and awaited him, and exhorting him to continue, (if he expected success,) unshaken in his firmness.

The solitary candidate now continues to traverse the gallery for some distance farther. On each side are placed in niches, colossal statues, in the attitude of mummies, awaiting the hour of resurrection. The lamp with which, at the commencement of the ceremonies, he had been furnished, casts but a glimmering light around, scarcely sufficient to make "darkness visible." Spectres seem to menace him at every step, but on his nearer approach they vanish into airy nothingness. At length he reaches an iron door guarded by three men armed with swords, and disguised in masks resembling the heads of jackals. One of them addresses him as follows: "We are not here to impede your passage. Continue your journey, if the gods have given you the power and strength to do so. But remember, if you once pass the threshold of that door, you must not dare to pause, or attempt to retrace your steps; if you do, you will find us here prepared to oppose your retreat, and to prevent your return." Having passed through the door, the candidate has scarcely proceeded fifty steps before he is dazzled by a brilliant light, whose intensity augments as he advances. He now finds himself in a spacious hall, filled with inflammable substances, in a state of combustion, whose flames pervade the whole apartment, and form a bower of fire on the roof above. Through this it is ne-

cessary that he should pass with the greatest speed, to avoid the
effects of the flames. To this peril succeeds another. On the
other side of this fiery furnace, the floor of the hall is garnished
with a huge net-work of red hot iron bars, the narrow interstices
of which afford the aspirant the only chances of a secure footing.
Having surmounted this difficulty by the greatest address, another
and unexpected obstacle opposes his farther progress. A wide
and rapid canal, fed from the waters of the Nile, crosses the passage he is treading. Over this stream he has to swim. Divesting himself, therefore, of his garments, he fastens them in a
bundle upon the top of his head, and holding his lamp, which
now affords him all the light that he possesses, high above the
water, he plunges in and boldly swims across.

On arriving at the opposite side, he finds a narrow landing
place, bounded by two high walls of brass, into each of which is
inserted an immense wheel of the same metal, and terminated by
an ivory door. This, of course, the aspirant attempts to open—
but his efforts are in vain. The door is unyielding. At length
he espies two large rings, of which he immediately takes hold, in
the expectation that they will afford him the means of effecting
an entrance. But what are his surprise and terror, when he beholds the brazen wheels revolve upon their axles with a formid-
able rapidity and stunning noise; the platform sinks from under
him, and he remains suspended by the rings, over a fathomless
abyss, from which issues a chilling blast of wind; his lamp is
extinguished, and he is left in profound darkness. For more
than a minute he remains in this unenviable position, deafened
by the noise of the revolving wheels, chilled by the cold current
of air, and dreading least his strength shall fail him, when he
must inevitably be precipitated into the yawning gulf below.
But by degrees the noise ceases, the platform resumes its former
position, and the aspirant is restored to safety. The ivory door
now spontaneously opens, and he finds himself in a brilliantly
illuminated apartment, in the midst of the priests of Isis, clothed
in the mystic insignia of their offices, who welcome him, and con-
11*

gratulate him on his escape from the dangers which have menaced him. In this apartment he beholds the various symbols of the Egyptian mysteries, the occult signification of which is by degrees explained to him.

But the ceremonies of initiation do not cease here. The candidate is subjected to a series of fastings, which gradually increase in severity for nine times nine days. During this period a rigorous silence is imposed upon him, which, if he preserve it inviolable, is at length rewarded by his receiving a full revelation of the esoteric knowledge of the rites. This instruction took place during what was called the twelve days of manifestation. He was conducted before the triple statue of Osiris, Isis, and Horus, where, bending the knee, he was clothed with the sacred garments, and crowned with a wreath of palm; a torch was placed in his hand and he was made to pronounce the following solemn obligation : "I swear never to reveal, to any of the uninitiated, the things that I shall see in this sanctuary, nor any of the knowledge that shall be communicated to me. I call as witnesses to my promise, the gods of heaven, of earth and hell, and I invoke their vengeance on my head, if I should ever wilfully violate my oath."

Having undergone this formality, the neophyte was introduced into the most secret part of the sacred edifice, where a priest instructed him in the application of their symbols to the doctrines of the mysteries. He was then publicly announced, amid the rejoicings of the multitude, as an initiated, and thus terminated the ceremonies of initiation into the *mysteries of Isis*, which were the first degree of the Egyptian rites.

The *mysteries of Serapis* constituted the second degree. Of these rites we know but little. Apuleius* alone, in his "Metamorphoses," has written of them, and what he has said is unimportant. He only tells us that they were celebrated at the summer

---

* It is indeed singular, that Herodotus, who treats circumstantially of the gods of the Egyptians and their religion, should make no mention of Serapis or his rites.

solstice, and at night; that the candidate was prepared by the usual fastings and purifications; and that no one was permitted to partake of them, unless he had previously been initiated into the mysteries of Isis.

The *mysteries of Osiris* formed the third degree or summit of the Egyptian initiation. In these, the legend of the murder of Osiris, by his brother Typhon, was represented, and the god was personated by the candidate. Osiris, according to the tradition, was a wise king of Egypt, who having achieved the reform of his subjects at home, resolved to spread the blessings of civilization in the other parts of the earth. This he accomplished, but on his return he found his kingdom, which he had left in the care of his wife Isis, distracted by the seditions of his brother Typhon. Osiris attempted, by mild remonstrances, to convince his brother of the impropriety of his conduct, but he fell a sacrifice in the attempt. For Typhon murdered him in a secret apartment, and cutting up the body, enclosed the pieces in a chest, which he committed to the waters of the Nile. Isis, searching for the body, found it, and entrusted it to the care of the priests, establishing at the same time the mysteries in commemoration of the foul deed. One piece of the body, however, she could not find, the *membrum virile.* For this she substituted a factitious representation, which she consecrated, and which, under the name of *phallus,* is to be found as the emblem of fecundity in all the ancient mysteries.

This legend was purely astronomical. Osiris was the sun, Isis the moon. Typhon was the symbol of winter, which destroys the fecundating and fertilizing powers of the sun, thus, as it were, depriving him of life. This was the catastrophe celebrated in the mysteries, and the aspirant was made to pass fictitiously through the sufferings and the death of Osiris.

The secret doctrines of the Egyptian rites related to the gods, the creation and government of the world, and the nature and condition of the human soul. In their initiations, says Oliver, they informed the candidate that the mysteries were received from Adam, Seth, and Enoch, and they called the perfectly initiated candidate *Al-om-jah*, from the name of the Deity. Secrecy was principally inculcated, and all their lessons were taught by symbols. Many of these have been preserved. With them, *a point within a circle*, was the symbol of the Deity surrounded by eternity; the *globe* was a symbol of the supreme and eternal God; a serpent with the tail in his mouth, was emblamatic of eternity; a child sitting on the lotos was a symbol of the sun; a palm tree, of victory; a staff, of authority; an ant, of knowledge; a goat, of fecundity; a wolf, of aversion; the right hand with the fingers open, of plenty; and the left hand closed, of protection.*

ELECT, PERFECT AND SUBLIME MASON. One who is in possession of the 14th degree of the ancient Scotch rite. See *Perfection*.

ELECT OF PERIGNAN. A French degree illustrative of the punishment inflicted upon certain criminals whose exploits constitute a portion of the legend of symbolic masonry. The counterpart of this degree is to be found in the Elected Knights of nine, and Illustrious Elected of Fifteen in the ancient Scotch rite.

ELECTED KNIGHTS OF FIFTEEN. See *Illustrious Elected of Fifteen*.

ELECTED KNIGHTS OF NINE. *Maitre élu des neufs.* The ninth degree in the ancient Scotch rite. There are but two officers: the Most Powerful, who represents Solomon, and one Warden in the West, representing Stokin. The meetings are called Chapters. In this degree is detailed the mode in which certain ****** ******, who just before the completion of the

* See, for the facts recorded in this article, Apuleius, Metamorph.; Clavel, Histoire de la Franc-Maçonrie; Oliver, Signs and Symbols; Pluche, Histoire du Ciel, etc.

Temple, had been engaged in an execrable deed of villany, received their punishment. It exemplifies the truth of the maxim, that the punishment of crime, though sometimes slow, is ever sure; and it admonishes us, by the historical circumstances on which it is founded, of the binding nature of our masonic obligations. The symbolic colours are red, white, and black. The white is emblematic of the purity of the knights; the red, of the crime which was committed; and the black, of grief. This degree, under the title of "Elu," constitutes the 4th degree in the French rite.

ELECTION. It is an ancient regulation that no candidate can be elected a member of our order, until strict enquiry shall have been made into his moral character. For this purpose, all letters of application, except those of transient persons, must lie over at least one month, during which time they are entrusted to a committee of investigation, whose unfavourable report is equivalent to a rejection by the lodge, and precludes the necessity of a ballot. If it be favourable, the ballot is then entered into. The reason why an unfavourable report of the committee is equivalent to a rejection, is, that as it takes two at least of the committee to make the report unfavourable, it is to be supposed that these two would of course black-ball the candidate. And as two black balls constitute a peremptory rejection, they may be considered as already given by the report. For the further regulation of the election, see the word *Ballot*.

The *election of the officers* of a lodge, must always take place before St. John the Evangelist's day, which is with us the commencement of the masonic year. Should it from any circumstances be postponed, it cannot afterward be entered into, except by dispensation from the Grand Master. Nominations of candidates are not permitted by the usages of masonry, but a short time previous to the election, the brethren should be called off to refreshment, for the purpose of interchanging their opinions. They are then called on, and each brother deposits in the ballot-

box the name of him whom he deems best qualified or most
worthy; and the votes being counted, the one who has received
the greatest number is declared elected.

ELEPHANTA. The cavern of Elephanta in Hindostan is
the most ancient temple in the world. It was the principal place
for the celebration of the mysteries of India.

ELEUSINIAN MYSTERIES. These were among the most
important of the ancient rites, and were hence often called emphatically "*the mysteries.*" Cicero speaks of them as "the sacred
and august rites of Eleusis, where men come from the remotest
regions to be initiated."* They were originally celebrated only at
Eleusis, a town of Attica in Greece, but they were extended to
Italy, and even to Britain. In these mysteries was commemorated the search of Ceres after her daughter Proserpine, who had
been ravished by Plato, and carried to the infernal regions. The
chief dispenser of the mysteries was called the Hierophant, or
revealer of sacred things; to him were joined three assistants,
the Daduchus or torch-bearer, the Ceryx or herald, and the Ho
epi bomo or altar-server. The mysteries were of two kinds, the
greater and lesser. The latter were merely preparatory, and consisted of a nine days lustration and purification succeeded by
sacrifices. A year after, those persons, who had passed through
the lesser were admitted into the greater, where a full revelation
was made of the secret doctrine. This, according to the opinion
of the learned Warburton, principally consisted in a declaration
of the unity of God, an opinion not with safety to be publicly promulgated, amid the errors and superstitions of ancient polytheism.†

---

* Eleusina sancta illa et augusta; ubi initiantur gentes orarum ultimæ.—
Nat. Deor. lib. i.

† The learned Faber believes there was an intimate connexion existing between the *Arkite* worship and the orgies of Eleusis, a connexion which he
traces through all the ancient mysteries.—*Faber's Cabiri and Origin of Pagan Idolatry.*

For, as Plato observes, in his Timæus, "it is difficult to discover the author and father of the Universe, and when discovered, impossible to reveal him to all mankind."

The herald opened the ceremonies of initiation into the greater mysteries by the proclamation, εχας, εχας, εστε βεβηλοι, "Retire, O ! ye profane." Thus were the sacred precincts tiled. The aspirant was presented naked. He was clothed with the skin of a calf. An oath of secrecy was administered, and he was then asked, "Have you eaten bread?" The reply to which was, "No, I have drunk the sacred mixture, I have been fed from the basket of Ceres; I have laboured, I have been placed in the calathius, and in the cystus." These replies proved that the candidate was duly and truly prepared, and that he had made suitable proficiency by a previous initiation in the lesser mysteries. The calf-skin was then taken from him, and he was invested with the sacred tunic, which he was to wear until it fell to pieces. He was now left in utter darkness, to await in the vestibule the time when the doors of the sanctuary should be opened to him. Terrific noises, resembling the roar of thunder, and the bellowing of mighty winds were heard; mimic lightning flashed, and spectres of horrible forms appeared. During this period, which, if the conjecture is correct, must have been the *funereal** part of the rites, it is supposed that the tragic end of Bacchus, the son of Semele, who was murdered by the Titans, was celebrated. The doors of the inner temple were at length thrown open, and the candidate beheld the statue of the goddess Ceres, surrounded by a dazzling light. The candidate, who had heretofore been called a mystes or novice, was now termed epoptes, an inspector or eye-witness, and the secret doctrine was revealed. The assembly was then closed with the Sanscrit words, "*konx om pax*," another proof, if another were wanting, of the Eastern origin of the Grecian mysteries.†

---

* "The mysteries of antiquity were all funereal."—*Oliver, Hist. of Initiation*, p. 314.

† The words *Candecha Om Pachsa*, of which konx om pax are a Grecian

The qualifications for initiation were maturity of age, and purity of conduct. A character, free from suspicion of immorality, was absolutely required in the aspirant. Nero, on this account, did not dare, when in Greece, to offer himself as a candidate for initiation. The privilege was at first confined to natives of Greece, but it was afterwards extended to foreigners. Significant symbols were used as means of instruction, and words of recognition were communicated to the initiated. In these regulations, as well as in the gradual advancement of the candidate from one degree to another, that resemblance to our own institution is readily perceived, which has given to these, as well as to the other ancient mysteries, the appropriate name of Spurious Freemasonry. The following passage of an ancient author, preserved by Stobæus, and quoted by Warburton in the 2d Book of his Divine Legation, is too interesting to Freemasons to be omitted:

"The mind is affected and agitated in death just as it is in initiation into the grand mysteries; and word answers to word, as well as thing to thing; for τελευτᾶν is to die; and τελεῖσθαι, to be initiated. The first stage is nothing, but errors and uncertainties; laborious wanderings; a rude and fearful march through night and darkness. And now arrived on the verge of death and initiation, every thing wears a dreadful aspect; it is all horror, trembling, sweating, and affrightment. But this scene once over, a miraculous and divine *light* displays itself, and shining plains, and flowery meadows, open on all hands before them. Here they are entertained with hymns and dances; with the sublime doctrines of faithful knowledge, and with reverend and holy

corruption, are still used, according to Capt. Wilford, at the religious meetings and ceremonies of the Brahmins. He gives the definition of the expression as follows: "*Candscha* signifies the object of our most ardent wishes. *Om* is the famous monosyllable used both at the beginning and conclusion of a prayer or religious rite like, *Amen*. *Pacsha* exactly answers to the obsolete Latin word *vix*; it signifies change, course, stead, place, turn of work, duty, fortune, &c." Asiatic Researches, vol. v. p. 300.

visions. And now become perfect and initiated, they are FREE, and no longer under restraint; but crowned and triumphant, they walk up and down the regions of the blessed; converse with pure and holy men, and celebrate the sacred mysteries at pleasure."

ELU. This, which may be translated "Elected Mason," is the fourth degree of the French rite. It is occupied in the details of the detection and punishment of certain traitors who, just before the completion of the Temple, were guilty of a henious crime.

ELUS. All the degrees, whose object is that detailed in the preceding article, are called "Elus," or "the degrees of the Elected." They are so numerous as to form, like Ecossaism, a particular system, which is to be found pervading every rite. In the York rite, the Elu is incorporated in the Master's degree; in the French, it occupies a distinct degree; in the ancient Scotch rite, it consists of three degrees, Elected Knights of Nine, Illustrious Elect of Fifteen, and Sublime Knights Elected. Ragon reckons the five preceding degrees among the Elus, but without reason, as they belong rather to the order of Masters, and are so classed by the chiefs of the Scotch rite.

Those higher Elus, in which the object of the election is changed and connected with Templar Masonry, are more properly called "Kadoshes."

EMBLEM. An occult representation of something unknown or concealed, by a sign that is known. In all the ancient mysteries, and in the philosophic school of Pythagoras, the mode of instruction adopted was by emblems. The same system is pursued in Freemasonry. The explanation of such of these emblems as it is lawful to divulge, will be found under the proper heads in this work. See, also, *Symbol.*

12

EMPERORS OF THE EAST AND WEST. In 1758 there was established in Paris a body called the "Council of Emperors of the East and West." The members assumed the titles of "Sovereign Prince Masons, Substitutes General of the Royal Art, Grand Superintendants and officers of the Grand and Sovereign Lodge of St John of Jerusalem." Their ritual consisted of twenty-five degrees, as follows: 1 to 19, the same as the Scotch Rite (which see.) 20, Grand Patriarch Noachite. 21, Key of Masonry. 22, Prince of Lebanon. 23, Knight of the Sun. 24, Kadosh. 25, Prince of the Royal Secret. In the same year the degrees were established in the city of Berlin, and adopted by the Grand Lodge of the Three Globes. Frederick II. King of Prussia, is said to have subsequently merged this body in the Ancient and Accepted Rite of which he was the head, adding eight degrees to the twenty-five they already possessed, so as to make the whole number thirty-three.

It is however a mistake to suppose, as has been asserted by Thory* and Ragon† that the Council of Emperors of the East and West was the origin of the Ancient and Accepted Rite. The former had originally adopted twenty-five of the degrees of the latter rite, but were subsequently reformed and reorganized by Frederick. Such at least is the theory now entertained by the possessors of the Ancient and Accepted Rite.

ENCAMPMENT. All regular assemblies of Knights Templars and Knights of Malta, are called Encampments. They should assemble at least quarterly, and must consist of the following officers: Grand Commander, Generalissimo, Captain General, Prelate, Senior Warden, Junior Warden, Treasurer, Recorder, Warder, Standard Bearer, Sword Bearer, and Sentinel. These Encampments derive their Warrants of Constitution from a Grand Encampment, or if there is no such body in the State in

* Acta Latomorum.
† Orthodoxie Maçonnique.

which they are organized, from the General Grand Encampment of the United States. They confer the degrees of Knight of the Red Cross, Knight Templar, and Knight of Malta.

In an Encampment of Knights Templars, the throne is situated in the East. Above it are suspended three banners : the centre one bearing a cross, surmounted by a glory; the left one having inscribed on it the emblems of the order, and the right one, a paschal lamb. The Grand Commander is seated on the throne; the Generalissimo, Prelate, and Past Grand Commanders on his right; the Captain General on his left; the Treasurer and Recorder, as in a symbolic lodge; the Senior Warden at the south-west angle of the triangle, and upon the right of the first division; the Junior Warden at the north-west angle of the triangle, and on the left of the third division; the Standard Bearer in the West, between the Sword Bearer on his right, and the Warder on his left; and in front of him is a stall for the initiate. The Knights are arranged in equal numbers on each side, and in front of the throne.*

ENCAMPMENT, GRAND. When three or more Encampments are instituted in a State, they may unite and form a Grand Encampment, having first obtained the consent of the General Grand Master, the Deputy General Grand Master, or the General Grand Encampment. They have the superintendence of all Councils of Knights of the Red Cross, and Encampments of Knights Templars, and Knights of Malta, that are holden in their respective jurisdictions.

A Grand Encampment meets, at least, annually, and consists of a Grand Master, Deputy Grand Master, Grand Generalissimo, Grand Captain General, Grand Prelate, Grand Senior and Junior Warden, Grand Treasurer, Grand Recorder, Grand Standard Bearer, and Grand Sword Bearer; all Past Grand Masters, Deputy Grand Masters, Grand Generalissimo, and Grand Captain

---

Cross, Templars' Chart, p. 41.

General, of any State Encampment wheresoever they may reside; the Grand Commander, Generalissimo, and Captain General for the time being, of the Encampments over which they shall respectively preside; and all Past Grand Commanders of such Encampments.*

ENCAMPMENT, GENERAL GRAND. The General Grand Encampment of the United States, was instituted on the 22d day of June, 1816. It consists of a General Grand Master, Deputy General Grand Master, and other General officers, similar to those of a Grand Encampment, with all Past General Grand Masters, Deputy General Grand Masters, General Grand Generalissimos, and General Grand Captain Generals, and the Grand Masters, Deputy Grand Masters, Grand Generalissimos, and Grand Captain Generals of all Grand Encampments held under its jurisdiction. The General Grand Encampment meets triennially.

ENOCH. Of Enoch, the father of Methuselah, the following tradition is interesting. When the increasing wickedness of mankind had caused God to threaten the world with universal destruction, Enoch became afraid that the knowledge of the arts and sciences would perish with the human race. To avoid this catastrophe, and to preserve the principles of the sciences for the posterity of those whom God should be pleased to spare, he erected two great pillars on the top of the highest mountain, the one of brass to withstand water, and the other of marble to withstand fire, for he was ignorant whether the destruction would be by a general deluge or a conflagration. On the marble pillar he engraved an historical direction in respect to a subterranean temple which he had built by the inspiration of the Most High, and on the pillar of brass he inscribed the principles of the liberal arts, and especially of masonry. In the flood which subsequently took place, the marble pillar was, of course, swept away, but by divine

---

* Constitution of the Gen. Grand Encamp. II. 2.

permission, the pillar of brass withstood the water, by which means the ancient state of the arts, and particularly of masonry, has been handed down to us. This tradition has been adopted into the Lodge of Perfection, (Scottish rite,) and forms a part of the degree of the Ancient Arch of Solomon, or Knights of the Ninth Arch.

According to the Greeks, Enoch was the same as Hermes Trismegistus. He taught, say they, the art of building cities, discovered the knowledge of the Zodiac, and the course of the planets, made excellent laws, and appointed festivals for sacrificing to the Sun, and instructed them in the worship of the true God. He, too, was the inventor of books, and the art of writing. "According to our traditions, Enoch was a very eminent Freemason, and the conservator of the true name of God, which was subsequently lost even among his favorite people the Jews."

ENTERED. We say of a candidate, who has received the first degree of masonry, that he has entered our society; whence the degree is called that of "Entered Apprentice."

ENTERED APPRENTICE. *Apprenti.* See *Apprentice.*

EPHOD. A garment worn by the high priest over the tunic and outer garment. It was without sleeves, and divided below the arm pits into two parts or halves, one falling before and the other behind, and both reaching to the middle of the thighs. They were joined above on the shoulders by buckles and two large precious stones, on which were inscribed the names of the twelve tribes, six on each. The Ephod was a distinctive mark of the priesthood. It was of two kinds, one of plain linen for the priests, and another, richer, and embroidered for the High Priest, which was composed of blue, purple, crimson, and fine linen.

EPOPT. This was the name given to one who had passed through the great mysteries, and been permitted to behold what was concealed from the *mystes*, who had only been initiated into the lesser. It signifies an eye-witness, and is derived from the Greek επωπτευω, *to look into, to behold*. The epopts repeated the oath of secrecy which had been administered to them on their initiation into the lesser mysteries, and were then conducted into the lighted interior of the sanctuary and permitted to behold what the Greeks emphatically termed "the sight," αυτοψία. The epopts alone were admitted to the sanctuary, for the mystæ were confined to the vestibule of the temple. The epopts were, in fact, the Master Masons of the Mysteries, while the mystæ were the Apprentices and Fellow Crafts.

ESOTERIC AND EXOTERIC MASONRY.*   From two Greek words signifying interior and exterior. The ancient philosophers, in the establishment of their respective sects, divided their schools into two kinds, *exoteric* and *esoteric*. In the exoteric school, instruction was given in public places; the elements of science, physical and moral, were unfolded, and those principles which ordinary intelligence could grasp, and against which the prejudices of ordinary minds would not revolt, were inculcated in places accessible to all whom curiosity or a love of wisdom congregated. But the more abstruse tenets of their philosophy were reserved for a chosen few, who, united in an esoteric school, received, in the secret recesses of the master's dwelling, lessons too strange to be acknowledged, too pure to be appreciated, by the vulgar crowd, who, in the morning, had assembled at the public lecture.

Thus, in some measure, is it with masonry. Its system, taken as a whole, is, it is true, strictly esoteric in its construction. Its disciples are taught a knowledge which is forbidden to the profane, and it is only in the adytum of the lodge that these lessons are bestowed; and yet, viewed in itself and unconnected with the

---

* See a Funeral Address delivered by the author in the year 1843, and published in Moore's Freemason's Mag. Vol. iii. No. 7.

world without, masonry contains within its bosom an exoteric and esoteric school, as palpably divided as were those of the ancient sects, with this simple difference, that the admission or the exclusion was in the latter case involuntary, and dependent solely on the will of the instructor, while in the former it is voluntary, and dependent only on the will and the wishes of the disciple. In the sense in which I wish to convey the terms, every Mason, on his initiation, is exoteric—he beholds before him a beautiful fabric, the exterior of which, alone, he has examined, and with this examination he may, possibly, remain satisfied—many, alas! too many, are. If so, he will remain an Exoteric Mason. But there are others, whose curiosity is not so easily gratified—they desire a further and more intimate knowledge of the structure than has been presented to their view—they enter and examine its internal form—they traverse its intricate passages, they explore its hidden recesses, and admire and contemplate its magnificent apartments—their knowledge of the edifice is thus enlarged, and with more extensive, they have purer views of the principles of its construction, than have fallen to the lot of their less enquiring brethren. These men become Esoteric Masons. The hidden things of the order are, to them, familiar as household words,—they constitute the Masters in Israel, who are to guide and instruct the less informed—and to diffuse light over paths which, to all others, are obscure and dark.

There is between these studious Masons, and their slothful, unenquiring brethren, the same difference in the views they take of masonry, as there is between an artist and a peasant in their respective estimation of an old painting—it may be of a Raphael or a Reubens. The peasant gazes with stupid wonder or with cold indifference, on the canvass redolent with life, without the excitation of a single emotion in his barren soul. Its colours mellowed to a rich softness, by the hand of time, are to him less pleasing than the gaudy tints which glare upon the sign of his village inn; and its subject, borrowed from the deep lore of history, or the bold imaginings of poesy, are less intelligible to him,

than the daubed print which hangs conspicuously at his cottage
fireside. And he is amazed to see this paltry piece of canvass
bought with the treasures of wealth, and guarded with a care
that the brightest jewel would demand in vain.

But to the eye of the artist, how different the impression conveyed! To him, every thing beams with light, and life, and
beauty. To him, it is the voice of nature, speaking in the language of art. Prometheus-like, he sees the warm blood gushing
through the blue veins, and the eye beaming with a fancied ani-
mation—the correctness of its outlines—the boldness of its fore-
shortenings, where the limbs appear ready to burst from the canvass,—the delicacy of its shadows, and the fine arrangement of
its lights, are all before him, subjects of admiration, on which he
could forever gaze, and examples of instruction which he would
fain imitate.

And whence arises this difference of impression, produced by
the same object on two different individuals? It is not from
genius alone, for that, unaided, brings no light to the mind,
though it prepares it for its reception. It is cultivation which
enlarges the intellect, and fits it as a matrix for the birth of those
truths which find in the bosom of ignorance no abiding place.

And thus it is with masonry. As we cultivate it as a science
its objects become extended—as our knowledge of it increases,
new lights burst forth from its inmost recess, which to the inqui-
sitive Mason, burn with bright effulgence; but to the inattentive
and unsearching, are but as dim and fitful glimmerings, only
rendering "darkness visible."

Let every Mason ask himself, if he be of the esoteric or the
exoteric school of masonry. Has he studied its hidden beauties
and excellencies? Has he explored its history, and traced out
the origin and the erudite meaning of its symbols? Or has he
supinely rested content with the knowledge he received at the
pedestal, nor sought to pass beyond the porch of the Temple?
If so, he is not prepared to find in our royal art those lessons
which adorn the path of life, and cheer the bed of death; and,

for all purposes, except those of social meeting, and friendly re
cognition, masonry is to him a sealed book.

But, if he has ever felt a desire to seek and cultivate the internal philosophy of masonry, let him advance in those rarely
trodden paths; the labour of such a pursuit is itself refreshment, and the reward great. Fresh flowers bloom at every step;
and the prospect on every side is so filled with beauty and en-
chantment, that, ravished at the sight, he will rush on with enthusiasm from fact to fact, and from truth to truth, until the
whole science of masonry lies before him invested with a new
form and sublimity.

ESQUIRE. A grade or rank in the degree of Knights Templars, according to the English organization. See *Knight Templar.*

ESSENES. A sect among the Jews, supposed by masonic
writers to have been the descendants of the Freemasons of the
Temple, and through whom the order was propagated to modern
times. See the article *"Antiquity of Masonry,"* in this work.
The real origin of the Essenes has been a subject of much dispute among profane writers; but there is certainly a remarkable
coincidence in many of their doctrines and ceremonies with those
professed by the Freemasons. They were divided into two classes,
speculatives and *operatives;* the former devoting themselves to a
life of contemplation, and the latter daily engaging in the practice of some handicraft. The proceeds of their labour were,
however, deposited in one general stock; for they religiously observed a community of goods. They secluded themselves from
the rest of the world, and were completely esoteric in their doctrines, which were also of a symbolic character. They admitted
no women into their order; abolished all distinctions of rank,
"meeting on the level," and giving the precedence only to
virtue. Charity was bestowed on their indigent brethren, and,
as a means of recognition, they adopted signs and other modes

similar to those of the Freemasons. Their order was divided into three degrees. When a candidate applied for admission, his character was scrutinized with the greatest severity. He was then presented with a girdle, a hatchet, and a white garment. Being thus admitted to the first degree, he remained in a state of probation for one year; during which time, although he lived according to their customs, he was not admitted to their meetings. At the termination of this period, if found worthy, he was advanced to the second degree, and was made a partaker of the waters of purification. But he was not yet permitted to live among them, but after enduring another probation of two years duration, he was at length admitted to the third degree, and united in full fellowship with them. On this occasion, he took a solemn oath, the principal heads of which, according to Josephus,[*] were as follows: To exercise piety toward God, and justice toward men; to hate the wicked and assist the good; to show fidelity to all men, obedience to those in authority, and kindness to those below him; to be a lover of truth, and a reprover of falsehood; to keep his hands clear from theft, and his soul from unlawful gains; to conceal nothing from his own sect, nor to discover any of their doctrines to others; to communicate their doctrines, in no otherwise than he had received them, himself; and lastly to preserve the books belonging to the sect, and the names of the angels in which he shall be instructed. Philo, of Alexandria, who, in two books written expressly on the subject of the Essenses, has given a copious account of their doctrines and manners, says, that when they were listening to the secret instructions of their chiefs, they stood with "the right hand on the breast a little below the chin, and the left hand placed along the side." A similar position is attributed by Macrobius to Venus, when deploring the death of Adonis, in those rites which were celebrated at Tyre, the birth-place of Hiram the Builder.

---

[*] Joseph. Bell. Jud. II. viii.

EUNUCH. No eunuch can be initiated as a Mason. The contempt in which these unfortunate beings are held by the rest of their fellow-creatures, unfits them for the close union of brotherly love which masonry inculcates; and the vicious and malignant disposition, which all experience teaches us is the characteristic of this isolated race, derived doubtless from their feeling of isolation, debars them from entrance into a society whose foundation is laid in religion and morality. The prohibition derives support, also, from the authority of Scripture. By the Jewish law, (Deut. xxiii. 1,) eunuchs are forbidden "to enter into the congregation of the Lord."

EXALTED. A candidate is said to be exalted, when he receives the degree of Holy Royal Arch, the seventh in York masonry. Exalted means *elevated* or *lifted up*, and is applicable both to a peculiar ceremony of the degree, and to the fact that this degree, in the rite in which it is practised, constitutes the summit of ancient masonry.

EXAMINATION. The due examination of strangers who claim the right of visit, should be entrusted only to the most skilful and prudent brethren of the lodge. And the examining committee should never forget, that no man applying for admission is to be considered as a Mason, however strong may be his recommendations, until by undeniable evidence he has proved himself to be such.

All the necessary forms and antecedent cautions should be observed. Enquiries should be made as to the time and place of initiation, as a preliminary step, the Tiler's O B, of course, never being omitted. Then remember the good old rule of "commencing at the beginning." Let every thing proceed in regular course, not varying in the slightest degree from the order in which it is to be supposed that the information sought was originally received. Whatever be the suspicions of imposture, let no expression of those suspicions be made until the final de-

cree for rejection is uttered. And let that decree be uttered in
general terms, such as, "I am not satisfied," or "I do not recognize you," and not in more specific language, such as "You
did not answer this enquiry," or "You are ignorant on that
point." The candidate for examination is only entitled to know
that he has not complied generally with the requisitions of his
examiner. To descend to particulars is always improper and
and often dangerous. Above all, never ask what the lawyers
call "leading questions," which include in themselves the answers, nor in any manner aid the memory or prompt the forget-
fulness of the party examined, by the slightest hints. If he has
it in him it will come out without assistance, and if he has it not,
he is clearly entitled to no aid. The Mason who is so unmindful
of his obligations as to have forgotten the instructions he has received, must pay the penalty of his carelessness, and be deprived
of his contemplated visit to that society, whose secret modes of
recognition he has so little valued as not to have treasured them
in his memory.

Lastly, never should an unjustifiable delicacy weaken the rigor
of these rules. Remember, that for the wisest and most evident
reasons, the merciful maxim of the law, which says that it is
better that ninety-nine guilty men should escape, than that one
innocent man should be punished, is with us reversed, and that
in masonry *it is better that ninety and nine true men should be
turned away from the door of a lodge, than that one cowan should
be admitted.*

EXCLUSION. See *Visit, Right of.*

EXOTERIC. See *Esoteric.*

EXPULSION. Expulsion is the highest masonic penalty
that can be imposed by a lodge, upon any of its delinquent members We shall, therefore, give it more than a passing notice,

and treat, 1st, of its effects; 2d, of the proper tribunal to impose it; 3d, of the persons who may be subject to it; and 4th, of the offences for which it may be inflicted.

1. Expulsion from a lodge deprives the party expelled of all the rights and privileges that he ever enjoyed, not only as a member of the particular lodge from which he has been ejected, but also of those which were inherent in him as a member of the fraternity at large. He is at once as completely divested of his masonic character, as though he had never been admitted, so far as regards his rights, while his duties and obligations remain as firm as ever, it being impossible for any human power to cancel them. He can no longer demand the aid of his brethren, nor require from them the performance of any of the duties to which he was formerly entitled, nor visit any lodge, nor unite in any of the public or private ceremonies of the order. He is considered as being without the pale, and it would be criminal in any brother, aware of his expulsion, even to hold communication with him on masonic subjects.

2. The only proper tribunal to impose this heavy punishment, is a Grand Lodge. A subordinate lodge tries its delinquent member, and if guilty declares him expelled. But the sentence is of no force until the Grand Lodge, under whose jurisdiction it is working, has confirmed it. And it is optional with the Grand Lodge to do so, or, as is frequently done, to reverse the decision and reinstate the brother. Some of the lodges in this country claim the right to expel independently of the action of the Grand Lodge, but the claim is not valid. The very fact that an expulsion is a penalty, affecting the general relations of the punished party with the whole fraternity, proves that its exercise never could with propriety be entrusted to a body so circumscribed in its authority as a subordinate lodge. Besides, the general practice of the fraternity is against it. The English Constitutions vest the power to expel exclusively in the Grand Lodge. "The subordinate lodge may suspend and report the case to the Grand

13

Lodge. If the offence and evidence be sufficient, expulsion is decreed."*

3. All Masons, whether members of lodges or not, are subject to the infliction of this punishment, when found to merit it. We have already said, under the article "*Demit*," that resignation or withdrawal from the order, does not cancel a Mason's obligations, nor exempt him from that wholesome control which the order exercises over the moral conduct of its members. The fact that a Mason, not a member of any particular lodge, but who has been guilty of immoral or unmasonic conduct, can be tried and punished by any lodge, within whose jurisdiction he may be residing, is without doubt. The remarks of Brother Moore[†] on this subject, are too valuable to be omitted. "Every member of the fraternity is accountable for his conduct as a Mason, to any regularly constituted lodge; but if he be a member of a particular lodge, he is more immediately accountable to that lodge. A Mason acquires some special privileges by becoming a member of a lodge, and he has to perform special services which he might not otherwise be subjected to. But he enters into no new obligations to the fraternity generally, and his accountability is not increased any further than regards the faithful performance of those special duties. Hence, the difference between those brethren who are members of a lodge, and those who are not, is, that the members are bound to obey the By-Laws of their own particular lodges, in addition to the general duty of the fraternity. Again, every Mason is bound to obey the summons of a lodge of Master Masons, whether he be a member or otherwise. This obligation on the part of an individual, clearly implies a power in the lodge to investigate and control his conduct, in all things which concern the interest of the institution. This power cannot be confined to those brethren who are members of lodges, for the obligation is general."

---

* Moore's Magazine, vol. 1, p. 356.
† Moore's Magazine, vol. 1, p. 36.

4. Immoral conduct, such as would subject a candidate for admission to rejection, should be the only offence visited with expulsion. As the punishment is general, affecting the relation of the one expelled with the whole fraternity, it should not be lightly imposed, for the violation of any masonic act not general in its character. The commission of a grossly immoral act is a violation of the contract entered into between each Mason and his order. If sanctioned by silence or impunity, it would bring discredit on the institution, and tend to impair its usefulness. A Mason who is a bad man, is to the fraternity what a mortified limb is to the body, and should be treated with the same mode of cure—he should be cut off, lest his example spread, and disease be propagated through the constitution. But it is too much the custom of lodges in this country, to extend this remedy to cases neither deserving nor requiring its application. I allude here, particularly, to expulsion for non-payment of lodge dues. Upon the principle just laid down, this is neither kind nor consistent. The payment of arrears is a contract, in which the only parties are a particular lodge and its members, of which contract the body at large know nothing. It is not a general masonic duty, and is not called for by any masonic regulation. The system of arrears was unknown in former years, and has only been established of late for the sake of convenience. Even now there are some lodges where it does not prevail ;* and no Grand Lodge has ever yet attempted to control or regulate it, thus tacitly admitting that it forms no part of the general regulations of the order. Hence the non-payment of arrears is a violation of a special and voluntary obligation to a particular lodge, and not of any general duty to the fraternity at large. The punishment therefore inflicted should be one affecting the relations of the delinquent with the particular

---

* I would cite, as an instance coming under my immediate and personal knowledge, the case of Union Kilwinning Lodge in Charleston, S. C., where every member pays a certain sum on his admission, and is forever afterwards exempt from contributions of any kind.

lodge, whose by-laws he has infringed, and not a general one affecting his relations with the whole order. But expulsion has this latter effect, and is therefore inconsistent and unjust. And as it is a punishment too often inflicted upon poverty, it is unkind. A lodge might in this case forfeit or suspend the membership of the defaulter in his own lodge, but such suspension should not affect the right of visiting other lodges, nor any of the other privileges inherent in him as a Mason. This is the practice, we are glad to say, pursued by the Grand Lodge of Massachusetts, one of the most enlightened masonic bodies in the Union. It is also the regulation of the Grand Lodge of England, from which most of our Grand Lodges derive, directly or indirectly, their existence. It is consonant with the ancient usages of the fraternity. And finally, it would produce all the good effects required by punishment, namely, reform and the prevention of crime, and ought to be adopted by every Grand Lodge, as a part of its constitution.

One other question arises. Does expulsion from one of what is called the higher degrees of masonry, such as a Chapter or an Encampment, affect the relations of the expelled party to Blue Masonry. We answer unhesitatingly, it does not. In this opinion, we are supported by the best authority, though the action of some Grand Lodges, as that of New York, is adverse to it. But the principle upon which our doctrine is founded, is plain. A Chapter of Royal Arch Masons, for instance, is not, and cannot be recognized as a masonic body, by a lodge of Master Masons. "They hear them so to be, but they do not know them so to be," by any of the modes of recognition known to masonry. The acts, therefore, of a Chapter, cannot be recognized by a Master Mason's lodge, any more than the acts of a literary or charitable society wholly unconnected with the order. Again. By the present organization of Freemasonry, Grand Lodges are the supreme masonic tribunals. If, therefore, expulsion from a Chapter of Royal Arch Masons involved expulsion from a Blue lodge, the right of the Grand Lodge to hear and determine causes, and to regulate the internal concerns of the Institution, would be interfered with by another body beyond its control. But the converse of this proposition does not hold good. Expulsion from a Blue lodge involves expulsion from all the higher degrees. Because, as they are composed of Blue Masons, the members could not of right sit and hold communications on masonic subjects with one who was an expelled Mason.

EXTENT OF THE LODGE. Boundless is the extent of a Mason's lodge—in height to the topmost heaven; in depth to the central abyss; in length from east to west; in breadth from north to south. Thus extensive is the limit of masonry, and thus extensive should be a Mason's charity. See more on this subject in the article *Form of the Lodge.*

F.

FAITH. The lowest round in the theological ladder, and hence symbolically instructing us that the first step in masonry, the first, the essential qualification of a candidate, is faith in God.

In the lecture of the E∴ A∴ it is said that "Faith may be lost in sight; Hope ends in fruition; but Charity extends beyond the grave, through the boundless realms of eternity." And this is said, because as faith is "the evidence of things not seen," when we see we no longer believe by faith but through demonstration, and as hope lives only in the expectation of possession, it ceases to exist when the object once hoped for is at length enjoyed, but charity, exercised on earth in acts of mutual kindness and forbearance, is still found in the world to come, in the sublimer form of mercy from God to his erring creatures.

FEAST, ANNUAL. The convocation of the craft together at an annual feast, for the laudable purpose of promoting social feelings, and cementing the bonds of brotherly love by the interchange of courtesies, is a time-honored custom, which is still, and we trust, will ever be observed. At this meeting, no business of any kind, except the installation of officers, should be transacted, and the day must be passed in innocent festivity. The election of officers always takes place at a previous meeting, in obedience to a regulation adopted by the Grand Lodge of England, in 1720, as follows: "It was agreed, in order to avoid disputes on the annual feast day, that the new Grand Master for the future shall be named and proposed to the Grand Lodge, some time before the feast." See *Anderson, Const.* p. 200.

FEELING. One of the five human senses, and, for well-known reasons, in great estimation among Masons.

FELLOW-CRAFT. *Compagnon.* The second degree of ancient craft masonry. It is particularly devoted to science. As in the first degree, those lessons are impressed, of morality and brotherly love, which should eminently distinguish the youthful apprentice; so in the second, is added that extension of knowledge, which enabled the original craftsmen to labor with ability and success, at the construction of the Temple. In the degree of Entered Apprentice, every emblematical ceremony is directed to the lustration of the heart; in that of Fellow-Craft, to the enlargement of the mind. Already clothed in the white garment of innocence, the advancing candidate is now invested with the deep and unalterable truths of science. At length he passes the porch of the Temple, and in his progress to the middle chamber is taught the ancient and unerring method of distinguishing a friend from a foe. His attention is directed to the wonders of nature and art, and the differences between operative and speculative masonry are unfolded, until by instruction and contemplation he is led to view with reverence and admiration the glorious works of the creation, and is inspired with the most exalted ideas of the perfections of his Divine Creator.

FESSLER'S RITE. A rite formerly practised by the Grand Lodge "Royal York à l'Amitié" at Berlin. It consisted of nine degrees, viz: 1, Apprentice; 2, Fellow-Craft; 3, Master; 4, Holy of Holies; 5, Justification; 6, Celebration; 7, True light; 8, Fatherland; 9, Perfection. They were drawn up, says Clavel, from the rituals of the Golden Rose Croix, of the rite of Strict Observance, of the Illuminated Chapter of Sweden, and the Ancient Chapter of Clermont at Paris. They are now practised by but few lodges, having been abandoned by the Grand Lodge which established them, for the purpose of adopting the ancient York rite under the Constitutions of England.*

FESTIVALS. The masonic festivals most generally celebrated, are those of St. John the Baptist, June 24, and St. John the Evangelist, December 27. These are the days kept in this country. Such, too, was formerly the case in England, but the annual festival of the Grand Lodge of England now falls on the Wednesday following St. George's day, April 23, that Saint being the patron of England. For a similar reason, St. Andrew's day, November 30, is kept by the Grand Lodge of Scotland.

FIDES. Fidelity; to which virtue, the ancients paid divine honours, under the name of the goddess of faith, oaths, and honesty. The oaths taken in the name of this goddess were held to be more inviolable than any others. Numa was the first who built temples, and erected altars to the goddess Fides or Fidelity. No animals were killed, and no blood shed in her sacrifices. The priests who celebrated them were clothed in white, and were conducted with much pomp to the place of sacrifice, in chariots, having their whole bodies and hands enveloped in their capacious

* Fessler's rite is perhaps the most abstrusely learned and philosophical of all the rites.

mantles. Fidelity was generally represented among the ancients
by two right hands joined, or by two human figures holding each
other by the right hand.   Horace calls incorruptible Fidelity the
sister of Justice, and Cicero makes them identical; those principles
of Justice, says he, which, when exercised toward God, are termed
Religion, and toward our parents, Piety, in matters of trust are
called Fidelity.*

FINANCES. The finances of the lodges are placed under
the charge of the Treasurer, who only pays them out on the order
of the Master, and with the consent of the brethren, previously
expressed in open lodge. By an unwritten law, the finances
should be first received by the Secretary, who then pays them
over to the Treasurer, taking his receipt for the same. A mutual
check is thus kept on each other by these officers.

FINES. Fines for non-attendance or neglect of duty, are not
usually imposed in masonic bodies, because each member is bound
to the discharge of these duties by a motive more powerful than
any that could be furnished by a pecuniary penalty. The imposition of such a penalty would be a tacit acknowledgment of
the inadequacy of that motive, and would hence detract from its
solemnity and its binding nature.

FIVE. One of the sacred numbers of Freemasonry. Its
symbolic properties are many and curious. It is formed by a
combination of the Duad with the Triad, of the first even number
with (excluding unity) the first odd one, 2 + 3. In the school
of Pythagoras, it represented Light, and among his disciples a
triple triangle, forming the outline of a five pointed star, was an
emblem of health, because being alternately conjoined within
itself, it constitutes a figure of *five* lines. Among the Cabbalists,

---

* Justitia erga Deos religio, erga parentes pietas,———creditis in rebus fides
nominatur.—*Orat.* 78.

the same figure, with the name of God written on each of its
points, and in the centre, was considered talismanic. The number
five was among the Hebrews a sacred round number, and is repeatedly used as such in the Old Testament, as, for example, in
Genesis xliii. 34, xlv. 22, xlvii. 2, Isaiah xvii. 6, xix. 18, xxx.
17. "This usage," says Gesenius, "perhaps passed over to the
Hebrews from the religious rites of Egypt, India, and other
oriental nations; among whom *five* minor planets and *five* elements,
and elementary powers, were accounted sacred." Among Freemasons, five is more particularly symbolical of the five orders of
architecture, and the five human senses, but still more especially
of the Five Points of Fellowship.

FIVE POINTS OF FELLOWSHIP. Masons owe certain
duties of brotherly love and fellowship to each other, the practice
of which, as the distinguishing principles of our order, are inculcated by the Master in the most impressive manner.

First. Indolence should not cause our footsteps to halt, or wrath
turn them aside, but with eager alacrity and swiftness of foot, we
should press forward in the exercise of charity and kindness to a
distressed fellow-creature.

Secondly. In our devotions to Almighty God, we should remember a brother's welfare as our own, for the prayers of a fer-
vent and sincere heart will find no less favour in the sight of heaven, because the petition for self is mingled with aspirations of
benevolence for a friend.

Thirdly. When a brother intrusts to our keeping the secret
thoughts of his bosom, prudence and fidelity should place a
sacred seal upon our lips, lest, in an unguarded moment, we betray the solemn trust confided to our honour.

Fourthly. When adversity has visited our brother, and his
calamities call for our aid, we should cheerfully and liberally
stretch forth the hand of kindness, to save him from sinking,
and to relieve his necessities.

Fifthly. While with candour and kindness we should admonish

a brother of his faults, we should never revile his character behind his back, but rather, when attacked by others, support and defend it.

FIVE SENSES. The five human senses, which are, Hearing, Seeing, Feeling, Smelling, and Tasting, are dilated on in the lecture of the Fellow Crafts' degree. See each word in its appropriate place in this Lexicon.

FLOATS. Pieces of timber, made fast together with rafters, for conveying burdens down a river with the stream.—*Bailey* The use of these floats in the building of the temple is thus described in the letter of King Hiram to Solomon : "And we will cut wood out of Lebanon, as much as thou shalt need; and we will bring it to thee in floats by sea to Joppa; and thou shalt carry it up to Jerusalem."—2 *Chron.* ii. 16.

FLOORING. A frame-work of board or canvas, on which the emblems of any particular degree are inscribed, for the assistance of the Master in giving a lecture. It is so called, because formerly it was the custom to inscribe these designs on the floor of the lodge room in chalk, which was wiped out when the lodge was closed. It is the same as the "Carpet," or "Tracing Board."

FORM OF THE LODGE. The form of the lodge is said to be an oblong square, having its greatest length from east to west, and its greatest breadth from north to south. According to Oliver, the form of the lodge ought to be a double cube, as an expressive emblem of the united powers of darkness and light in the creation, and because the ark of the covenant and the altar of incense were both of that figure. But these two theories of its form are not inconsistent with each other, for, taken in its solid dimensions, the lodge is a double cube, while its surface is a parallelogram or oblong square.

This oblong form of the lodge has, I think, a symbolic allusion, which has not been heretofore adverted to, so far as I am aware, by any masonic writer.

If, on a map of the world, we draw lines which shall circumscribe just that portion which was known and inhabited at the time of the building of Solomon's temple, these lines, running a short distance north and south of the Mediterranean Sea, and extending from Spain to Asia Minor, will form an *oblong square*, whose greatest length will be from east to west, and whose greatest breadth will be from north to south, as is shown in the annexed diagram.

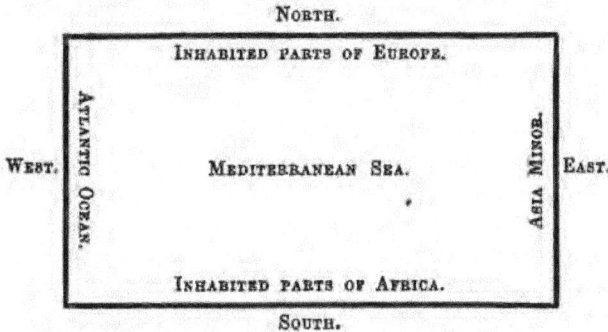

NORTH.

	INHABITED PARTS OF EUROPE.	
WEST. ATLANTIC OCEAN.	MEDITERRANEAN SEA.	ASIA MINOR. EAST.
	INHABITED PARTS OF AFRICA.	

SOUTH.

The oblong square which thus enclosed the whole habitable part of the globe, would represent the form of the lodge to denote the universality of masonry, since the world constitutes the lodge; a doctrine that has since been taught in that expressive sentence: In every clime the Mason may find a home, and in every land a brother.

FORTITUDE. One of the four cardinal virtues, whose excellencies are dilated on in the first degree. It not only instructs the worthy Mason to bear the ills of life with becoming resignation, "taking up arms against a sea of trouble," but, by its intimate connection with a portion of our ceremonies, it teaches him to let no dangers shake, no pains dissolve the inviolable fidelity he owes to the trusts reposed in him.

FORTY-SEVENTH PROBLEM. The forty-seventh problem of Euclid's first book, which has been adopted as an emblem in the Master's degree, is thus enunciated. "In any right angled triangle, the square which is described upon the side subtending the right angle, is equal to the squares described upon the sides which contain the right angle." This interesting problem, on account of its great utility in making calculations, and drawing plans for buildings, is sometimes called the "carpenter's theorem."

For the demonstration of this problem, the world is indebted to Pythagoras, who, it is said, was so elated after making the discovery, that he made an offering of a hecatomb, or a sacrifice of a hundred oxen to the gods.* The devotion to learning which this religious act indicated, in the mind of the ancient philosopher, has induced Masons to adopt the problem as a memento, instructing them to be lovers of the arts and sciences.

The triangle, whose base is 4 parts, whose perpendicular is 3, and whose hypotenuse is 5, and which would exactly serve for a demonstration of this problem,† was, according to Plutarch, a symbol frequently employed by the Egyptian priests, and hence it is called by M. Jomard,‡ the Egyptian triangle. It was, with the Egyptians, the symbol of universal nature, the base representing Osiris, or the male principle, the perpendicular, Isis, or the female principle, and the hypotenuse, Horus, their son, or

---

* The well-known aversion of Pythagoras to the shedding of blood has led to the supposition that the sacrifice consisted of small oxen, made of wax, and not of living animals.

† For the square of the base is 4 × 4, or 16, the square of the perpendicular is 3 × 3, or 9, and the square of the hypotenuse is 5 × 5, or 25; but 25 is the sum of 9 and 16, and therefore the square of the longest side is equal to the sum of the squares of the other two, which is the forty-seventh problem of Euclid.

‡ In his "Exposition du Système Métrique des Anciens Egyptiens."

the produce of the two principles. They added that 3 was the first perfect odd number, that 4 was the square of 2, the first even number, and that 5 was the result of 3 and 2.

But the Egyptians made a still more important use of this triangle. It was the standard of all their measures of extent, and was applied by them to the building of the pyramids. The researches of M. Jomard, on the Egyptian system of measures, published in the magnificent work of the French savans on Egypt, has placed us completely in possession of the uses made by the Egyptians of this forty-seventh problem of Euclid, and of the triangle which formed the diagram by which it was demonstrated.

If we inscribe within a circle a triangle, whose perpendicular shall be 300 parts, whose base shall be 400 parts, and whose hypothenuse shall be 500 parts, which of course bear the same proportion to each other as 3, 4 and 5; then, if we let a perpendicular fall from the angle of the perpendicular and base to the hypothenuse, and extend it through the hypothenuse to the circumference of the circle, this chord or line will be equal to 480 parts, and the two segments of the hypothenuse, on each side of it, will be found equal, respectively, to 180 and 320. From the point where this chord intersects the hypothenuse, let another line fall perpendicularly to the shortest side of the triangle, and this line will be equal to 144 parts, while the shorter segment, formed by its junction with the perpendicular side of the triangle, will be equal to 108 parts. Hence, we may derive the following measures from the diagram : 500, 480, 400, 320, 180, 144, and 108, and all these without the slightest fraction. Supposing, then, the 500 to be cubits, we have the measure of the base of the great pyramid of Memphis. In the 400 cubits of the base of the triangle, we have the exact length of the Egyptian stadium. The 320 give us the exact number of Egyptian cubits contained in the Hebrew and Babylonian stadium. The stadium of Ptolemy is represented by the 480 cubits, or length of the line falling from the right angle to the circumference of the circle, through the hypothenuse. The number 180, which expresses the smaller segment of the hypothenuse, being doubled, will give 360 cubits, which will be the stadium of Cleomedes. By doubling the 144, the result will be 288 cubits, or the length of the stadium of Archimedes, and by doubling the 108, we produce 216 cubits, or the precise value of the lesser Egyptian stadium. In this manner, we obtain from this triangle all the measures of length that were in use among the Egyptians; and since this triangle, whose sides are equal to 3, 4, and 5, was the very one that most naturally would be used in demonstrating the forty-seventh problem of Euclid; and since by these three sides the Egyptians symbolized Osiris, Isis, and Horus, or the two producers and the product, the very principle, expressed in symbolic language, which constitutes the terms of the problem as enunciated by Pythagoras, that the sum of the squares of the two sides will produce the square of the third, we have no reason to doubt that the forty-seventh problem was perfectly known to the Egyptian priests, and by them communicated to Pythagoras.

FREE BORN. The constitutions of our order require that every candidate shall be free born. And this is necessary, for, as admission into the fraternity involves a solemn contract, no one can bind himself to its performance who is not the master of his own actions; nor can the man of servile condition or slavish mind be expected to perform his masonic duties with that "freedom, fervency, and zeal," which the laws of our institution require. Neither, according to the authority of Dr. Oliver,* "can any one, although he have been initiated, continue to act as a Mason, or practise the rites of the order, if he be temporarily deprived of his liberty or freedom of will." On this subject, the Grand Lodge of England, on the occasion of certain Masons having been made in the King's Bench prison, passed a special resolution in November, 1783, declaring "That it is inconsistent with the principles of masonry for any Freemason's lodge to be

---

* Historical Landmarks, i. 110.

held, for the purpose of making, passing, or raising Masons, in any prison or place of confinement."*

The same usage existed in the spurious Freemasonry of the ancient mysteries, where slaves could not be initiated, the requisites for initiation being that a man must be a free-born denizen of the country, as well as of irreproachable morals.

FREEMASON. The word "free," in connection with "Mason," originally signified that the person so called was free of the company or guild of incorporated Masons. For those operative Masons who were not thus made free of the guild, were not permitted to work with those who were. A similar regulation still exists in many parts of Europe, although it is not known to this country. The term appears to have been first thus used in the tenth century, when the travelling Freemasons were incorporated by the Roman Pontiff. See *Travelling Freemasons.*

FREEMASONRY. "A beautiful system of morality, veiled in allegory, and illustrated by symbols." To this sublime definition of our order, borrowed from the lectures of our English brethren, and prefixed by Dr. Oliver, as a motto to one of his most interesting works, I shall take the liberty of adding an exposition of its principles from the pen of De Witt Clinton, as pure a patriot as ever served his country, and as bright a Mason as ever honoured the fraternity.

"Although," says he, "the origin of our fraternity is covered with darkness, and its history is, to a great extent, obscure, yet we can confidently say, that it is the most ancient society in the world—and we are equally certain that its principles are based on pure morality—that its ethics are the ethics of Christianity—its doctrines, the doctrines of patriotism and brotherly love—and its sentiments, the sentiments of exalted benevolence. Upon these points, there can be no doubt. All that is good, and kind,

---

* Minutes of the Grand Lodge, quoted by Oliver, *ut supra.*

nnd charitable, it encourages; all that is vicious, and cruel, and oppressive, it reprobates."*

FRENCH RITE. *Rite Français ou moderne.* The French or Modern rite is one of the three principal rites of Freemasonry. It consists of seven degrees, three symbolic and four higher, viz. 1. Apprentice; 2. Fellow Craft; 3. Master; 4. Elect; 5. Scotch Master; 6. Knight of the East; 7. Rose Croix. This rite is practised in France, in Brazil, and in Louisiana. It was founded in 1786, by the Grand Orient of France, who, unwilling to destroy entirely the high degrees which were then practised by the different rites, and yet anxious to reduce them to a smaller number, and to greater simplicity, extracted these degrees out of the rite of Perfection, making some few slight modifications. Most of the authors who have treated of this rite have given to its symbolism an entirely astronomical meaning, Among these writers, we may refer to Ragon, in his "Cours Philosophique," as probably the most scientific.

FUNERAL RITES. None but Master Masons can be interred with the funeral honours of masonry, and even then the performance of the service is subjected to certain unalterable restrictions. No Mason can be buried with the formalities of the order, except by his own request, preferred, while living, to the Master of the lodge of which he was a member, strangers and the higher officers of the order excepted. No public procession can take place, nor can two or more lodges assemble for this purpose, until a dispensation has been granted by the Grand Master. The ceremonies practised on the interment of a brother are to be found in all the Monitors. It is unnecessary, therefore, to specify them here.

---

* Address at the installation of Grand Master Van Rensselaer, New York, 1852.

FURNITURE OF A LODGE. Every well-regulated lodge must contain a Bible, square, and compasses, which are technically said to constitute its furniture, and which are respectively dedicated to God, the Master of the lodge, and the Craft. Our English brethren differ from us in their explanation of the furniture. Oliver gives their illustration, from the English lectures, as follows:

"The Bible is said to derive from God to man in general, because the Almighty has been pleased to reveal more of his divine will by that holy book, than by any other means. The compasses being the chief implement used in the construction of all architectural plans and designs, are assigned to the Grand Master in particular, as emblems of his dignity, he being the chief head and ruler of the craft. The square is given to the whole masonic body, because we are all obligated within it, and are consequently bound to act thereon."

G.

GAVEL. The common gavel is one of the working tools of an Entered Apprentice. It is made use of by the operative Mason to break off the corners of the rough ashlar, and thus fit it the better for the builder's use, and is therefore adopted as a symbol in speculative masonry, to admonish us of the duty of divesting our minds and consciences of all the vices and impurities of life, thereby fitting our bodies as living stones for that spiritual building not made with hands, eternal in the heavens.

Hence, too, we see the propriety of adopting the gavel as the instrument for maintaining order in the lodge. For, as the lodge is an imitation of the temple, and each member represents a stone thereof, so, by the influence of the gavel, all the ebullitions of

14*

temper, and the indecorum of frivolity are restrained, as the material stones of that building were, by the same instrument, divested of their asperities and imperfections.

In the first edition of this work, I confessed myself at a loss for the derivation of the word "gavel." I have, however, no longer any doubt that it borrows its name from its shape, being that of the *gable* or *gavel* end of a house, and this word again comes from the German *gipfel*, a summit, top, or peak,—the idea of a pointed extremity being common to all.

In the name, as well as the application of this implement, error has crept into the customs of the lodges. The implement employed by many Masters is not a gavel, but a mallet, (the French Masons, in fact, make use of the word "maillet,") and is properly not one of the working tools of an E∴ A∴, but a representation of the *setting-maul*, one of the emblems of the third degree. The two implements and the two names are entirely distinct, and should never be confounded; and I am surprised to see so learned a Mason as Brother Oliver, falling into this too usual error, and speaking of "the common gavel or setting-maul," as synonymous terms.*

The true form of the gavel is that of the stone-mason's hammer. It is to be made with a cutting edge, as in the annexed engraving, that it may be used "to break off the corners of rough stones," an operation which could never be effected by the common hammer or mallet. The gavel, thus shaped, will give, when looked at in front, the exact representation of the *gavel* or *gable* end of a house, whence, as I have already said, the name is derived.

---

* In my labours, as Grand Lecturer of South-Carolina, I have succeeded, in many instances, in correcting this error, and placing the common gavel in the hands of the Master and Wardens, for the government of the lodge, while the mallet or setting-maul remains in the archives of the lodge, to be used only as an emblem of the third degree.

The gavel of the Master is also called a " Hiram," for a reason which will be explained under that word.

GENERALISSIMO. The second officer in an Encampment of Knights Templars, and one of its representatives in the Grand Encampment. His duty is to receive and communicate all orders, signs, and petitions; to assist the Grand Commander, and, in his absence, to preside over the Encampment. His station is on the right of the Grand Commander, and his jewel is a square, surmounted by a paschal lamb.

GENUFLEXION. Bending the knees has, in all ages of the world, been considered as an act of reverence and humility, and hence Pliny, the Roman naturalist, observes, that " a certain degree of religious reverence is attributed to the knees of man." Solomon placed himself in this position when he prayed at the consecration of the temple, and Masons use the same posture in some portions of their ceremonies, as a token of solemn reverence.

GEOMETRY. Geometry is defined to be that science which teaches the nature and relations of whatever is capable of measurement. It is one of the oldest and most necessary of sciences; is that upon which the whole doctrine of mathematics is founded, and is so closely connected with the practice of operative masonry, that our ancient brethren were as often called geometricians as Masons. It was, indeed, in such great repute among the wise men of antiquity, that Plato placed over the portals of the academy this significant inscription: Οὐδεὶς ἀγεωμέτρητος εἰσίτω, "Let none enter who is ignorant of geometry."

The first inhabitants of the earth must have practised the simplest principles of geometry in the construction of even the rude huts which were intended to shelter them from the inclemencies of the weather; and afterward, when they began to unite in communities, and to exercise the right of property in lands, this science must have been still further developed, as a

necessary means of measuring and distinguishing each person's
particular domain. Land-surveying, indeed, seems to have been
the most important purpose to which geometry was originally
applied : a fact warranted also by the derivation of the word, whose
roots, in the Greek language, signify " a measure of the earth."
But as operative masonry and architecture improved, and, in the
construction of edifices, elegance was added to strength, and ornament to utility, geometry began, too, to be extended in its
principles, and perfected in its system. The Egyptians were
undoubtedly one of the first nations who cultivated geometry as
a science. " It was not less useful and necessary to them," as
Goguet observes,* " in the affairs of life, than agreeable to their
speculatively philosophical genius."   From Egypt, which was the
parent both of the sciences and the mysteries of the Pagan world,
it passed over into other countries, and geometry and operative
masonry have ever been found together, the latter carrying into
execution those designs which were first traced according to the
principles of the former.

Speculative masonry is, in like manner, intimately connected
with geometry. In deference to our operative ancestors, and, in
fact, as a necessary result of our close connection with them,
speculative Freemasonry derives its most important emblems from
this parent science. As the earthly temple was constructed under the correcting application of the plumb, the level, and the
square, by which its lines and angles were properly admeasured,
so we are accustomed, in the construction of the great moral edifice of our minds, symbolically to apply the same instruments, in
order to exhibit our work on the great day of inspection as "true
and trusty."

The explanation of the principal geometrical figures given by
Pythagoras, may be interesting to the masonic student. According to the Grecian sage, the point is represented by unity, the
line by the duad, the surface by the ternary, and the solid by

the quarternary. The circle, he says, is the most perfect of cur-
vilinear figures, containing the triangle in a concealed manner.
The triangle is the principle of the generation and formation of
bodies, because all bodies are reducible to this figure, and the elements are triangular. The square is the symbol of the divine
essence.

GIBALIM OR GIBLIM. These were the inhabitants of the
Phenician city of Gebal, called by the Greeks Byblos. The Phenician word, נבל, "gebal," (of which נבלים, "gibalim," or "giblim," is the plural,) signifies a Mason, or stone-squarer. Gesenius[*]
says, that the inhabitants of Gebal were seamen and builders; and
Sir William Drummond asserts that "the Gibalim were Master
Masons, who put the finishing hand to Solomon's temple."[†]

GLOBE. In the Egyptian mysteries, the globe was a symbol
of the Supreme and Eternal God. Among the Mexicans, it represented universal power. Among Freemasons, the globes,
celestial and terrestrial, are emblems of the universal extension
of the institution, and remind us also of the extensive claims of
that charity we are called on to practise.

GLOVES. White gloves form a part of a Freemason's costume, and should always be worn in the lodge.[‡] An instance of
the antiquity of this dress is given in this work, under the article
"Clothed." In an institution so symbolical as ours, it is not
unreasonable to suppose that the white gloves are to remind us,
that "without a pure heart and *clean* hands," no one can "stand
in the holy place." And this is the emblematic use of the gloves
in the French rite, where every Apprentice, on his initiation, is

---

* Heb. Lex. in voc.

† Origines, vol. iii., b. v., ch. iv., p. 192.

‡ I regret to say, that this rule is too much neglected in our American
lodges.

presented with two pair, one for himself, and one for his wife or mistress.

GOD. Freemasons have always been worshippers of the one true God. "This," says Hutchinson,* "was the first and corner-stone on which our originals thought it expedient to place the foundation of masonry." While the world around them was polluted with sun-worship, and brute-worship, and all the absurdities of polytheism, masonry, even in its spurious forms, as the ancient mysteries have appropriately been styled, was alone occupied in raising altars to the one I AM, and declaring and teaching the unity of the Godhead. Josephus, in his defence of the Jews against Apion, sums up in a few words this doctrine of the mysteries, and its conformity with the Jewish belief, which was, of course, identical with that of the Freemasons. "God, perfect and blessed, contains all things, is self-existent and the cause of existence to all, the beginning, the middle, and the end of all things."†

GOLGOTHA. A Hebrew word, signifying "a skull." It was the name given by the Jews to Mount Calvary, where Christ was crucified, and where his sepulchre was situated.

GOTHIC CONSTITUTIONS. Those regulations of the craft, which were adopted in 926, at the General Assembly in the city of York, under Prince Edwin, and to which additions were made from time to time, at other annual assemblies of the fraternity, are called the Gothic Constitutions, from the fact that they were written in the old Gothic character. Several copies of them were in existence at the revival of masonry in 1717. In 1721, they were digested by Dr. Anderson, in a new and better method, and form the foundation of the Book of Constitutions, the first edition of which was published in 1722.

* Spirit of Masonry, p. 6.
† Joseph. contra Ap., lib. ii., cap. 2.

GOOD SAMARITAN. See *Samaritan.*

GRAMMAR. One of the seven liberal arts and sciences, which forms, with Logic and Rhetoric, a triad, dedicated to the cultivation of language. "God," says Sanctius, "created man the participant of reason; and as he willed him to be a social being, he bestowed upon him the gift of language, in the perfecting of which there are three aids. The first is *Grammar*, which rejects from language all solecisms and barbarous expressions; the second is *Logic*, which is occupied with the truthfulness of language; and the third is *Rhetoric*, which seeks only the adornment of language."*

GRAND HONOURS. See *Honours.*

GRAND INQUISITOR. *Grand inspecteur-inquisiteur-commandeur.* The 31st degree of the Ancient Scotch rite. It is not a historical degree, but simply administrative in its character,—the duties of the members being to examine and regulate the proceedings of the inferior lodges and chapters. Its place of meeting is called a tribunal, its decorations are white, and its presiding officer is called a President, who is elected for life.

GRAND LODGES, HISTORY OF. The present organization of Grand Lodges is by no means coeval with the origin of our institution. Every lodge was originally independent; and a sufficient number of brethren meeting together, were empowered to practise all the rights of masonry without a warrant of constitution. This privilege, as Preston remarks, was inherent in them as individuals. The brethren were in the custom of meeting annually, at least as many as conveniently could, for the purpose of conference on the general concerns of the order, and on this occasion a Grand Master, or superintendent of the whole

* Sanct. Minut., lib. i., cap. 2, apud Harris, Hermes. I. c. i.

fraternity, was usually chosen. These meetings were not, however, called Grand Lodges, but "Assemblies." This name and
organization are as old as the fourth century of the Christian
era; for, in a MS.* once in the possession of Nicholas Stone, a
sculptor under the celebrated Inigo Jones, it is stated that "St
Albans (who was martyred in 306) loved Masons well, and
cherished them much ****. And he got them a charter from the
king and his counsell, for to holde a generall counsel and gave itt
to name Assemblie." The privilege of attending these annual
assemblies was not restricted, as it now is, to the Grand Officers,
and Masters, and Wardens of subordinate lodges, but constituted
one of the obligatory duties of every Mason. Thus, among the
ancient masonic charges, in possession of the Lodge of Antiquity,
at London, is one which declares that "every Master and Fellow
shall come to the assemblie, if itt be within fifty miles of him, and
if he have any warning. And if he have trespassed the craft,
to abide the award of Masters and Fellows."

England. The next† charter granted in England to the Masons,
as a body, was bestowed by King Athelstane, in 926, upon the
application of his brother, Prince Edwin. "Accordingly, Prince
Edwin summoned all the Masons in the realm to meet him in a
congregation at York, who came and composed a General Lodge,
of which he was Grand Master; and having brought with them
all the writings and records extant, some in Greek, some in Latin,
some in French, and other languages, from the contents thereof
that assembly did frame the constitution and charges of an English lodge."‡

From this assembly at York, the true rise of masonry in England is generally dated; from the statutes there enacted, are
derived the English Masonic Constitutions; and from the place

---

* Quoted by Preston.
† And if the anecdote of St. Albans be not authentic, the first.
‡ Elias Ashmole's MS.

of meeting, the ritual of the English lodges is designated as the
"Ancient York Rite."

For a long time, the York assembly exercised the masonic
jurisdiction over all England; but, in 1567, the Masons of the
southern part of the island elected Sir Thomas Gresham, the
celebrated merchant, their Grand Master. He was succeeded
by the illustrious architect, Inigo Jones. There were now two
Grand Masters in England who assumed distinctive titles; the
Grand Master of the north being called Grand Master of all
England, while he who presided in the south was called Grand
Master of England.

In the beginning of the 18th century, masonry in the south
of England had fallen into decay. The disturbances of the revolution, which placed William III. on the throne, and the subsequent warmth of political feelings which agitated the two parties
of the state, had given this peaceful society a wound fatal to its
success. Sir Christopher Wren, the Grand Master in the reign
of Queen Anne, had become aged, infirm, and inactive, and
hence the general assemblies of the Grand Lodge had ceased to
take place. There were, in the year 1715, but four lodges in
the south of England, all working in the city of London.
These four lodges, desirous of reviving the prosperity of the
order, determined to unite themselves under a Grand Master,
Sir Christopher Wren being now dead, and none having, as yet,
been appointed in his place. They, therefore, "met at the
Apple tree tavern; and having put into the chair the oldest Master Mason, (being the Master of a lodge,) they constituted themselves a Grand Lodge, *pro tempore*, in due form, and forthwith
revived the quarterly communication of the officers of lodges,
(called the Grand Lodge,) resolved to hold the annual assembly
and feast, and then to choose a Grand Master from among themselves, till they should have the honour of a noble brother at
their head."*

---

* Anderson's Constitutions, p. 197.
15

Accordingly, on St. John the Baptist's day, 1717, the annual assembly and feast were held, and Mr. Anthony Sayer duly proposed and elected Grand Master. The Grand Lodge adopted, among its regulations, the following: "That the privilege of assembling as Masons, which had hitherto been unlimited, should be vested in certain lodges or assemblies of Masons, convened in certain places; and that every lodge to be hereafter convened, except the four old lodges at this time existing, should be legally authorized to act by a warrant from the Grand Master, for the time being, granted to certain individuals by petition, with the consent and approbation of the Grand Lodge in communication, and that, without such warrant, no lodge should be hereafter deemed regular or constitutional."

In compliment, however, to the four old lodges, the privileges which they had always possessed under the old organization were particularly reserved to them; and it was enacted that "no law, rule, or regulation, to be hereafter made or passed in Grand Lodge, should ever deprive them of such privilege,* or encroach on any landmark which was at that time established as the standard of masonic government."

The Grand Lodges of York and of London kept up a friendly intercourse, and mutual interchange of recognition, until the latter body, in 1725, granted a warrant of constitution to some Masons who had seceded from the former. This unmasonic act was severely reprobated by the York Grand Lodge, and produced the first interruption to the harmony that had long subsisted between them. It was, however, followed some years after by another unjustifiable act of interference. In 1725, the Earl of Crawford, Grand Master of England, constituted two lodges within the jurisdiction of the Grand Lodge of York, and granted, without its consent, deputations for Lancashire, Durham, and

---

* Among these privileges, were those of assembling without a warrant of constitution, and raising Masons to the Master's degree, a power for a long time exercised only by the Grand Lodge.

Northumberland. "This circumstance," says Preston, "the Grand Lodge at York highly resented, and ever afterward viewed the proceedings of the brethren in the south with a jealous eye. All friendly intercourse ceased, and the York Masons, from that moment, considered their interests distinct from the Masons under the Grand Lodge in London.*

Three years after, in 1738, several brethren, dissatisfied with the conduct of the Grand Lodge of England, seceded from it, and held unauthorized meetings for the purpose of initiation. Taking advantage of the breach between the Grand Lodges of York and London, they assumed the character of York Masons. On the Grand Lodge's determination to put strictly in execution the laws against such seceders, they still further separated from its jurisdiction, and assumed the appellation of "*Ancient York Masons.*" They announced that the ancient landmarks were alone preserved by them; and, declaring that the regular lodges had adopted new plans, and sanctioned innovations, they branded them with the name of "*Modern Masons.*" In 1739, they established a new Grand Lodge in London, under the name of the "Grand Lodge of Ancient York Masons," and, persevering in the measures they had adopted, held communications and appointed annual feasts. They were soon afterward recognized by the Masons of Scotland and Ireland, and were encouraged and fostered by many of the nobility. The two Grand Lodges continued to exist, and to act in opposition to each other, extending their schisms into other countries,† until the year 1813, when, under the Grand Mastership of the Duke of Sussex, they were happily united, and discord, we trust, forever banished from English Masonry.‡

---

* Preston's Illustrations, p. 184.

† For instance, there were, originally, in Massachusetts and South Carolina, two Grand Lodges, claiming their authority from these discordant bodies. In the former State, however, they were united in 1792, and in the latter in 1817.

‡ We may as well mention here, that the rites and ceremonies of these bodies were essentially the same, and that the landmarks were equally preserved by them.

Scotland. Freemasonry was introduced into Scotland by the architects who built the Abbey of Kilwinning; and the village of that name bears the same relation to Scottish masonry, that the city of York does to English. Assemblies, for the general government of the craft, were frequently held at Kilwinning. In the reign of James II., the office of Grand Master of Scotland was granted to William St. Clair, Earl of Orkney and Caithness, and Baron of Roslin, "his heirs and successors," by the king's charter.* But, in 1736, the St. Clair who then exercised the Grand Mastership, "taking into consideration that his holding or claiming any such jurisdiction, right, or privilege, might be prejudicial to the craft and vocation of masonry,"† renounced his claims, and empowered the Freemasons to choose their Grand Master. The consequence of this act of resignation was the immediate organization of the Grand Lodge of Scotland, over whom, for obvious reasons, the late hereditary Grand Master was unanimously called to preside.

Ireland. In 1729, the Freemasons of Dublin held an assembly, and organized the "Grand Lodge of Ireland." The Earl of Kingston was elected the first Grand Master.

France. In the beginning of the 18th century, Freemasonry in France was in a state of great disorder. Every lodge acted independently of all others; the Masters were elected for life, and exercised the privileges and powers which are now confined to Grand Lodges; there was no masonic centre, and consequently no masonic union.

In 1735, there were six lodges in Paris, and several others in the different provincial towns. The Earl of Derwentwater, the celebrated Jacobite, who afterward was beheaded at London, for his adherence to the house of Stuart, exercised the functions of Grand Master by a tacit consent, although not by a formal election. In the following year, Lord Harnouster was elected by

---

* See the MS. in the Edinburgh Advocates' Library, quoted by Lawrie.

† See the deed of resignation in Lawrie's Hist. Masonry.

GRA   173

the Parisian lodges Grand Master; and in 1738, he was succeeded by the Duc d'Antin. On his death, in 1743, the Count
de Clermont was elected to supply his place.

Organized Freemasonry in France dates its existence from this
latter year. In 1735, the lodges of Paris had petitioned the Grand
Lodge of England for the establishment of a Provincial Grand
Lodge, which, on political grounds, had been refused. In 1743,
however, it was granted, and the Provincial Grand Lodge of
France was constituted under the name of the "Grand Loge
Anglaise de France." The Grand Master, Clermont, was, however, an inefficient officer; anarchy and confusion once more invaded the fraternity; the authority of the Grand Lodge was prostrated; and the establishment of mother lodges in the provinces,
with the original intention of superintending the proceedings of
the distant provincial lodges, instead of restoring harmony, as
was vainly expected, widened still more the breach. For, assuming the rank, and exercising the functions, of Grand Lodges,
they ceased all correspondence with the metropolitan body, and
became in fact its rivals.

Under these circumstances, the Grand Lodge declared itself
independent of England in 1756, and assumed the title of the
"Grand Lodge of France." It recognized only the three degrees of Apprentice, Fellow-Craft, and Master Mason, and was
composed of the grand officers to be elected out of the body of
the fraternity, and of the Masters for life of the Parisian lodges;
thus formally excluding the provincial lodges from any participation in the government of the craft.

But the proceedings of this body were not less stormy than
those of its predecessor. We have stated that the Count de
Clermont proved an inefficient Grand Master. He had appointed,
in succession, two deputies, both of whom had been displeasing
to the fraternity. The last, Lacorne, was a man of such low
origin and rude manners, that the Grand Lodge refused to meet
him as their presiding officer. Irritated at this pointed disre-
spect, he sought in the taverns of Paris those Masters who had

made a traffic of initiations, but who, heretofore, had submitted
to the control, and been checked by the authority, of the Grand
Lodge. From among them he selected officers devoted to his
service, and undertook a complete reorganization of the Grand
Lodge.

The retired members, however, protested against these illegal
proceedings; and in the subsequent year, the Grand Master consented to revoke the authority he had bestowed upon Lacorne,
and appointed as his deputy, M. Chaillon de Jonville. The
respectable members now returned to their seats in the Grand
Lodge; and in the triennial election which took place in June,
1765, the officers who had been elected during the Deputy Grand
Mastership of Lacorne were all removed. The displaced officers
protested, and published a defamatory memoir on the subject,
and were in consequence expelled from masonry by the Grand
Lodge. Ill feeling on both sides was thus engendered, and carried to such a height, that, at one of the communications of the
Grand Lodge, the expelled brethren, attempting to force their
way in, were resisted with violence. The next day the lieutenant
of police issued an edict, forbidding the future meetings of the
Grand Lodge.

The expelled party, however, still continued their meetings.
The Count de Clermont died in 1771: and the excluded brethren
having invited the Duke of Chartres, (afterwards Duke of Orleans,)
to the Grand Mastership, he accepted the appointment. They
now offered to unite with the Grand Lodge, on condition that
the latter would revoke the decree of expulsion. The proposal
was accepted, and the Grand Lodge went once more into
operation.

Another union took place, which has since considerably influenced the character of French masonry. During the troubles of
the preceding years, masonic bodies were instituted in various
parts of the kingdom, which professed to confer degrees, of a
higher nature, than those belonging to craft masonry, and which
have since been known by the name of the Ineffable degrees.

These chapters assumed a right to organize and control symbolic or blue lodges, and this assumption had been a fertile source of controversy between them and the Grand Lodge. By the latter body they had never been recognized, but the lodges under their direction had often been declared irregular, and their members expelled. They now, however, demanded a recognition, and proposed, if their request was complied with, to bestow the government of the "hauts grades" upon the same person who was at the head of the Grand Lodge. The compromise was made, the recognition was decreed, and the Duke of Chartres was elected Grand Master of all the councils, chapters, and Scotch lodges of France.

But peace was not yet restored. The party who had been expelled, moved by a spirit of revenge for the disgrace formerly inflicted on them, succeeded in obtaining the appointment of a committee which was empowered to prepare a new constitution. All the lodges of Paris and the provinces were requested to appoint deputies, who were to form a convention to take the new constitution into consideration. This convention, or, as they called it, national assembly, met at Paris, in December, 1771. The Duke of Luxemburg presided, and on the 24th of that month, the ancient Grand Lodge of France was declared extinct, and in its place another substituted, with the title of *Grand Orient de France*.

Notwithstanding the declaration of extinction by the national assembly, the Grand Lodge continued to meet and to exercise its functions. Thus the fraternity of France continued to be harrassed, by the bitter contentions of these rival bodies, until the commencement of the revolution compelled both the Grand Orient and the Grand Lodge to suspend their labours.

On the restoration of civil order, both bodies resumed their operations, but the Grand Lodge had been weakened by the death of many of the perpetual Masters, who had originally been attached to it; and a better spirit arising, the Grand Lodge was, by a solemn and mutual declaration, united to the Grand Orient on the 28th of June, 1799.

Dissensions, however, continued to arise between the Grand Orient and the different chapters of the higher degrees. Several of those bodies had at various periods given in their adhesion to the Grand Orient, and again violated the compact of peace. Finally, the Grand Orient perceiving that the pretensions of the Scotch rite Masons would be a perpetual source of disorder, decreed on the 16th of September, 1805, that the Supreme Council of the 33d degree should thenceforth become an independent body, with the power to confer warrants of constitution for all the degrees superior to the 18th, or Rose Croix; while the chapters of that and the inferior degrees were placed under the exclusive control of the Grand Orient.

But a further detail of the dissensions which obscured masonry in France, would be painful as well as tedious. They were renewed in 1821, by the reorganization of the Supreme Council, which had been dormant since 1815. But in 1842 an advance towards a reconciliation was made by the Supreme Council, which has at length been met by the Grand Orient. The friendship was consummated in 1842, and peace now reigns, at last, among the Masons of France.

Germany. The first German lodge was established at Cologne, in 1716, but it died almost as soon as it was born. Seventeen years afterward, (in 1733,) according to Preston,[*] a charter was granted by the Grand Lodge of England, to eleven German Masons in Hamburg. In 1738, another lodge was established in Brunswick, under the authority of the Grand Lodge of Scotland. This lodge, which was called "The Three Gloves," united with the lodges of "The Three White Eagles," and "The Three Swans," to organize, in 1741, a Grand Lodge, the first established in Germany. This Grand Lodge still exists, and has under its jurisdiction eighty-eight subordinate lodges. There is

---

Illustrations, p. 183, ed. 1804.

another Grand Lodge at Brunswick, which was established in
1768, by the Grand Lodge of England, and which is considered
as the metropolitan Grand Lodge of Germany. It has under its
jurisdiction fifty-three subordinate lodges.

Prussia. The Royal York Grand Lodge of Prussia is situated
at Berlin. It was established as a subordinate lodge, in 1752.
In 1765 it initiated the Duke of York, and then assumed the
name of "Royal York in Friendship." It had under its jurisdiction, in 1840, twenty-seven lodges. The "Grand Lodge of
the Three Globes" was founded in 1740, and has under its jurisdiction one hundred and seventy-seven lodges. There are now
three Grand Lodges in Prussia, the "Three Globes," the "Royal
York," and the "National," which was founded, in 1770, by a
warrant from the Grand Lodge of England; every lodge in
Prussia derives its warrant from one of these Grand Lodges.

Saxony. The first lodge in Saxony was the Three White
Eagles, which was formed in 1738 at Dresden. In 1741 another
was formed at Leipsig, and a third in the following year at Al-
tenburg. The Grand Lodge of Saxony was establised in 1812.
It has adopted the system of Ancient Craft, or St. John's masonry,
for its rite, and under this all its subordinates, except two, profess
to work.

Belgium. In 1721, the Grand Lodge of England constituted
the lodge of "Perfect Union," at Mons, and in 1730, another at
Ghent. The former was afterward erected into a Grand Lodge.
The present Grand Orient of Belgium has its seat at Brussels.

Holland. The first lodge established in Holland, was at the
Hague in 1731, under the warrant of the Grand Lodge of England.
It was, however, only a lodge of emergency, having been called
to initiate the Duke of Tuscany, afterward Francis the First,
Emperor of Germany. After the ceremony had been performed
by the Earl of Chesterfield, the lodge was closed. The first regular lodge was established at the same place in 1734, which five
years after took the name of "Mother Lodge." In 1735, a lodge
was opened at Amsterdam. The National Grand Lodge was esta-

blished on the 18th December, 1757, and now has about seventy lodges under its register.

Denmark. The Grand Lodge of Denmark was instituted in 1743. It derived its existence from the Grand Lodge of Scotland. It is situated at Copenhagen. Masonry in this country is in a flourishing condition; it is recognized by the state, and the reigning king is Grand Master.

Sweden. In no country has the progress of masonry been more prosperous than in Sweden. It arose there in 1754, under the charter of the Grand Lodge of Scotland. The seat of the Grand Lodge is at Stockholm, and the king is at the head of the craft.

Russia. An English lodge was constituted at St. Petersburg, in 1740, under a warrant from the Grand Lodge of England, and masonry soon afterwards began to increase with great rapidity throughout the empire. In 1772, the Grand Lodge of England established a Provincial Grand Mastership, and lodges were constituted successively at Moscow, Riga, Jassy, and in various parts of Courtland. The order was patronized by the throne, and, of course, by the nobility. But, unfortunately, politics began to poison, with its pollutions, the pure atmosphere of masonry, and the order rapidly declined. Lodges are, however, still privately held in various parts of the empire.

Poland. In 1739, Freemasonry was suppressed in this kingdom by an edict of King Augustus II. In 1781, however, it was revived under the auspices of the Grand Orient of France; who, upon the application of three lodges at Warsaw, established lodges at Wilna, Dubno, Posen, Grodno, and Warsaw. These united in 1784, to form a Grand Orient, whose seat is at the last named city. Masonry in Poland is now in a flourishing condition.

Bohemia. Freemasonry was instituted in Bohemia, in 1749, by the Grand Lodge of Scotland. In 1776 it was highly prosperous, and continued so until the commencement of the French revolution, when it was suppressed by the Austrian government. Its present condition I have no means of ascertaining.

Switzerland. In 1737, the Grand Lodge of England granted a patent to Sir George Hamilton, by authority of which he instituted a Provincial Grand Lodge at Geneva. Two years afterwards the same body bestowed a warrant of constitution on a lodge situated at Lausanne. Masonry continued to flourish in Switzerland until 1745, when it was prohibited by an edict of the Council of Berne. From this attack, however, it recovered in 1764. The lodges resumed their labours, and a Grand Lodge was organized at Geneva. But Switzerland, like France, has been sorely visited with masonic dissensions. At one time there existed not less than three conflicting masonic authorities in the republic. Peace has, however, been restored, and the National Grand Lodge of Switzerland, seated at Berne, now exercises sole masonic jurisdiction, under the name of Alpina. The Book of Constitutions is similar to that of England. The Grand Lodge Alpina recognizes only the three degrees of Ancient Craft Masonry.

Italy. The enmity of the Roman church towards Freemasonry, has ever kept the latter institution in a depressed state in Italy. A lodge existed at Florence, as early as 1733, established by Lord Charles Sackville, the son of the Duke of Dorset, and lodges still are to be found at Leghorn, Turin, Genoa, and the other principal cities, but their meetings are held with great secrecy.

Spain. The first lodge established in Spain was in 1726, at Gilbraltar. Another was constituted the year following, at Madrid. A third was formed at Andalusia, in 1731. The persecutions of the priests and government were always obstacles to the successful propagation of masonry in this kingdom. Lodges, however, still exist and work in various parts of Spain, but their meetings are in private.

Portugal. What has been said of Freemasonry in Italy and Spain, is equally applicable to Portugal. Though lodges were established as early as 1727, they always were, and continue to be, holden with great secrecy. One, however, of the influences of the French invasion, was the dissemination of Freemasonry among the Portuguese, and there are now, or were within a few years, not less than four Grand Lodges existing in that kingdom.

Turkey. Of the state of masonry in the Ottoman Empire, we know but little. Clavel says, that lodges were established at Constantinople, Smyrna and Aleppo, in 1738, but of their present existence we have no information.

Asia. Freemasonry was introduced into India, in 1728, by Sir George Pomfret, who established a lodge at Calcutta. Another was formed in 1740, and in 1779, there was scarcely a town in Hindostan in which there was not a lodge. In that year, Omdit ul Omrah Bahauder, the eldest son of the nabob of the Carnatic, was initiated at Trinchinopoly. Masonry still exists in a prosperous condition, in Asia Minor and all the English settlements. The lodges are under the jurisdiction generally of the Grand Lodge of England.

Africa. Freemasonry was introduced into Africa, in 1736, by the establishment of lodges at Cape Coast on the Gambia River. Lodges have since been constituted at the Cape of Good Hope; in the islands of Mauritius, Madagascar, and St. Helena; and at Algiers, Tunis, Morocco, Cairo, and Alexandria.

Oceanica. Into these remote regions has the institution of Freemasonry extended. Lodges have existed since 1828, at Sidney, Paramatta, Melbourne, and in many other of the English colonies.

America. The first lodge established in Canada, was at Cape Breton, in the year 1745. Lodges existed from as early a period in the West India Islands. On the establishment of the Brazilian Empire, a Grand Lodge was instituted, and, in 1825, Don Pedro the First was elected its Grand Master. In 1825, the Grand Lodge of Mexico was organized; and in 1837, that of Texas was instituted. Long before these periods, however, lodges had been constituted in both these countries, under charters from different Grand Lodges in the United States.

United States. The first notice that we have of Freemasonry

in the United States, is in 1729, in which year, during the Grand
Mastership of the Duke of Norfolk, Mr. Daniel Cox was appointed Provincial Grand Master for New Jersey. I have not,
however, been able to obtain any evidence that he exercised his
prerogative by the establishment of lodges in that province,
although it is probable that he did. In the year 1733 the " St.
John's Grand Lodge" was opened in Boston in consequence of a
charter granted, on the application of several brethren residing in
that city, by Lord Viscount Montacute,* Grand Master of England.

This charter is dated on the 30th of April, in the same year,
and appointed the R. W. Henry Price, Grand Master in North
America, with power to appoint his Deputy, and the other officers
necessary for forming a Grand Lodge, and also to constitute lodges
of Free and Accepted Masons as often as occasion should require.
The first charter granted by this body was to " St. John's Lodge"
in Boston, which lodge is still in existence. In the succeeding
year, it granted a charter for the constitution of a lodge in Philadelphia, of which the venerable Benjamin Franklin was the first
Master. This Grand Lodge, however, descending from the Grand
Lodge of England, was, of course, composed of Modern Masons.†
A number of brethren, there, residing in Boston, who were Ancient Masons, applied to and received a dispensation from
Lord Aberdour, Grand Master of Scotland, constituting them a
regular lodge, under the designation of St. Andrew's Lodge,
No. 82, and the Massachusetts Grand Lodge, descending from
the Grand Lodge of Scotland, was established on the 27th December, 1769. On the 19th June, 1792, the two Grand Lodges
were united, and all the distinctions of Ancient and Modern Masons abolished.

---

* I am indebted to my esteemed friend and learned brother A. O. Sullivan,
Grand Secretary of Missouri, for calling my attention to the inadvertence I have
committed in previous editions of spelling this name *Montague* instead of
Montacute. But I may console myself with the rather selfish reflection that
nearly all of my contemporaries have fallen into the same error.

† See the article *Modern Masons.*

In 1735, Freemasonry was introduced into South-Carolina by the constitution of "Solomon's Lodge, No. 1," under a Warrant from Lord Montague, Grand Master of Free and Accepted Masons of England. This was, therefore, the fourth lodge organized in the United States.* Three other lodges were soon afterwards constituted. In 1754, on the 30th of March, the Marquis of Carnarvon, Grand Master of England, issued his Warrant, constituting a Provincial Grand Lodge in the province, and appointing Chief Justice Leigh, Provincial Grand Master. On the 24th of December, in the same year, the Grand Lodge was solemnly constituted at Charleston. In 1787 a Grand Lodge of Ancient York Masons was also established at Charleston, and in the course of the succeeding years, many disagreeable dissensions occurred between this and the Grand Lodge of Free and Accepted Masons which had been organized in 1754. These, however, at length, happily terminated, and an indissoluble union took place between the two bodies in December, 1817, which resulted in the formation of the present "Grand Lodge of Ancient Freemasons."

In 1764, the Grand Lodge of Pennsylvania was established by a Warrant issued from the Grand Lodge of England. Subsequently, the Grand Lodge of North Carolina was constituted in 1771; that of Virginia in 1778; and that of New York in 1781.

These Grand Lodges were, until the close of the Revolutionary War, held under the authority of Charters granted either by the Grand Lodge of England, or that of Scotland. But, on the confirmation of our political independence, the brethren, desirous of a like relief from the thraldom of a foreign power, began to organize Grand Lodges in their respective limits, and there now exist such bodies in every State and Territory in the Union, the last formed being that of Minnesota in 1853.

---

* It ranked as No. 45, on the Register of England, while Solomon's lodge in Savannah, which preceded it in time of constitution, held the number 46. See Hutchinson's List.

GRA   183

GRAND LODGES, JURISDICTION OF. A Grand Lodge
is invested with power and authority over all the craft within its
jurisdiction. It is the Supreme Court of Appeal in all masonic
cases, and to its decrees unlimited obedience must be paid, by
every lodge and every Mason situated within its control. The
government of Grand Lodges is, therefore, completely despotic.
While a Grand Lodge exists, its edicts must be respected and
obeyed without examination by its subordinate lodges. Yet should
a Grand Lodge decree wrongfully or contrary to the ancient constitutions, though there be no redress for its subordinates, the
Grand Lodges in other States may declare its proceedings irregular, and even put it out of the pale of masonry, by refusing to
hold communion with it. But in this case, the Grand Lodge
does not suffer more than the craft in general working under it :
for every Mason who should then acknowledge its authority, would
be placed under the same ban of masonic outlawry. Grand Lodges
are, however, exceedingly scrupulous in exercising this interference
with the masonic authorities of other jurisdictions, reserving the
exertion of this power only for cases in which there has been a
manifest violation of the ancient landmarks. An instance of this
kind has lately occurred in this country. In 1828, the labours
of the Grand Lodge of Michigan, in consequence of the anti-masonic excitement then at its height, were suspended, and the
lodges under its jurisdiction dissolved. In 1841, masonry having
revived in that State, the Masons of Michigan met in convention,
and without the existence of a single subordinate lodge, proceeded
to institute a Grand Lodge. This was in palpable derogation of
the fundamental laws of the order. Consequently, the other supreme masonic bodies in the Union refused to acknowledge the
Grand Lodge of Michigan. Afterwards (in 1844) this body,
submitting very properly to the general opinion of the fraternity,
proceeded to organize according to the legitimate mode, by the
convention of the constitutional number of lodges, and it is now
recognized as a regularly constituted Grand Lodge.

This supreme power that is vested in Grand Lodges, by which

they are constituted as the sole judges and exponents, for their
respective jurisdictions, of the ancient landmarks and usages of
the fraternity, is derived from the fundamental laws of masonry.
It is based, too, upon sound sense and expediency. For without
a governing power, so large a body as the craft would soon run
into anarchy. But this power could not be placed in the hands
of subordinate lodges, or individual brethren, for that would create
endless confusion. Grand Lodges are, therefore, its proper depositories, since they contain within themselves the united wisdom
and prudence of many subordinate lodges. And so careful has
our institution been of the preservation of this power to Grand
Lodges, that according to the Ancient Charges, the master of
every lodge is called upon, previous to his installation, to give
his assent to the following propositions:

"You agree to hold in veneration, the original rulers and patrons of the order of Freemasonry, and their regular successors,
supreme and subordinate, according to their stations; and to
submit to the awards and resolutions of your brethren in Grand
Lodge convened, in every case, consistent with the constitutions
of the order.

"You promise to pay homage to the Grand Master for the time
being, and to his officers when duly installed, and *strictly to conform to every edict of the Grand Lodge.*"

GRAND LODGES, ORGANIZATION OF. Grand Lodges
are organized in the following manner. Three or more legally
constituted lodges working in any state, kingdom, or other independent political division, where no Grand Lodge already exists, may meet in convention, adopt by-laws, elect officers, and
organize a Grand Lodge. The lodges within its jurisdiction then
surrender their Warrants of Constitution to the Grand Lodges
from which they respectively had received them, and accept others
from the newly organized Grand Lodge, which thenceforward exercises all masonic jurisdiction over the state in which it has been
organized.

A Grand Lodge thus organized, consists of the Masters and Wardens of all the lodges under its jurisdiction, and such Past Masters as may enrol themselves or be elected as members. Past Masters are not, however, members of the Grand Lodge by inherent right, but only by courtesy, and no Past Master can remain a member of the Grand Lodge unless he is attached to some subordinate lodge in its jurisdiction.

All Grand Lodges are governed by the following officers: Grand Master, Deputy Grand Master, Senior and Junior Grand Wardens, Grand Treasurer, and Grand Secretary. These are usually termed the Grand officers; in addition to them there are subordinate officers appointed by the Grand Master and the Grand Wardens, such as Grand Deacons, Grand Stewards, Grand Marshal, Grand Pursuivant, Grand Sword Bearer, and Grand Tyler; but their number and titles vary in different Grand Lodges.

GRAND MASTER. The presiding officer of the masonic fraternity, to whom is entrusted the execution of important duties, and who is consequently invested with extensive powers, should always be selected for his respectability, virtue, and learning. For the first, that the dignity of the fraternity may not suffer under his administration; for the second, that he may afford an example worthy of imitation to his brethren; for the last, that he may be enabled to guide and control the craft with proper skill and accuracy.

The powers of the Grand Master during the recess of the Grand Lodge are very extensive. He has full authority and right not only to be present, but also to preside in every lodge, with the Master of the lodge on his left hand, and to order his Grand Wardens to attend him, and act as Wardens in that particular lodge.* He has the right of visiting the lodges and inspecting their books and mode of work as often as he pleases, or if unable to do so, he may depute his grand officers to act for him. He has the power of granting dispensations for the formation of new

* General Regulations, 1757, Art. 5, in Anderson Const. 337.
16*

lodges, which dispensations are of force until revoked by himself
or the Grand Lodge. He may also grant dispensations for several other purposes, for which see the article "*Dispensation.*"
Formerly, the Grand Master appointed his Grand officers, but
this regulation has been repealed, and the Grand officers are now
all elected by the Grand Lodge.

When the Grand Master visits a lodge, he must be received
with the greatest respect, and the Master of the lodge should
always offer him the chair, which the Grand Master may or may
not accept at his pleasure.

Should the Grand Master die, or be absent from the jurisdiction
during his term of office, the Deputy Grand Master assumes his
powers, or if there be no Deputy, then the Grand Wardens according to seniority.

GRAND MASTER ARCHITECT. *Grand Master Architect.*
The 12th degree in the Ancient Scotch rite. This is strictly a
scientific degree, resembling in that respect the degree of Fellow
Craft. In it the principles of architecture and the connection of
the liberal arts with masonry, are unfolded. Its officers are three,
a Most Powerful and two Wardens. The chapter is decorated
with white and red hangings, and furnished with the five orders
of architecture and a case of mathematical instruments. The
jewel is a gold medal, on both sides of which are engraved the
orders of architecture. It is suspended by a stone colored
ribbon.

GRAND MASTER OF ALL SYMBOLIC LODGES.
Vénérable maître de toutes les loges. The 20th degree in the
Ancient Scotch rite. The presiding officer is styled Venerable
Grand Master, and represents Cyrus Artaxerxes. He is seated
in the east on a throne elevated upon nine steps, and is assisted
by two Wardens in the west. The decorations of the lodge are
blue and yellow. The lecture of the degree contains some interesting instructions respecting the first and second temple.

Among the traditions preserved by the possessors of this degree, is one which states that after the third temple was destroyed by Titus, the son of Vespasian, the Christian Freemasons who were then in the Holy Land, being filled with sorrow, departed from home with the determination of building a fourth,* and that, dividing themselves into several bodies, they dispersed over the various parts of Europe. The greater number went to Scotland, and repaired to the town of Kilwinning, where they established a lodge and built an abbey, and where the records of the order were deposited.

GRAND OFFERINGS. See *Ground Floor of the Lodge.*

GRAND PONTIFF. *Grand Pontife ou Sublime Ecossais.* The 19th degree of the Ancient Scotch rite. The degree is occupied in an examination of the Apocalyptic mysteries of the New Jerusalem. Its officers are a Thrice Puissant and one Warden. The Thrice Puissant is seated in the east on a throne canopied with blue, and wears a white satin robe. The Warden is in the west, and holds a staff of gold. The members are clothed in white, with blue fillets embroidered with twelve stars of gold, and are called True and Faithful Brothers. The decorations of the lodge are blue sprinkled with gold stars

GREEN. The emblematic color of a Knight of the Red Cross, and of a Perfect Master.
The Red Cross Knight is reminded by this color that Truth is a divine attribute, and that like the green Bay tree it will flourish in perpetual verdure.
The Perfect Master is admonished by it, that being dead in sin, he must hope to revive in virtue.

GROUND FLOOR OF THE LODGE. Mount Moriah, on which the Temple of Solomon was built, is symbolically called

_____
* This was to be a spiritual one.

the *ground floor of the lodge*, and hence it is said that "the lodge rests on holy ground." This ground floor of the lodge is remarkable for three great events recorded in Scripture, and which are called "the three grand offerings of masonry." It was here that Abraham prepared, as a token of his faith, to offer up his beloved son Isaac—this was the *first grand offering ;* it was here that David, when his people were afflicted with a pestilence, built an altar, and offered thereon peace offerings and burnt offerings to appease the wrath of God—this was the *second grand offering ;* and lastly, it was here, that when the Temple was completed, King Solomon dedicated that magnificent structure to the service of Jehovah, with the offering of pious prayers and many costly presents—and this was the *third grand offering.*

This sacred spot was once the threshing floor of Ornan the Jebusite, and from him David purchased it for fifty shekels of silver.* The Cabbalists delight to invest it with still more solemn associations, and declare that it was the spot on which Adam was born and Abel slain. To the Mason it is sufficiently endeared by the collection that it was here that after a long night of darkness, *language was restored and masonry found.*

GUAGE. See *Twenty-four inch Gauge.*

GUARDS OF THE CONCLAVE. See *Knights of the Christian Mark.*

GUTTURAL. Belonging to the throat; from the Latin *guttur,* the throat. The throat is that avenue of the body which is most employed in the sins of intemperance, and hence it suggests to the Mason certain symbolic instructions in relation to the virtue of temperance.

---

* 1 Chronicles xxi. 25.

H.

HAGGAI. Haggai was the first of the three prophets who flourished after the captivity. He was most probably born at Babylon, whence he accompanied Zerubbabel to Jerusalem to rebuild the second temple. In the Royal Arch he is represented by the Scribe, because he expounded the law to Zerubbabel and Joshua, which was the proper duty of a Scribe. (See *Scribe.*) He reproved the people for their neglect in rebuilding the temple, and incited them to the work, by the promise of God's assistance. His intimate connection with the King and High Priest, and the masonic authority for placing him in the council with Zerubbabel and Johsua, are confirmed by the first verse of the Book of Haggai: "In the second year of Darius the king, in the sixth month, in the first day of the month, came the word of the Lord *by Haggai* the Prophet unto Zerubbabel, the son of Shealtiel, governor of Judah, and to Johsua the son of Josedech the High Priest, saying," etc.

HAH. The Hebrew definite article, ה, signifying "the."

HAIL, or HALE. This word is used among Masons with two very different significations. 1. When addressed as an inquiry to a visiting brother, it has the same import as that in which it is used under like circumstances by mariners. Thus: "Whence do you hail?" that is, "of what lodge are you a member?" Used in this sense, it comes from the Saxon term of salutation "HÆL," and should be spelt "hail." 2. Its second use is confined to what Masons understand by the "*tie,*" and in this sense it signifies to *conceal*, being derived from the Saxon word "HELAN,"* to hide. By the rules of etymology, it should be spelt "hale." The preservation of this Saxon word in the masonic dialect, while

---

* E, in Anglo-Saxon, is to be pronounced as a in the word *fate.*

it has ceased to exist in the vernacular, is a striking proof of the antiquity of the order and its ceremonies, in England.*

HAND. See *Right Hand*.

HARMONY. Harmony is the chief support of every well regulated institution. Without it, the most extensive empires must decay; with it, the weakest nations may become powerful. The ancient philosophers and poets believed, that the prototype of harmony was to be found in the sublime music of the spheres, and that man, copying nature, has attempted to introduce this divine melody into human life.† And thus it proves its celestial origin, by the heavenly influence it exerts on earth. Sallust represents the good king Micipsa as saying, that "by concord small things increase; by discord the greatest fall gradually into ruin."‡ Let every Mason, anxious for the prosperity of his order, feel the truth of the maxim, and remember that *for* harmony should his lodge be opened—*in* harmony should it work—and *with* harmony be closed.

HARODIM. A Hebrew word, signifying *princes* or *rulers*. In 1 Kings v. 16, it is said that Solomon had 3300 chief officers who ruled over the people, and in 2 Chronicles ii. 18, we read as follows: "and he set three score and ten thousand of them to be bearers of burdens, and four score thousand to be hewers in the mountain, and three thousand and six hundred overseers to set the people at work." The difference between the 3600 overseers mentioned in this place, and the 3300 recorded in the book of Kings, arises from the fact that in the former place 300 chief

---

* "In the western parts of England," says Lord King, "at this very day to *hele* over any thing signifies among the common people to cover it; and he that covereth an house with tile or slate is called a helliar."—*Critical Hist. of the Apostle's Creed*, p. 178.

† See Cicero, Somnium Scipionis.

‡ Concordia parvæ res crescunt, discordia maxume dilabuntur. Bell. Jugurth. ? 18.

overseers are included that are not alluded to in the latter. These
300 overseers were the Harodim, or Provosts, or Princes.*

HARODIM, GRAND CHAPTER OF. An institution
opened in London, in 1787, whose nature is thus defined by
Preston, who is said to have been its founder: "The mysteries
of this order are peculiar to the institution itself, while the lectures
of the chapter include every branch of the masonic system, and
represent the art of masonry in a finished and complete form."†
In other words, it was a school of instruction organized upon a
peculiar plan. Different classes were established, and particular
lectures restricted to each class. The lectures were divided into
sections, and the sections into clauses. The presiding officer was
called the Chief Harod. He annually distributed the various
sections to skilful members, who were called Sectionists, and these
divided the different clauses among others who were denominated
Clauseholders. When a member became possessed of all the
sections, he was denominated a Lecturer. The whole system was
admirably adapted to the purposes of masonic instruction. This
body, I believe, (though I cannot speak with certainty,) no longer
exists. Dr. Oliver, however, writes of it in 1846 as if it were
still in operation.

HEAL. A Mason who has received the degrees in a clandestine lodge, or in an irregular manner, is not permitted to enjoy
the privileges of masonry, until he has passed through the ceremonies in a legally constituted lodge, or if it be the higher degrees,
in a chapter or encampment. After passing through this process,
for which the expense is generally reduced, the brother is said *to
be healed*.

---

* These passages are thus ably explained by Brother Kleinschmidt in his
" Constitutionensbuch der Freimaurer." v. 1, p. 17. Frankfort, 1784.
† Illust. of Masonry, p. 254.

HEARING. One of the five human senses, and highly important to Masons as one of the modes through which the universal language of masonry may be communicated. But the contemplation of this subject also conveys to us two invaluable lessons First, that we should always listen with humility to the lessons of instruction that come from the lips of those wiser than ourselves; and secondly, that our ears should ever be open to the calls for assistance, which the worthy and destitute may make upon our charity.

HEREDOM, RITE OF. See *Perfection, rite of.*

HERMAPHRODITE. Strictly, this word should have no place in a Masonic Lexicon; but as I have heard many unskilful brethren make use of it, and refer to it, with much gravity in certain parts of the ceremony of initiation, I will avail myself of this opportunity, to announce a fact to them, which has long since been received as indisputable, by the whole medical world. The hermaphrodite is a monster, the belief in which has long been exploded; no such being ever existed, and every instance of the pretended conformation of both sexes in one animal, has upon inspection proved to be nothing more than a variety in the structure of the female organs.

HERMETIC RITE. This is the name of a spurious system of Freemasonry, established by one Pernetti, in 1770, at Avignon in France. Its object was to teach symbolically the pretended arts of the alchemists, the transmutation of metals, and the composition of the universal panacea, and of the elixir of life. It is now extinct, or exists only in its modification, the " Philosophic Scoth rite," (which see.)

HERODEM, ROYAL ORDER OF. This is an order which is said to have been founded in the year 1314, by King Robert Bruce. It is almost confined to Scotland, out of which country

it is hardly known. The best account of it that I can find, is the
following, given by Dr. Oliver in his "Historical Landmark,"
vol. ii. p. 12.

"Its history, in brief, relates to the dissolution of the Order
of the Temple. Some of these persecuted individuals took refuge
in Scotland, and placed themselves under the protection of Robert
Bruce, and assisted him at the battle of Bannockburn, which was
fought on St. John's day, 1314. After this battle, the Royal
Order was founded; and, from the fact of the Templars having
contributed to the victory, and the subsequent grants to their
order by King Robert, for which they were formally excommu-
nicated by the Church, it has by some persons been identified
with that ancient military order. But there are sound reasons
for believing that the two systems were unconnected with each
other.

"The Royal Order of H. R. D. M.[*] had formerly its chief seat
at Kilwinning, and there is reason to think that it and St. John's
masonry were then governed by the same Grand Lodge. But
during the sixteenth and seventeenth centuries, masonry was at
a very low ebb in Scotland, and it was with the greatest difficulty
that St. John's masonry was preserved. The Grand Chapter of
H. R. D. M. resumed its functions about the middle of the last
century at Edinburg; and, in order to preserve a marked distinction between the Royal Order and Craft Masonry, which had
formed a Grand Lodge there in 1736, the former confined itself
solely to the two degrees of H. R. D. M. and R. S. Y. C. S.[†]

"The first of these degrees may not have been originally masonic. It appears rather to have been connected with the ceremonies of the early Christians. The second degree, which was
termed the Grade de la Tour, is honorary; the tradition being
that it was an order of knighthood, conferred on the field of Bannockburn, and subsequently in Grand Lodge, opened in the Abbey

---

* That is, *Herodem.*
† That is, *Herodem* and *Rosy Cross.*

17

of Kilwinning. It is purely Scotch, and given to Scotch Masons
only ; or to those who become so by affiliation, on being registered
in the books of the Grand Chapter. But no one is regarded as a
lawful Brother of H. R. D. M. or Knight of R. S. Y.C. S., until
he be acknowledged by the Grand Chapter of Scotland."

In a note to his assertion that the Degree of H. R. D. M. "was
connected with the ceremonies of the early Christians," Dr. Oliver
says that "these ceremonies are believed to have been introduced by
the Culdees, in the second or third centuries of the Christian era."
Some light may be thrown upon this supposition, by the following
extract from a MS. in my possession relating to this degree.

"Q. In what place was this order first established ?

"A. First at I-colmb-kill, or I-columb-kill, and afterwards at
Kilwinning, where the Kings of Scotland presided in person as
Grand Master."

I-colm-kill, it will be recollected, was one of the principal seats
of the Culdees.

HERODEN. "Heroden," says a MS. of the ancient Scotch
rite in my possession, " is a mountain situated in the N. W. of
Scotland, where the first or metropolitan lodge of Europe was held.
Hence the term Sovereign Prince of Rose Croix de Heroden."
The French Masons spell it "Hérédom," which, I imagine, is
simply a Gallic mode of expressing the Scottish title *Heroden*.*
I refer for further explanation to the preceding article.

---

* Since the 2d edition of this work was issued, Ragon has published a new
and elaborate treatise entitled "Orthodoxie Maçonnique," in which he asserts
that the word "Heredom," was invented between 1740 and 1745, by the adherents
of Charles Stuart the Pretender at the Court of St. Germain, the residence, during
that period, of that unfortunate prince, and that it is only a corruption of the
mediæval Latin word, "hœredum," signifying "an heritage, " and alluded to the
castle of St. Germain. But as Ragon's favorite notion is that the Scotch rite,
for which he has but little friendship, was instituted for the purpose of aiding
the Stuarts in a restoration to the throne of their ancestors, his theories and de-
rivations must be taken with some grains of allowance. The suggestion is, however, an ingenious one.

HEROINE OF JERICHO. A side degree, instituted in this country, and, like the French masonry of adoption, common to both men and women. None but Royal Arch Masons, their wives and widows, are qualified to receive it. It is by no means extensively known, though there are some females in the Northern and Western States upon whom it has been conferred.

HESED. A Hebrew word, חֶסֶד, pronounced hes-ed, signifying "mercy."

HIGH PLACES. The Hebrews, as well as other ancient nations, were accustomed to worship on the tops of "the highest hills," and sacrifices offered from these elevated positions were superstitiously supposed to be most acceptable to the Deity. So tenacious were the Jews of the observance of this custom, that even after the completion of the temple, they continued, notwithstanding the prohibition in Deuteronomy, to erect chapels on the mountains around Jerusalem, and to offer sacrifices in them. Even Solomon went to Gibeon to sacrifice, and the reason assigned is, because "it was the great high place."*

"The highest hills and the lowest valleys," says Hutchinson, "were from the earliest times esteemed sacred, and it was supposed that the spirit of God was peculiarly diffusive in those places." Bryant says that high places were always dedicated to Sun worship, which was the spurious Freemasonry.

Oliver† mentions a tradition among the Masons of Scotland, that the brethren of the ancient lodges of Kilwinning, Stirling, Aberdeen, &c., used formerly to assemble in the monasteries in foul weather; but in fair weather, especially on the day of St. John the Evangelist, they met on the tops of the neighbouring hills.

HIGH PRIEST. The presiding officer of a Chapter of Royal

---

* 1 Kings iii. 4.   † Landmarks I, 352.

Arch Masons. He is the representative of Joshua, the High Priest, who, with Zerubbabel, Prince of Judah, and Haggai the the Scribe, laid the foundations of the second temple, and resumed the worship of the Lord.

HIGH PRIEST OF THE JEWS. The office of High Priest among the Jews, was, on its first institution, confined to the house of Aaron in the line of his eldest son, though it was afterwards transferred to the family of Judas Maccabeus. The High Priest was at the head of religious affairs, and was the ordinary judge, not only of ecclesiastical matters, but even of the general justice of the Jewish nation. He was consecrated to his sacred office with the most imposing ceremonies, such as investiture, anointing, and sacrifices. The first of these, as it is imitated in the vestments of the High Priest of a Royal Arch Chapter, requires some notice here.

The garments worn by the High Priest were as follows: he was first clothed in a pair of linen drawers. Over this was a coat or shirt of fine linen reaching to his feet, and with sleeves extending to his wrists. Over this again was a robe of blue, called the coat of ephod. It was without sleeves, but consisted of two pieces, one before and another behind, having a large opening in the top for the passage of the head, and another on each side to admit the arms. It extended only to the middle of the legs, and its skirt was adorned with little golden bells and pomegranates. Above all these vestments was placed the ephod, which has already been described as a short garment coming down only to the breast before, but somewhat longer behind, without sleeves, and artificially wrought with gold, and blue, and purple, and scarlet, in embroidery of various figures. It was looped on the shoulders with two onyx stones, on each of which was inscribed the names of six of the tribes. On the front of the ephod he wore the breast plate, which has already been described.* The High Priest also

---

* See article *Breast Plate.*

wore, at his solemn ministration, a mitre of fine linen of a blue colour. This was wrapt in several folds, and worn about his head in the manner of a Turkish turban, except that it was without a crown, being open on top, and sitting on his head like a garland. In front of it there hung down upon his forehead a square plate of gold, called the plate of the golden crown, upon which were inscribed the words HOLINESS TO THE LORD.*

These vestments, as we have before observed, are worn by the High Priest of a Chapter of Royal Arch Masons, and each of them conveys to the possessor a portion of symbolical instruction. The various colours of the robes are emblematic of the graces and virtues which should adorn the human mind; the white, of innocence and purity; the scarlet, of fervency and zeal; the purple, of union; and the blue, of friendship. The mitre is to remind him of the dignity of his office, and the inscription on its plate to admonish him of his dependence on God. Lastly, the breast plate, upon which is engraved the names of the twelve tribes, is to teach him that he is always to bear in mind his responsibility to the laws and ordinances of the institution, and that the honour and interests of the chapter and its members should always be near his heart.†

HIGH PRIESTHOOD, ORDER OF. This is an honorary degree, conferred only on the High Priest of a Royal Arch

---

* See Home's Scripture History of the Jews. B. 1. Ch. 3. Sect. 4.

† According to Josephus, the ancient Jews gave a different symbolic interpretation to these vestments. The breast plate in the middle of the ephod was emblematic of the earth placed in the centre, while the surrounding ocean was represented by the zone or girdle of the High Priest. The two onyx stones were symbols of the sun and moon, and the twelve stones in the breast plate of the twelve zodiacal signs. The blue mitre with its sacred inscription was emblematic of heaven and the Deity who resided there.—*Antiq. Judaic. lib. iii. c. 7.* We may observe further of the mitre, that in the form of the Persian tiara or Phrygian bonnet, it was worn by the priests of Egypt, from whom the Jews, doubtless, borrowed it, and by those of the god Mithras. Its pyramidal shape made it symbolical of the beams of the sun. Maurice, in his "Indian Antiquities," suggests that the word *mitre* may be derived from *Mithra.*

Chapter. It may be conferred by three High Priests, but when the ceremonies are performed in ample form, the presence of at least nine High Priests is required. This degree is to the office of High Priest what that of Past Master is to the office of Worshipful Master of a symbolic lodge. In it is commemorated an ancient circumstance which occurred to a priest of God. The ceremonies, when duly performed, are exceedingly impressive.

HIRAM. A name given to the gavel of the Worshipful Master, because, as Solomon controlled and directed the workmen in the temple by the assistance of Hiram the Builder, so does the Master preserve order in the lodge by the aid of the gavel.

HIRAM, KING OF TYRE. He was the contemporary of Solomon, and assisted him in the construction of the Temple : furnishing him with timber, stone, and artificers, and loaning him one hundred and twenty talents of gold, equal in Federal currency, to about two and a half millions of dollars. Upon Solomon's accession to the throne of Israel, Hiram sent ambassadors to congratulate him on this event. Solomon, in reply, made known to Hiram his intention of carrying into effect the long contemplated object of his father David, by the erection of a Temple to Jehovah, and he requested the assistance of the King of Tyre. Hiram, in his answer, expressed his willingness to grant the required assistance, and said, "I will do all thy desire concerning timber of cedar, and timber of fir. My servants shall bring them down from Lebanon unto the sea; and I will convey them by sea in floats, unto the place that thou shalt appoint me, and will cause them to be discharged there, and thou shalt receive them; and thou shalt accomplish my desire in giving food for my brotherhood."* The timber which was cut in Lebanon, was accordingly sent in floats to Joppa, the seaport of Jerusalem, whence it was conveyed by land to that city. Solomon, in return for this kindness,

---

* See 1 Kings v. 8. 9.

gave King Hiram yearly twenty thousand measures* of wheat, and twenty thousand measures of pure oil, besides liberally supporting the artificers and laborers with whom the King of Tyre had supplied him. Solomon also presented him with twenty cities in Galilee, with which, however, he was not satisfied, and a masonic tradition informs us, that he visited the King of Israel, to expostulate with him on his injustice. Dius and Menander, two heathen historians inform us that Hiram and Solomon corresponded frequently, and attempted to puzzle each other by subtile questions.

HIRAM THE BUILDER. 'Among the workmen sent by Hiram, King of Tyre, to Solomon, was one whom he styles "a cunning man, endued with understanding,"† and he is in another place described as "a widow's son of the tribe of Naphthali, and his father was a man of Tyre, a worker in brass; and he was filled with wisdom and understanding, and cunning to work in all works in brass."‡ This is the workman to whom Solomon was indebted for the construction of all the ornaments of the Temple. Hiram calls him *Huram abi*, that is, "Hiram my father; which is an evidence of his high standing at the Tyrian Court; for the title *ab*, or father, was among the Hebrews often bestowed as a title of honour and dignity, on the chief advisers and intimate friends of the king. Thus Joseph, according to some commentators, is called, *Abrech*, or the "father of the king," and this very Hiram is spoken of in Chronicles§ in the following words: *gnasah Huram Abif l'melech Shlomo*, that is, "did Huram his father, make to King Solomon." The name given to this architect in the lodges, is derived from this passage, *Huram abif*, meaning in Hebrew, Hiram his father.

This Hiram, from his profession as an architect, and his birth

---

* The word which in our Bibles is translated "measure," is, in the original, *corim*. The cor was a measure containing ten ephahs or baths, and equal to a little more than seventy-five wine gallons.

† 2 Chronicles ii. 13.   ‡ 1 Kings viii. 14.   § 2 Chronicles iv. 16.

as a Tyrian, was, in all probability, acquainted with the Dionysian fraternity, which society had extended itself to Tyre, and if so, the union in his person of the Tyrian and Israelitish races, must have afforded him a favourable opportunity, as we have already suggested, of communicating the mysteries of that fraternity to the Jewish builders of the Temple.*

HIRAMITES. A name bestowed upon Freemasons, to indicate their descent from Hiram, the chief builder at King Solomon's Temple. More particularly is the term used in the degree of Patriarch Noachite, (the twenty-first degree of the Scotch rite,) to distinguish Master Masons from the brethren of that degree, who profess to descend immediately, and without connection with Temple masonry, from the sons of Noah. Some learned writers, however, embrace all Masons under the general term of Noachites.

HISTORY. The history of the order, since it has assumed its present organization, will be found in the article *Grand Lodges*; its antecedent history must be sought for under the head of *Antiquity of Masonry*.

HOLINESS TO THE LORD. *Kodesh ladonai*. This was the inscription worn by the High Priest on his forehead, in obedience to the command of God, expressed in Exodus. "And they made the plate of the holy crown of pure gold, and wrote upon it a writing, like to the engraving of a signet, HOLINESS TO THE LORD." xxxix. 30.

HOLY OF HOLIES. See *Temple*.

HONOURABLE. This was the title formerly given to the degree of Fellow Craft.

---

* There is a masonic tradition that he married the sister of Adoniram, and that his widow survived him many years.

HONORARY DEGREE. The degrees of Past Master and High Priesthood, are styled honorary, because each is conferred as an " honorarium," or reward attendant upon certain offices; that of Past Master upon the elected Master of a symbolic lodge, and that of the High Priesthood upon the presiding officer of a Chapter of Royal Arch Masons. The degree of Mark Master, it 'appears to me, is called an honorary degree, because it was intended originally to be conferred only on worthy Fellow Crafts. It certainly should, consistently with its own tradition, precede the degree of Master Mason. The side degrees are also sometimes called honorary degrees.

HONOURS, GRAND. The Grand Honours of masonry are those peculiar acts and gestures, by which the craft have always been accustomed to express their homage, their joy, or their grief on memorable occasions. They are of two kinds, the private and public, and each of them are used on different occasions and for different purposes.

The private Grand Honours of masonry are performed in a manner known only to Master Masons, since they can only be used in a Master's lodge. They are practised by the craft only on four occasions: when a masonic hall is to be consecrated, a new lodge to be constituted, a Master elect to be installed, or a Grand Master or his Deputy to be received on an official visitation to a lodge. They are used at all these ceremonies as tokens of congratulation and homage. And as they can only be given by Master Masons, it is evident that every consecration of a hall, or constitution of a new lodge, every installation of a Worshipful Master, and every reception of a Grand Master, must be done in the third degree. It is also evident from what has been said, that the mode and manner of giving the private Grand Honours can only be personally communicated to Master Masons. They are among the *aporreta* —the things forbidden to be divulged.

The public Grand Honours, as their name imports, do not partake of this secret character. They are given on all public

occasions, in the presence of the profane as well as the initiated.
They are used at the laying of corner-stones of public buildings,
or in other services in which the ministrations of the fraternity
are required, and especially in funerals.   They are given in the
following manner : Both arms are crossed on the breast, the left
uppermost, and the open palms of the hands sharply striking the
shoulders, they are then raised above the head, the palms striking
each other, and then made to fall smartly upon the thighs.   This
is repeated three times, and as there are three blows given each
time, namely on the-breast, on the palms of the hands, and on the
thighs, making nine concussions in all, the Grand Honours are
technically said to be given "by three times three."   On the
occasion of funerals, each one of these honours is accompanied by
the words " *the will of God is accomplished ; so mote it be*,"
audibly pronounced by the brethren.

These Grand Honours of masonry have undoubtedly a classical
origin, and are but an imitation of the plaudits and acclamations
practised by the ancient Greeks and Romans, in their theatres,
their senates, and their public games.   There is abundant evidence
in the writings of the ancients, that in the days of the empire,
the Romans had circumscribed the mode of doing homage to their
emperors and great men when they made their appearance in public, and of expressing their approbation of actors at the theatre,
within as explicit rules and regulations as those that govern the
system of giving the Grand Honours in Freemasonry.   This was
not the case in the earlier ages of Rome, for Ovid, speaking of
the Sabines, says that when they applauded, they did so without
any rules of art :

"In medio plausu, plausus tunc arte carebat."

And Propertius speaks, at a later day, of the ignorance of the
country people, who, at the theatres, destroyed the general harmony, by their awkward attempts to join in the modulated ap-
plauses of the more skilful citizens.

The ancient Romans had carried their science on this subject to such an extent, as to have divided these *honours* into three kinds, differing from each other in the mode in which the hands were struck against each other, and in the sound that thence resulted. Suetonius, in his life of Nero, (cap. xx.,) gives the names of these various kinds of applause, which he says were called *bombi, imbrices* and *testæ;* and Seneca, in his "Naturales Quæstiones," gives a description of the manner in which they were executed. The "bombi," or *hums,* were produced by striking the palms of the hands together, while they were in a hollow or concave position, and doing this at frequent intervals, but with little force, so as to imitate the humming sound of a swarm of bees. The "imbrices," or *tiles,* were made, by briskly striking the flattened and extended palms of the hands against each other, so as to resemble the sound of hail pattering upon the tiles of a roof. The "testæ," or *earthen vases,* were executed by striking the palm of the left hand, with the fingers of the right collected into one point. By this blow a sound was elicited, which imitated that given out by an earthen vase, when struck by a stick.

The Romans, and other ancient nations, having invested this system of applauding with all the accuracy of a science, used it in its various forms, not only for the purpose of testifying their approbation of actors in the theatre, but also bestowed it, as a mark of respect, or a token of adulation, on their emperors, and other great men, on the occasion of their making their appearance in public. Huzzas and cheers have, in this latter case, been generally adopted by the moderns, while the manual applause is only appropriated to successful public speakers and declaimers. The Freemasons, however, have altogether preserved the ancient custom of applause, guarding and regulating its use by as strict, though different rules, as did the Romans; and thus showing, as another evidence of the antiquity of their institution, that the "Grand Honours" of Freemasonry are legitimately derived from the "plausus," or applaudings, practised by the ancients on public occasions.

HOPE. The second round in the theological and masonic ladder, and appropriately placed there. For having attained the first, or *faith in God*, we are led by a belief in his wisdom and goodness, to the *hope of immortality*. This is but a reasonable expectation; without it, virtue would lose its necessary stimulus, and vice its salutary fear; life would be devoid of joy, and the grave but a scene of desolation.

HOST, CAPTAIN OF THE. An officer in a Chapter of Royal Arch Masons, whose duties are of a peculiar nature, resembling in some degree those of a Master of Ceremonies. The person, who in Scripture is called Captain of the Host, occupied a station somewhat similar to that of a modern general, having the whole army under his command.

HOUR GLASS. An emblem in the third degree, reminding us, by the quick passage of its sands, of the transitory nature of human life.

HOURS OF WORK. Lodge hours, or hours of work, before or after which time no business should be transacted in the lodge, are prescribed in the Book of Constitutions. They are, from the vernal to the autumnal equinox, between the hours of seven and ten, and from the autumnal to the vernal, between six and nine.

In this selection of the hours of night and darkness for initiation, the usual coincidence will be found between the ceremonies of Freemasonry and those of the Ancient Mysteries, showing their evident derivation from a common origin.

In the "Bacchæ" of Euripides, that author introduces the god Bacchus, the supposed inventor of the Dionysian Mysteries, as replying to the question of King Pentheus, in the following words:

"*Pentheus.*—By night or day, these sacred rites perform'st thou?
Bacchus.—Mostly by night, for venerable is darkness;"*

---

* ΠΕΝ. Τά δ'ιερά νύκτωρ, ἢ μεθ' ἡμέραν τελεις;
ΔΙΟ. Νύκτωρ τα πολλά σεμνότητ' ἔχει σκοτος.
[*Eurip. Bacch. Act. ii. l.* 485.

and in all the other mysteries the same reason was assigned for
nocturnal celebrations, since night and darkness have something
solemn and august in them which is disposed to fill the mind with
sacred awe. And hence, black, as an emblem of darkness and
night, was considered as the colour appropriate to the mysteries.

In the mysteries of Hindostan, the candidate for initiation,
having been duly prepared by previous purifications, was led at
the dead of night to the gloomy cavern, in which the mystic rites
were performed.

The same period of darkness was adopted for the celebration
of the mysteries of Mithras, in Persia. Among the Druids of
Britain and Gaul, the principal annual initiation commenced at
"low twelve," or midnight of the eve of May-day. In short it
is indisputable, that the initiations in all the ancient mysteries were
nocturnal in their character.

The reason given by the ancients for this selection of night as
the time for initiation, is equally applicable to the system of
Freemasonry. "Darkness," says Oliver, "was an emblem of
death, and death was a prelude to resurrection. It will be at
once seen, therefore, in what manner the doctrine of the resurrection was inculcated and exemplified in these remarkable
institutions."

Death and the resurrection were the doctrines taught in the
ancient mysteries; and night and darkness were necessary to add
to the sacred awe and reverence which these doctrines ought
always to inspire in the rational and contemplative mind. The
same doctrines form the very ground-work of Freemasonry, and
as the Master Mason, to use the language of Hutchinson, "represents a man saved from the grave of iniquity and raised to
the faith of salvation," darkness and night are the appropriate
accompaniments to the solemn ceremonies which demonstrate this
profession.

18

I.

IDIOT. Idiocy is one of the mental disqualifications for initiation. This does not, however, include a mere dullness of intellect and indocility of apprehension. These amount only to stupidity, and "the judgment of the heavy or stupid man," as Dr. Good has correctly remarked, "is often as sound in itself as that of a man of more capacious comprehension." The idiot is characterized by "a general obliteration of the mental powers and affections, a paucity or destitution of ideas, an obtuse sensibility, a vacant, countenance, an imperfect or broken articulation, with occasionally transient and unmeaning gusts of passion."* A being thus mentally afflicted, is incompetent to perform the duties, to observe the obligations, or to appreciate the instructions of Freemasonry, and to such a being the ancient constitutions of our order have wisely forbidden access to our portals.

ILLUMINATI. *Illuminées* (Signifying in Latin *enlightened*.) This was a secret society instituted in Bavaria, in 1776, by Adam Weishaupt, Professor of Canon Law in the University of Ingoldstat. Weishaupt was a radical in politics, and an infidel in religion; and he organized this association, not more for the purpose of aggrandizing himself, than of overturning Christianity and the institutions of society. With the view of carrying his objects more completely into effect, he united himself with a lodge of Freemasons in Munich, and attempted to graft his system of Illuminism upon the stock of Freemasonry. Many Freemasons, misled by the construction of his first degrees, were enticed into the order, but the developments made in the higher degrees, so averse from all the virtuous and loyal principles of Masonry, soon taught them the error they had committed, and caused them to abandon Illuminism with greater rapidity than that with which

* I quote the specific definition of the enlightened writer already cited.

they had embraced it. Among those who had abandoned the order, some went so far as to betray its secret principles. The Elector of Bavaria becoming alarmed at the political tenets which were said to be taught in their assemblies, instituted a judicial examination into the merits of the charges made against them, and the consequence was, that the Illuminati were completely extinguished in his territories.* The serpent had, however, only been scotched, not killed; and the order afterwards made rapid progress in other parts of Germany, and especially in France, where it had been introduced in 1787, two years before the execution of Louis XVI. It was an institution created at the period, when the locust plague of infidelity and atheism was blighting, with its destructive influences, the peace and order of Europe; and with the return of sense and virtue, it ceased to exist. Illuminism belongs only to the history of the past.

Illuminism was by its founder arranged systematically into classes, each of which was again subdivided into degrees, in the following manner :

NURSERY,
Preparation,
Novice,
Minerval,
Illuminatus Minor.

MASONRY,
Symbolic { Entered Apprentice, Fellow Craft, Master Mason.
Scotch { Illuminatus Major or Scotch Novice, Illuminatus Dirigens or Scotch Knight.

MYSTERIES,
Lesser { Presbyter, Priest, Prince, Regent,
Greater { Magus, Rex.

* See Robison's "Proofs of a Conspiracy," which, although the work of an enemy to our order, contains a very excellent exposition of the nature of this pseudo-masonic institution.

ILLUMINATED THEOSOPHISTS. A modification of the above society, instituted at Paris by one Chastanier, who succeeded in introducing his system in London.

ILLUMINATI OF AVIGNON. A species of Freemasonry instituted in 1760, by Pernetti, a Benedictine monk, and Gabrianca, a Polish nobleman, in which the reveries of Swedenborg were mingled with the principles of masonry.

ILLUSTRIOUS ELECTED OF FIFTEEN. *Maîtres élus des quinze.* The tenth degree in the ancient Scotch rite. The place of meeting is called a chapter; the emblematic colour is black, strewed with tears; and the principal officers are a Most Illustrious, a Grand Inspector and a Junior Warden. The history of this degree developes the continuation and conclusion of the punishment inflicted on three traitors, who, just before the conclusion of the Temple, had committed a crime of the most atrocious character.

IMMANUEL. A Hebrew word signifying "God with us," from עִמָּנוּ, *immanu* "with us," and אֵל, *el* "God." A name applied to Christ.

IMMORTALITY OF THE SOUL. A belief in this doctrine is inculcated in masonry by several expressive emblems, but more especially by the second round of Jacob's ladder, and by the sprig of acacia. Its inculcation is also the principal symbolic object of the third or Master Mason's degree.

The teaching of this doctrine was one of the most important of the Ancient Mysteries. They symbolized the resurrection and new birth of the spirit by that final part of the ceremonies of their legend which celebrated the restoration of their hero to life, as in the case of Bacchus among the Dionysians, or the finding of the mutilated body, as in that of Osiris among the Egyptians. Such was the groping in darkness after truth among the disciples

of the spurious Freemasonry; and we now teach the same truth
in the Master's degree, but aided by a better light.

On this subject a learned brother* thus describes the differences between the spurious and true Freemasonry:

"Whereas the heathens had taught this doctrine only by the
application of a fable to their purpose; the wisdom of the pious
Grand Master of the Israelitish Masons took advantage of
a real circumstance which would more forcibly impress the sublime truths he intended to inculcate upon the minds of all
brethren."

IMMOVABLE JEWELS.   According to the old system
used in England, the immovable jewels of the lodge are the
Rough Ashlar, Perfect Ashlar, and Trestle Board; but in this
country, by the decision of the Baltimore Masonic Convention in
1843, they are made to consist of the Square, Level, and Plumb.
See *Jewels of the Lodge.*

IMPLEMENTS.   The implements made use of in operative
masonry are all adopted by speculative masonry, for the purpose
of symbolical instruction.   Each will be discussed in its proper
place, throughout this work.   But I may here be permitted to
recount the mode in which they are distributed among the different degrees, and the reasons for this distribution.   The twenty-
four inch gauge and gavel are bestowed upon the Entered Apprentice, because these are the implements used in the quarries
in hewing the stones and fitting them for the builder's use, an
occupation which, for its simplicity, is properly suited to the
unskilled apprentice.   The square, level, and plumb are employed
in the still further preparation of these stones and in adjusting
them to their appropriate positions.   This is the labour of the
craftsmen, and hence to the Fellow Craft are they presented.
But the work is not completed, until the stones thus adjusted

---

* Archdeacon Mant, quoted by Dr. Oliver, Landmarks, II. 2.

have been accurately examined by the master workman and
permanently secured in their places by cement. This is accomplished by the trowel, and hence this implement is entrusted to
the Master Mason. Thus the tools attached to each degree admonish the Mason, as an Apprentice, to prepare his mind for the
reception of the great truths which are hereafter to be unfolded
to him; as a Fellow Craft to mark their importance and adapt
them to their proper uses; and as a Master to adorn their beauty
by the practice of brotherly love and kindness, the cement that
binds all Masons in one common fraternity.

INDENTED TESSEL. The ornamented border which surrounds the Mosaic pavement. See *Tessellated Border.*

INDUCTION. Candidates who have been initiated into a
council of the " Holy and Thrice Illustrious Order of the Cross"
are said to be inducted. Past Masters are said to be inducted
into the Oriental Chair of King Solomon.

INDIA, MYSTERIES OF. Though the mysteries of Greece
and Rome were modelled after those of Egypt, these last undoubtedly derived their existence from the East, where the priests
first began to conceal their doctrines under the form of mysterious
rites, and to reveal them only to those who underwent a process
of initiation. The western philosophers derived much, if not all
of their learning from the gymnosophists or sages of India, who
were not more celebrated for the extent of their knowledge, than
for the simplicity of their lives. They inculcated a belief in the
triad of gods, Brahma, Vishnu, and Siva, the first being the supreme, eternal, uncreated god. It was from the gymnosophists
that the philosophers of other nations acquired their idea of the
existence of a Supreme Being, and of the immortality of the soul.
The instructions of the gymnosophists were oral, and secret. They
were communicated only after a process of initiation, which is said
to have been extremely severe in its trials.

The ceremonies of initiation into the mysteries of ancient India, have been collected from various sources with great industry and research by Dr. Oliver. "They formed," says he, "one of the earliest corruptions of the pure science, which is now denominated Freemasonry, and bore a direct reference to the happiness of man in paradise, the subsequent deviations from righteousness, and the destruction accomplished by the general deluge."* The scenes of initiation were in-spacious caverns, the principal of which were Elephanta and Salsette, both situated near Bombay. The mysteries were divided into four degrees, and the candidate was permitted to perform the probation of the first at the early age of eight years. It consisted simply in the investiture with the linen garment, and Zennar or sacred cord, composed of nine threads, and suspended from the left shoulder across the breast to the right side; of sacrifices accompanied by aqueous ablutions; and of an explanatory lecture delivered to the juvenile aspirant by the priest. He was now delivered into the care of a Brahmin, who thenceforth became his spiritual guide, and prepared him by repeated instructions and a life of austerity for admission into the second degree. To this, if found qualified, he was admitted at the requisite age. The probationary ceremonies of this degree consisted in an incessant occupation in prayers, fastings, ablutions, and the study of astronomy. Having undergone these austerities for a sufficient period, after having been placed in the Pastos, he was led at night to the gloomy caverns of initiation, which had been duly prepared for his reception.

The interior of this cavern was brilliantly illuminated, and there sat the three chief hierophants, in the east, west, and south, representing the gods Brahma, Vishnu, and Siva, surrounded by the attendant mystagogues, dressed in appropriate vestments. After an invocation to the Sun, the aspirant was called upon to promise that he would be obedient to his superiors, keep his body

---

* Hist. Initiat. lect. ii. p. 41.

pure, and preserve inviolable secrecy on the subject of the mysteries. He was then sprinkled with water, an invocation of the
deity was whispered in his ear, he was divested of his shoes, and
made to circumambulate the cavern three times, in imitation of
the course of the Sun, whose rising was personated by the hierophant representing Brahma, stationed in the east, whose meridian
height by the representative of Siva in the south, and whose
setting by the representative of Vishnu in the west. He was then
conducted through seven ranges of dark and gloomy caverns, during which period the wailings of Mahadeva for the loss of Siva
was represented by dismal howlings. The usual paraphernalia
of flashes of light, of dismal sounds and horrid phantoms, was
practised to intimidate or confuse the aspirant. After the
performance of a variety of other ceremonies, many of which
we can only conjecture, the candidate reached the extremity
of the seven caverns; he was now prepared for enlightenment
by requisite instruction and the administration of a solemn oath.

This part of the ceremonies being concluded, the sacred conch
was blown, the folding doors were suddenly thrown open, and the
aspirant was admitted into a spacious apartment filled with dazzling light, ornamented with statues and emblematical figures, richly
decorated with gems, and scented with the most fragrant perfumes.
This was a representation of Paradise.

The candidate was now supposed to be regenerated, and he
was invested by the chief Brahmin with the white robe and
tiara; a cross was marked upon his forehead, and a tau upon his
breast, and he was invested with the signs, tokens, and lectures
of the order. He was presented with the sacred belt, the magical
black stone, the talismanic jewel to be worn upon his breast, and
the serpent stone, which, as its name imported, was an antidote
against the bite of serpents. And lastly, he was entrusted with
the sacred name, known only to the initiated. This ineffable name
was AUM, which, in its triliteral form, was significant of the
creative, preservative, and destroying power, that is, of Brahma,
Vishnu, and Siva. It could not be pronounced, but was to be the

subject of incessant silent contemplation. The emblems around and the *aporreta* or secret things of the mysteries were now explained.

Here ended the second degree. The third took place when the candidate had grown old and his children had all been provided for. This consisted in a total exclusion in the forest, where as an anchorite he occupied himself in ablutions, prayers, and sacrifices.

In the fourth degree, he underwent still greater austerities, the object of which was to impart to the happy sage who observed them, a portion of the divine nature, and to secure him a residence among the immortal gods.

The object of the Indian mysteries appears to have been to teach the unity of God, and the necessity of virtue. The happiness of our first parents, the subsequent depravity of the human race, and the universal deluge were described in a manner which showed that their knowledge must have been derived from an authentic source.

INEFFABLE. From the Latin word "ineffabilis," not to be spoken or expressed. The degrees above the Master Mason in the French and Scotch rites, are thus called, in allusion to the sanctity and sublimity of the secrets they contain. But in this sense of the word, all masonry is equally ineffable, though the term is technically confined to these higher degrees.

INFORMATION, LAWFUL. One of the modes of recognising a stranger as a true brother, is from the "lawful information" of a third party. No Mason can lawfully give information of another's qualifications unless he has actually tested him by the strictest trial and examination, or knows that it has been done by another. But it is not every Mason who is competent to give "lawful information." Ignorant and unskilful brethren cannot do so, because they are incapable of discovering truth or of detecting error. A "rusty Mason" should never attempt to

examine a stranger, and certainly if he does his opinion as to the
result is worth nothing. If the information given is on the
ground that the party who is vouched for, has been seen sitting
in a lodge, care must be taken to inquire if it was a "just and
legally constituted lodge of Master Masons." A person may
forget from the lapse of time, and vouch for a stranger as a Master Mason, when the lodge in which he saw him was only opened
in the first or second degree. Information given by letter, or
through a third party, is irregular. The person giving the information, the one receiving it, and the one of whom it is given,
should all be present at the same time, for otherwise there would
be no certainty of identity. The information must be positive,
not founded on belief or opinion, but derived from a legitimate
source. And, lastly, it must not have been received casually, but
for the every purpose of being used for masonic purposes. For
one to say to another, in the course of a desultory conversation,
" A. B. is a Mason," is not sufficient. He may not be speaking
with due caution, under the expectation that his words will be considered of weight. He must say something to this effect, " I
know this man to be a Master Mason, for such or such reasons,
and you may safely recognise him as such." This alone will
ensure the necessary care and proper observance of prudence.

INITIATION. The reception into the first degree of masonry is thus called. It is derived from the Latin word *initia*,
which signifies the first principles of a science. The same
term was used by the ancients to designate admission into the
mysteries of their Pagan rites. Thus Justin, speaking of
Mida, King of Phrygia, says he was initiated into the mysteries by Orpheus. "Ab Orpheo sacrorum solennibus initiatus."
Lib. xi. c. 7.

INNOVATIONS. Nothing is more offensive to the true Mason than any innovations on the ancient usages and customs of
the order. It is in consequence of this conservative principle

that masonry, notwithstanding many attempts have been made to
alter, or as it was supposed, to amend it, still remains unchanged
—now, as it has always been.

The middle of the eighteenth century was the most prominent
era of those attempted innovations.

After the downfall of the house of Stuart, and the defeat of the
Pretender's hopes in 1715, his adherents vainly endeavoured to
enlist Freemasonry as a powerful adjunct to his cause. For this
purpose it was declared by those who had enlisted in this design,
that the great legend of masonry alluded to the violent death of
Charles I., and Cromwell and his companions in rebellion were
execrated as the arch traitors whom the lodges were to condemn.
To carry out these views, new degrees were now for the first time
manufactured, under the titles of *Irish Master, Perfect Irish Mas-*
ter, Puissant Irish Master, and others of similar appellations.

The Chevalier Ramsay, so well known in masonic history, soon
after made his appearance in the political world, and having
attached himself to the house of Stuart, he endeavoured more
effectually to carry out these views by reducing the whole system
to perfect order, and giving to it the appearance of plausibility.
For this purpose he invented a new theory on the subject of the
origin of Freemasonry.

He declared that it was instituted in the Holy Land at the time
of the Crusades, where the Knights Templars had associated themselves together for the purpose of rebuilding those churches and
other sacred edifices which had been destroyed by the Saracens.
These latter, however, having discovered this holy design, and
being determined to thwart it, had employed emissaries who, secretly mingling with the Christian workmen, materially impeded
and often entirely paralyzed their labours. The Christians, as a
security against this species of treason, then found it necessary to
invent signs and other modes of recognition by which intruders
might be detected.

When compelled by the failure of the Crusaders to leave the
Holy Land, these pious as well as warlike knights were invited

by a king of England to retire to his dominions, where they devoted themselves to the cultivation of architecture and the fine arts.

Ramsay pretended that the degrees originally established by the Templars were those of Scotch Master, Novice, and Knight of the Temple, and he even had the audacity to propose, in 1728, to the Grand Lodge of England to substitute them for the three primitive degrees of symbolical masonry, a proposition which met with no more success than it deserved.

In Paris, however, he was more fortunate, for there his degrees were adopted, not, indeed, as a substitute for, but as an addition to Ancient Craft Masonry.

These degrees became popular on the Continent, and in a short time gave birth to innumerable others, which attempted to compensate for their want of consistency with the history, the traditions, and the principles of the ancient institution, by splendour of external decorations and gorgeousness of ceremonies. Happily, however, the existence of these innovations has been but ephemeral. They are no longer worked as degrees, but remain only in the library of the masonic student as subjects of curious inquiry. The "hautes grades" of the French, and the Philosophic degrees of the Ancient and Accepted Scotch rite, are not innovations on, but illustrations of, pure symbolic masonry, and as such will be found to be the depositories of many interesting traditions and instructive speculations, which are eminently useful in shedding light upon the character and objects of the institution.

I. N. R. I.   The initials of the Latin sentence which was placed upon the Cross: *Jesus Nazarenus Rex Judæorum.* The Rosicrucians used them as the initials of one of their hermetic secrets: *Igne Natura Renovatur Integra*—"By fire nature is perfectly renewed."[*] They also adopted them to express the names of their three elementary principles, salt, sulphur, and mercury, by making them the initials of the sentence, *Igne Nitrum Roris*

---

[*] Cours Philosophique et Interprétatif des Initiations, p. 323.

INS—INT   217

Invenitur. Ragon finds in the equivalent Hebrew letters יַנְרֵי the initials of the Hebrew names of the ancient elements; *Iaminim*, water, *Nour*, fire, *Ruach*, air, and *Iebschah*, earth.

These speculations may afford some interest to the Rose Croix Mason and the Knight Templar.

INSPECTOR. See *Sovereign Grand Inspector General.*

INSTALLATION. The officers of a lodge, before they can proceed to discharge their functions, must be installed. The officers of a new lodge are installed by the Grand Master, or by some Past Master deputed by him to perform the ceremony. Formerly the Master was installed by the Grand Master, the Wardens by the Grand Wardens, and the Secretary and Treasurer by the Grand Secretary and Treasurer, but now this custom is not continued. At the election of the officers of an old lodge, the Master is installed by his predecessor or some Past Master present, and the Master elect them instals his subordinate officers. No officer after his installation can resign. At his installation the Master receives the degree of Past Master. It is a law of masonry that all officers hold on to their respective offices until their successors are installed.

INSTRUCTION, LODGE OF. These are assemblies of brethren congregated without a warrant of constitution, under the direction of a Lecturer or skilful brother for the purpose of improvement in masonry, which is accomplished by the frequent rehearsal of the work and lectures of each degree. These bodies should consist exclusively of Master Masons, and though they possess no masonic power, it is evident to every Mason that they are extremely useful, as schools of preparation for the duties that are afterwards to be performed in the regular lodge.

INTENDANT OF THE BUILDINGS. *Intendant des Batiments.* This degree is sometimes called "Master in Israel."
19

It is the eighth in the Ancient Scotch rite. Its emblematic colour is red, and its principal officers are a Thrice Puissant representing Solomon, a Senior Warden representing the illustrious Tito, one of the Harodim, and a Junior Warden representing Adoniram the son of Abda. In the history of the degree, we are told that it was instituted to supply a great loss well known to Master Masons.

INTIMATE SECRETARY. *Secretaire intime.* The sixth degree in the ancient Scotch rite. Its emblematic colour is black, strewed with tears, and its collar and the lining of the apron are red. Its officers are only three: Solomon, King of Israel; Hiram, King of Tyre; and a Captain of the Guards. Its history records an instance of unlawful curiosity, the punishment of which was only averted by the previous fidelity of the offender.

INVESTITURE. See *Apron.*

IONIC ORDER. Next to the Doric the oldest order among the Greeks. It is more delicate and graceful than the Doric, and more majestic than the Corinthian. Its column is fluted with twenty-four channels, the abacus is scooped on the side, and the principal ornaments of its capital are its two spiral volutes. The architectural judgment and skill displayed in its composition as an intermediate order, between the rude massiveness of the Doric and the extraneous beauty of the Corinthian, has occasioned it to be adopted as the column of Wisdom that supports the lodge. Its appropriate situation and symbolic officer are in the E.∴.

IRISH DEGREES. The establishment of certain degrees, called by this title, such as the Irish Master, Perfect Irish Master, Puissant Irish Master, and many others of a similiar nature, was an attempt on the part of the adherents of the exiled house of Stuart, to give to Freemasonry a political bias, and to enlist the

members of the fraternity on the side of King James, and his son
the pretender.

ISH CHOTZEB. The hewers who were engaged in felling
timber on Mt. Lebanon for the building of Solomon's temple.
They amounted to 80,000. See 1 Kings v. 15, and 2. Chron.
ii. 18. Webb calls them Fellow Crafts, but Webb's arrangement
of the workmen at the temple is not a correct one.

ISH SABAL. The bearers of burdens at the building of the
temple. They amounted to 70,000. See 1 Kings v. 15, and 2.
Chron. ii. 18. They are the Entered Apprentices of Webb, but
the old writers say that they were not masons, but the descendants of the ancient Canaanites.

ISH SOUDY. It is a corrupted form of the Hebrew אִישׁ
סוֹדִי, *ish sodi*, "a man who is my confidant or familiar friend;"
and hence it is masonically interpreted to signify "a man of my
choice" or "a select mason." A similar expression is to be found
in Job. xix. 19, *mati sodi*, that is," the men of my intimacy, "or
as it has been translated in the common version "my inward
friends."

IZABUD. Properly *Zabud*. He is mentioned in 1 Kings,
iv. 5, as "the principal officer and the king's friend." Kitto,
speaking of the position held by Izabud or Zabud in the household of Solomon, says that the term "king's friend" implies the
possession of the utmost confidence of, and familiar intercourse
with, the monarch, to whose person "the friend" at all times has
access, and whose influence is therefore often greater, even in matters of state, than that of the recognised ministers of government."*
Zabud, under the corrupted name of Izabud, is an important per-

---

* Cycloped. Bib. Literat. in voc. *Zabud*. See also Jahn, Bib. Archæol.
§ 236. IV.

sonage in the degree of Select Master, where his peculiar position
in the household of King Solomon is correctly defined according to
the definition of Kitto.

J.

JACHIN. The name of the right hand pillar that stood at the
porch of King Solomon's temple. It is derived from two Hebrew
words, יה *jah*, "God" and יהכין *iachin*, "will establish." It
signifies, therefore, "God will establish."

JACOB'S LADDER. When Jacob, by the command of his
father Isaac, was journeying towards Padan-aram, while sleeping
one night with the bare earth for his couch and a stone for his
pillow, he beheld the vision of a ladder whose foot rested on the
earth and its top reached to heaven. Angels were continually
ascending and descending upon it, and promised him the blessing
of a numerous and happy posterity. When Jacob awoke, he was
filled with pious gratitude, and consecrated the spot as the house
of God."*

This ladder, so remarkable in the history of the Jewish people,
has also occupied a conspicuous place among the symbols of masonry. Its true origin was lost among the worshippers of the
Pagan rites, but the symbol itself, in various modified forms, was
retained. Among them it was always made to consist of seven
rounds, which might, as Oliver suggests, have been in allusion
either to the seven stories of the Tower of Babel, or to the Sab-
batical period. In the Persian mysteries of Mithras, the ladder
of seven rounds was symbolical of the soul's approach to perfection. These rounds were called *gates*, and in allusion to them

* Genesis, ch. xxviii.

the candidate was made to pass through seven dark and winding
caverns, which process was called the ascent of the ladder of perfection. Each of these caverns was the representative of a world,
or state of existence through which the soul was supposed to pass
in its progress from the first world to the last, or the world of
truth. Each round of the ladder was said to be of metal of increasing purity, and was dignified also with the name of its protecting planet. Some idea of the construction of this symbolic
ladder may be obtained from the following table :

7	Gold,	Sun,	Truth.
6	Silver,	Moon,	Mansion of the Blessed.
5	Iron,	Mars,	World of Births.
4	Tin,	Jupiter,	Middle World.
3	Copper,	Venus,	Heaven.
2	Quicksilver,	Mercury,	World of Pre-existence.
1	Lead,	Saturn,	First World.

Thus, too, in all the mysteries of the ancients, we find some
allusion to this sacred ladder, requiring, it is true, in some instances, considerable ingenuity to trace the identity. Even in the
Edda of the Scandinavians we find the great tree Ydrasil, which
Dr. Oliver concludes, for the most sufficient reasons, to be ana-
logous with the ladder of Jacob.

Among the Hebrews the staves of the ladder were originally
supposed to be infinite. The Essenians first reduced them to
seven, which were called the Sephiroth, whose names were
Strength, Mercy, Beauty, Eternity, Glory, the Foundation, and
the Kingdom.

Among Freemasons the principal rounds only are named, and
they are Faith, Hope, and Charity, because masonry is founded
upon Faith in God, Hope of Immortality, and Charity to all
mankind. But of these, Charity is the greatest; for Faith ends
in sight, Hope terminates in fruition, but Charity extends beyond
the grave. It is by the practice of these virtues that the Mason
expects to find access to Him who is the subject of Faith, the
object of Hope, and the eternal fountain of Charity. Hence it is

symbolically said, that Masons hope to reach the clouded canopy of their lodge by the assistance of Jacob's Theological Ladder.

JACQUES DE MOLAY. The celebrated Grand Master of the Knights Templar at the time of their suppression by Philip the Fair and Pope Clement V. De Molay was elected Grand Master in 1297, and suffered martyrdom by being burnt to death on the 18th of March, 1314. See *Knights Templar*.

JAH. The Syriac name of God. It was also used by the Hebrews as an abbreviation of *Jehovah*, and seems to have been well known to the Gentile nations as the triliteral name of God; for, although biliteral among the Hebrews, it assumed among the Greeks the triliteral form, as IAΩ. Macrobius, in his Saturnalia, says that this was the sacred name of the Supreme Deity, and the Clarian Oracle being asked which of the gods was Jao, replied, "The initiated are bound to conceal the mysterious secrets. Learn thou that IAΩ is the Great God Supreme who ruleth over all." See the word *Jehovah*.

JEHOSAPHAT. The Valley of Jehosaphat is situated east of Jerusalem, between Mount Zion and the Mount of Olives. In the ancient rituals of our order the Valley of Jehosaphat played an important part, but it is now very much neglected in the modern working of the lodges. It has been supposed, in consequence of the prophecy of Joel (iii. 13,) that this valley is to be the scene of the final judgment. The word itself denotes "the Lord judgeth," and hence Hutchinson says that the spiritual lodge is placed in the Valley of Jehosaphat to imply that the principles of masonry are derived from the knowledge of God, and are established in the judgments of the Lord.

JEHOVAH. The ineffable name of God. In Hebrew, it consists of four letters יהוה, and is hence called the *nomen tetragrammaton* or quadriliteral name. It is derived from the

substantive verb הָוָה *havah*, TO BE; and, as it combines in itself
the present, past, and future forms of the verb, it is to be considered as designating God as immutable, eternal, the only being
who can say forever, "I AM THAT I AM." This name was first announced to Moses by God, when he appeared to him in the burning bush; on which occasion he said, "this is my name forever,
and this is my memorial unto all generations." (Ex. iii. 15.)
It was considered unlawful to pronounce this name of God, except
on one sacred occasion, (the day of the atonement,) when it was
only uttered by the High Priest in the holy of holies, amid the
sound of trumpets and cymbals, which prevented the people from
hearing it. This custom no doubt originally arose from a wish to
prevent its becoming known to the surrounding nations, and being
by them blasphemously applied to their idols. Some of the Jews
afterward attempted, by an ingenious corruption of the text of
Exodus above quoted, to defend the custom by the authority of
Scripture. By the change of a single letter, they made the word
l'olam, which signifies "forever," read *l'alam*, that is, "to be
concealed," and hence the passage was translated, "this is my
name to be concealed," instead of "this is my name forever."
And thus Josephus, in writing upon this subject, uses the following expressions: "Whereupon God declared to Moses his holy
name which had never been discovered to men before; concerning
which it is not lawful for me to say any more."* In obedience
to this law, whenever the word Jehovah occurs to a Jew in reading, he abstains from pronouncing it, and substitutes in its place
the word *Adonai* or *Lord*. In consequence of the people thus
abstaining from its utterance, the true pronunciation of the name
was at length lost. Nor is the question yet definitely settled, some
Orientalists contending, on orthographical grounds, that JEHOVAH
is the true pronunciation, while others, on the authority of certain
ancient writers, assert that it was pronounced JAO.†

---

* Antiquities of the Jews. Whiston's trans.; B. II. c. 12.

† The task is difficult to make one, unacquainted with the structure of the
Hebrew language, comprehend how the pronunciation of a word, whose letters

Some learned Jews even doubt whether Jehovah be the true
name of God, which they consider to have been irrecoverably lost,
and they say that this is one of the mysteries that will be revealed only at the coming of the Messiah.   They attribute this loss
to the sinful habit of applying the masoretic points to so sacred a
name, in consequence of which the true vowels were lost.   They
even relate the legend of a celebrated Hebrew scholar whom God
permitted to be burnt by a Roman emperor, because he had been
heard to pronounce the holy name with these points.*

This dispute is not likely to be terminated by a reference to
ancient authorities, among whom there is too great a discrepancy in
relation to the name to be easily reconciled.   Irenæus calls it
Jaoth, Isidore says it is *Jodjod*, Diodorus Siculus, *Jao*, Clemens
of Alexandria, *Jau*, and Theodoret says that the Hebrews pronounced it *Ja*, and the Samaritans *Javah.*

---

are preserved, can be wholly lost.   It may be attempted, however, in the following manner.   The Hebrew alphabet consists entirely of consonants.   The
vowel sounds were originally supplied by the reader while reading, he being
previously made acquainted with the correct pronunciation of each word, and
if he did not possess this knowledge the letters before him could not supply it, and
he was, of course, unable to pronounce the word.   Every Hebrew, however, knew
from practice, the vocal sounds with which the consonants were pronounced
in the different words, in the same manner as every English reader knows
the different sounds of *a* in *hat, hate, all, was,* and that *knt* is pronounced *knight.*
The words " God save the republic," written in the Hebrew method, would appear thus: " Gd sv th rpblc."   Now this incommunicable name of God consists, as we have already observed, of four letters, Yod, He, Vav, and He, equivalent, in English, to the combination JHVH.   It is now, we presume, evident,
that these four letters cannot, in our own language, be pronounced, unless at
least two vowels be supplied.   Neither can they in Hebrew.   In other words
the vowels were known to the Jew, because he heard the words continually
pronounced, just as we know that *Mr.* stand for *Mister,* because we continually
hear this combination so pronounced.   But the name of God, of which these
four letters are symbols, was never pronounced, but another word, *adonai,* substituted for it; and hence, as the letters themselves have no vocal power, the
Jew, not knowing the implied vowels, was unable to supply them, and thus the
pronunciation of the word was, in time, entirely lost.

 * Oliver, Insignia of the Royal Arch, p. 15.

The Grand, Elect, Perfect and Sublime Masons tell us that the pronunciation varied among the patriarchs in different ages. Methuselah, Lamech, and Noah pronounced it *Juha*;[*] Shem, Arphaxad, Selah, Heber and Peleg pronounced it *Jeva*; Reu, Serug, Nahor, Terah, Abraham, Isaac and Judah called it *Jova*; by Hezrom and Ram it was pronounced *Jevo*; by Aminadab and Nasshon, *Jevah*; by Salmon, Boaz, and Obed, *Johe*; by Jesse and David, *Jehovah*. And they imply that none of these was the right pronunciation, which was only in the possession of Enoch, Jacob, and Moses, whose names are, therefore, not mentioned in this list.

Lanci[†] says that the word should be read from left to right, and pronounced HO–HI, that is to say, "He-She;" *ho* being in Hebrew the masculine pronoun, and *hi* the feminine. Ho–Hi, (*hi* pronounced *he*,) therefore, denotes the male and female principle, the vis genitrix, the phallus and lingam, the point within the circle, the notion of which, in some one form or another of this double gender, pervades all the ancient systems as the representative of the creative power.

Thus one of the names given by the mythological writers to the Supreme Jupiter, was ἀῤῥενοθηλυς, the *man-woman*. In one of the Orphic hymns we find the following line :

Ζευς αρσην γενετο, Ζευς αμβροτος επλετο νυμφη.
Jove is a male, Jove is an immortal virgin.

And Plutarch, in his Isis and Osiris, says "God, who is a male and female intelligence, being both life and light, brought forth another intelligence, the Creator of the world." All the Pagan

[*] In all these names the J is to be pronounced as Y, the A as *a* in *father*, the E as *a* in *mate*; thus *Jehova* must be pronounced as if written Ya-ho-vah.

[†] This speculation of Michæl Angelo Lanci, one of the greatest Orientalists of the present day, I have at second-hand. His great work—intended to be, indeed, an opus magnum—has not been published, and I am indebted for this, as well as many other of his investigations, to my learned friend, George R. Gliddon, Esq., who was a pupil of this illustrious scholar.

gods and goddesses, however various their appellation, were but different expressions for the male and female principle. "In fact," says Russel,[*] "they may all be included in the one great Hermaphrodite, the ἀρρενόθηλυς; who combines in his nature all the elements of production, and who continues to support the vast creation which originally proceeded from his will."

The Jews believed that this holy name, which they held in the highest veneration, was possessed of unbounded powers. "He who pronounces it," say they, "shakes heaven and earth, and inspires the very angels with astonishment and terror. There is a sovereign authority in this name; it governs the world by its power. The other names and surnames of the Deity are ranged about it like officers and soldiers about their sovereigns and generals; from this king-name, they receive their orders and obey."[†] The Rabbins call it *shem hamphorash*, the unutterable name, and say that David found it engraved on a stone while he was digging the foundations of the earth.

Manasseh Ben Israel states it as the opinion of the Cabbalists, that Jehovah is not only the name of the divine essence, but that it also denotes the Aziluthic world, or world of emanations, which contains the ten Sephiroth, or emanations from the Deity which compose the universe, according the Rabbinical philosophy.

The Hebrew substantive verb I AM, which is אהיה, is said by the Talmudists to be equivalent to יהוה, and the four letters of which it is formed possess peculiar properties. א is in Hebrew numerically equivalent to 1, and י to 10, which is equal to 11, a result also obtained by taking the second and third letters of the holy name, or ה and ו, which are 5 and 6, amounting to 11. But the 5 and 6 invariably produce the same number in their multiplication, for 5 times 5 are 25, and 6 times 6 are 36, and this invariable product of ה and ו was said to denote the unchangeableness of the First Cause. Again I am אהיה commences with

---

* Connection of Sacred and Profane History, vol. I. p. 402.

† Calmet, Dict. Bib. I. 751.

א or 1, the beginning of numbers, and *Jehovah*, יְהוָֹה with י or
10, the end of numbers, which signified that God was the beginning and end of all things.* There are many other Talmudical
exercitations on the ineffable name which it is unnecessary to
dwell upon. To the Hebrew student most of them are familiar;
to any other they would be uninteresting or inexplicable.

The pronunciation of the name was preserved and transmitted
by the Essenes, who always communicated it to each other in a
whisper, and in a such a form, that while its component parts
were known, its connected whole still remained a mystery.

It is said, too, to have been the pass-word in the Egyptian
Mysteries, by which the candidate was admitted to the chambers
of initiation. The modern Jews say it was engraved on the rod
of Moses, and enabled him to perform his miracles, and they
attribute all the wonderful works of Jesus Christ to the potency
of this incommunicable name, which they say he stole out of the
temple and wore about him.

The Jews had four symbols by which they expressed this ineffable name of God; the first and most common was two Jods with
a Sheva, and the point Kametz underneath, thus ּיְיִ ; the second
was three points in a radiated form like a diadem, thus יְיִ
to represent, in all probability, the sovereignty of God; the third
was a Jod within an equilateral triangle thus, △ which the Cabbalists explained as a ray of light whose lustre was too transcen-
dent to be contemplated by human eyes; and the fourth was the
letter שׁ, which is the initial letter of *Shadai*, "the Almighty,"
and was the symbol usually placed upon their phylacteries. Bux-
torf mentions a fifth method, which was by three Jods with a
Kametz underneath inclosed in a circle.

Of the varieties of this sacred name in use among the different
nations of the earth, three particularly merit the attention of Royal
Arch Masons.

---

* For these Talmudical remarks, I am indebted to my learned friend, W. S.
Rockwell, Esq., of Milledgeville, Ga.

1. JAH. This name of God is found in the 68th Psalm, v. 4: "Extol him that rideth upon the heavens by his name JAH." It is the Syriac name of God, and is still retained in some of the Syriac forms of doxology, according to Gesenius.

2. BEL, or BAAL. This word signifies a *lord*, *master*, or *possessor;* and hence it was applied by many of the nations of the East, to denote the Lord of all things, and the Master of the world. Baal was worshipped by the Chaldeans, the Moabites, the Phenicians, the Assyrians, and sometimes even by the Hebrews. It has been supposed that the first Baal was the Chaldean Nimrod. This word is repeatedly met with in the Scriptures, both in allusion to the idolatrous worship of this god, and in connection with other words, to denote the names of places.

3. ON. This was the name by which Jehovah was worshipped among the Egyptians. It is this God of whom Plato speaks in his Timæus, when he says, "tell me of the God ON; which IS and never knew beginning." The Egyptians gave to this God the same attributes that the Hebrews bestowed upon Jehovah, and though we are unable to say what was the signification of On in the ancient Egyptian, we know that this word in Greek, ΩN, has the same signification of being or existence as יְהוָֹה has in Hebrew. The Hindoos used the word AUM or AUN.

I have made these remarks on the three names of God in Syriac, Chaldaic, and Egyptian, JAH, BEL, and ON, in the expectation that my Royal Arch companions will readily recognise them in a corrupted form, and thus be enabled to understand a mystery which, I confess, was to me, at first, unintelligible.

JERUSALEM. The capital of Judea and the city of the Holy Temple—memorable as the scene of many events that are dear to the Mason's memory. At the time that the Israelites entered the Promised Land, the city was in possession of the Jebusites, from whom, after the death of Joshua, it was conquered, and afterwards inhabited by the tribes of Judah and Benjamin, although Mount Zion for a long period subsequent continued to

be occupied by the descendants of Jebus, and in the reign of
David that monarch is said to have purchased Mount Moriah
from Ornan the Jebusite, who had used it as a threshing floor.
Here, afterwards, Solomon was permitted to build a temple to
the Lord.

JEWELS. Every lodge is furnished with six jewels, three
of which are movable and three immovable. The movable
jewels, so called because they are not confined to any particular
part of the lodge, are the rough ashlar, the perfect ashlar, and
the trestle board. The immovable jewels are the square, the level,
and the plumb. They are termed immovable, because they are
appropriated to particular parts of the lodge, where alone they
should be found, namely, the square to the east, the level to the
west, and the plumb to the south.

Jewels are also the names applied to the emblems worn by the
officers of Masonic bodies as distinctive badges of their offices.
For the purpose of reference the jewels worn in symbolic lodges,
in chapters, councils, and encampments, are here appended.

1. *In Symbolic Lodges.*

W∴ Master	wears	a square.
Senior Warden	"	a level.
Junior Warden	"	a plumb.
Treasurer	"	cross keys.
Secretary	"	cross pens.
Senior Deacon	"	square and compass, sun in the centre.
Junior Deacon*	"	square and compass moon in the centre.
Steward	"	a cornucopia.
Tyler	"	cross swords.

The jewels are of silver in a subordinate lodge, and of gold in
a Grand Lodge.

_____

* In English lodges the jewel of the Deacons is a dove.
20

2. In Royal Arch Chapters.

High Priest	wears	a mitre.
King	"	a level surmounted by a crown.
Scribe	"	a plumb-rule surmounted by a turban.
Captain of the Host	"	a triangular plate inscribed with a soldier.
Principal Sojourner	"	a triangular plate inscribed with a pilgrim.
Royal Arch Captain	"	a sword.
Grand Master of the Veils	"	a sword.

The other officers as in a symbolic lodge. All the jewels are of gold, and suspended within an equilateral triangle.

3. In Royal and Select Councils.

T. I. Grand Master	wears	a trowel and square.
I. Hiram of Tyre	"	a trowel and level.
Principal Conductor of the works.	"	a trowel and plumb.
Treasurer	"	a trowel and cross keys.
Recorder	"	a trowel and cross pens.
Captain of the Guards	"	a trowel and sword.
Steward	"	a trowel and cross swords.
Marshal	"	a trowel and baton.

If a conductor of the Council is used, he wears a trowel and baton and then a scroll is added to the Marshal's baton to distinguish the two officers.

All the jewels are of silver and are enclosed within an equilateral triangle.

4. In Encampments of Knights Templars.

Grand Commander	wears	a cross surmounted by rays of light.
Generalissimo	"	a square surmounted by a paschal lamb.
Captain General	"	a level surmounted by a cock.

Prelate	wears	a triple triangle.
Senior Warden	"	a hollow square and sword of justice.
Junior Warden	"	eagle and flaming sword.
Treasurer	"	cross keys.
Recorder	"	cross pens.
Standard Bearer	"	a plumb surmounted by a banner.
Warder	"	a square plate inscribed with a trumpet and cross swords.
Three Guards	"	a square plate inscribed with a battle-axe.

The jewels are of silver.

JEWEL OF AN ANCIENT GRAND MASTER. A masonic tradition informs us that the Jewel of an ancient Grand Master at the Temple was the square and compass with the letter G between. This was the jewel worn by Hiram Abif on the day which deprived the craft of his invaluable services, and which was subsequently found upon him.

JOABERT. This was the name of the chief favourite of Solomon, who, according to the traditions of masonry, incurred the displeasure of Hiram of Tyre on a certain occasion, but was subsequently pardoned; and, on account of the great attachment he had shown to the person of his master, was appointed the Secretary of Solomon and Hiram in their most intimate relations. He was afterward still further promoted by Solomon, and appointed with Tito and Adoniram a Provost and Judge. He distinguished himself in his successful efforts to bring certain traitors to condign punishment, and although by his rashness he at first excited the anger of the king, he was subsequently forgiven, and eventually received the highest reward that Solomon could bestow, by being made an Elect, Perfect, and Sublime Mason.

JOHANNITE MASONRY. That system of masonry which contends for the dedication of all symbolic lodges to St. John the Baptist and St. John the Evangelist. This is the system now practised in the United States, and formerly in England. Since the union in 1813, a change has been effected in the latter country, in whose lodges the "lines parallel" are said to represent Moses and King Solomon. But this is admitted to be an innovation, and the most celebrated masonic writer of England, Dr. Oliver, has written a series of "Letters on Johannite Masonry," in which he strongly argues for the restoration of the ancient parallelism.

JOHN'S BROTHERS. In a curious masonic document, entitled the Charter of Cologne, it is said that before the year 1440, the Society of Freemasons were known by no other name than that of "John's Brothers;" that they then began to be called at Valenciennes, Free and Accepted Masons; and that at that time, in some parts of Flanders, by the assistance and riches of the brotherhood, the first hospitals were erected for the relief of such as were afflicted with St. Anthony's fire.

JOPPA. A town of Palestine and the seaport of Jerusalem, from which it is distant about forty miles in a westerly direction. It was here that the King of Tyre sent ships laden with timber and marble to be forwarded overland to Solomon for the construction of the Temple. Its shore is exceedingly rough and much dreaded by navigators, who, on account of its exposure and the perpendicularity of its banks, are compelled to be perpetually on their guard. The following extract from the narrative of the Baron Geramb, a Trappist, who visited the Holy Land in 1842, will be interesting to Mark Masters. "Yesterday morning at daybreak, boats put off and surrounded the vessel to take us to the town (of Joppa,) *the access to which is difficult on account of the numerous rocks that present to view their bare flanks.* The walls were covered with spectators, attracted by curiosity. The boats being much lower than the bridge, *upon which one is obliged to climb*, and having no ladder, *the landing is not effected without danger*. More than once it has happened, that passengers in springing out have broken their limbs, and we might have met with the like accident, *if several persons had not hastened to our assistance*."* The place is now called Jaffa.

JOSHUA, or JESHUA. The High Priest who with Zerubbabel the Prince of Judah, superintended the re-building of the Temple, after the Babylonian captivity. He was the High Priest by lineal descent from the Pontifical family; for he was the son of Josadek, who was the son of Seraiah, who was the High Priest when the Temple was destroyed by the Chaldeans.

JUDAH. The whole of Palestine was sometimes called the Land of Judah, because Judah was a distinguished tribe in obtaining possession of the country. The tribe of Judah bore a Lion in their standard, and hence the masonic allusion to the Lion of the tribe of Judah. See also Genesis xlix. 9. "Judah is a lion's whelp."

JUDAH AND BENJAMIN. Of the twelve tribes of Israel who were, at various times carried into captivity, only two, those of Judah and Benjamin, returned under Zerubbabel to rebuild the second temple.

JUNIOR WARDEN. See *Wardens*.

JURISDICTION. The jurisdiction of a Grand Lodge extends over every lodge working within its territorial limits, and over all places not already occupied by a Grand Lodge. The territorial limits of a Grand Lodge are determined in general by the political boundaries of the country in which it is placed. Thus the territorial limits of the Grand Lodge of South Carolina are circum-

---

* Pilgrimage to Jerusalem and Mount Sinai. Vol. i. p. 27.

scribed within the settled boundaries of that State. Nor can its jurisdiction extend beyond these limits into the neighbouring States of North Carolina or Georgia. The Grand Lodge of South Carolina could not, therefore, without an infringement of masonic usage, grant a warrant of constitution to any lodge located in either of these latter States. It might, however, charter a lodge in Oregon Territory, because there is not in existence a Grand Lodge of that Territory. Thus the lodges of France held of the Grand Lodge of England, until the formation of a Grand Lodge of France, and the Grand Lodges of both England, Scotland, and France, granted warrants to various lodges in America, until after the Revolution, when the States began to organize Grand Lodges for themselves. For the purpose of avoiding collision and unfriendly feeling, it has become the settled usage, that when a Grand Lodge has been legally organized in a State, all the lodges within its limits must surrender the charters which they have received from foreign bodies, and accept new ones from the recently established Grand Lodge.

JUSTICE. One of the four cardinal virtues, the practice of which is inculcated in the first degree. The Mason who remembers how emphatically he has been charged to preserve an upright position in all his dealings with mankind, should never fail to act justly to himself, to his brethren, and to the world. This is the corner-stone on which alone he can expect " to erect a superstructure alike honourable to himself and to the fraternity."

K.

KADOSH. This is the name of a very important degree in many of the rites of masonry. The word is Hebrew, and signifies *holy, consecrated, separated,* and is intended to denote the

elevated character of the degree and the sublimity of the truths
which distinguish it and its possessors from the other degrees.
Pluche says that in the East, a person preferred to honours bore
a sceptre, and sometimes a plate of gold on the forehead, called
a *Kadosh*,* to apprise the people that the bearer of this mark or
rod was a public person who possessed the privilege of entering
into hostile camps without the fear of losing his personal liberty.

The degree of Kadosh, though found in many of the rites and
in various countries, seems, in all of them, to have been more or
less connected with the Knights Templars. In some of the rites
it was placed at the head of the list, and was then dignified as
the "*ne plus ultra*" of masonry.

It was sometimes given as a separate order or rite within
itself, and then it was divided into the three degrees of Illustrious Knight of the Temple, Knight of the Black Eagle, and
Grand Elect.

Oliver enumerates six degrees of Kadosh: the Knight
Kadosh; Kadosh of the Chapter of Clermont; Philosophical
Kadosh; Kadosh Prince of Death; and Kadosh of the Ancient
and Accepted Scotch rite.

Ragon speaks of a Kadosh which is said to have been established at Jerusalem in 1118, but I imagine that this can be no
other than the order of Knights Templars.

Of these degrees, we need pay little attention to any except that
of the Ancient and Accepted Scotch rite, the most important
of the few that continue to be worked. See *Knight of Kadosh.*

KASSIDEANS. (Heb. *chasidim, pious.*) The Kassideans
or Assideans, (though the etymology of the word indicates that
the former is the better spelling,) are described in the 1st Book
of Maccabees ii. 42, as "mighty men of Israel, such as were
voluntarily devoted unto the law." They were a fraternity eminently pious and charitable, who devoted themselves particularly
to repairing the Temple and keeping it in order. They were,

* Whence probably is derived the *Caduceus* of Mercury.

therefore, not only content to pay the usual tribute, but charged themselves with greater expense on that account. Their usual oath was " by the temple." This sect arose either during the captivity, or soon after the restoration. Scaliger contends that they were the source whence, in after times, sprung the Essenes, that body whose close connection with the Freemasons has been so much insisted on by certain writers. Hence Lawrie infers their relationship to the architects who built the house of the Lord for Solomon, and calls them "Knights of the Temple of Jerusalem." They were, in fact, the conservators of masonry among the Jews, and deposited it with their successors, the Essenians, who brought it down beyond the times of Christ.

KEY. The key was anciently an emblem of power, and as such has been adopted as the jewel of the Treasurer in a Blue lodge, because he has the purse under his command. The key is also a symbol of silence and circumspection, and as such has been adopted as one of the emblems of the Royal Arch Tracing Board. "The key," says Dr. Oliver, "is one of the most important symbols of Freemasonry. It bears the appearance of a common metal instrument, confined to the performance of one simple act. But the well instructed brother beholds in it the symbol which teaches him to keep a tongue of good report, and to abstain from the debasing vices of slander and defamation."*

KEY OF MASONRY. See *Knight of the Sun.*

KEY-STONE. That stone placed in the centre of an arch which preserves the others in their places, and secures firmness and stability to the arch. As it was formerly the custom of operative masons to place a peculiar mark on each stone of a building to designate the workman by whom it had been adjusted, so the Key-Stone was most likely to receive the most prominent mark, that of the superintendent of the structure.

* Historical Landmarks, I. 180.

Such is related to have occurred to that Key-Stone which plays so important a part in the legend of the Royal Arch degree.

The objection has sometimes been made, that the arch was unknown to the times of Solomon. But this objection has been completely laid at rest by the researches of antiquaries and travellers within a few years past. Wilkinson discovered arches with regular key-stones in the doorways of the tombs of Thebes, the construction of which he traced to the year 1540, B. C., or 460 years before the building of the Temple of Solomon. And Dr. Clark asserts that the Cycoplean gallery of Tyrius exhibits lancet-shaped arches almost as old as the times of Abraham. In fact, at the era of the building of the Temple, the construction of the arch was a secret, which was, however, known to the Dionysian Artificers, many of whom were present and engaged in the works of the Temple, and of which society we have elsewhere said that there was every reason to believe that Hiram Abif was a member.

KILWINNING. As the city of York claims to be the birthplace of masonry in England, the obscure little village of Kilwinning is entitled to the same honour with respect to the origin of the order in the sister kingdom of Scotland. A place, in itself small and wholly undistinguishable in the political, the literary, or the commercial annals of its country, has become of great importance in the estimation of the masonic antiquary from its intimate connection with the history of the institution.

The abbey of Kilwinning is situated in the bailiwick of Cunningham, about three miles north of the royal burgh of Irving, near the Irish Sea. The abbey was founded in the year 1140, by Hugh Morville, Constable of Scotland, and dedicated to St. Winning, being intended for a company of monks of the Tyronesian order, who had been brought from Kelso. The edifice must have been constructed at great expense, and with much magnificence, since it is said to have occupied several acres of ground in its whole extent.

Laurie says, that, by authentic documents as well as by. other collateral arguments which amount almost to a demonstration, the existence of the Kilwinning lodge has been traced back as far as the end of the fifteenth century, But we know that the body of architects who perambulated the continent of Europe, under the name of "Travelling Freemasons," flourished at a much earlier period; and we learn, also, from Laurie himself, that several of these Masons travelled into Scotland, about the beginning of the twelfth century.* Hence, we have every reason to suppose that these men were the architects who constructed the abbey at Kilwinning, and who first established the institution of Freemasonry in Scotland. If such be the fact, we must place the origin of the first lodge in that kingdom at an earlier date, by three centuries, than that claimed for it by Laurie, which would bring it much nearer, in point of time, to the great Masonic Assembly, convened in the year 926, by Prince Edwin, at York, in England.

There is some collateral evidence to sustain the probability of this early commencement of masonry in Scotland. It is very generally admitted that the Royal Order of Herodem was founded by King Robert Bruce, at Kilwinning. Thory, in the "Acta Latamorum," gives the following chronicle : " Robert Bruce, King of Scotland, under the title of Robert I., created the order of St. Andrew of Chardon, after the battle of Bannockburn, which was fought on the 24th of June, 1314. To this order was afterward united that of Herodem, for the sake of the Scotch Masons, who formed a part of the thirty thousand troops with whom he had fought an army of one hundred thousand Englishmen. King Robert reserved the title of Grand Master to himself and his successors forever, and founded the Royal Grand Lodge of Herodem at Kilwinning.

Dr. Oliver says that "the Royal Order of Herodem had formerly its chief seat at Kilwinning; and there is every reason

* History of Freemasonry, p. 89.

to think that it and St. John's masonry were then governed by the same Grand Lodge."

In 1820, there was published, at Paris, a record which states that in 1286, James, Lord Stewart, received the Earls of Gloucester and Ulster into his lodge at Kilwinning, which goes to prove that a lodge was then existing and in active operation at that place.

I confess that I am disposed to give some credit to the authority of these documents. They, at least, furnish the evidence that there has been a general belief among the fraternity of the antiquity of the Kilwinning Lodge. Those, however, whose faith is of a more hesitating character, will find the most satisfactory testimonies of the existence of that lodge in the beginning of the fifteenth century. At that period, when James II. was on the throne, the Barons of Roslin, as hereditary Grand Masters of Scotland, held their annual meetings at Kilwinning, and the lodge at that place granted warrants of constitution for the formation of subordinate lodges in other parts of the kingdom. The lodges thus formed, in token of their respect for, and submission to, the mother lodge, whence they derived their existence, affixed the word Kilwinning to their own distinctive name, many instances of which are still to be found on the register of the Grand Lodge of Scotland—such as Cannongate Kilwinning, Greenock Kilwinning, Cumberland Kilwinning, &c.

But, in process of time, this Grand Lodge at Kilwinning ceased to retain its supremacy, and finally its very existence. As in the case of the sister kingdom, where the Grand Lodge was removed from York, the birthplace of English masonry, to London, so in Scotland, the supreme seat of the order was at length transferred from Kilwinning to the metropolis; and hence, in the document entitled the "Charter of Cologne," which purports to have been written in 1535, we find, in a list of nineteen Grand Lodges in Europe, that that of Scotland is mentioned as sitting at Edinburg, under the Grand Mastership of John Bruce. In 1743, the Lodge of Kilwinning, although universally admitted to have been the cradle of Scottish masonry, was compelled to content itself with the second number on the register of the Grand Lodge, in consequence of its records having been destroyed by fire, while the lodge of St. Mary's Chapel, having been more fortunate in preserving its archives as far back as the year 1598, received the first number and the precedence among the lodges of Scotland.

Here terminates the connection of Kilwinning as a place of any importance with Scottish masonry. A lodge long continued to exist there, and may probably still remain; but its honours and dignities consist only in the recollections of its venerable origin, and in the union of its name with many of the most opulent and respectable lodges of Scotland. As for the abbey, the stupendous fabric which was executed by the Freemasons who first migrated into Scotland, its history, like that of the lodge which they founded, is one of decline and decay. In 1560 it was in a great measure demolished by Alexander, Earl of Glencairne, in obedience to an order from the States of Scotland, in the exercise of their usurped authority during the imprisonment of Mary Stuart. A few years afterward, a part of the abbey chapel was repaired and converted into the parish church, and was used as such until about the year 1775, when, in consequence of its ruinous and dangerous state, it was pulled down and an elegant church erected, in the modern style. In 1789, so much of the ancient abbey remained as to enable Grose, the antiquary, to take a sketch of the ruins; but now, not a vestige of the building is to be found, nor can its exact site be ascertained with any precision.

KING. The second officer in a Royal Arch Chapter. He is the representative of Zerubbabel, prince or governor of Judah. When the chapter meets as a lodge of Mark, Past, or Most Excellent Masters, the King acts as Senior Warden. See *Zerubbabel*.

After the rebuilding of the second temple, the government of the Jews was administered by the High Priests as the vice-

gerents of the Kings of Persia, to whom they paid tribute.
This is the reason that the High Priest is the presiding officer in
a chapter, and the King only a subordinate.

KNEELING. See *Genuflection.*

KNIGHTHOOD, ORDERS OF. In the article on the
Crusades, I have stated the impossibility of admitting that we
are indebted to them for the introduction of masonry into Europe, and the reason assigned was its inconsistency with historical
facts. The objection, however, does not exist against the opinion
that the orders of knighthood assumed the masonic character
from the influence of these wars. On the contrary, we have
every reason for believing that the knights who visited Palestine
organized their chivalric system upon the model of the masonic
institutions which existed there, and into which, we may also
presume, that most of them were admitted. Upon this subject
we have something more than mere conjecture to direct us, for
we are informed by Adler, who wrote an account of the Association of Druses on Mount Libanus, that the Knights Templars
were actually members of the Syriac fraternities.[*]

The oldest order of masonic knighthood is said by a writer in
the Freemason's Quarterly Review, to be the Rosy Cross of Scotland,[†] and the fact that it unites the Trowel with the Sword, an
union which the more modern orders have sought to avoid, is adduced as evidence of this antiquity. The same union of the
Sword and Trowel is likewise adopted by the Knights of the
East, who also claim to be the most ancient order of masonic
knighthood.

KNIGHT OF THE BRAZEN SERPENT. *Chevalier du
Serpent d'airain.* The 25th degree in the Ancient Scotch rite.

_____

[*] Adler, de Drusis Mont. Liban.

[†] This is not the same degree as the Rose Croix of the Ancient and
Accepted rite. For some account of it, see the word *Heredom* in this Lexicon.

The history of this degree is founded upon the circumstances related in numbers, ch. xxi. ver. 6–9: "And the Lord sent fiery serpents among the people, and they bit the people; and much people of Israel died. Therefore the people came to Moses, and said, We have sinned; for we have spoken against the Lord, and against thee: pray unto the Lord that he take away the serpents from us. And Moses prayed for the people. And the Lord said unto Moses, make thee a fiery serpent, and set it upon a pole: and it shall come to pass, that every one that is bitten, when he looketh upon it shall live. And Moses made a serpent of brass, and put it upon a pole; and it came to pass, that if a serpent had bitten any man, when he beheld the serpent of brass, he lived." The hangings of the lodge are red and blue. A transparency, representing the Burning Bush with the Incommunicable name in the centre, is placed over the throne. A conical mount, elevated on five steps, is placed in the centre of the room. The lodge has but one light. It is named the Court of Sinai. The presiding officer is styled "Most Powerful Grand Master," and represents Moses; the Wardens are called "Ministers," and represent Aaron and Joshua; the Orator is styled "Pontiff," and the Secretary "Grand Graver." The candidate is called "A Traveller." The jewel is a serpent entwined around a tau cross, standing upon a triangle, with the inscription יהוה. It is suspended from a white ribbon.

The knights say that this degree was founded in the time of the Crusades, by John Ralph, who established the order in the Holy Land as a military and monastic society, and gave it the name of the Brazen Serpent, because it was a part of their obligation to receive and gratuitously nurse sick travellers, to protect them against the attacks of the Saracens, and escort them safely to Palestine; thus alluding to the healing and saving virtues of the Brazen Serpent among the Israelites in the wilderness.

KNIGHT OF THE AMERICAN EAGLE. A side degree,

of a military character, which was invented, I think, in Texas or some of the Western States.

KNIGHT OF THE CHRISTIAN MARK, AND GUARD OF THE CONCLAVE. The first degree in a Council of the Trinity. This order is said to have been organized by Pope Alexander for the defence of his person, and to have been originally selected from the most worthy Knights of St. John of Jerusalem. Their ceremonies are founded on certain passages in the Books of Ezekiel and Jeremiah. The officers are an Invincible Knight, Senior and Junior Knight, six Grand Ministers, Recorder, Treasurer, Conductor, and Guard. The jewel is a triangular plate of gold, with the letter G within a five-pointed star engraved on one side, and seven eyes on the other. The motto of the order is, "Christus regnat, vincit, triumphat. Rex regnantium, Dominus dominantium." Christ reigns, conquers and triumphs. King of Kings and Lord of Lords. -

The degree is given in New-York Encampments of Knights Templar, after the Knight of Malta.

KNIGHT OF CONSTANTINOPLE. A side degree, instituted, doubtless, by some Lecturer, teaching, however, an excellent moral lesson of humility. Its history has no connection whatever with masonry. The degree is not very extensively diffused, but several Masons, especially in the Western States, are in possession of it. It may be conferred by any Master Mason on another, although the proper performance of the ceremonies requires the assistance of several. When the degree is formally conferred, the body is called a Council, and consists of the following officers: Illustrious Sovereign, Chief of the Artizaus, Seneschal, Conductor, Prefect of the Palace, and Captain of the Guards.

KNIGHT OF THE EAGLE. See *Rose Croix.*

KNIGHT OF THE EAST. *Chevalier d' Orient.* The 15th degree in the Ancient Scotch rite. This is a very interesting degree. It is founded upon the circumstance of the assistance rendered by Darius to the Jews, who had been liberated from their captivity at Babylon, and who had been prevented after the death of Cyrus, by their enemies, from completing their purpose of rebuilding the temple. The meetings are called "Councils." The hangings of the council chamber are water-coloured, interspersed with red, in allusion to certain events that occurred at the river Euphrates, on the return of the Israelites from captivity. It is illuminated by seventy-two lights, in memory of the seventy-two years of captivity, and also for another reason.

All the Knights are decorated with a green watered ribbon from the right shoulder to the left hip, a wooden bridge being painted on the front of it, with the letters Y and H upon it. It is also painted over with the heads and limbs of bodies newly slain. The apron is lined with red, and bordered with green, having three heaps of triangular chains painted on it, and on the flap a bloody head between two swords in saltire. The officers are : 1, Cyrus or Sovereign ; 2, Nehemias or Grand Keeper of the Seals ; 3, Sathrabuzanes or Grand General; 4, Mithridates or Grand Treasurer; 5, Sidrus or Minister of State. The Knights of the East afterwards, in Palestine, assumed the name of Knights of the Red Cross, under which name a degree is now given, as preparatory to that of Knight Templar.

Scripture and the traditions of the order furnish us with many interesting facts in relation to this degree. The Knights of the East are said to derive their origin from the captivity of the Israelites in Babylon. After seventy-two years of servitude, they were restored to liberty by Cyrus, king of Persia, through the intercession of Zerubbabel, a prince of the tribe of Judah, and Nehemias, a holy man of a distinguished family.

Cyrus then permitted the Jews to return to Jerusalem, for the purpose of rebuilding the temple, and he caused all the holy vessels and ornaments which had been carried away at its destruction by Nebuzaradan, to be restored to them.

He entrusted the command of the returning captives to Zerubbabel, and issued an edict for their free passage from Syria to Jerusalem. Zerubbabel then assembled the Israelites, to the number of 42,360, exclusive of slaves and servants, and having armed those Masons who had escaped the fury of the enemy at the destruction of the old temple, amounting to 7000, he placed them at the head of the people to fight such as should oppose their return to Judea. The march was prosperous as far as the banks of the Euphrates, where Zerubbabel first found armed troops to oppose their passage. A battle now ensued, and all the enemy, to a man, were either drowned in the river or cut to pieces at the passage of the bridge.

After a march of four months, the Israelites arrived at Jerusalem on the 22d of June. Seven days after they began to lay out the work of the new temple. The workmen were divided, as at the building of the old temple, into classes, over which a chief with two assistants presided; every degree of each class was paid according to its rank, and each class had its distinctive modes of recognition.

The works had scarcely been begun, before the workmen were disturbed by the persecutions of the neighbouring Samaritans, who, influenced by envy, were determined to oppose the reconstruction of the edifice. But Zerubbabel ordered, as a measure of precaution, that the Masons should work with a sword in one hand and a trowel in the other, that they might be able at any moment to defend themselves from the attacks of their enemies.

This second temple occupied forty-six years in its construction, having been begun in the reign of Cyrus and completed in that of Artaxerxes. It was consecrated in the same manner as Solomon had consecrated the first. From the Masons who constructed it, and who were created Knights of the East by Cyrus, the present order of knights claim their descent.

The degree of Knights of the East constitutes the 6th degree

21*

of the French rite. It does not differ in essentials from the same degree of the Ancient and Accepted Scotch rite.

KNIGHT OF THE EAST AND WEST. *Chevalier d' Orient et d' Occident.* The 17th degree in the Ancient Scotch rite, called a Council. This is a degree of chivalry, unconnected by its history with Freemasonry. The knights assert, that upon their return from the Holy Land, in the age of the Crusaders, their ancestors organized this order; and that, in the year 1118, the first knights, to the number of eleven, took their vows of secrecy, friendship and discretion, between the hands of Garinus, patriarch and prince of Jerusalem. The presiding officer is called Most Powerful; the Wardens and twenty-one knights, Worshipful Ancients; and the rest of the brethren, Worshipful Knights.

The jewel is a heptagon of silver, at each angle a star of gold, and one of these letters B. D. W. P. H. C. S.; in the centre is inscribed a lamb on a book with seven seals. On the reverse of the jewel are the same letters, but the device is a two-edged sword between the scales of a balance.

The apron is white, lined with red, and inscribed with a two-edged sword.

KNIGHT OF THE HOLY SEPULCHRE. This order was instituted by St. Helena, the mother of Constantine the Great, in 302, after she had visited Jerusalem, and, according to the traditions of the Roman Church, discovered the true cross. In 304, the order was confirmed by Pope Marcellinus. During the times of the Christian Kings of Jerusalem, the Knights of the Holy Sepulchre were eminent for their courage and fidelity. Upon the loss of the Holy Land, they took refuge in Perugia, and were afterwards incorporated with the Knights of Rhodes. Curzon, in his "Visits to Monasteries in the Levant," states that the order is still conferred in Jerusalem, but only on Roman Catholics of noble birth, by the Reverendissimo or Superior of the Franciscans, and that the *accolade*, or blow of knighthood, is bestowed with the sword of Godfrey de Bouillon, which is preserved, with his spurs, in the sacristy of the Church of the Holy Sepulchre. The degree is now given in Councils of the Trinity, next after the Knight of the Christian Mark; and also in the New-York Encampments of Knights Templar. The presiding officer is called " Right Reverend Prelate."

The council chamber is decorated with black ornaments; the altar is covered with black, and has three lights, a crucifix, and skull and cross bones.

KNIGHT OF K——H. Grand Elected Knight of Kadosh. *Grand élu Chevalier Kadosch.* The 29th degree in the Ancient Scotch rite. This degree is intimately connected with the ancient order of the Knights Templar, a history of whose destruction, by the united efforts of Philip, King of France, and Pope Clement V. forms a part of the instructions given to the candidate. The dress of the knights is black, as an emblem of mourning for the extinction of the Knights Templar, and the death of Jacques de Molay, their last Grand Master. They wear a red cross suspended by a black ribbon from the left shoulder to the right side. The presiding officer is styled Most Illustrious Grand Commander.

KNIGHT OF THE LILIES OF THE VALLEY. This was a degree conferred by the Grand Orient of France as an appendage to Templarism. The Knights Templar who received it were constituted Knights Commanders.

KNIGHT OF MALTA. The Knights of St. John of Jerusalem, or Hospitallers of St. John, afterwards called Knights of Rhodes, and finally Knights of Malta, were founded about the commencement of the Crusades, as a military and religious order. In 1048, some pious merchants from Amalfi, in the kingdom of Naples, built a church and monastery at Jerusalem, which they dedicated to St. John the Almoner. The monks were hence called Brothers of St. John, or Hospitallers, and it was their duty

to assist those sick and needy pilgrims whom a spirit of piety had
led to the Holy Land. They assumed the black habit of the
hermits of St. Augustine, distinguished only by a white cross of
eight points on the left breast. They rapidly increased in numbers and in wealth, and at the beginning of the twelfth century,
were organized as a military order by Raymond du Puy, who
added to their original vows of chastity, obedience, and poverty, the
obligation of defending the church against infidels. Raymond
then devided them into three classes : Knights, who alone bore
arms ; Chaplains, who were regular ecclesiastics ; and Servitors,
who attended to the sick. After long and bloody contests with
the Turks and Saracens, they were finally driven from Palestine
in the year 1191. Upon this, they attacked and conquered Cyprus, which, however, they lost after eighteen years occupation ;
they then established themselves at the Island of Rhodes, under
the Grand Mastership of Fulk de Villaret, and assumed the title'
of Knights of Rhodes. On the 15th of December, 1442, after a
tranquil occupation of this island for more than two hundred
years, they were finally ejected from all their possessions by the
sultan, Soliman the Second. After this disaster, they successively
retired to Castro, Messina, and Rome, until the Emperor Charles
V., in 1530, bestowed upon them the Island of Malta, upon the
condition of their defending it from the depredations of the Turks,
and the corsairs of Barbary, and of restoring it to Naples, should
they ever succeed in recovering Rhodes. They now took the name
of Knights of Malta, by which title they have ever since been
designated. Here the organization of the order was as follows :
The chief of the order was called " Grand Master of the Holy
Hospital of St. John of Jerusalem, and Guardian of the army of
Jesus Christ." He was elected for life, and resided at the city
of Valette. He was addressed by foreign powers with the title
of "altezza eminentissima," and enjoyed an annual revenue of
about one million of guilders.* The knights were divided into

* The Grand Master's election was regulated in the following manner, when
Clark wrote his "History of Knighthood." The several seminaries named two

eight languages, according to their respective nations. The languages were those of Provence, Auvergne, France, Italy, Arragon, Germany, Castile, and England. Upon the extinction of the language of England, that of Anglo-Bavaria was substituted. The Grand Officers were also eight in number, and consisted of the chiefs of the different languages, as follows:

1. The chief of the language of Provence was Grand Commander.
2. " " Auvergne " Marshal.
3. " " France " Hospitaller.
4. " " Italy " Grand Admiral.
5. " " Arragon " Grand Conservator.
6. " " Germany " Grand Bailiff.
7. " " Castile " Grand Chancellor.
8. " " England " Turcopolier or Captain [General of the Cavalry.

The knights, in time of war, wore over their usual garments a scarlet surcoat, embellished before and behind with a broad white cross of eight points. In times of peace, the dress of ceremony was a long black mantle, upon which the same cross of white linen was sowed.

In 1565, the Island of Malta was beleagured by Soliman the Second, on which occasion the knights suffered immense loss, from which they never entirely recovered. Of the eight languages, the English became extinct in the sixteenth century, those of France, Auvergne, and Provence, perished in the anarchy of the French revolution, Castile and Arragon were separated at the peace of Amiens, and the remaining two have been since abolished. The order, therefore, as respects its ancient constitution, has now ceased to exist.

In 1798, the knights chose Paul I., Emperor of Russia, as their Grand Master, who took them under his protection. Upon his death they elected Prince Carracciolo. Upon the reduction

knights each, allowing also two for the English; those sixteen, from among themselves chose eight: those eight chose a knight, a priest, and a serving brother; and they three, out of the sixteen great crosses, elected the Grand Master.

of the Island of Malta by the English in 1800, the chief seat
of the order was transferred to Catanea in Sicily, whence in 1826
it was removed by the authority of the Pope to Ferrara. The
last public reception of the order took place at Sonneburg in 1800,
when Leopold, the present King of Belgium, and Prince Ernest
of Hesse Philippsthal Barchfeld, with several other knights, were
created.

In 1841, Ferdinand I., Emperor of Austria, issued a decree
restoring the order in Italy, and endowing it with a moderate revenue.* But the wealth, the power, and the magnificence of the
order have passed away with the age and the spirit of chivalry
which gave it birth.

Ancient Ceremonies of Reception.—They were simple and impressive. "The novice was made to understand that he was
'about to put off the old man, and to be regenerated;' and having
received absolution, was required to present himself in a secular
habit, without a girdle, in order to appear perfectly free on entering into so sacred an engagement, and with a burning taper in his
hand, representing charity. He then received the holy communion, and afterwards presented himself 'most respectfully before
the person who was to perform the ceremony, and requested to be
received into the company of brothers and into the holy order of
the Hospital of Jerusalem.' The rules of the order, the obligations
he was about to take upon himself, and the duties that would be
required of him, being explained, an open Missal was then presented to him, on which he placed both of his hands, and made his
profession in the following terms :

"'I, N., do vow and promise to Almighty God, to the eternal
Virgin Mary, mother of God, and to St. John the Baptist, to render henceforward, by the grace of God, perfect obedience to the
superior placed over me by the choice of the order, to live without
personal property, and to preserve my chastity.'

"Having taken his hands from the book, the brother who re-

---

* See Moore's Magazine for a copy of this decree.

ceived him said as follows: 'We acknowledge you the servant of
the poor and sick, and as having consecrated yourself to the service of the Church.' To which he answered: 'I acknowledge
myself as such.' He then kissed the Missal and returned it to
the brother who received him, in token of perfect obedience. He
was then invested with the mantle of the order, in such a manner
as that the cross fell on his left breast. A variety of other minor
ceremonies followed, and the whole was concluded with a series
of appropriate and solemn prayers."*

As a masonic grade, the degree of Knight of Malta is in this
country communicated in an Encampment of Knights Templar,
as an appendant order thereto.

KNIGHT OF THE MEDITERRANEAN PASS. This
is an honorary degree, conferred only on Knights Templar as
Knights of Malta. It is conferred by Inspectors of the 33d degree
of the Ancient and Accepted rite, though, I suppose, it may also
be conferred by Encampments of Knights Templar that are in
possession of it, upon their members.

The degree is said to have been founded by the Knights of
Malta, about the year 1367. In an excursion of a party of Maltese knights, they were attacked while crossing the river Offanto,†
in Italy, by a very superior force. Notwithstanding the disparity
of numbers, the knights succeeded in obtaining a signal victory,
and routed the Turks, with an immense loss, the river being
literally stained with their blood.

As a reward of their valour, the knights who had thus distinguished themselves were affranchised on all the Mediterranean
shores; that is to say, they received permission to pass and repass,
wherever and whenever it seemed to them good, and this was the

---

* Moore's Magazine, vol. ii, p. 133–4.

† This is the ancient Aufidius, memorable for the battle of Cannæ fought on
its banks, between Hannibal and the Romans, in which the latter were defeated
with the loss of 45,000 men.

origin of the degree which was instituted in commemoration of these circumstances. Such is the legend of the knights of this degree. It is by no means to be confounded with the side degree of the "Mediterranean Pass," conferred on Royal Arch Masons, which resembles it only in the name.

KNIGHT OF THE NINTH ARCH. *Royal Arche.* The 13th degree in the Ancient Scotch rite, sometimes called the "Ancient Royal Arch of Solomon." This is, without question, the most interesting and impressive of what are called the ineffable degrees. The historical portions of this degree are copious, and afford us much information in relation to Enoch, and the mode in which, notwithstanding the destructive influence of the deluge and the lapse of ages, he was enabled to preserve important secrets eventually to be communicated to the first possessors of this degree. Its officers are a Most Potent Grand Master, representing Solomon K. of I., a Grand Warden, representing Hiram K. of T., a Grand Inspector, Grand Treasurer, and Grand Secretary.

The apron of this degree is lined with yellow, and has on it a triangle.

The jewel is a medal of gold. On one side is a representation of two people letting down a third through a square hole into arches, and round the edge these letters: "R. S. S. G. I. E. S. I. P. A. T. S. R. E., A. M. 2995." They are the initials of the following sentence: "Regnante Sapientissimo Salamone, G—— J—— et S—— Invenerunt Pretiosissimum Artificum Thesaurum, Subter Ruinas Enoch, Anno Mundi 2995."

KNIGHT OF THE PELICAN. One of the titles by which the Princes of Rose Croix are designated.

KNIGHT OF THE RED CROSS. This is strictly a masonic order of knighthood, and its history is intimately connected with the circumstances related in the Royal Arch degree. It has no analogy to the degrees of chivalry, dating its existence long before the Crusades, or even the Christian era, as far back, indeed, as the reign of Darius, by whom it is said to have been founded. It is, however, always conferred in an Encampment of Knights Templar, and is given preparatory to communicating that degree, though there is no connection whatsoever between the two. After the death of Cyrus, the Jews, who had been released by him from their captivity, and permitted to return to Jerusalem, for the purpose of re-building the temple, found themselves obstructed in the undertaking by the neighbouring nations, and especially by the Samaritans. Hereupon, they sent an embassy, at the head of which was their prince Zerubbabel, to Darius the successor of Cyrus, to crave his interposition and protection. Zerubbabel, awaiting a favourable opportunity, succeeded not only in obtaining his request, but also in renewing the friendship which formerly existed between the king and himself. In commemoration of these events, Darius is said to have instituted a new order, and called it the Knights of the East. They afterwards assumed their present name from the red cross borne in their banners. The historical circumstances connected with this degree will be found in Josephus, and in the 3d and 4th chapters of the 1st book of Esdras. It is asserted that this order has been long known in Europe, under different names, though its introduction into this country is of comparatively recent date. A council of Knights of the Red Cross is composed of the following officers: a Sovereign Master, Chancellor, Master of the Palace, Prelate, Master of Despatches, Master of Calvary, Master of Infantry, Standard-Bearer, Sword-Bearer, Warder, and Sentinel.

KNIGHT OF THE ROYAL AXE, OR PRINCE OF LIBANUS. *Royal-Hache, ou Prince du Liban.* The 22d degree in the Ancient Scotch rite. It was instituted to record three memorable services rendered to masonry by the "mighty cedars of Lebanon," and its history furnishes some interesting information on the subject of the Sidonian architects.

22

We learn from this degree that the Sidonians were employed in cutting cedars, on Mount Libanus or Lebanon, for the construction of Noah's ark. Their descendants subsequently cut cedars from the same place for the ark of the covenant; and the descendants of these were again employed in the same offices, and in the same place, in obtaining materials for building Solomon's temple. Lastly, Zerubbabel employed them in cutting the cedars of Lebanon for the use of the second temple. This celebrated nation formed colleges on Mount Libanus, and in their labours always adored the Great Architect of the Universe. I have no doubt that this last sentence refers to the Druses, that secret sect of Theists, who still reside upon Mount Libanus, and in the adjacent parts of Syria and Palestine, and whose mysterious ceremonies have attracted so much of the curiosity of Eastern travellers.

Thory* says that Pierre Riel, Marquis of Beurnonville, who died in Paris in 1821, having gone to the island of Bourbon, was there elected Grand Master of all the lodges of India, in 1778, and then instituted this degree.

The apron of the Knights of the Royal Axe is white, lined and bordered with purple. On it is painted a round table, on which are laid several architectural plans. On the flap is a three-headed serpent. The jewel is a golden axe, having on the handle and blade the initials of several personages illustrious in the history of masonry

KNIGHT OF THE ROSY CROSS. See *Heredom, Royal Order of.*

KNIGHTS OF ST. JOHN OF JERUSALEM. According to a tradition of the Rose Croix, 27,000 of the descendants of the Masons who, at the destruction of Jerusalem by Titus, had fled to Scotland, being desirous of uniting in the war of the Crusades, obtained permission of the Scotch monarch, and, on their arrival in Palestine, performed so many deeds of valour as

---

* Chronologie, tome i., p. 311.

to attract the admiration of the Knights of St. John of Jerusalem, who, as a token of their esteem, requested to be initiated into the masonic order, whence arose the connection of that body with the Freemasons.

KNIGHT OF THE SUN. *Chevalier du Soliel.* The 28th degree of the Ancient Scotch rite, sometimes called by other names, as Prince of the Sun, Prince Adept, and Key of Masonry, or Chaos Disentangled. This is a philosophical degree. Its ceremonies and lecture are employed in giving a history of all the preceding degrees, and in explaining the emblems of masonry. Its great object is the inculcation of TRUTH. The principal officers are styled Thrice Perfect Father Adam and Brother Truth; the other officers are named after the seven chief angels, and the brethren are called Sylphs. The jewel is a gold medal, with a sun on one side surrounded by rays, and on the reverse a globe. There is but one light in the lodge, which shines from behind a globe of water.

Ragon,* speaking of this degree, says that it is not, like many of the high degrees, a modern invention, but is of the highest antiquity, and was, in fact, the last degree of initiation, teaching, as it did, the doctrines of natural religion, which formed an essential part of the ancient mysteries.

KNIGHT OF THE THREE KINGS. A side degree sometimes given by Lecturers. Its history connects it with the dedication of the first temple, the conferrer of the degree representing King Solomon. Its moral tendency appears to be the inculcation of reconciliation of grievances among Masons by friendly conference. It may be conferred by any Master Mason on another.

KNIGHT TEMPLAR. In the early ages of the Christian church, a holy veneration for the scenes which had been conse-

---

* Cours Philosophique, p. 361.

crated by the sufferings and death of the founder of our religion,
led thousands of pious pilgrims to visit Jerusalem, for the purpose of offering up their devotions at the sepulchre of the Lord.
To such a height did this religious enthusiasm arrive, that, in
1064, not less than seven thousand pilgrims assembled from all
parts of Europe around the tomb of Christ. At a time when
the facilities of intercourse which now exist were unknown, the
journey must have always been attended with difficulties and
dangers, to which the youthful, the aged, and the infirm, must
often have been sacrificed. But when Palestine was conquered
by the Arabs, and the land of pilgrimage became infested by
hordes of barbarous fanatics, inspired with the most intense hatred towards Christianity, these difficulties and dangers were
eminently increased. The tale of the sufferings inflicted on the
pilgrims by the Mussulman possessors of Jerusalem excited in
Europe an enthusiastic indignation, which led to the institution
of the Crusades, wars undertaken solely for the purpose of recovering the Holy Land from the followers of Mahomet. In 1099,
the city of Jerusalem was captured by the Crusaders, the consequence of which was an increase in the zeal of pilgrimage, which
had been gathering intensity during its long suppression by the
barbarities of the Turcomans. But, although the infidels had
been driven out of Jerusalem, they had not been expelled from
Palestine, but they still continued to infest the lofty mountains
bordering on the sea-coast, from whose inaccessible strongholds
they were wont to make incursions into the roads surrounding
the Holy City, and pillage every unguarded traveller.

To protect the pious pilgrims thus exposed to plunder and death,
nine noble knights, who had previously distinguished themselves
at the siege of Jerusalem, united in a brotherhood, and bound
themselves by a solemn compact to aid one another in clearing the
highways of infidels and robbers, and in protecting the pilgrim
through the passes and defiles of the mountains to the Holy City.[*]

* The Knight Templars, by C. G. Addison, Esq., of the Inner Temple. F.
6, London, 1842.

These knights called themselves the *Poor Fellow Soldiers of Jesus Christ*. Baldwin, King of Jerusalem, gave them, in 1118, for a dwelling, a part of the church which had been built by the Emperor Justinian within the site on which the temple of Solomon had been erected on Mount Moriah, and adjoining to the temple which had been built by the Caliph Omar. Thenceforth they assumed the title of "Poor Fellow Soldiers of Christ and of the temple of Solomon."* The views of the order now became more extensive, and they added to their profession of protecting poor pilgrims, that of defending the kingdom of Jerusalem, and the whole Eastern church, from the attacks of infidels. Hugh de Payens was chosen by the knights their leader, under the title of the " Master of the Temple." Their name and reputation spread rapidly through Europe, and many of the nobles of the West, who had visited Palestine as pilgrims, aspired to become members of the order. In 1128, they received a rule or system of regulations from the pope, which had been drawn expressly for them by St. Bernard. In the same year Hugh de Payens visited various parts of Europe, and received from different princes and nobles many liberal donations of land and money. In England, especially, where the amount granted was large, he established a branch of the order, placing a Knight Templar at its head, as his procurator and vicegerent, with the title of Prior of the Temple. As the English domains became enlarged, this title was successively changed to that of Grand Prior, and then to that of Master of the Temple in England. At this time, the rule of St. Bernard, which had been adopted for their government, prescribed to them a dress, consisting of a white mantle, "that those," as the rule expressed it, " who have cast behind them a dark life, may know that they are to commend themselves to their creator by a pure and white life."† To this, Pope Eugenius some years afterwards added a red cross, as a symbol of martyrdom. Their banner was half black, half

---

* Pauperos Commilitiones Christi et Templi Salomonis.
† Regula. cap xx.

white, called Beauseant, "that is to say, in the Gallic tongue, Bien-seant, (*well-becoming*,) because they are fair and favourable to the friends of Christ, but black and terrible to his enemies."*

The knights, engaged in continual wars with the infidels, continued to increase their reputation, and enlarge their possessions, which are esteemed by Dugdale to have produced, in 1185, the enormous annual sum of six millions sterling. But in the beginning of the 14th century, the avarice of Philip le Bel, and the weakness and perfidy of Clement V., conspired to give a blow to their order, from which it never recovered. Before adverting to that catastrophe, I shall occupy a few moments in examining the organization of the order during the most prosperous period of its existence.

The order of the Temple, in the 12th century, was divided into three classes : knights, priests, and serving brethren. Every candidate for admission into the first class must have received the honour of knighthood in due form, and according to the laws of chivalry, and consequently the Knights Templar were all men of noble birth. The second class, or the priests, were not originally a part of the order, but by the bull of Pope Alexander, known as the bull *omne datum optimum*, it was ordained that they might be admitted, to enable the knights more commodiously to hear divine service, and to receive the sacraments. Serving brothers, like the priests, were not a part of the primitive institution. They owed their existence to the increasing prosperity and luxury of the order.

Over this society, thus constituted, was placed a presiding officer, with the title of Grand Master. His power, though great, was limited. He was, in war, the commander-in-chief of all the forces of the Temple. In his hands was placed the whole patronage of the order, and as the vicegerent of the pope, he was the spiritual head and bishop of all the clergy belonging to the society. He was, however, much controlled and guided

---

* James de Vitry. Hist. Hierosol.

by the chapter, without whose consent he was never permitted to draw out or expend the money of the order.

The Grand Master resided originally at Jerusalem ; afterwards, when that city was lost, at Acre, and finally at Cyprus. His duty always required him to be in the Holy Land; he consequently never resided in Europe. He was elected for life from among the knights in the following manner. On the death of the Grand Master, a Grand Prior was chosen to administer the affairs of the order until a successor could be elected. When the day which had been appointed for the election arrived, the chapter usually assembled at the chief seat of the order; three or more of the most esteemed knights were then proposed, the Grand Prior collected the votes, and he who had received the greatest number was nominated to be the electing Prior. An Assistant was then associated with him in the person of another knight. These two remained all night in the chapel engaged in prayer. In the morning, they chose two others, and these four, two more, and so on until the number of twelve (that of the apostles) had been selected. The twelve then selected a chaplain. The thirteen then proceeded to vote for a Grand Master, who was elected by a majority of the votes. When the election was completed, it was announced to the assembled brethren, and when all had promised obedience, the Prior, if the person was present, said to him, " In the name of God the Father, the Son, and the Holy Ghost, we have chosen, and do choose thee, brother N., to be our Master." Then, turning to the brethren, he said, " Beloved sirs and brethren, give thanks unto God, behold here our Master."*

The remaining officers were a Marshal, who was charged with the execution of the military arrangements on the field of battle. The Prior of Jerusalem, called the Grand Preceptor of the Temple, was the Treasurer of the order, and had charge of all the receipts and expenditures. The Draper had the care of the clothing department, and distributed the garments to all the

* See N. Americ. Quart. Mag. vol. vii. p. 328.

brethren. The Standard-Bearer bore the glorious Beauseant to the field. The Turcopilar was the commander of a body of ligh-horse called Turcopoles, who were employed as skirmishers and light cavalry. And lastly, to the Guardian of the Chapel was entrusted the care of the portable chapel, which was always car-ried by the Templars into the field.*

Each province of the order had a Grand Prior, who was in it the representative of the Grand Master; and each house was governed by a Prior or Preceptor, who commanded its knights in time of war, and presided over its chapter in peace.

The mode of reception into the order is described to have been exceedingly solemn. A novitiate was enjoined by the canons; though practically, it was in general dispensed with. The can-didate was received in a chapter assembled in the chapel of the order, all strangers being rigorously excluded. The Preceptor opened the business with an address to those present, demanding if they knew of any just cause or impediment why the candi-date should not be admitted. If no objection was made, the candidate was conducted into an adjacent chamber, where two or three of the knights, placing before his view the rigour and aus-terities of the order, demanded if he still persisted in entering it. If he persisted, he was asked if he was married or betrothed, had made a vow in any other order, if he owed more than he could pay, if he was of sound body, without any secret infirmity, and free? If his answers proved satisfactory, they left him and returned to the chapter, and the Preceptor again asked, if any one had any thing to say against his being received. If all were silent, he asked if they were willing to receive him. On their assenting, the candidate was led in by the knights who had questioned him, and who now instructed him in the mode of asking admission. He advanced, and kneeling before the Pre-ceptor with folded hands, said, "Sir, I am come before God, and before you and the brethren; and I pray and beseech you,

---

* This list is given on the authority of Addison. Other writers vary slightly in the names and number of these officers.

for the sake of God, and our sweet lady, to receive me into your
society and the good works of the order, as one who, all his life
long, will be the servant and slave of the order." The Preceptor then inquired of him if he had well considered all the
trials and difficulties which awaited him in the order, adjured
him on the Holy Evangelists to speak the truth, and then put to
him the questions which had already been asked of him in the
preparation room, further inquiring if he was a knight, and the
son of a knight and gentlewoman, and if he was a priest. He
then asked him the following questions: "Do you promise to
God and Mary, and our dear lady, obedience, as long as you live,
to the Master of the Temple, and the Prior who shall be set over
you; do you promise chastity of the body; do you further promise a strict compliance with the laudable customs and usages of
the order now in force, and such as the Master and knights may
hereafter add; will you fight for and defend, with all your
might, the holy land of Jerusalem, and never quit the order but
with the consent of the Master and Chapter; and lastly, do you
agree that you never will see a Christian unjustly deprived of his
inheritance, nor be aiding in such a deed?" The answers to all
these questions being in the affirmative, the Preceptor then said:
"In the name of God, and of Mary, our dear lady, and in the
name of St. Peter of Rome, and of our Father the Pope, and in
the name of all the brethren of the Temple, we receive you to
all the good works of the order, which have been performed from
the beginning, and will be performed to the end, you, your
father, your mother, and all those of your family whom you let
participate therein. So you, in like manner, receive us to all the
good works which you have performed and will perform. We
assure you of bread and water, the poor clothing of the order,
and labor and toil enow." The Preceptor then took the white
mantle, with its ruddy cross, placed it about his neck and bound
it fast. The Chaplain repeated the 133d Psalm: *Behold how
good and how pleasant it is for brethren to dwell together in
unity;*" and the prayer of the Holy Spirit, " *Deus qui corda*

fidelium; each brother said a *Pater*, and the Preceptor and Chaplain kissed the candidate. He then placed himself at the feet of the Preceptor, who exhorted him to peace and charity, to chastity, obedience, humility, and piety, and so the ceremony was ended.*

But to resume the history of the order. From the time of Hugh de Payens, to that of Jacques de Molay, the Templars continued to be governed by a succession of the noblest and bravest knights of which the chivalry of Christendom could boast. They continued to increase in power, in fame and in wealth, and, what is unfortunately too often the concomitants of these qualities, in luxury and pride. In the beginning of the 14th century, the throne of France was filled by Philip the Fair, an ambitious, a vindictive, and an avaricious prince. In his celebrated controversy with Pope Boniface, the Templars had, as was usual with them, sided with the Pontiff and opposed the King; this act excited his hatred: the order was enormously wealthy; this aroused his avarice: their power interfered with his designs of political aggrandizement; and this alarmed his ambition. He, therefore, secretly concerted with Pope Clement V. a plan for their destruction, and the appropriation of their revenues. Clement, by his direction, wrote in June, 1306, to De Molay, the Grand Master, who was then at Cyprus, inviting him to come and consult with him on some matters of great importance to the order. De Molay obeyed the summons, and arrived in the beginning of 1307 at Paris, with sixty knights and a large amount of treasure. He was immediately imprisoned, and, on the 13th of October following, every knight in France was, in consequence of the secret orders of the King, arrested on the pretended charge of idolatry, and other enormous crimes, of which a renegade and expelled Prior of the order was said to have confessed that the knights were guilty in their secret chapters. On the 12th of May, 1310, fifty-four of the knights were, after a mock trial, publicly burnt, and on the 18th of March,

---

* N. Am. Quart. Mag. ut supra.

1314, De Molay, the Grand Master, and the three principal dignitaries of the order, suffered the same fate. They died faithfully asserting their innocence of all the crimes imputed to them.
The order was now, by the energy of the King of France, assisted by the spiritual authority of the Pope, suppressed
throughout Europe. But it was not annihilated. De Molay, in
anticipation of his fate, had appointed John Mark Larmienus as
his successor in office, and from that time to the present there
has been a regular and uninterrupted succession of Grand
Masters. Of the names of these Grand Masters, and the date
of their election, I annex a list for the gratification of the
curious.*

1.	Hugh de Payens,	1118.
2.	Robert of Burgundy,	1139.
3.	Everard de Barri,	1147.
4.	Bernard de Trenellape,	1151.
5.	Bertrand de Blanchefort,	1154.
6.	Andrew de Montbar	1165.
7.	Philip of Naplus,	1169.
8.	Odo de St. Amand,	1171.
9.	Arnold de Troye,	1180.
10.	John Terricus,	1185.
11.	Gerard Ridefort,	1187.
12.	Robert Sablaeus,	1191.
13.	Gilbert Gralius,	1196.
14.	Philip de Plessis,	1201.
15.	William de Carnota,	1217.
16.	Peter de Montagu,	1218.
17.	Armaud de Petragrossa,	1229.
18.	Herman de Petragrorius,	1237.
19.	William de Rupefort,	1244.

---

* It may be as well to observe that this is the list given by the order of the
Temple at Paris, who claim to be the lineal descendants of the ancient order.
Other Templars, who do not admit the legality of the Grand Mastership of
Larmenius, give different catalogues of Grand Masters.

20.	William de Sonnac,	1247.
21.	Reginald Vichierius,	1250.
22.	Thomas Beraud,	1257.
23.	William de Beaujeau,	1274.
24.	Theobald Gaudinius,	1291.
25.	Jacques de Molay,	1298.
26.	John Mark Larmienus.	1314.
27.	Thomas Theobald Alexandrinus,	1324.
28.	Arnold de Braque,	1340.
29.	John de Claremont,	1349.
30.	Bertrand du Guesclin,	1357.
31.	John Arminiacus,	1381.
32.	Bernard Arminiacus,	1392.
33.	John Arminiacus,	1419.
34.	John de Croy,	1451.
35.	Bernard Imbault,	1472.
36.	Robert Senoncourt,	1478.
37.	Galeatius de Salazar,	1497.
38.	Philip Chabot,	1516.
39.	Gaspard de Jaltiaco Tavanensis,	1544.
40.	Henry de Montmorency,	1574.
41.	Charles de Valois,	1615.
42.	James Ruxellius de Granceio,	1651.
43.	Duc de Duras,	1681.
44.	Philip Duke of Orleans,	1705.
45.	Duc de Maine,	1724.
46.	Louis Henry Bourbon,	1737.
47.	Louis Francis Bourbon,	1741.
48.	Duc de Cosse Brissac,	1776.
49.	Claude M. R. Chevillon,	1792.
50	Bernard R. F. Palaprat,	1804.
51.	Sir Sidney Smith,	1838.

Notwithstanding, therefore, the efforts of the King and the Pope, the order of Templars was not entirely extinguished. In France it still exists, and ranks among its members some of the most influential noblemen of the kingdom. In Portugal, the name of the order has been changed to that of the "Knights of Christ," and its Cross is frequently conferred by the government as the reward of distinguished merit. In England, the Encampment of Baldwin, which was established at Bristol by the Templars who returned with Richard I. from Palestine, still continues to hold its regular meetings, and is believed to have preserved the ancient costume and ceremonies of the order. This encampment, with another at Bath, and a third at York, constituted the three original encampments of England. From these have emanated the existing encampments in the British Islands and in the United States, so that the order, as it now exists in Britain and America, is a lineal descendant of the ancient order.

The connection between the Knights Templar and the Freemasons has been repeatedly asserted by the enemies of both institutions, and as often admitted by their friends. Lawrie, on this subject, holds the following language: "We know that the Knight Templars not only possessed the mysteries, but performed the ceremonies, and inculcated the duties of Freemasons;"[*] and he attributes the dissolution of the order to the discovery of their being Freemasons, and their assembling in secret to practise the rites of the order. He further endeavours to explain the manner in which they became the depository of the masonic mysteries by tracing their initiation to the Druses, a Syriac fraternity, which, at the time of the Crusades, and long after, existed on Mount Libanus.[†]

Costume.—At the conclusion of this article, a few remarks on the costume of the order may be acceptable. The present *black* dress of the Templars is derived from the Knights of Malta, to whom, with the Teutonic Knights, their estates were assigned by Pope Clement on the dissolution of the order, and with whom many of the knights united themselves. But originally, as we

---

[*] Hist. of Freemasonry, p. 58.
[†] Hist. of Freemasonry, p. 88.

have already observed, their costume was *white*. In the Statutes of the order, as established in Scotland, which were revised in 1843, the ancient costume was exactly adopted. According to these regulations the dress of the Knights Templar is as follows :

A white woollen mantle to reach the knee in front, and taper away to the ankle behind, fastened with white cord and tassel, and with a red cross *patée* on the left shoulder; white woollen tunic, reaching to about three or four inches above the knee, with the cross upon the left breast; white stock with falling white shirt collar; tight white pantaloons; buff boots, with buff tops turned over five inches broad, no tassels; spurs gilt, with red leathers; sash of white silk, half a yard in breadth, tied in a knot in front; the ends edged with a white silk fringe hanging down, and a small red cross near the extremities; white woollen cap with red leather band, or, if he has obtained a diploma from the Grand Master, a red velvet cap; no feather; cross-hilted sword with brass guard, and white ivory hilt; scabbard of red morocco; belt of red leather, with gilt buckle; buff gauntlets, with a red cross on the wrist; badge, and enamelled black cross, with white orle, and a small red cross enamelled thereon, suspended from the neck by a red ribbon with white edges, about two inches broad, passing through the ring of the badge.

In America the dress is very different from that of the ancient knights. The suit is black, with black gloves. A black velvet sash, trimmed with silver lace, crosses the body from the left shoulder to the right hip, having at its end a cross-hilted dagger, a black rose on the left shoulder, and a Maltese cross at the end. Where the sash crosses the left breast, is a nine-pointed star in silver, with a cross and serpent of gold in the centre, within a circle, around which are the words, "*in hoc signo vinces.*" The apron is of black velvet, in triangular form, to represent the delta, and edged with silver lace. On its flap is placed a triangle of silver, perforated with twelve holes, with a cross and serpent in the centre; on the centre of the apron are a skull and cross-bones, between three stars of seven points, having a red cross in the centre of each. The belt is black, to which is attached a cross-hilted sword. The caps vary in form and decoration in different encampments. The standard is black, bearing a nine-pointed cross of silver, having in its centre a circle of green, with the cross and serpent in gold, and the motto around "*in hoc signo vinces.*"

L.

LABOUR. From the time of opening to that of closing, a lodge is said to be at labour. This is but one of the numerous instances in which the terms of operative masonry are symbolically applied to speculative; for, as our operative ancestors, when congregated in lodge, were engaged in the building of material edifices, so Free and Accepted Masons are supposed to be employed in the erection of a superstructure of virtue and morality, upon the foundation of the masonic principles which they were taught at their admission into the order. Extending the allusion, the lodge is said "to be called from labour to refreshment," whenever, in the course of the meeting, it adjourns for a definite period, or takes a recess of a few minutes. During this time, the Junior Warden presides over the craft.

LADDER. See *Jacob's Ladder.*

LANDMARKS. In ancient times, it was the custom to mark the boundaries of lands by means of stone pillars, the removal of which, by malicious persons, would be the occasion of much confusion, men having no other guide than these pillars by which to distinguish the limits of their property. To remove them, therefore, was considered a heinous crime. "Thou shalt not," says the Jewish law, "remove thy neighbour's landmark, which they of old time have set in thine inheritance."[*] Hence those peculiar marks of distinction by which we are separated from the profane world, and by which we are enabled to designate our inheritance as the "sons of light," are called the landmarks of the order. The *universal language* and the *universal laws*[†] of masonry are landmarks, but not so are the local ceremonies, laws, and usages, which vary in different countries. To attempt to alter or remove these sacred landmarks, by which we examine and prove a brother's claims to share in our privileges, is one of the most heinous offences that a Mason can commit.

There are, however, certain forms and regulations, which, although not constituting landmarks, are nevertheless so protected by the venerable claim of antiquity, that they should be guarded by every good Mason with religious care from alteration. It is not in the power of any body of men to make innovations in masonry.

LANGUAGE, UNIVERSAL. Freemasons boast, with truth, that they possess an universal language, which men of all languages can understand. "An universal language," says Mr. Locke,[‡] "has been much desired by the learned of many ages. It is a thing rather to be wished than hoped for. But it seems the Masons pretend to have such a thing among them." We who possess that language, can estimate its value, for we know that its eloquent tones have often won sympathy from the most unfeeling, and converted the indifferent stranger into the faithful brother.

LAPICIDA. A Freemason. See *Latomus.*

---

[*] Deuteronomy xix. 14.

[†] It has been supposed, by some authorities, that all laws which were in existence in 1717, at the re-organization of the Grand Lodge in the south of England, are to be considered as landmarks.

[‡] That is, if Leland's Manuscript be authentic.

LATIN LODGE. In the year 1784, Brown, the celebrated physician, organized the Roman Eagle lodge at Edinburgh, the whole work of which was conducted in the Latin language.

LATOMUS. A Latin term derived from the Greek λατομος a *stone-cutter*. It is used in the sense of a Freemasons in Molart's Latin Register, quoted in the notes to Preston, note 17. A purer Latin word is *lapicida*, which Ainsworth defines "a stone-cutter, a Freemason."* *Architecto* is used by some writers.

LAWS OF MASONRY. The laws of masonry are of two kinds, local and universal. The local laws are those enacted by Grand and subordinate lodges for the government of their members. These, of course, may be altered or annulled at the pleasure of the bodies who originally framed them. The universal laws are those handed down by universal consent from times immemorial, and which govern the fraternity throughout the world. These are irrevocable, for they constitute a part of the ancient landmarks. We will give an example of each kind. The rule regulating the amount of the fee to be paid on the admission of candidates is a local law, and varies in every country. But the law which declares that no woman can be admitted, is universal, and controls every lodge on the face of the globe.

LEBANON or LIBANUS. A mountain, or rather a range of mountains in Syria, extending from beyond Sidon to Tyre, and forming the northern boundary of Palestine. Lebanon is celebrated for the cedars which it produces, many of which are from 50 to 80 feet in height, and cover with their branches a space of ground, the diameter of which is still greater. Hiram, King of

---

* The "Acta Latomorum," a modern French work, states that the word latimus was first applied by the Jesuits to designate a Freemason. The use of it in 1429, by Molart, proves that this is not so. Ragon has very truly said that the statements of the "Acta Latomorum" require verification before they can be received as authentic.

23*

Tyre, in whose dominions Mount Lebanon was situated, furnished
* these trees for the building of the temple of Solomon.

LECTURE. Each degree of masonry contains a course of
instruction, in which the ceremonies, traditions, and moral instruction appertaining to the degree, are set forth. This arrangement is called a lecture. Each lecture, for the sake of convenience, and for the purpose of conforming to certain divisions
in the ceremonies, is divided into sections, the number of which
have varied at different periods, although the substance remains
the same. According to Preston, the lecture of the first degree
contains six sections; that of the second, four; and that of the
third, twelve. But according to the arrangment adopted in this
country, there are three sections in the first degree, two in the
second, and three in the third.

In the Entered Apprentice's degree, the first section describes
the proper mode of initiation, and supplies the means of qualify-
ing us for our privileges, and of testing the claims of others. The
second section rationally accounts for all the ceremonies peculiar
to this degree. The third section explains the nature and principles of our institution, and instructs us in the form and construction of the lodge, furnishing, in conclusion, some important
lessons on the various virtues which should distinguish a Freemason.

In the Fellow Craft's degree, the first section recapitulates the
ceremonies of passing a candidate. The second section gives an
account of the ancient division of our institution into operative
and speculative Masons, and, by striking emblems, directs the
candidate to an attentive study of the liberal arts and sciences.

In the Master's degree, the first section illustrates the ancient
and proper mode of raising a candidate to this sublime degree.
In the second section, the historical traditions of the order are
introduced, and an important instance of masonic virtue is exemplified. In the third section, our emblems are explained, and
the construction of Solomon's Temple described.

There does not seem to have been any established system of lectures, such as now exist, previous to the revival of masonry in the beginning of the eighteenth century. In 1720, Desaguliers and Anderson, the compilers of the Book of Constitutions, arranged the lectures for the first time in a catechetical form, from the old Charges and other masonic documents that were then extant. Of this system, Dr. Oliver informs us that "the first lecture extended to the greatest length, but the replies were circumscribed within a very narrow compass. The second was shorter, and the third, called 'the Master's Part,' contained only seven questions, besides the explanations and examinations."* The imperfection of these lectures loudly called for a revision of them, which was accordingly accomplished in 1732 by brother Martin Clare, a man of talent, and afterwards a Deputy Grand Master. Clare's amendments, however, amounted to little more than the addition of a few moral and scriptural admonitions, and the insertion of a simple allusion to the human senses, and to the theological ladder.

Subsequently, Thomas Dunckerley, who was considered as the most intelligent Mason of the day, extended and improved the lectures, and among other things first gave to the theological ladder its three most important rounds.

The lectures thus continued until 1763, when Hutchinson gave them an improved form, which was still further extended in 1772, by Preston, who remained for a long time the standard. But at the union of the two Grand Lodges of England, in 1813, Dr. Hemming established that system which is now generally practised in the English lodges.

The lectures of Preston were early introduced into this country, having been, however, much modified by T. S. Webb, whose system has been the basis of all those taught since his day in the lodges of the United States. No changes of any importance have been made in the lectures, in this country, since their first introduction.

---

* Symbol of Glory, Lect. I., p. 17.

These constitute the simple text of masonry, while the ex
tended illustrations which are given to them by an intelligent
Master or Lecturer, and which he can only derive from a careful
study of scripture, of history, of the manuscript lectures of the
philosophical degrees, and lastly, of the published works of
learned masonic writers, constitute the commentary, without
which the simple text would be comparatively barren and unin-
structive. These commentaries are the philosophy of masonry,
and without an adequate knowledge of them no brother can be
entitled to claim our technical title of "a bright Mason."   In
relation to this subject, the following extract from the Freemason's Quarterly Review, published at London, deserves preservation.*

"Our masonic society has to this day retained many interesting symbols in its instructions, when properly explained by a
scientific Lecturer, and not garbled by ignorant pretenders, who,
by dint merely of a good memory and some assurance, intrude
themselves on a well-informed assembly of brethren, by giving a
lecture not composed by themselves, but taught them *verbatim*."

LECTURER. A brother of skill and intelligence, entrusted
with the task of instructing the lodges in the proper mode of
work, in the ceremonies, usages, legends, history, and science of
the order.   When the appointment emanates, as it always should,
from a Grand Lodge, he is called a Grand Lecturer.

LEGEND. A legend may properly be defined a traditional
tale.† All countries and all religions have their legends. In
the ancient mysteries there was always a legend on which much
symbolical instruction was based. These legends of the mysteries, although they varied as to the subject of the history in

---

* Vol. ii. p. 274.

† The word is derived from the Latin *legenda*, "things to be read," because
it was formerly the custom to read portions of some of the religious legends,
which abound in the Roman Church to people at morning prayer.

each, yet all agree in this, that they were funereal in their character—that they commemorated the death by violence, and the
subsequent resurrection, of some favourite hero or hero-god—and
that beginning with lamentation they ended in joy.

"In like manner Freemasonry has its legends and allegorical
references, many of them founded in fact, and capable of un-
questionable proof, while others are based on Jewish traditions,
and only invested with probability, while they equally inculcate
and enforce the most solemn and important truths."* Of these
legends, the one which may, by way of excellence, be called
"*The* Legend," and which more particularly is connected with
the Master's degree, it may be supposed was substituted by our
ancient brethren, when they united themselves at the Temple
with the Dionysians, for the pagan and apocryphal legend of
Bacchus, celebrated by that society.†

LEVEL. An emblem of equality. In the sight of God,
who alone is great, all men are equal, subject to the same infirmities, hastening to the same goal, and preparing to be judged by
the same immutable law. In this sense only do Masons speak
of the equality which should reign in the lodge; but as "peaceable subjects to the civil powers," they deny the existence of
that revolutionary equality, which, levelling all distinctions of
ranks, would tend to beget confusion, insubordination, and anarchy in the state.

The level is one of the working tools of a Fellow Craft, admonishing him, by its peculiar uses, of that vast level of time
on which all men are travelling, to its limit in eternity.

The level is also the jewel worn by the Senior Warden, as the
distinctive badge of his office, reminding him that while he presides over the labours of the lodge, as the Junior Warden does
over its refreshments, it is his duty to see that every brother

---

* Oliver's Landmarks, vol. p. 399.

† See the account of the union of the Dionysians with the Masons at the
Temple, in the article "Antiquity of Masonry," in this work.

meets upon the level, and that the principle of equality is preserved during the work, without which, harmony, the chief support of our institution, could not be preserved.

LEWIS, or LOUVETEAU. The words lewis and louve-
teau, which, in their original meanings, import two very different
things, have in masonry an equivalent signification—the former
being used in England, and the latter in France, to designate
the son of a mason.   .

The English word *lewis* is a term belonging to operative masonry, and signifies an iron cramp, which is inserted in a cavity
prepared for the purpose in any large stone, so as to give attachment to a pulley and hook, whereby the stone may be conveniently raised to any height, and deposited in its proper position.
In this country, the lewis has not been adopted as a symbol of
Freemasonry, but in the English ritual it is found among the
emblems placed upon the Tracing Board of the Entered Apprentice, and is used in that degree as a symbol of strength, because
by its assistance the operative mason is enabled to lift the heaviest
stones with a comparatively trifling exertion of physical power.
Extending the symbolic allusion still further, the son of a Mason
is in England called a *lewis*, because it is his duty to support the
sinking powers and aid the failing strength of his father, or, as
Oliver has expressed it, "to bear the burden and heat of the
day, that his parents may rest in their old age; thus rendering
the evening of their lives peaceful and happy."

By the constitutions of England, a lewis, or son of a Mason,
may be initiated at the age of eighteen, while it is required of
all other candidates that they shall have arrived at the maturer
age of twenty-one. The Book of Constitutions had prescribed
that no lodge should make "any man under the age of twenty-
one years, *unless by a dispensation* from the Grand Master or
his deputy." The Grand Lodge of England, in its modern regulations, has availed itself of the license allowed by this dis-

pensing power, to confer the right of an earlier initiation on the sons of Masons.

The word *louveteau*, signifies, in French, a young wolf. The application of the term to the son of a Mason, is derived from a peculiarity in some of the initiations into the ancient mysteries. In the mysteries of Isis, which were practised in Egypt, the candidate was made to wear the mask of a wolf's head. Hence, a wolf and a candidate in these mysteries were often used as synonymous terms. Macrobius, in his Saturnalia, says, in reference to this custom, that the ancients perceived a relationship between the sun, the great symbol in these mysteries, and a wolf, which the candidate represented at his initiation. For, he remarks, as the flocks of sheep and cattle fly and disperse at the sight of the wolf, so the flocks of stars disappear at the approach of the sun's light. The learned reader will also recollect that in the Greek language *lukos* signifies both the sun and a wolf.

Hence, as the candidate in the Isaic mysteries was called a wolf, the son of a Freemason in the French lodges is called a young wolf or a *louveteau*.

The louveteau in France, like the lewis in England, is invested with peculiar privileges. He also is permitted to unite himself with the order at the early age of eighteen years. The baptism of a louveteau is sometimes performed by the lodge, of which his father is a member, with impressive ceremonies. The infant, soon after birth, is taken to the lodge room, where he receives a masonic name, differing from that which he bears in the world; he is formally adopted by the lodge as one of its children, and should he become an orphan, requiring assistance, he is supported and educated by the fraternity, and finally established in life.

In this country these rights of a lewis or a louveteau are not recognised, and the very names were, until lately, scarcely known, except to a few masonic scholars.

LIBANUS. The Latin name of Lebanon, which see.

LIBATION. The libation was a very ancient ceremony, and among the Greeks and Romans constituted an essential part of every sacrifice. The material of the libation differed according to the different deities in honour of whom they were made, but wine was the most usual. Libations are still used in some of the higher degrees of masonry.

LIBERTINE. The man who lives without the restraint of conscience, licentiously violating the moral law, and paying no regard to the precepts of religion, is unworthy to become a member of that institution which boasts that its principles are intended to make all its members *good men and true;* and hence our Old Charges lay down a rule that " a Mason is obliged, by his tenure, to obey the moral law; and if he rightly understands the art, he will never be a stupid atheist nor an irreligious liber tine." The word "libertine" in this passage is used in its primitive signification of a freethinker or disbeliever in the truths of religion.

LIGHT. Light was the object, and its attainment the end, of all the ancient mysteries. In the Grecian system of initiation, the hierophant declared that all mankind, except the initiated, were in darkness. In the Persian rites, the *Divine Lights* were displayed before the aspirant at the moment of illumination, and he was instructed by the Archimagus, that, at the end of the world, the bad should be plunged with Ahriman into a state of perpetual darkness, while the good should ascend with Yazdan, upon a ladder, to a state of eternal light.* The Persians consecrated fire, as containing the principle of light, and the Druids worshipped the Sun as its eternal source.

Freemasons, too, travel in search of spiritual light, which can be found only in the East, from whence it springs, and having attained its possession, they are thenceforth called " the sons of light." But the light of masonry is pure, as emanating from

---

* Oliver, Signs and Symbols, p. 107.

the source of all purity and perfection; and Masons, remember-ing that they are brought out of darkness into light, are admon-ished to let the light which is in them so shine before all men, that their good works may be seen, and the great fountain of that light be glorified. See *Darkness.*

LILY. The white lily is one of the field-flowers of Judea, and is repeatedly alluded to in the Scriptures, as an emblem of purity. It occupied a conspicuous place among the ornaments of the temple furniture. The brim of the molten sea was wrought with flowers of lilies, the chapiters on the tops of the pillars at the porch, and the tops of the pillars themselves, were adorned with the same plant. Sir Robert Ker Porter, describing a piece of sculpture which he found at Persepolis, says, "Almost every one in this procession holds in his hand a figure like the lotos. This flower was full of meaning among the ancients, and occurs all over the East. Egypt, Persia, Palestine, and India, present it every where over their architecture, in the hands and on the heads of their sculptured figures, whether in statue or in bas relief. We also find it in the sacred vestments and architec-ture of the tabernacle and temple of the Israelites, and see it mentioned by our Saviour, as an image of peculiar beauty and glory, when comparing the works of nature with the decorations of art. It is also represented in all pictures of the salutation of Gabriel to the Virgin Mary; and, in fact, has been held in mys-terious veneration by people of all nations and times. 'It is the symbol of divinity, of purity, and abundance, and of a love most complete in perfection, charity, and benediction; as in Holy Scripture, that mirror of purity, Susanna is defined *Susa*, which signified the lily flower, the chief city of the Persians, bearing that name for excellency. Hence, the lily's three leaves in the arms of France, meaneth Piety, Justice, and Charity.' So far, the general impression of a peculiar regard to this beautiful and fragrant flower; but the early Persians attached to it a peculiar sanctity."

LINE. The line is a cord, to the end of which a piece of lead is attached, so that it may hang perpendicularly. The line is one of the working tools of a Past Master. Operative masons make use of the line to prove that their work is duly perpendicular, but by it the Past Master is taught the criterion of moral rectitude, to avoid dissimulation in conversation and action, and to direct his steps to the path which leads to a glorious immortality.

LINES PARALLEL. See *Parallel lines.*

LINGAM. See *Phallus.*

LION OF THE TRIBE OF JUDAH. See *Judah.*

LODGE. The room in which a regularly constituted body of Freemasons assemble, for the purposes connected with the institution, is called a lodge.* The term is also used to designate the collection of Masons thus assembled; just as we use the word "church" to signify the building in which a congregation of worshippers assembles, as well as the congregation itself.

Our English brethren, in their lectures, define a lodge to be "an assembly of Masons, just, perfect, and regular, who are met together to expatiate on the mysteries of the order; *just*, because it contains the volume of the sacred law, unfolded; *perfect*, from its numbers, every order of masonry being virtually present by its representatives, to ratify and confirm its proceedings; and *regular*, from its Warrant of Constitution, which implies the sanction of the Grand Master for the country where the lodge is held."

A lodge of Freemasons must be *legally constituted;* that is, it

---

* Ragon (Cours Philosophique) says that the word lodge is derived from the Sanscrit *loga*, which signifies the *world*. This is illustrated by our article on the *Form of the Lodge*.

must be in possession of a Charter or Warrant of Constitution, emanating from the Grand Lodge in whose jurisdiction it is situated. This warrant must also be in full force, for if it has been revoked or recalled by the Grand Lodge from which it emanated, the lodge ceases to be legally constituted, and all its proceedings are void. A body of Masons assembled to transact masonic business, without the authority of a warrant of constitution, or under a warrant whose authority has been revoked, is styled a "Clandestine Lodge," and its members are called "Clandestine Masons." In thus meeting, they are guilty of a high masonic misdemeanor, and become, by the very act itself, expelled from the order.

This restriction in respect to the constitution of a lodge did not always exist. Formerly any number of brethren* might assemble at any place for the performance of work, and when so assembled, were authorized to receive into the order, brothers and fellows, and to practice the rites of masonry. The ancient charges were the only standard for the regulation of their conduct. The Master of the lodge was elected *pro tempore*, and his authority terminated with the dissolution of the meeting over which he had presided, unless the lodge was permanently established at any particular place. To the general assembly of the craft, held once or twice a year, all the brethren indiscriminately were amenable, and to that power alone. But on the formation of Grand Lodges, this inherent right of assembling was voluntarily surrendered by the brethren and the lodges, and vested in the Grand Lodge. And from this time warrants of constitution date their existence.†

In addition to this charter or warrant of constitution, every well regulated lodge is also furnished with a Bible, square, and compasses, which by their symbolic signification enlighten the

---

* Our unwritten laws say that three must rule a lodge, five may hold a lodge, but only seven can make a lodge perfect.

† The first warrant granted by the Grand Lodge of England, after its organization in 1717, is dated 1718.

mind of the Mason and guide him in the path of his duty. A
lodge has also a peculiar form, support, and covering, and is supplied with furniture, ornaments, lights and jewels, all of which
afford means of symbolic instruction, and are explained in the third
section of the first lecture.

Officers.—A lodge of Ancient York Masons is composed of
the following officers. A Worshipful Master, a Senior and a
Junior Warden, Treasurer, Secretary, Senior and Junior Deacon,
and a Tiler. The latter is not necessarily a member of the lodge.
To these, some lodges add two Stewards, and sometimes a Chaplain. The Senior Deacon is always appointed by the Master, and
the Junior by the Senior Warden. The Stewards are generally
appointed by the Junior Warden. The Tiler is sometimes elected
by the lodge, and sometimes appointed by the Master. The rest
of the officers are always elected annually.

The officers in a lodge of the French rite are more numerous, some
corresponding, and others bearing no analogy to those in a York
lodge. They are as follows: Le Venerable or Worshipful Master,
Premier and Second Surveillants or Senior and Junior Wardens,
Orator, Treasurer, Secretary, Hospitaler or collector of alms, the
Expert, combining the duties of the Senior Deacon and an
examining committee, Master of Ceremonies, Architecte, who
attends to the decoration of the lodge, and superintends the finan-
cial department, Archiviste or Librarian, Keeper of the Seal,
Master of the Banquets or Steward, and Guardian of the Temple
or Tiler.

In lodges of the Scotch rite, there are, in addition to these, two
Deacons, a Standard Bearer, and a Sword Bearer.

In the rite of Misraim, the Wardens are called Assessors, and
the Deacons, Acolytes.

Symbolic Signification of the Lodge.—Symbolically a Mason's
lodge is a representation of the world. Its clouded canopy is an
emblem of those mansions of unutterable bliss, where the Grand
Master of the Universe forever reigns, whose all-seeing eye beholds, with unceasing complacency, the efforts of his creatures to

do his will. To that abode of the blessed the Mason it taught to aspire, while the path is indicated by the theological ladder, whose principal rounds are faith, hope, and charity. The Sun, the eternal fountain of light, the unwearied ruler of the day, shines in the lodge, a bright exponent of his Creator's power, while the Moon, the glorious orb of night, repeats the lesson of divine munificence. Here, too, are we taught, that the vast universe over which this Omnipotence presides, was no work of chance, but that its foundations are laid in wisdom, supported by strength, and adorned with beauty. And as the presence of the Almighty illuminates with refulgent splendour the most distant recesses of the universe, so is the lodge enlightened by the presence of his revealed will. And hence the Bible, as it is of all lights the most pure, is to the Mason the most indispensable. And, finally, as this world, vast in its extent and complicated in its motions, is governed and regulated with unceasing concord and harmony, so is the lodge controlled and directed by the same spirits of peace, which, emanating in brotherly love, relief, and truth, find their full fruition in universal charity.

The *lodge*, technically speaking, is a piece of furniture made in imitation of the Ark of the Covenant, which was constructed by Bazaleel, according to the form prescribed by God himself, and which, after the erection of the Temple, was kept in the Holy of Holies. As it contained the table of the laws, the *lodge* contains the Book of Constitutions and the warrant of constitution granted by the Grand Lodge.

LODGE ROOM. The Masons on the continent of Europe have a prescribed form or ritual of building, according to whose directions it is absolutely necessary that every hall for masonic purposes shall be erected. No such regulation exists among the fraternity of this country or Great Britain. Still the usages of the craft, and the objects of convenience in the administration of our rites, require that certain general rules should be followed in the construction of a lodge room.   These rules relate to its position, its form, and its decorations.

A lodge room should always, if possible, be situated due east and west. This position is not absolutely necessary, and yet it is so far so as to demand that some sacrifices should be made, if possible, to obtain so desirable a position. It should also be isolated, where it is practicable, from all surrounding buildings, and should always be placed in an upper story. No lodge should ever be held on the ground floor.

The form of a lodge room should be that of a parallelogram or oblong square, at least one-third larger from east to west than it is from north to south. The ceiling should be lofty, to give dignity to the appearance of the hall, as well as for the purposes of health, by compensating, in some degree, for the inconvenience of closed windows, which necessarily will deteriorate the quality of the air in a very short time in a low room. The approaches to the lodge room, from without should be angular, for, as Oliver says, "A straight entrance is unmasonic, and cannot be tolerated."* There should be two entrances to the room, which should be situated in the west, and on each side of the Senior Warden's station. The one on his right hand is for the introduction of visitors and members, and leading from the Tiler's room, is called the Tiler's, or the outer door; the other, on his left, leading from the preparation room, is known as the "inner door," and sometimes called the "northwest door." The situation of these two doors, as well as the rooms with which they are connected, and which are essentially necessary in a well-constructed lodge room, may be seen from the diagram in the following page, which also exhibits the seats of the officers and the arrangement of the altar and lights.

The whole of the east end of the lodge should be elevated from the floor by a platform running across the room, and ascended by three steps. The windows should be either in the roof of the building, or at least very high from the floor. The

* Book of the Lodge, p. 47.

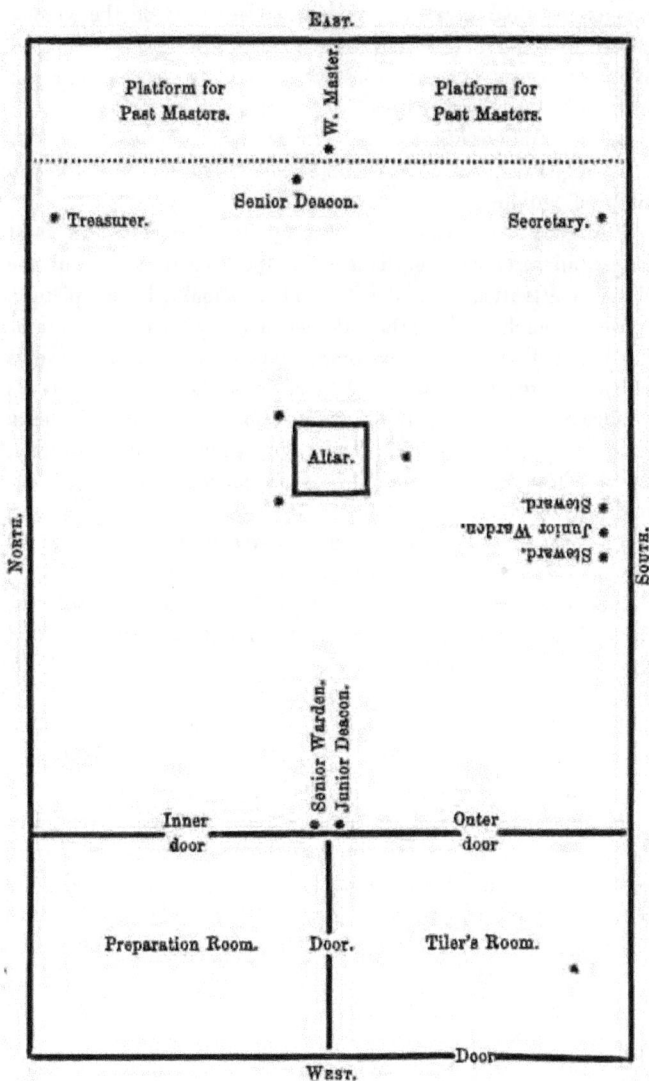

Helvetian ritual prescribes that the lower part of the window should be seven and a half feet from the surface of the floor. By these means our mysteries are adequately secured from the profanation of "prying eyes."

The decorations of a lodge should be altogether masonic. The following directions on this subject are given in the Helvetian ritual of building:

"A good lodge may be known by its ornaments. In most lodges, all sorts of decorations are heaped together, without the slightest attention to propriety. There should be no picture, statue or emblem of heathen deities, nor any bust or picture of heathen philosophers. The proper images or emblems are to be taken from the Bible, which alone contains the authentic records of ancient masonry. The decorations should be masonic emblems, intersecting triangles, the triple tau, square and compasses, death's head, &c.; these, if properly managed, can be made highly ornamental."

The floor of the lodge should be covered with a carpet or oil cloth, made of a Mosaic pattern; and the ceiling, if painted, should represent the "clouded canopy." The curtains, cushions, &c., of a symbolic lodge, should be of light or sky blue, and those of a chapter room scarlet.

LOGIC. The art of reasoning, and one of the seven liberal arts and sciences, whose uses are inculcated in the second degree. The power of right reasoning, which distinguishes the man of sane mind from the madman and the idiot, is deemed essential to the Mason, that he may comprehend both his rights and his duties. And hence the unfortunate beings just named, who are without this necessary mental quality, are denied admission into the order.

LOUVETEAU. See *Lewis*.

LOWEN. An old word, signifying, most probably, a disreputable person. Webster defines *lown*, which seems to be the same word, without the old Saxon termination *en*, "a low fellow," The word is found in the "Ancient Charges at the constituting of a Lodge," belonging to the Lodge of Antiquity, London. "Twelvethly, That a Master or Fellow make not a mould stone, square, nor rule, to no *lowen*, nor let no *lowen* worke within their lodge, nor without to mould stone."

LUSTRATION. A purification by water. This was an indispensable pre-requisite to initiation into all the ancient mysteries. The lustration in Freemasonry is mental. No aspirant can be admitted to participate in our sacred rites until he is thoroughly cleansed from all pollution of guilt. In some of the higher degrees of the Ancient and Accepted rite a lustration or ablution is practised.

LUX. *Light.* Freemasonry anciently received, among other names, that of "Lux," because it is to be regarded as the doctrine of Truth, and in this sense may be said to be coeval with creation, as an emanation from the Divine Intelligence. Among the Rosicrucians, light was the knowledge of the philosopher's stone, and Mosheim says that in chemical language the cross $+$ was an emblem of light, because it contains within its figure the forms of the three letters, of which LVX or light is composed

LUX E TENEBRIS. *Light out of darkness.* A masonic motto, expressive of the object of masonry, and of what the true Mason supposes himself to have attained.

M.

MAACHA. In the 10th degree of the Scotch Rite we are informed that certain traitors fled to " Maacha king of Cheth," by whom they were delivered up to King Solomon on his sending for them. In 1 Kings ii. 39, we find it recorded that two of the servants of Shimei fled from Jerusalem to "Achish, son of Maacha king of Gath." I am inclined to believe from this passage, that the carelessness of the early copyists of the ritual led to the double error of putting *Cheth* for *Gath* and of supposing that Maacha was its king instead of its king's father. The manuscripts of the Scotch or Ancient and Accepted rite, too often copied by unlearned persons, show many such corruptions of Hebrew names, which modern researches must eventually correct.

MAC. A Hebrew word which is said to signify "is smitten," from the verb נכה *nacha* to smite. This is not however a pure derivation. It may be the word מק *mak*, " rottenness," and in its appropriate place would then signify "*there is rotteness*," or "*he is rotten.*"

MAH. The Hebrew interrogative pronoun מה signifying "*what?*"

MAHER–SHALAL–HASH–BAZ. Four Hebrew words which the prophet Isaiah was ordered to write upon a tablet, and which were afterwards to be the name of his son. They signify, "make haste to the prey, fall upon the spoil," and were prognostic of the sudden attack of the Assyrians. They may be said, in their masonic use, to be symbolic of the readiness for action which should distinguish a warrior.

MAKE. "To make Masons" is a very ancient term, used

in the oldest charges extant, as synonymous with the verb
"initiate."

MALLET. One of the working tools of a Mark Master,
having the same emblematic meaning as the common gavel in
the Entered Apprentice's degree. It teaches us to correct the
irregularities of temper, and, like enlightened reason, to curb
the aspirations of unbridled ambition, to depress the malignity
of envy, and to moderate the ebullition of anger. It relieves
the mind from all the excrescences of vice, and fits it, as a well
wrought stone, for that exalted station in the great temple of
nature, to which, as an emanation of the Deity, it is entitled.

The mallet or setting maul is also an emblem of the third
degree, and is said to have been the implement by which the
stones were set up at the temple. It is often improperly confounded with the common gavel.

MANUAL. Belonging to the hand, from the Latin *manus*,
a hand. Masons are, in a peculiar manner, reminded by the
hand, of the necessity of a prudent and careful observance of
all their pledges and duties, and hence this organ suggests
certain symbolic instructions in relation to the virtue of prudence.

MARK. It is a plate of gold or silver, worn by Mark
Masters. The form is generally that of a Mark Master's key-
stone, within the circular inscription there being engraved a
device, selected by the owner. This mark, on being adopted by
a Mark Master, is recorded in the Book of Marks, and it is not
lawful for him ever afterwards to exchange it for any other.
It is a peculiar pledge of friendship, and its presentation by a
destitute brother to another Mark Master, claims from the latter
certain offices of friendship and hospitality, which are of solemn
obligation among the brethren of this degree.

Marks or pledges of this kind were of frequent use among

the ancients, under the name of *tessera hospitalis* and "arrhabo." The nature of the *tessera hospitalis*, or, as the Greeks
called it, συμβολον, cannot be better described than in the words
of the Scholiast on the Media of Euripides, v. 613, where Jason
promises Medea, on her parting from him, to send her the symbols of hospitality which should procure her a kind reception in
foreign countries. It was the custom, says the Scholiast, when a
guest had been entertained, to break a die in two parts, one of
which parts was retained by the guest, so that if, at any future
period he required assistance, on exhibiting the broken pieces of
the die to each other, the friendship was renewed. Plautus, in
one of his comedies, gives us an exemplification of the manner
in which these *tesseræ* or pledges of friendship were used at
Rome, whence it appears that the privileges of this friendship
were extended to the descendants of the contracting parties.
Pœnulus is introduced, inquiring for Agorastocles, with whose
family he had formerly exchanged the tessera.

"*Ag.* Antidimarchus' adopted son,
If you do seek, I am the very man.
    Pœn. How! do I hear aright?
    Ag. I am the son
Of old Antidamus.
    Pœn. If so, I pray you
Compare with me the hospitable die.
I've brought this with me.
    Ag. Prithee, let me see it.
It is, indeed, the very counterpart
Of mine at home.
    Pœn. All hail, my welcome guest,
Your father was my guest, Antidamus.
Your father was my honoured guest, and then
This hospitable die with me he parted."*

---

* *Ag.* Siquidem Antidimarchi quæris adoptatitium.
Ego sum ipsus quem tu quæris.
    Pœn. Hem! quid ego audio?

These tesseræ, thus used, like the Mark Master's mark, for
the purposes of perpetuating friendship and rendering its union
more sacred, were constructed in the following manner: they took
a small piece of bone, ivory or stone, generally of a square or
cubical form, and dividing it into equal parts, each wrote his own
name, or some other inscription, upon one of the pieces; they
then made a mutual exchange, and, lest falling into other hands
it should give occasion to imposture, the pledge was preserved
with the greatest secrecy, and no one knew the name inscribed
upon it except the possessor.

The primitive Christians seem to have adopted a similar practice, and the tessera was carried by them in their travels, as a
means of introduction to their fellow Christians. A favourite inscription with them were the letters Π. Υ. Α. Π., being the initials
of Πατηρ, Υιος, Αγιον Πνευμα, or Father, Son, and Holy Ghost.
The use of these tesseræ, in the place of written certificates, continued, says Dr. Harris, until the 11th century, at which time
they are mentioned by Burchardus, Archbishop of Worms, in a
visitation charge.*

The arrhabo was a similar keepsake, formed by breaking a
piece of money in two. The etymology of this word shows distinctly that the Romans borrowed the custom of these pledges
from the ancient Israelites. For it is derived from the Hebrew
arabon, a pledge.

With this detail of the customs of the ancients before us, we
can easily explain the well-known passage in Revelation, ii. 17.
" To him that overcometh will I give a white stone, and in it a

---

Ag. Antidamæ me gnatum esse.
Pœn. Si ita est, tesseram
Conferre si vis hospitalem, eccam, attuli.
    Ag. Agedum huc ostende; est per probe; nam habeo domum.
    Pœn. O mi hospes, salve multum; nam mihi tuus pater,
Pater tuus ergo hospes, Antidamas fuit:
Hæc mihi hospitalis tessera cum illo fuit.
Pœnul. act. v., s. c. 2, ver. 85.
* Harris, Diss. on the Tess. Hospit., ¿ vi.

new name written, which no man knoweth saving he that re-
ceiveth it." That is, to borrow the interpretation of Harris,
"To him that overcometh will I give a pledge of my affection,
which shall constitute him my friend, and entitle him to privileges and honours, of which none else can know the value or the
extent.*

MARK MAN. According to masonic tradition, the Mark
Men were the Wardens, as the Mark Masters were the Masters
of the Fellow Craft lodges,† at the building of the Temple.
They distributed the marks to the workmen, and made the first
inspection of the work, which was afterwards to be approved
by the overseers. As a degree, the Mark Man is not recognised
in America, and I am not aware that it is worked as such in
England, although Carlyle gives us its ritual. Oliver, at least,
mentions it only incidentally in his chronological catalogue.

MARK MASTER. The 4th degree in the York rite. We
are told in Holy Writ, that Solomon employed not less than
113,600 craftsmen in the construction of the Temple. To control this vast multitude of workmen, to inspect their work with
accuracy, and to pay their wages with punctuality and correctness, so that harmony might continue to exist among all, must
have required a judicious system of government, in which every
avenue to imposition was guarded with unceasing vigilance, and
the very best means adopted of rewarding the industrious, and
of discovering and punishing the idle. With such a system
alone was it possible to construct an edifice of the size of Solomon's Temple in but little more than seven years, while the
Temple of Diana, at Ephesus, in every respect inferior to it, oc-

---

* Harris, Diss. on the Tess. Hospit., § vii
† Only those working in the quarries were, I suppose, thus governed. The
Fellow Crafts on Mount Lebanon were differently arranged. This is, however,
all supposition, though a different theory would be incongruous with the history
of the Mark degree.

cupied the amazing period of two hundred and twenty years in building. This system of government, Mark Masters assert, is preserved in their degree, and its historical ceremonies consist principally in a recapitulation of the manner in which this work was conducted, exemplifying, by the relation of an event which is said to have occurred, the necessity of circumspection on the one part, and of honest industry on the other. The degree also inculcates the virtue of charity, and draws still closer the bonds of mutual friendship, which unite us into one common brotherhood of love.

In this country, the Mark Master's is the first degree given in a Royal Arch Chapter. Its officers are a Right Worshipful Master, Senior and Junior Wardens, Secretary, Treasurer, Senior and Junior Deacons, Master, Senior and Junior Overseers. The degree cannot be conferred when less than six are present, who, in that case, must be the first and last three officers above named. The working tools are the Mallet and indenting Chisel, (which see.)

Until lately the degree was not given in England, and Royal Arch Masons, arriving from that country, were obliged to be marked, before they could be permitted to enter the American chapters. Uniformity is, however, now beginning to prevail, as Mark Masonry is practised in many of the English lodges or chapters, although it is rather by the tolerance than the sanction of the Grand Lodge. Mark Masters' lodges were formerly sometimes organized independently of chapters, deriving their warrants directly from a Grand Chapter. But such lodges have lately been forbidden by the revised constitution of the General Grand Chapter of the United States, and no longer exist in the States which acknowledge the supremacy of that body.

MARK OF THE CRAFT. Masonic tradition informs us that, at the building of King Solomon's temple, every Mason was provided with a peculiar mark, which he placed upon his work, to distinguish it from that of his fellows. By the aid of these marks the overseers were enabled, without difficulty, to trace any piece of defective work to the faulty workman, and every chance of imposition, among so large an assemblage of craftsmen as were engaged at the Temple, was thus effectually prevented.

History confirms the truth of this tradition, because it clearly shows that a similar usage has always existed among operative Masons. These marks have been found at Spire, Worms, Strasburg, Rheims, Basle, and other places; and M. Didron, who reported a series of observations,* on the subject of these Masons' marks, to the *Comité Historique des Arts et Monumens*, of Paris, believes that he can discover in them references to distinct schools or lodges of Masons. He divides them into two classes: those of the overseers and those of the men who worked the stones. The marks of the first class consist of monogrammatic characters; those of the second, are of the nature of symbols, such as shoes, trowels, mallets, &c.

A correspondent of the Freemason's Quarterly Review states that similar marks are to be found on the stones which compose the walls of the fortress of Allahabad, which was erected in 1542, in the East Indies. "The walls," says this writer, "are composed of large oblong blocks of red granite, and are almost every where covered by masonic emblems, which evince something more than mere ornament. They are not confined to one particular spot, but are scattered over the walls of the fortress, in many places as high as thirty or forty feet from the ground. It is quite certain that thousands of stones on the walls, bearing these masonic symbols, were carved, marked, and numbered in the quarry, previous to the erection of the building."

In the ancient buildings of England and France, these marks are to be found in great abundance. In a communication, on this subject, to the London Society of Antiquaries, Mr. Godwin states, "that, in his opinion, these marks, if collected and com-

---

* Quoted by Godwin, in the Archæological Transactions, and by Oliver, in his Historical Landmarks.

pared, might assist in connecting the various bands of operatives, who, under the protection of the church—mystically united—spread themselves over Europe during the Middle Ages, and are known as Freemasons."* Mr. Godwin describes these marks, as varying in length from two to seven inches, and as formed by a single line, slightly indented, consisting chiefly of crosses, known masonic symbols, emblems of the Trinity and of eternity, the double triangle, trowel, square, &c.

The same writer observes that, in a conversation, in September, 1844, with a Mason at work on the Canterbury Cathedral, he "found that many Masons (all who were Freemasons) had their mystic marks handed down from generation to generation; this man had his mark from his father, and he received it from his grandfather."†

MARSHAL. An officer common to several masonic bodies, whose duty is to regulate processions and other public solemnities

MARTINISM. A rite or modification of masonry, instituted at Lyons, in France, towards the end of the last century, by the Marquis de St. Martin. St. Martin was a disciple of Paschalis, the rite established by whom, in 1754, he attempted to reform.‡ The degrees in Martin's rite were ten, divided into two classes or temples. The first temple comprised the degrees of Apprentice, Fellow Craft, Master, Ancient Master, Elect, Grand Architect,

---

* The Travelling Freemasons, who are described in this work under that title.

† I refer the masonic student, who desires still further to investigate this interesting subject, to the 15th Lecture of Bro. Oliver's Historical Landmarks; a work to which I have been deeply indebted in the course of my masonic studies. Godwin has also written learnedly on this topic, in various articles in the Archæological Transactions, the Builder, and other periodicals. One of his articles I have caused to be re-published in the Southern and Western Masonic Miscellany, vol. ii. No. 12.

‡ See the word Paschalis.

and Master of the Secret. The degrees of the second temple were Prince of Jerusalem, Knight of Palestine, and Knight Kadosh. Martinism extended from Lyons into the principal cities of France, Germany, and even Russia.*

MASON, DERIVATION OF. The etymology of the words mason and masonry have afforded masonic writers an ample opportunity of exhibiting their research and ingenuity. Some have derived them from the Persian Magi, or disciples of Zoroaster; while Hutchinson offers the conjecture, that they are corrupted from the Greek Μυστηριον, a mystery, and Μυστης, one initiated into the ancient mysteries. He seems, too, to think that *Mason* may probably come from *Μαω Σοον, I seek what is safe,* and *masonry* from *Μεσουρανεω, I am in the midst of heaven,* or from the Hebrew Greek *Μαζουραθ,* one of the constellations of the zodiac. A writer in the European Magazine, for February, 1792, who signs himself George Drake, attributing to masonry a Druidical origin, derives Mason from what he calls *may's on,* or the men of May, *on* being *men* as in the French *on dit,* and *may's on* are, therefore, the Druids, whose principal celebrations were in the month of May. Lastly, we may add, as a curious coincidence, at least, that the Hebrew מסע, *massang* or *masan,* signifies a stone quarry. All these suggestions, however, seem to me to be more fanciful than true; it is more probable that the word must be taken in its ordinary signification of a worker in stone, and thus it indicates the origin of the order from a society of practical artificers.

MASONRY. Masonry is of two kinds, operative and speculative. Operative masonry is engaged in the construction of material edifices, by means of stone and marble; speculative masonry is occupied in the erection of a spiritual temple, by means of symbolic instruction. The latter, which is also called Freemasonry, adopts and symbolizes, for its sacred purpose, the im-

---

* Clavel, Hist. Pitt., p. 170.

plements and materials which are used in the former. Hence
operative masonry is an art, and speculative, a science; and while
the objects of the one are profane and temporal, those of the other
are sacred and eternal.

MASON'S DAUGHTER. This is an androgynous degree,
invented in the Western States, and given to Master Masons,
their wives, and unmarried sisters and daughters. It refers to
circumstances recorded in the xi. and xii. chapters of the Gospel
of St. John.

MASTER AD VITAM. Another name for the degree of
Grand Master of all symbolic lodges, which see.

MASTER, GRAND. See *Grand Master*.

MASTER IN ISRAEL. See *Intendant of the Building*.

MASTER MASON. The third degree in all the different
rites. In this, which is the perfection of symbolic or ancient
craft masonry, the purest of truths are unveiled amid the most
awful ceremonies. None but he who has visited the holy of
holies, and travelled the *road of peril*, can have any conception
of the mysteries unfolded in this degree. Its solemn observances
diffuse a sacred awe, and inculcate a lesson of religious truth—
and it is not until the neophyte has reached this summit of our
ritual, that he can exclaim with joyful accents, in the language
of the sage of old, "*Eureka, Eureka*," I have found at last the
long-sought treasure. In the language of the learned and zealous
Hutchinson, somewhat enlarged in its allusion, "the Master Mason
represents a man under the doctrine of love, saved from the grave
of iniquity, and raised to the faith of salvation. It testifies our
faith in the resurrection of the body, and, while it inculcates a
practical lesson of prudence and unshrinking fidelity, it inspires .

the most cheering hope of that final reward which belongs alone
to the "just made perfect."

This was the last and highest of the three degrees in existence
at the construction of the first temple, and it is, therefore, called
"the perfection of ancient craft masonry." From the sublimity
of the truths developed in it, and from the solemn nature of the
ceremonies, it has received the appellation of the "sublime degree." From this degree alone can the officers of a lodge be
chosen; and, though Fellow Crafts are permitted to speak, the
privilege of voting is confined to Master Masons.

MASTER OF A LODGE. The presiding officer, in a blue
or symbolic lodge, is called "the Worshipful Master." In the
French lodges, he is styled "*Le Vénérable*," when the lodge is
opened in the first or second degree, and "*Le très Vénérable*,"
when in the third. The power of a Master in his lodge is absolute.
He is the supreme arbiter of all questions of order, so far as the
meeting is concerned, nor can any appeal be made from his decision to that of the lodge. He is amenable for his conduct to
the Grand Lodge alone, and to that body must every complaint
against him be made. For no misdemeanor, however great, can
he be tried by his lodge, for, as no one has a right to preside there
in his presence except himself, it would be absurd to suppose that
he could sit as the judge in his own case. This is the decision
that has been made on the subject by every Grand Lodge in the
United States which has entertained the question, and it may be
now considered as a settled law of masonry. He is elected annually, but must have previously presided as a Warden, except
in the case of a newly constituted lodge, or where every Past Master and Warden, as well as the present Master, have refused to
serve, or have died, resigned, or been expelled. He is, with his
Wardens, the representative of his lodge in the Grand Lodge,
and is there bound to speak, act, or vote, as the lodge shall, by
resolution, direct him. The right of instruction forms a part of
our ancient regulations. He is to be treated with the utmost re-

verence and respect while in the chair, and his commands must
be implicitly obeyed. The ancient charges on this subject are explicit. "You are not to hold private committees, or separate conversation, without leave from the Master, nor to talk of any thing
impertinent or unseemly, nor interrupt the Master; * * * * * but
to pay due reverence to your Master, Wardens and Fellows, and
put them to worship."—*Ancient Charges*, § vi. 1.

The jewels and furniture of the lodge are placed under the
care of the Master, he being responsible to the lodge for their
safe custody. It is his duty to see that the landmarks of the
order be not infringed, that the regulations of the Grand Lodge
and the by-laws of his own lodge be strictly enforced, that all his
officers faithfully perform their duties, and that no ineligible candidate be admitted. He has the right of congregating his lodge
whenever he thinks proper, and of closing it at any time that in
his judgment may seem best.

With respect to the removal of the lodge, the Master possesses
peculiar privileges according to the regulations of the Grand
Lodge of England, adopted in 1735. By these no motion for
removal of the lodge can be made during the absence of the Master. But this is a merely local regulation, and does not appear,
generally, to have been adopted by the fraternity in America.

Lastly, the Master has particularly the charge of the warrant
of constitution, and is empowered to select his Senior Deacon from
among the Master Masons of the lodge.

The jewel of the Master is a square; because, as the square is
employed by operative Masons to fit and adjust the stones of a
building, so that all the parts shall properly agree, so the Master
of the lodge is admonished, by the symbolic meaning of the
square upon his breast, to preserve that moral deportment among
the members, which should ever characterize good Masons, so
that no ill-feeling or angry discussions may arise to impair the
harmony of the meeting.

I cannot better close this article than with the following extract from the writings of Dr. Oliver, in relation to the qualifi-

cations of a Master of a lodge. "I am decidedly of opinion that much general knowledge is necessary to expand the mind, and familiarize it with masonic discussions and illustrations, before a brother can be pronounced competent to undertake the arduous duty of governing a lodge. A Master of the work ought to have nothing to learn. He should be fully qualified, not only to instruct the younger brethren, but to resolve the doubts of those who are more advanced in masonic knowledge; to reconcile apparent contradictions; to settle chronologies, and to elucidate obscure facts or mystic legends, as well as to answer the objections and to render pointless the ridicule of our uninitiated adversaries."*

MASTER OF CAVALRY. An officer in a Council of Knights of the Red Cross, whose duties are, in some respects, similar to those of a Junior Deacon in a symbolic lodge.

MASTER OF CEREMONIES. An officer found in many of the lodges of England, and in all of those of the Continent. His duties are principally those of a conductor of the candidate. The office is not recognised in the York ritual as practised in this country, though I think it is to be found in some of the lodges of New York, and perhaps occasionally elsewhere.

MASTER OF DISPATCHES. The Secretary of a Council of Knights of the Red Cross.

MASTER OF FINANCES. The Treasurer of a Council of Knights of the Red Cross.

MASTER OF INFANTRY. An officer in a Council of Knights of the Red Cross, whose duties are, in some respects, similar to those of a Senior Deacon in a symbolic lodge.

---

* Hist. of Initiation, Pref., p. x.

MASTER OF THE PALACE. An officer in a Council of Knights of the Red Cross, whose duties are peculiar to the degree.

MEDITERRANEAN PASS. A side degree, sometimes conferred in this country on Royal Arch Masons. It has no lecture or legend.

MEETINGS OF A LODGE. The meetings of lodges are regular, and extra or emergent. Regular meetings are held under the provision of the by-laws, but extra meetings are called by the order of the Worshipful Master. It is one of the ancient laws, that no extra meeting can alter, amend, or expunge the proceedings of a regular meeting. The meetings of lodges are termed "communications," and this word should always be used in the minutes, summonses, and other masonic documents.

MELCHISEDEK. King of Salem, and a Priest of the Most High God, of whom all that we know is to be found in the passages of Scripture read at the conferring of the degree of High Priesthood. Some theologians have supposed him to have been Shem, the son of Noah.

MELITA. The ancient name of the island of Malta.

MEMPHIS, RITE OF. A Masonic rite, established at Paris, in 1839, by J. A. Marconis and E. N. Mouttet. It afterwards extended to Brussels and Marseilles. It was composed of ninety-one degrees, and is said to have been a modification of the rite of Misriam. Its existence has been ephemeral, for it is now extinct.

MENATZCHIM. The overseers at the building of the Temple, amounting to 3300. See 1 Kings v. 15, and 2 Chron. ii. 18.

MIDDLE CHAMBER. The middle chamber is thus described in the 1st book of Kings. "And against the wall of the house he built chambers round about, against the walls of the house round about, both of the temple and of the oracle: and he made chambers round about: the nethermost chamber was five cubits broad, and the middle was six cubits broad, and the third was seven cubits broad: for without in the wall of the house he made narrowed rests round about, that the beams should not be fastened in the walls of the house. The door for the *middle chamber* was in the right side of the house: and they went up with *winding stairs* into the middle chamber, and out of the middle into the third."—1 *Kings*, vi. 5, 6, 8.

These chambers, after the temple was completed, served for the accommodation of the priests when upon duty; in them they deposited their vestments and the sacred vessels. But the knowledge of the purpose to which the middle chamber was appropriated, while the temple was in the course of construction, is only preserved in masonic tradition.

MINUTES. The minutes of the proceedings of the lodge should always be read just before closing, that any alterations or amendments may be proposed by the brethren; and again immediately after opening at the next communication, that they may be confirmed. But the minutes of a regular communication are not to be read at a succeeding extra one, because, as the proceedings of a regular communication cannot be discussed at an extra, it would be unnecessary to read them; for, if incorrect, they could not be amended until the next regular communication.

MISRAIM, RITE OF. This rite was composed, in 1805,*

---

* Oliver says it was founded in 1782, but I think he confounds the Egyptian masonry, of Cagliostro, with the rite of Misraim. Clavel is my authority for the date.

by several Masons who had been refused admission into the
Supreme Council of the Scotch rite, which had been organized
during that year, at Milan. In 1814, it was established in
France, and, in the following year, the lodge of *"Arc-en-ciel"*
was constituted at Paris. Unsuccessful attempts were made to
extend this rite, during the succeeding years, to Belgium, Sweden, and Switzerland; and, in 1820, it was carried over to Ireland, where it is said still to exist, but in a languishing condition. At present but three lodges at Paris acknowledge this
rite, whose *"Puissance Suprême,"* or centre of government, is
placed in that city. The Grand Orient of France has never
recognised this rite as a part of masonry. The rite of Misriam,
or, as it is sometimes called, the rite of Egypt, consists of 90
degrees, divided into 4 series and 17 classes. Some of these
degrees are entirely original, but many of them are borrowed
from the Scotch rite.

For the gratification of the curious inspector, the following list
of these degrees is subjoined. The titles are translated as literally as possible from the French.

I. SERIES—SYMBOLIC.

1st Class: 1, Apprentice; 2, Fellow Craft; 3, Master. *2d
Class:* 4, Secret Master; 5, Perfect Master; 6, Master through
Curiosity; 7, Master in Israel; 8, English Master. *3d Class:*
9, Elect of Nine; 10, Elect of the Unknown; 11, Elect of
Fifteen; 12, Perfect Elect; 13, Illustrious Elect. *4th Class:*
14, Scotch Trinitarian; 15, Scotch Fellow Craft; 16, Scotch
Master; 17, Scotch panisière; 18, Master of the Scottish rite;
19, Elect of three; Scotch Master of the sacred vault of James
VI.; 21, Scotch Master of St. Andrew. *5th Class:* 22, Archi-
tect; 23, Grand Architect; 24, Architecture; 25, Apprentice
Perfect Architect; 26, Fellow Craft Perfect Architect; 27,
Master Perfect Architect; 28, Perfect Architect; 29, Sublime
Scotch Master; 30, Sublime Scotch Master of Heroden. *6th*

Class: 31, Royal Arch; 32, Grand Axe; 33, Sublime Knight of Election, Chief of the 1st Series.

II. SERIES—PHILOSOPHIC.

7th Class: 34, Knight of the Sublime Election; 35, Prussian Knight; 36, Knight of the Temple; 37, Knight of the Eagle; 38, Knight of the Black Eagle; 39, Knight of the Red Eagle; 40, White Knight of the East; 41, Knight of the East. *8th Class:* 42, Commander of the East; 43, Grand Commander of the East; 44, Architect of the Sovereign Commanders of the Temple; 45, Prince of Jerusalem. *9th Class:* 46, Sovereign Prince Rose Croix of Kilwinning and Heroden; 47, Knight of the West; 48, Sublime Philosophy; 49, Chaos the first, discreet; 50, Chaos the second, wise; 51, Knight of the Sun. *10th Class:* 52, Supreme Commander of the Stars; 53, Sublime Philosopher; 54, First degree of the Key of Masonry, Minor; 55, Second degree, Washer; 56, Third degree, Bellows-blower; 57, Fourth degree, Caster; 58, Freemason Adept; 59, Sovereign Elect; 60, Sovereign of Sovereigns; 61, Master of Lodges; 62, Most High and Most Powerful; 63, Knight of Palestine; 64, Knight of the White Eagle; 65, Grand Elect Knight K———H; 66, Grand Inquiring Commander, Chief of the 2d Series.

III. SERIES—MYSTICAL.

11th Class: 67, Benevolent Knight; 68, Knight of the Rainbow; 69, Knight of B. or Hhanuka, called Hynaroth; 70, Most wise Israelitish prince; *12th Class:* 71, Sovereign Prince Talmudim; 72, Sovereign Prince Zadkim; 73, Grand Haram. *13th Class:* 74, Sovereign Grand Prince Haram; 75, Sovereign Prince Hassidim. *14th Class:* 76, Sovereign Grand Prince Hasidim; 77, Grand Inspector Intendant, Regulator-General of the Order, Chief of the 3d Series.

IV. SERIES—CABALISTIC.

15th and *16th Classes:* 78, 79, 80, 81, 82, 83, 84, 85, 86, degrees whose names are concealed from all but the possessors. *17th Class:* 87, Sovereign Grand Princes, constituted Grand

Masters, and legitimate representatives of the order for the First Series; 88, Ditto for the Second Series; 89, Ditto for the Third Series; 90, Absolute Sovereign Grand Master, Supreme Power of the Order, and Chief of the 4th Series.

The chiefs of this rite claim the privilege, which, of course, has never been conceded to them, of directing and controlling all the other rites of Freemasonry, as their common source. From an examination of a part of its ritual, and the perusal of some of its official publications, I am inclined to believe the assertion of its friends, who claim for it an eminently philosophical character. The organization of the rite is, however, too complicated and diffuse to have ever been practically convenient. Many of its degrees were founded upon, or borrowed from, the Egyptian rites, and its ritual is said to be a very close imitation of the ancient system of initiation.

The legend of the third degree in this rite is abolished. HAB is said to have returned to his family, after the completion of the Temple, and to have passed the remainder of his days in peace and opulence. The legend, substituted by the rite of Misraim for that admitted by all the other rites, is carried back to the days of Lamech, whose son Jubal, under the name of Hario-Jubal-Abi, is reported to have been slain by three traitors, Hagava, Hakina, and Haremda.*

MITHRAS, MYSTERIES OF. The mysteries of Mithras were celebrated in Persia. They were instituted by Zeradusht, or Zoroaster, an Eastern sage, concerning whose era the learned are unable to agree, some placing it in the reign of Darius Hystaspes, and others contending that he lived centuries before the reign of that monarch. Zoroaster reformed the doctrines of the Magi, and established a theology which was adopted as the religion of the Persians, Chaldeans, Parthians, Medes, and other

---

* See a singular work, published in 1835, at Paris, by Marc Bedarride, one of the chiefs of the rite, under the title of "*De l'Ordre Maconnique de Misraim*," pp. 25 and 118.

neighbouring nations. According to the Zend Avesta, the sacred book in which these doctrines are contained, the Supreme Being, whose name signifies "Time without bounds," created *Light* in the beginning; out of this light proceeded Ormuzd, or the principle of light, who, by his omnific word, created the world. He produced also the superior genii, Amshaspands, who surround his throne, as the messengers of his will, and the inferior genii, Izeds, who are the guardian angels of the world, and whose chief is Mithras. The Supreme Being also created Ahriman, the principle of darkness, and the Dives, or evil genii under him. These are incessantly at war with Ormuzd, endeavouring to corrupt the virtue and destroy the happiness of the human race. But their efforts, the Zend Avesta declares, are vain; for, assisted by the Izeds, the triumph of the good principle has been resolved in the secret decrees of the Supreme Being.

Mithras resided in the sun, and hence that luminary was worshipped as the abode of the God of Light. He was represented as a young man covered with a Phrygian turban, and clothed in a mantle and tunic. He presses with his knee upon a bull, one of whose horns he holds in his right hand, while with the right he plunges a dagger into his neck. This was an evident allusion to the power of the sun when he is in the zodiacal sign of Taurus. In Persia, the mysteries of Mithras were celebrated at the winter solstice; in Rome, where they were introduced in the time of Pompey, at the vernal equinox.

They were divided into seven degrees, and the initiation consisted of the most rigorous trials, sometimes even terminating in the death of the aspirant. No one, says Gregory Nazianzen, could be initiated into the mysteries of Mithras, unless he had passed through all the trials, and proved himself passionless and pure.* The aspirant at first underwent the purifications by

---

* Orat. Cont. Julian. Appropriately does he call these trials κοyαστις, or *punishments.*

water, by fire, and by fasting; after which he was introduced into
a cavern representing the world, on whose walls and roof were
inscribed the celestial signs.† Here he submitted to a species
of baptism, and received a mark on his forehead. He was presented with a crown on the point of a sword, which he was to
refuse, declaring at the same time, "Mithras alone is my
crown." He was prepared, by anointing him with oil, crowning
him with olive, and clothing him in enchanted armour, for the
seven stages of initiation through which he was about to pass.
These commenced in the following manner: In the first cavern
he heard the howling of wild beasts, and was enveloped in total
darkness, except when the cave was illuminated by the fitful
glare of terrific flashes of lightning. He was hurried to the
spot whence the sounds proceeded, and was suddenly thrust by
his silent guide through a door into a den of wild beasts, where
he was attacked by the initiated in the disguise of lions, tigers,
hyenas, and other ravenous beasts. Hurried through this apartment, in the second cavern he was again shrouded in darkness,
and for a time in fearful silence, until it was broken by awful
peals of thunder, whose repeated reverberations shook the very
walls of the cavern, and could not fail to inspire the aspirant
with terror. He was conducted through four other caverns, in
which the methods of exciting astonishment and fear were ingeniously varied. He was made to swim over a raging flood; was
subjected to a rigorous fast; exposed to all the horrors of a
dreary desert; and finally, if we may trust the authority of Ni-
cætas, after being severely beaten with rods, was buried for many
days up to the neck in snow. In the seventh cavern or Sacellum,
the darkness was changed to light, and the candidate was introduced into the presence of the Archimagus, or chief priest,
seated on a splendid throne, and surrounded by the assistant dis-
pensers of the mysteries. Here the obligation of secrecy was

---

† According to Tertullian, his entrance was opposed by a drawn sword,
from which, in the obstinacy of his perseverance, he often received more than
one wound.

administered, and he was made acquainted with the sacred
words, among which the Tetractys or ineffable name of God was
the principal.   He received also the appropriate investiture,* and
was instructed in the secret doctrines of the rites of Mithras, of
which the history of the creation, already recited, formed a part.
The mysteries of Mithras passed from Persia into Europe, and
were introduced into Rome in the time of Pompey.   Here they
flourished with various success, until the year 378, when they
were prescribed by a decree of the Senate, and the sacred cave,
in which they had been celebrated, was destroyed by the Preto-
rian prefect.

MITRE.   One of the vestments of the High Priest of a
Royal Arch Chapter.   See *High Priest of the Jews.*

MODERN MASONS.   The terms, *Ancient* and *Modern Masons*, are no longer known to the craft as distinctive appellations
of any classes of the fraternity ; but the time has not long past
when the masonic world was convulsed by the controversies of
the two bodies who assumed these titles.   As an important part
of the history of our order, it is therefore necessary that I should
briefly relate the origin of the words, *Modern* and *Ancient Masons.*†

In the commencement of the eighteenth century, the universal
name by which the whole mystic family was known, was that of

---

* This investiture consisted of the Kara or conical cap, and *candys* or loose
tunic of Mithras, on which was depicted the celestial constellations, the zone,
or belt, containing a representation of the figures of the zodiac, the pastoral
staff or crozier, alluding to the influence of the sun in the labours of agricul-
ture, and the golden serpent, which was placed in his bosom as an emblem of
his having been regenerated and made a disciple of Mithras, because the serpent, by casting its skin annually, was considered in these mysteries as a
symbol of regeneration.—See *Maurice's Indian Antiquities,* vol. v., ch. 4.

† The subject has already been alluded to in the article on *Grand Lodges*
and it is, therefore, unavoidable, that I should here be guilty of repetition for
the purposes of facility of reference, and to preserve the continuity of the
narrative.

"Free and Accepted Masons." At that period there were in England two Grand Lodges, the Grand Lodge of England, seated at London, and governing the southern part of the kingdom, and the Grand Lodge of all England, placed at York, and extending its jurisdiction over the northern counties. These bodies at first maintained a friendly intercourse, which was, however, at length interrupted by the officious interference of the Grand Lodge at London, in granting warrants to lodges under the jurisdiction of the Grand Lodge at York. At this time, in 1738, under the Grand Mastership of the Marquis of Carnarvon, some of the brethren, becoming dissatisfied with certain proceedings of the Grand Lodge of England, seceded from that body, and assumed, without authority, the title of York Masons. In the next year, Lord Raymond being Grand Master, the secessions continuing, the Grand Lodge of England attempted to check the evil by passing votes of censure on the most refractory, and by enacting laws to discourage these irregular associations. In consequence of these measures, the seceders immediately declared themselves independent, and assumed the appellation of *Ancient* Masons. They propagated an opinion, that the ancient tenets and usages of masonry were preserved by them, and that the regular lodges, being composed of *Modern* Masons, had adopted new plans, and were not to be considered as acting under the old establishment.*

They, therefore, organized a Grand Lodge, the authority for which they professed to derive from the ancient body at York; called themselves "Ancient York Masons;" and constituted several subordinate lodges. The brethren who still adhered to the Grand Lodge of England, continued to style themselves "Free and Accepted Masons," but were stigmatized by their opponents with the name of *Moderns,* the most opprobrious epithet that can be applied to a masonic body. The dissensions between these bodies were disseminated into foreign countries, where each body constituted lodges, and were continued in

---

* Preston, Illust. of Masonry, p. 189.

England until the year 1813, when they were happily united
during the Grand Mastership of the Duke of Sussex. Before
that period, in some countries, and shortly after it in others, the
union had elsewhere taken place,* and the two terms of Ancient
and Modern Masons now exist only in the records of the past.

With respect to the real differences between these two bodies,
they appear to have existed rather in name, than in fact. Dermott, an Ancient Mason, with an illiberal desire of injuring the
reputation of his opponents, asserts that "a very material difference exists between the Ancient and Modern Masons;" but
Dalcho, who was also an Ancient York, but acquainted with
both systems, declares that "the difference in point of importance, was no greater than it would be to dispute, whether *the
glove should be placed first upon the right hand, or on the left.*"
The question, however, is definitely settled by the report of the
Committees of Conference of the two Grand Lodges of Ancient
York, and Free and Accepted Masons, of South Carolina, who
met for the purpose of mutually examining the work, preparatory to the confirmation of the articles of the Union, which took
place between these bodies in 1817. On that occasion the joint
committees reported, "That from the reciprocal examinations by
the several committees already had in Grand Lodge, it doth appear that there *exists no difference* in the mode of entering, passing and raising, instructing, obligating, and clothing brothers, in
the respective Grand Lodges."

MONITOR. Those manuals, published for the convenience
of lodges, and containing the charges, general regulations, emblems, and account of the public ceremonies of the order, are
called Monitors. The instruction in these works is said to be
Monitorial, to distinguish it from esoteric instruction, which is
not permitted to be written, and can be obtained only in the precincts of the lodge.

---

* They were united in Massachusetts as early as 1792, and in South Carolina in 1817.

MONITOR, SECRET. See *Secret Monitor*.

MOON. If the moon is found in our lodges bestowing her light upon the brethren, and instructing the Master to imitate, in his government, the precision and regularity with which she presides over the night, we shall find her also holding a conspicuous place in the worship of the first seceders from the true spirit of Freemasonry. In Egypt, Osiris was the sun, and Isis the moon; in Syria, Adonis was the sun, and Ashtoroth the moon; the Greeks adored her as Diana, and Hecate; in the mysteries of Ceres, while the hierophant or chief priest represented the Creator, and the torch bearer the sun, the *ho epi bomos*, or officer nearest the altar, represented the moon. In short, moon-worship was as widely disseminated as sun-worship. Masons retain her image in their rites, because the lodge is a representation of the universe, where as the sun rules over the day, the moon presides over the night; as the one regulates the year, so does the other the months, and as the former is the king of the starry hosts of heaven, so is the latter their queen; but both deriving their heat, and light, and power from him, who, as a third and the greatest light, the master of heaven and earth, controls them both.

MOPSES. In 1738 Pope Clement XII. had issued a Bull, condemning and forbidding the practice of the rites of Freemasonry. Several brethren in the Catholic States of Germany, unwilling to renounce the order, and yet fearful of offending the ecclesiastical authority, formed in 1740, under the name of *Mopses*, what was pretended to be a new association, devoted to the papal hierarchy, but which was in truth nothing else than Freemasonry under a less offensive appellation. It was patronized by the most illustrious persons of Germany, and many Princes of the Empire were its Grand Masters. The title is derived from the German word *mops*, signifying a young mastiff, and was indicative of the mutual fidelity and attachment of the brethren, these virtues being characteristic of that noble animal.

In 1776, the Mopses became an androgynous order, and admitted females to all the offices, except that of Grand Master, which was held for life. There was, however, a Grand Mistress, and the male and female heads of the order alternately assumed, for six months each, the supreme authority.

MORALITY OF FREEMASONRY. No one who reads our ancient charges can fail to see that Freemasonry is a strictly moral institution, and that the principles which it inculcates inevitably tend to make the brother, who obeys their dictates, a more virtuous man. What this morality is, has been so well defined in a late address before one of our Grand Lodges, that nothing I could say would add strength to the sentiment, or beauty to the language.

"The morality of masonry requires us to deal justly with others; not to defraud, cheat, or wrong them of their just dues and rights. But it goes farther; regarding all as the children of one great father, it regards man as bound by piety, *masonic* morality, and fraternal bonds, to minister to the wants of the destitute and afflicted; and that we may be enabled to fulfil this high behest of humanity, it strictly enjoins industry and frugality, that so our hands may ever be filled with the means of exercising that charity to which our hearts should ever dispose us."*

MORIAH, MOUNT. A hill on the north-east side of Jerusalem, once separated from the hill of Acra, by a valley, which was filled up by the Asmoneans, and the two hills converted into one. In the time of David, it stood apart from the city and was under cultivation, for here was the threshing floor of Ornan the

---

* Address before the Grand Lodge of Kentucky, by Rev. M. M. Henkle, G. O. 1844.

Jebusite, which David bought for the purpose of erecting on it an altar to God. Here also Abraham is supposed to have been directed to offer up his son Isaac. On Mount Moriah, Solomon afterwards erected the Temple, when it was included within the walls of the city. Mount Gihon, the Hill of Gareb, and especially Mount Calvary, are to *the westward of Mount Moriah.*

Mount Moriah is represented by the ground floor of the lodge, and on it the three grand offerings of masonry were made. See *Ground Floor of the Lodge.*

MOSAIC PAVEMENT. Mosaic work consists of innumerable little stones, of different colours, closely united together, so as to imitate a painting. The floor of the tabernacle, and the pavement of Solomon's temple, are said to have been thus constructed.* The Mosaic pavement, in imitation of this pavement of the temple, is an ornament of the lodge, and is illustrated in the Entered Apprentice's degree. It is surrounded by a richly inlaid or *tessellated border,* commonly called the *indented tessel,* and has in its centre a *blazing star.* The variety of colours in the pavement, is a fit emblem of human life, a mingled scene of virtue and vice, of happiness and misery; to-day "our feet tread in prosperity, to-morrow we totter on the uneven paths of weakness, temptation, and adversity;" the tessellated border, rich in the adornments of figure and colour, represents the many blessings which surround us, and of which not even the most lowly are entirely destitute; while the blazing star, like that bright meteor which of old directed the steps of the wise men of the East, still points to that eternal source from which each blessing flows.

MOST EXCELLENT. The style given to a Royal Arch Chapter, and to its presiding officer, the High Priest.

---

* The term *Mosaic* is supposed to have been derived from the fact that Moses thus constructed the floor of the tabernacle. Mosaic or tesselated pavements were very common among the ancients.

MOST EXCELLENT MASTER. The 6th degree in the York rite. Its history refers to the dedication of the Temple by King Solomon, who is represented by its presiding officer, under the title of Most Excellent. Its officers are the same as those in a symbolic lodge.

MOST WORSHIPFUL. The style given to a Grand Lodge, and to its presiding officer, the Grand Master.

MUSIC. One of the seven liberal arts and sciences, whose beauties are inculcated in the Fellow Craft's degree. Music is recommended to the attention of Masons, because as the "concord of sweet sounds" elevates the generous sentiments of the soul, so should the concord of good feeling reign among the brethren, that by the union of friendship and brotherly love, the boisterous passions may be lulled, and harmony exist throughout the craft.

MUSTARD SEED, ORDER OF. *Ordre de la graine de Sénéve.* This association, whose members also called themselves "The fraternity of Moravian Brothers of the order of Religious Freemasons," was one of the first innovations introduced into German Freemasonry. It was instituted in the year 1739. Its mysteries were founded on that passage in the 4th chapter of St. Mark's gospel, in which Christ compares the kingdom of heaven to a mustard seed. The brethren wore a ring, on which was inscribed, "No one of us lives for himself." The jewel of the order was a cross of gold, surmounted by a Mustard plant, with the words, "What was it before? Nothing." This was suspended from a green ribbon.

MYSTAGOGUE. The one who presided at the Ancient Mysteries, and explained the sacred things to the candidate. He was also called the hierophant.

MYSTERIES. This is the name given to those religious assemblies of the ancients, whose ceremonies were conducted in secret, whose doctrines were known only to those who had obtained the right of knowledge by a previous initiation, and whose members were in possession of signs and tokens by which they were enabled to recognise each other.* For the origin of these mysteries we must look to the Gymnosophists of India, from whom they passed through Egpyt into Greece and Rome, and from whom likewise they were extended, in a more immediate line, to the northern part of Europe and to Britain. The most important of these mysteries were those of Mithras, celebrated in Persia; of Osiris and Isis, celebrated in Egypt; of Eleusis, instituted in Greece; and the Scandinavian and Druidical rites, which were confined to the Gothic and Celtic tribes. In all these various mysteries, we find a singular unity of design clearly indicating a common origin, and a purity of doctrine as evidently proving that this common origin was not to be sought for in the popular theology of the Pagan world. The ceremonies of initiation were all funereal in their character. They celebrated the death and the resurrection of some cherished being, either the object of esteem as a hero, or of devotion as a god. Subordination of degrees was instituted, and the candidate was subjected to probations varying in their character and severity; the rites were practised in the darkness of night, and often amid the gloom of impenetrable forests or subterranean caverns; and the full fruition of knowledge, for which so much labour was endured, and so much danger incurred, was not attained until the aspirant, well tried and thoroughly purified, had reached the place of wisdom and of light.

These mysteries undoubtedly owed their origin to the desire

---

* Warburton's definition of the Mysteries is as follows: " Each of the pagan gods had (besides the *public* and *open*) a *secret worship* paid unto him; to which none were admitted but those who had been selected by preparatory ceremonies, called INITIATION. This *secret worship* was termed the MYSTE-RIES."—*Divine Legation, Vol.* 1, *B. ii.* § 4, *p.* 189.

on the part of the priests of establishing an esoteric philosophy, in which should be taught the sublime truths which they had derived, (though they themselves at length forgot the source,) from the instruction of God himself through the ancient patriarchs. By this confinement of these doctrines to a system of secret knowledge, guarded by the most rigid rites, could they only expect to preserve them from the superstitions, innovations, and corruptions of the world as it then existed. "The distinguished few," says Oliver, "who retained their fidelity, uncontaminated by the contagion of evil example, would soon be able to estimate the superior benefits of an isolated institution, which afforded the advantage of a select society, and kept at an unapproachable distance the profane scoffer, whose presence might pollute their pure devotions and social converse, by contumelious language or unholy mirth."* And doubtless the prevention of this intrusion, and the preservation of these sublime truths, was the original object of the institution of the ceremonies of initiation, and the adoption of other means by which the initiated could be recognised, and the uninitiated excluded. Such was the opinion of Warburton, who says that "the mysteries were at first the retreats of sense and virtue, till time corrupted them in most of the gods."†

The Abbe Robin, in a learned work‡ on this subject, places the origin of the initiations at that remote period when crimes first began to appear upon earth. The vicious, he remarks, were urged by the terror of guilt to seek among the virtuous for intercessors with the deity. The latter, retiring into solitude to avoid the contagion of growing corruption, devoted themselves to a life of contemplation and the cultivation of several of the useful sciences. The periodical return of the seasons, the revolution of the stars, the productions of the earth, and the various phenomena of nature, studied with attention, rendered them useful guides to

---

* History of Initiation, p. 2.　　　　　† Spence's Anecdotes, p. 309.
‡ Recherches sur les Initiations Anciennes et Modernes. Paris. 1780.

men, both in their pursuits of industry and in their social duties.
These recluse students invented certain signs to recall to the remembrance of the people the times of their festivals and of their
rural labours, and hence the origin of the symbols and hieroglyphics that were in use among the priests of all nations. Having
now become guides and leaders of the people, these sages, in order
to select as associates of their learned labours and sacred functions
only such as had sufficient merit and capacity, appointed strict
courses of trial and examination, and this, our author thinks, must
have been the source of the initiations of antiquity. The Magi,
Brahmins, Gymnosophists, Druids, and priests of Egypt, lived
thus in sequestered habitations and subterranean caves, and obtained
great reputation by their discoveries in astronomy, chemistry and
mechanics, by their purity of morals, and by their knowledge of
the science of legislation. It was in these schools, says M. Robin,
that the first sages and legislators of antiquity were formed, and
in them he supposes the doctrines taught to have been the unity of
God and the immortality of the soul; and it was from these mysteries, and their symbols and hieroglyphics, that the exuberant
fancy of the Greeks drew much of their mythology.*

The candidates for initiation were not only expected to be of a
clear and unblemished character, and free from crime, but their
future conduct was required to be characterized by the same
purity and innocence. They were, therefore, obliged, by solemn
engagements, to commence a new life of piety and virtue, upon
which they entered by a severe course of penance.†

The mysteries were held in the highest respect, by both the
government and the people. It was believed that he who was
initiated would not only enjoy an increased share of virtue and
happiness in this world, but would be entitled to celestial honours
in the next. "Thrice happy they," says Sophocles, "who de-

---

* I give these ingenious speculations of the Abbe Robin, although I dissent
from much of his doctrine, because they add another item to the history of the
theories on this interesting subject.

† Warburton, Divine Legation, B. ii., Sect. 4.

scended to the shades below after having beheld these rites; for
they alone have life in Hades, while all others suffer there every
kind of evil." And Isocrates declares that "those who have been
initiated in the mysteries, entertain better hopes, both as to the
end of life and the whole of futurity."

The ancient historians relate many circumstances in illustration
of the sanctity in which the mysteries were held. Livy tell us
the following story : Two Acarnanian youths who had not been
initiated, accidentally entered the temple of Ceres, during the days
of the mysteries. They were soon detected by their absurd questions, and being carried to the managers of the temple, though it
was evident that they had come there by mistake, they were put
to death for so horrible a crime.*

Plutarch records the fact that Alcibiades was indicted for sacri-
lege, because he imitiated the mysteries of Eleusis and exhibited
them to his companions in the same dress in which the hierophant
showed the sacred things, and called himself the hierophant, one
of his companions the torch bearer, and the other the herald.†

Lobeck, one of the most learned writers on this subject, has collected several examples of the reluctance with which the ancients
approached a mystical subject, and the manner in which they
shrunk from divulging any explanation or fable which had been
related to them at the mysteries.‡

To divulge them was considered a sacrilegious crime, the prescribed punishment for which was immediate death. I would not,
says Horace, dwell beneath the same roof, nor trust myself in the
same frail bark, with the man who has betrayed the secrets of the
Eleusinian rites.§

---

* Liv. Hist. xxi. 14.   † Plut. Alcibiad. 22.
‡ Lobeck's Aglaophamus, vol. i. app. 131, 151; vol. ii. p. 1287.
      §   Vetabo, qui Cereris sacrum
      Vulgârit arcanæ, sub iisdem
      Sit trabibus, fragilemque mecum
      Solvat phaselum.
                          [*Carm.* iii. 3, 26.

On the subject of their relation to the rites of Freemasonry, to which they bear in many respects so remarkable a resemblance, that some connection seems necessarily implied, there are two principal theories. The one, is that embraced and taught by Dr. Oliver, namely, that they are but deviations from that common source, both of them and of Freemasonry, the patriarchal mode of worship established by God himself. With this pure system of truth, he supposes the science of Freemasonry to have been coeval and identified. But the truths thus revealed by divinity, came at length to be doubted or rejected through the imperfection of human reason, and though the visible symbols were retained in the mysteries of the Pagan world, their true interpretation was lost.*

That the instruction communicated in the mysteries of Paganism were an impure derivation from the sublime truths of the patriarchal theology, I have no hesitation in believing. But that they were an emanation from Freemasonry, as we now understand the terms, I am not yet prepared to admit, notwithstanding the deep veneration in which I hold the learning of Dr. Oliver. I prefer, therefore, the second theory, which, leaving the origin of the mysteries to be sought in the patriarchal doctrines, where Oliver has placed it, finds the connection between them and Freemasonry commencing at the building of King Solomon's Temple. Over the construction of this building, Hiram, the Architect of Tyre, presided. At Tyre the mysteries of Bacchus had been introduced by the Dionysian Artificers, and into their fraternity Hiram, in all probability, had, as I have already suggested, been admitted.†
Freemasonry, whose tenets had always existed in purity among the immediate descendants of the patriarchs, added now to its doctrines the guard of secrecy, which, as Dr. Oliver himself remarks, was necessary to preserve them from perversion or pollution.†

This, then, it seems to me, is the true connection between the

---

* Signs and Symbols, p. 217.
† See *Antiquity of Masonry*, and *Hiram the Builder*, in this work.
‡ Hist. of Initiation, p. 2.

mysteries and speculative Freemasonry. They both emanated
from one common source, but the former soon losing much of
their original purity, were compelled, in order to preserve the little
that was left, to have recourse to the invention of ceremonies and
modes of recognition, and a secret doctrine, by means of which
all but a select and worthy few were excluded. These ceremonies,
and especially this symbolic or secret mode of communicating instruction, so admirable in themselves, were afterwards adopted by
the Freemasons, who had retained the ancient tenets in their
original purity, but they divested them of their heathen allusions,
and adapted them to the divine system which they had preserved
unimpaired.

A third theory has been advanced by the Abbe Robin, in
which he connects Freemasonry indirectly with the mysteries,
through the intervention of the Crusaders. In the work already
cited, he attempts to deduce from the ancient initiations, the orders of Chivalry, whose branches, he says, produced the institution of Freemasonry. But this theory is utterly untenable and
inconsistent with the facts of history, since Freemasonry preceded, instead of following, the institution of Chivalry, as I have
elsewhere shown, and could not, therefore, have been indebted to
this system for its primal organization.

These mysteries, so important from their connection with
Freemasonry, deserve a still further examination of their origin
and design.

Faber, who sought an Arkite origin for every thing, says that
"the initiations into the mysteries scientifically represented the
mythic descent into Hades and the return from thence to the
light of day, by which was meant the entrance into the ark and
the subsequent liberation from its dark enclosure. They all
equally related to the allegorical disappearance, or death, or descent of the great father, at their commencement; and to his invention, or revival, or return from Hades, at their conclusion."[*]

---

* Origin of Pagan Idolatry, vol. ii., b. iv., ch. v., p 384.

"They were," says Warburton, "a school of morality and religion, in which the vanity of polytheism and the unity of the First Cause were revealed to the initiated."[†] This opinion of the learned Bishop of Gloucester is not gratuitous; it is supported by the concurrent testimony of the ancient writers. "All the mysteries," says Plutarch, "refer to a future life and to the state of the soul after death."[‡] In another place, addressing his wife, he says, "we have been instructed in the religious rites of Dionysus, that the soul is immortal, and that there is a future state of existence."[§] Cicero tells us, that in the mysteries of Ceres at Eleusis, the initiated were taught to live happily and to die in the hope of a blessed futurity.[||] And, finally, Plato informs us, that the hymns of Musæus, which were sung in the mysteries, celebrated the rewards and pleasures of the virtuous in another life, and the punishments which awaited the wicked.[¶]

These sentiments, so different from the debased polytheism which prevailed among the uninitiated, are the most certain evidence that the mysteries arose from a purer source than that which gave birth to the religion of the vulgar. That purer source was the common original of them and of Freemasonry.

I conclude with a notice of their ultimate fate. They continued to flourish until long after the Christian era. But they, at length, degenerated. In the fourth century, Christianity had begun to triumph. The Pagans, desirous of making converts, threw open the hitherto inaccessible portals of their mysterious rites. The strict scrutiny of the candidate's past life, and the demand for proofs of irreproachable conduct, were no longer deemed indispensable. The vile and the vicious were indiscriminately, and even with avidity, admitted to participate in privileges which were once granted only to the noble and the virtuous. The sun of Paganism was setting, and its rites had become con-

---

† Divine Legislation.   ‡ Plut. de Oraculis.
§ Plut. Consol. ad uxorem. || Cic. de Legibus.
¶ Plato in Phædone.

temptible and corrupt. Their character was entirely changed, and the initiations were indiscriminately sold by peddling priests, who wandered through the country, to every applicant who was willing to pay a trifling fee for that which had once been refused to the entreaties of a monarch. At length these abominations attracted the attention of the emperors, and Constantine and Gratian forbade their celebration at night, excepting, however, from these edicts, the initiations at Eleusis. But finally Theodosius, by a general edict of proscription, ordered the whole of the Pagan mysteries to be abolished, in the four hundred and thirty-eighth year of the Christian era, and eighteen hundred years after their first establishment in Greece.*

MYSTES. The Mystes was one who had been initiated only into the lesser mysteries, and who was therefore permitted to proceed no farther than the vestibule or porch of the Temple. When admitted into the greater mysteries, and allowed to enter the adytum, or sanctuary, he was called an *epopt*. A female initiate was called a *mystis*.

MYSTIC TIE. That sacred and inviolable bond which unites men of the most discordant opinions into one band of brothers, which gives but one language to men of all nations, and one altar to men of all religions, is properly, from the mysterious influence it exerts, denominated the mystic tie, and Freemasons, because they alone are under its influence, or enjoy its benefits, are called "Brethren of the mystic tie."

---

* It was not, however, says Clavel, until the era of the restoration, that the mysteries entirely ceased. During the Middle Ages, the mysteries of Diana, under the name of the *Courses of Diana*, and those of Pan, under the name of *Sabbats*, were practised in the country.

N.

NABIIM, SCHOOLS OF THE. We repeatedly meet in the Old Testament with references to the *Beni Hanabiim*, or sons of the prophets.* These were the disciples of the prophets, or wise men of Israel, who underwent a course of esoteric-instruction in the secret institutions of the Nabiim or prophets, just as the disciples of the Magi did in Persia, or of Pythagoras in Greece. Of these institutions, Oliver says, that "though little is known of their internal económy, their rites and ceremonies being strictly concealed, there can be no doubt that they were in many respects similar to our masonic lodges, and in some of their features they bore a resemblance to the collegiate institutions of our own country."†

NAHARDA, FRATERNITY OF. The Jewish Rabbins tell us, that the tribes which were carried into captivity on the destruction of the first temple, founded a fraternity at Naharda, on the river Euphrates, for the preservation of traditional knowledge, and which they transmitted to a few initiates, and that on the restoration of the Jews by Cyrus, Zerubbabel, with Joshua and Esdras, carried all this secret instruction to Jerusalem, and established a similar fraternity in that city. Oliver says that during the captivity, the Jews practised Freemasonry in regular lodges, until the time of their deliverance, and they had for this purpose three Colleges or Grand Lodges, which were situated at Sora, Pompeditha, and Naharda.

NAME OF GOD. In addition to what has been said upon this subject in the article *Jehovah*, we may observe, that an allu-

---

* I refer the reader for this expression to the Second Book of Kings, chap. ii., verses 3, 5, 7, 12, 15.

† Historical Landmarks, ii., p. 374. Note.

sion to the unutterable name of God, is to be found in the doctrines and ceremonies of other nations, as well as the Jews. It is said to have been used as the pass-word in the Egyptian mysteries. In the rites of Hindostan, it was bestowed upon the aspirant, under the triliteral form AUM,* at the completion of his initiation, and then only by whispering it in his ear. The Cabalists reckoned seventy-two names of God, the knowledge of which imparted to the possessor magical powers. The Druids invoked the omnipotent and all-preserving power, under the symbol I. O. W. The Mohammedans have a science called Ism Allah, or the science of the name of God. "They pretend," says Niebuhr, "that God is the lock of this science, and Mohammed the key; that consequently none but Mohammedans can attain it; that it discovers what passes in different countries; that it familiarizes the possessors with the genii who are at the command of the initiated, and who instruct them; that it places the winds and the seasons at their disposal, and heals the bites of serpents, the lame, the maimed, and the blind."

Besides the Tetragrammaton, or incommunicable name, there are other expressive but less holy names of Deity. Maimonides, for instance, mentions a twelve lettered and a forty-two lettered name.†

Rosenberg gives the following twelve Cabalistic names : Ehie,

---

* Sir William Jones, speaking of this Hindoo name of God, says: "It forms a mystical word which never escapes the lips of the pious Hindoo. They meditate on it in silence."—*Dissertations relative to Asia*, vol. i., p. 33. The Brahmins make a great secret of it, and the "Institutes of Menu" are continually referring to its peculiar efficacy as an *omnific* word. "All rites ordained in the Veda," says this book, "oblations to fire and solemn sacrifices pass away, but that which passes not away is the syllable AUM, thence called *aishara*, since it is a symbol of God, the Lord of created beings."—*Instit. of Menu*, p. 28.

† Urquhart (Pillars of Hercules, vol. ii., p. 67) mentions one name of God among the Hebrews, which I have met with nowhere else. viz., EL GIBAL, *the master builder.*

Jehovah, Elohim, El, Gibbor, Eloah, Sabaoth, Tsebaoth, Shaddai, Adonai, Makom, Agla.

Lanci, whose researches on this subject have been surpassed by no other scholar, and equalled by few, extends his list of divine names to twenty-six, which, with their signification, are as follows :*

1. *At.* The Aleph and Tau, that is, Alpha and Omega. A name figurative of the Tetragrammaton.

2. *Ihoh.* } The eternal, absolute principle of creation and
3. *Hohi.* } destruction, the male and female principle, the author and regulator of time and motion.

4. *Jah.* The Lord and Remunerator.

5. *Oh.* The severe and punisher.

6. *Jao.* The author of life.

7. *Azazel.* The author of death.

8. *Jao-Sabaoth.* God of the co-ordinations of loves and hatreds. Lord of the solstices and the equinoxes.

9. *Ehie.* The Being; the Ens.

10. *El.* The first cause. The principle or beginning of all things.

11. *Elo-hi.* The good principle.

12. *Elo-ho.* The evil principle.

13. *El-raccum.* The succouring principle.

14. *El-cannum.* The abhorring principle.

15. *Ell.* The most luminous.

16. *Il.* The omnipotent.

17. *Ellohim.* The omnipotent and beneficent.

18. *Elohim.* The most beneficent.

19. *Elo.* The Sovereign, the Excelsus.

20. *Adon.* The Lord, the dominator.

21. *Eloi.* The illuminator, the most effulgent.

22. *Adonai.* The most firm, the strongest.

23. *Elion.* The most high.

---

* I am indebted to my friend, Mr. Gliddon, for this interesting list.

24. *Shaddai.* The most victorious.

25. *Yeshurun.* The most generous.

26. *Noil.* The most sublime.

The ineffable degrees of masonry record a great variety of the names of God; making the whole system, like the Mohammedan *Ism Allah,* a science of the name of God. In fact, the name of God must be taken in Freemasonry as symbolical of truth, and then the search for it will be nothing else but the search after truth, the true end and aim of the masonic science. The subordinate names are the subordinate modifications of truth, but the ineffable tetragrammaton will be the sublimity and perfection of Divine Truth, to which all good Masons and all good men are seeking to approach, whether it be by the aid of the theological ladder, or passing through the pillars of Strength and Establishment, or wandering in the mazes of darkness, beset on all sides by dangers, or travelling weary and worn over rough and rugged roads, whatever be the direction of our journey or how accomplished, light and truth, the Urim and Thummin, are the ultimate objects of our search as Freemasons.

NEBUCHADNEZZAR. A king of Babylon, who in the eleventh year of the reign of Zedekiah, King of Judah, having, after a siege of about twelve months, taken Jerusalem, commanded Nebuzaradan, one of his generals, to set fire to and utterly consume the temple, to reduce the city to desolation, and to carry the citizens captive to Babylon. See the entire history under the title of *Royal Arch.*

NEBUZARADAN. One of the generals of the King of Babylon, who by his order entered Jurusalem with a Chaldean army, and after having taken away every thing that was valuable, burned the city and temple, and carried all the inhabitants, except a few husbandmen, as captives to Babylon.

NEOPHYTE. (From the Greek νεον φυτον, a new plant.)

In the primitive church it signified one who had recently abandoned Judaism or Paganism, and embraced Christianity; whence
it was afterwards applied to the young disciple of any art or
science. Freemasons thus sometimes designate the uninstructed
candidate.

NE VARIETUR. *"Lest it should be changed."* These
words refer to the masonic usage of requiring a brother, when he
receives a certificate from a lodge, to affix his name, in his own
hand-writing, in the margin, as a precautionary measure, in
enabling distant brethren to recognise the true and original owner
of the certificate, and to detect any impostor who may surrepti-
tiously have obtained one.

NINE. If the number three is sacred among Masons, the number nine, or three times three, is scarcely less so. The Pythagoreans, remarking that this number has the power of always re-
producing itself by multiplication,* considered it as an emblem
of matter which, though continually changing its form, is never
annihilated. It was also consecrated to the spheres, because the
circumference of a sphere is 360 degrees, and 3 and 6 and 0 are
equal to 9.

In Freemasonry, 9 derives its value from its being the product
of 3 multiplied into itself, and consequently in masonic language
the number 9 is always denoted by the expression 3 times 3. For
a similar reason, 27, which is 3 times 9, and 81, which is 9
times 9, are esteemed as sacred numbers in the higher degrees.

---

* Thus 2 9—18, and 1 and 8—9.
     3 9—27, and 2 and 7—9.
     4 9—36, and 3 and 6—9.
     5 9—45, and 4 and 5—9.
     6 9—54, and 5 and 4—9.
     7 9—63, and 6 and 3—9.
     8 9—72, and 7 and 2—9.
     9 9—81, and 8 and 1—9.

NOACHIDÆ, or NOACHITES. The descendants of Noah. A term applied to Freemasons. Noah having alone preserved the true name and worship of God, amid a race of impious idolaters, Freemasons claim to be his descendants, because they still preserve that pure religion which distinguished this second father of the human race from the rest of the world. And even when his descendants began again, in the plains of Shinar, to forget the Almighty, and to wander from the path of purity, the principles of Noah were still perpetuated by that portion of his race whom the Freemasons of the present day regard as their early predecessors. Hence, Freemasons call themselves Noachidæ, or the sons of Noah.

This respect for Noah, as the father and founder of the masonic system of theology, was not confined to the pure Freemasons, but extended, even unconsciously, to the seceders from its spirit, those whom Oliver calls the spurious Freemasons of antiquity. In all their mysteries, they commemorated, even after they had lost the true history, the descent of Noah into the ark, and his subsequent exodus. The entrance into initiation was symbolic of his entrance into the vessel of his salvation; his detention in the ark was represented by the darkness and the pastos, coffin, or couch in which the aspirant was placed, and the exit of Noah, after the forty days of deluge, was seen in the manifestation of the candidate, when, being fully tried and proved, he was admitted to full light, amid the rejoicings of the surrounding initiates, who received him in the sacellum or holy place.

NOACHITE, or PRUSSIAN KNIGHT. *Noachite ou Chevalier Prussien.* The 21st degree of the Ancient Scotch rite, called by its possessors not a degree, but "the very Ancient Order of Noachites." In this degree the Knights celebrate the destruction of the Tower of Babel, and for this purpose they meet on the night of the full moon of each month. No other light is permitted in the lodge than what proceeds from that satellite. The records of the order furnish us with the following history. The

Noachites, at this day called Prussian Knights, are the descendants of Peleg, Chief Architect of the Tower of Babel. Thus
they trace the origin of their order to a more ancient date than
the descendants of Hiram, for the Tower of Babel was built many
ages before the Temple of Solomon. And formerly it was not
necessary that candidates for this degree should be Hiramites or
Blue Masons. But a different regulation was afterwards adopted,
and to receive the degree of Noachite, it is now necessary that the
candidate shall have performed the duties of a worthy office in a
regularly constituted lodge of Blue Masons. The order of Noachites was established in Prussia in 1755, and inducted into France
by the Count St. Gelaire in 1757.

NOAH, PRECEPTS OF. The precepts of the patriarch
Noah, which were preserved as the constitutions of our ancient
brethren, are seven in number, and are as follows :

1. Renounce all idols.
2. Worship the only true God.
3. Commit no murder.
4. Be not defiled by incest.
5. Do not steal.
6. Be just.
7. Eat no flesh with blood in it.

The "proselytes of the gate," as the Jews termed those who
lived among them without undergoing circumcision, or observing
the ceremonial law, were bound to obey the seven precepts of
Noah.

NOMINATION. The nomination of officers, previous to an
election, is contrary to true masonic usage. Officers should be
elected in the manner prescribed under the article *Election*.

NORTH. The north is masonically called a place of darkness. I doubt whether I am at liberty to explain the reason.
But I may make this general explanation. The sun in his pro-

gress through the ecliptic, never reaches farther than 23° 28′ north of the equator. A wall being erected on any part of the earth farther north than that, will, therefore, receive the rays of the sun only on its south side, while the north will be entirely in shadow at the hour of meridian.

NUMBERS. The mystical meaning and divine virtue of numbers formed an important part of the philosophy of Pythagoras, and from him have been transmitted to the masonic system of symbolism. Pythagoras doubtless brought his doctrines on this subject from Egypt, in which country he long resided, and with whose wisdom he was richly embued. In numbers Pythagoras saw the principle of all things; he believed that the creation of the world was produced by their harmonious combination, and that they existed before the world.

According to the doctrine of this sage, numbers are of two kinds, intellectual and scientific.

Intellectual number has always existed in the divine mind; it is the basis of universal order, and the link which binds all things.

Scientific number is the generative cause of multiplicity, which proceeds from and is the result of unity. Scientific numbers are equal or odd.

Equal numbers are said to be female, and odd ones, male; because even numbers admit of division or generation, which odd ones do not. Odd numbers, however, are the most perfect.

To each number Pythagoras ascribed a peculiar character and quality.

ONE,—the Monad,—represented the central fire, or God, without beginning and without end, *the point within the circle.* It also denoted love, concord, piety, and friendship, because it is indivisible. It was the symbol of identity, equality, existence, and universal preservation and harmony.

Two was unlucky, and as one denoted light and the good principle or God, two denoted darkness and the evil principle.

Hence it was that the Romans dedicated the second month of the year to Pluto, the god of hell, and the second day of that month to the manes of the dead.

THREE referred to harmony, friendship, peace, concord, and temperance, and was so highly esteemed among the Pythagoreans that they called this number "perfect harmony."

FOUR was a divine number; it referred to Deity, and among the ancients many nations gave to God a name of four letters, as the Hebrews יהוה, the Assyrians ADAD, the Egyptians AMUM, the Persians SYRE, the Greeks ΘΕΟΣ, and the Latins DEUS. This, which was the Tetragrammaton of the Hebrews, the Pythagoreans called Tetractys, and used it as a most solemn oath.*

FIVE denoted light, nature, marriage; the latter, because it was made up of the female two and the male three, whence it is sometimes called a hemaphrodite number. The triple triangle, which was a figure of five lines uniting into five points, was among the Pythagoreans an emblem of health.

SIX was also an emblem of health, and it was also the symbol of justice, because it was the first perfect number, that is, one whose aliquot parts being added together make itself, for the aliquot parts of six, which are three, two and one, are equal to six.

SEVEN was highly esteemed, and called a venerable number, because it referred to the creation of the world.

EIGHT was esteemed as the first cube, $(2 \times 2 \times 2)$ and signified friendship, prudence, counsel, and justice. It designated the primitive law of nature, which supposes all men to be equal.

NINE was called τελειος, or *perfect, finished*, because nine months is the period required for the perfection of a human being in the womb before birth.

TEN was denominated heaven, because it was the perfection and consummation of all things, and was constituted by the union of ONE, the monad or active principle, TWO, the duad or

---

* See *Tetractys.*

28*

passive principle, THREE, the triad or world proceeding from their union, and FOUR, the sacred tetractys, thus $1 + 2 + 3 + 4 = 10$. Hence Ten contained all the relations, numerical and harmonic.

The Pythagoreans extended still farther their speculations on the first three numbers, the monad, the duad, and the triad.

The monad was male, because its action produces no change *in* itself, but only out of itself. It represented the creative principle.

The duad, for a contrary reason, was female, being ever changing by addition, substraction, or multiplication. It represents matter capable of form.

The union of the monad and duad produces the triad, which signifies the world formed by the creative principle out of matter. This world Pythagoras represented by the right angled triangle, because the square of the longest side is equal to the squares of the two other sides, and the world as it is formed is equal to the formative cause and matter clothed with form. Thus :

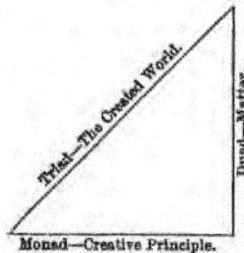

In symbolic masonry, three, five, and seven, are mystic numbers, as is nine in Royal Arch Masonry. In the ineffable degrees, nine, with its products, such as twenty-seven and eighty-one are sacred.

For further observations on some of these numbers, see in this work, the words, *Five, Nine, Seven, Three* and *Tetractys*.

O.

OBEDIENCE. Submission to the constituted authorities, both in the state and in the craft, is a quality inculcated upon all Masons. With respect to the state, a Mason is charged to be "a peaceable subject to the civil powers, wherever he resides or works, and never to be concerned in plots or conspiracies against the peace and welfare of the nation, nor to behave himself undutifully to inferior magistrates."[*] And with respect to the craft, he is directed "to pay due reverence to his Master, Wardens, and Fellows, and to put them to worship."[†] And another part of the same regulations directs, that the rulers and governers, supreme and subordinate, of the ancient lodge, are to be obeyed in their respective stations, by all the brethren, with all humility, reverence, love, and alacrity."[‡]

Oliver, commenting on the emblematic allusion of the Master to the Sun and Moon, says : "Hence we find that the Master's authority in the lodge, is despotic as the sun in the firmament, which was placed there by the Creator, never to deviate from its accustomed course till the declaration is promulgated that time shall be no more."[§]

This spirit of obedience runs through the whole system, and constitutes one of the greatest safeguards of our institution. The Mason is obedient to the Master; the Master and the lodge to the Grand Lodge; and this, in its turn, to the old landmarks and ancient regulations of the order. Thus is a due degree of subordination kept up and the institution preserved in its pristine purity.

OBLONG SQUARE. A parallelogram or four sided figure,

---

[*] Old Charges, Sect. 1.   [†] Ibm., Sect. 2.   [‡] Ibm., Sect. 4.
[§] Signs and Symbols, p. 205.

all of whose angles are equal, but two of whose sides are longer than the others.

This is the symbolic form of a masonic lodge, and it finds its prototype in many of the structures of our ancient brethren. The ark of Noah, the camp of the Israelites, the ark of the Covenant, the Tabernacle, and lastly, the Temple of Solomon, were all oblong squares. See *Ground Floor of the Lodge.*

OBSERVANCE, RITE OF STRICT. The rite of Strict Observance was a modification of masonry, based on the order of Knights Templar, and introduced into Germany in 1754 by its founder, the Baron Hunde. It was divided into the following seven degrees : 1. Apprentice ; 2. Fellow Craft ; 3. Master ; 4. Scotch Master ; 5. Novice ; 6. Templar ; 7. Professed Knight.

According to the system of the founder of this rite, upon the death of Jacques Molay, the Grand Master of the Templars, Pierre d'Aumont, the Provincial Grand Master of Auvergne, with two commanders and five knights, retired for purposes of safety into Scotland, which place they reached disguised as operative Masons, and there finding the Grand Commander, George Harris, and several Knights, they determined to continue the order Aumont was nominated Grand Master, at a chapter held on St. John's day, 1313. To avoid persecution, the Knights became Freemasons. In 1361, the Grand Master of the Temple removed his seat to Old Aberdeen, and from that time the order, under the veil of masonry, spread rapidly through France, Germany, Spain, Portugal, and elsewhere. These events constituted the principal subject of many of the degrees of the rite of Strict Observance. The others were connected with alchemy, magic, and other superstitious practices. The great doctrine contended for, by the followers of the rite, was, "that every true Mason is a Knight Templar."[*]

OBSERVANCE, CLERKS OF RELAXED. The Clerks

Clavel, p. 184.

of Relaxed Observance were a schism from the order of Strict Observance, described above. They claimed a pre-eminence over not only the latter rite, but over all masonry. The rite was divided into ten degrees, called Apprentice, Fellow-Craft, Master, African Brother, Knight of St. Andrew, Knight of the Eagle, Scotch Master, Sovereign Magus, Provincial Master of the Red Cross, and Knight of Light. This last degree was divided into five sections, comprehending Knight Novice of the third year, Knight of the fifth year, Knight of the seventh year, Knight Levite, and Knight Priest. To be initiated into the mysteries of the Clerks, it was necessary to be a Roman Catholic, and to have taken all the military degrees of the rite of Strict Observance. Alchemy was one of the objects of their secret instruction.*

OFFERINGS, THE THREE GRAND. See *Ground Floor of the Lodge.*

OFFICERS. See *Installation, Jewels, Lodge.*

OIL. The Hebrews anointed their kings, prophets, and high priests, with oil mingled with the richest spices. They also anointed themselves with oil on all festive occasions, whence the expression in Psalms xlv. 7, "God hath anointed thee with the oil of gladness." See *Corn.*

ON. An ancient Egyptian word signifying the Sun, which was at one time worshipped by the Egyptians as the Supreme Deity. The city of On, in Lower Egypt, which contained a temple dedicated to the worship of this divinity is called, in the septuagint, "Heliopolis," or the city of the Sun, and by Jeremiah (xliii. 13,) "Beth-shemesh," which has the same signification. In Genesis (xli. 45–50.) we are informed that Pharaoh

---

gave Joseph for his wife Asenath, "the daughter of Potipherah, priest of On." *On* may therefore be considered as the equivalent for Jehovah among the Egyptians, as *Jah* was among the Syrians and *Bel* among the Chaldees. The modern masonic corruption of this word into "Lun" is sheer nonsense.

OPENING OF THE LODGE. The ceremony of opening the lodge is solemn and impressive. Every brother is reminded by it of his duties and obligations. The necessary precautions are employed to avoid the intrusion of the profane, and every member being compelled to assume a share of the necessary forms, is thus admonished, that masonry is a whole, of which each Mason forms a part.

The manner of opening in each degree slightly varies. In the English system, which seems, according to the "Trestle Board" published under the sanction of the late Baltimore Masonic Convention, to have been adopted by that body, the lodge is opened in the first degree "in the name of God and Universal Benevolence;" in the second, "on the square, in the name of the Great Geometrician of the Universe;" and in the third, "on the centre, in the name of the Most High."*

OPERATIVE MASONRY. See *Masonry.*

ORATOR. An officer in a lodge of the French rite, whose principal duty is to give instruction to the newly initiated. The duties of the office are those of a Lecturer.

ORDER. An order is defined by Johnson, to be, among other things, "a regular government, a society of dignified persons, distinguished by marks of honour, and a religious fraternity." In all of these senses, masonry may be styled an order. Its government is of the most regular and systematic character;

* See Moore and Carnegy's Trestle Board, ch. iii.

men the most eminent for dignity and reputation, have been its members, and if it does not constitute a religion in itself, it is at least religion's hand-maid.

The word was first used by the ecclesiastical writers of the tenth century to signify a certain form or rule of monastic discipline, and was in that sense applied to the different sects of monks.

ORDERS OF ARCHITECTURE. A system of the several members, ornaments, and proportions of columns and pilasters, is called an order. There are five orders of columns, three of which are Greek, the Doric, Ionic, and Corinthian; and two Italian, the Tuscan and Composite. See these respective titles.

ORDO AB CHAO. *Order out of Chaos.* A motto of the 33d degree, and having the same allusion as *lux e tenebris,* which see.

ORIENT. The East. The place where a lodge is situated is called its Orient. The seat of the Grand Lodge is called the Grand Orient.* But on the continent of Europe, some of the supreme masonic bodies are called Grand Orients. In these instances, Grand Orient is equivalent to Grand Lodge.

ORIENTAL CHAIR OF SOLOMON. The seat of the W∴ M∴ in a symbolic lodge, and so called because the Master is supposed symbolically to fill the place over the craft once occupied by King Solomon.

ORNAMENTS OF A LODGE. These are the Mosaic pavement, the indented tessel, and the blazing star. See *Mosaic Pavement.*

---

* The term is thus used, because in masonry the East is the seat of light and of authority. It is the station of the Worshipful Master.

ORNAN THE JEBUSITE. He was an inhabitant of Jerusalem, at the time that city was called Jebus, from the son of Canaan, whose descendants peopled it. He was the owner of the threshing floor, situated on Mount Moriah, in the same spot on which the temple was afterwards built. This threshing floor David bought to erect on it an altar to God. (2 Chron. xxi. 18–25.) On the same spot Solomon afterwards built the temple.

ORPHIC MYSTERIES. These Grecian rites were only a modification of the mysteries of Bacchus or Dionysus, and were thus called, because it was said that Orpheus first introduced the worship of Bacchus into Greece from Egypt. They differed, however, from the other pagan rites, in not being confined to the priesthood, but in being practised by a fraternity who did not possess the sacerdotal functions. The initiated commemorated in their ceremonies, which were performed at night, the murder of Bacchus by the Titans, and his final restoration to the supreme government of the universe, under the name of Phanes.

Demosthenes, while reproaching Eschines for having engaged with his mother in these mysteries, gives us some notion of their nature.

In the day, the initiates were crowned with fennel and poplar, and carried serpents in their hands, or twined them around their heads, crying with a loud voice, *enos, sabos,* and danced to the sound of the mystic words, *hyes, attes, attes, hyes.* At night the mystes was bathed in the lustral water, and having been rubbed over with clay and bran, he was clothed in the skin of a fawn, and having risen from the bath, he exclaimed, " I have departed from evil and have found the good."*

The Orphic initiation, because it was not sacerdotal in its character, was not so celebrated among the ancients, as the other mysteries. It, nevertheless, existed until the first ages of the Christian era, and fell, with the remaining rites of paganism, a

---

* Demosth. contra Ctesiph. Orat. pp. 568–9.

victim to the rapid and triumphant progress of the new religion.

OSIRIS. For the legend of Osiris, see *Egyptian Mysteries.*

OVERSEER. The title of three officers in a Mark Lodge, who are distinguished as the Master, Senior and Junior Overseer. The jewel of their office is a square. In Mark lodges attached to chapters, the duties of these officers are performed by the three Grand Masters of the veils.

P.

PARALLEL LINES. In every well-regulated lodge, there is found a point within a circle, which circle is embordered by two perpendicular parallel lines. These lines are representatives of St. John the Baptist, and St. John the Evangelist, the two great patrons of masonry, to whom our lodges are dedicated, and who are said to have been "perfect parallels in Christianity, as well as Masonry." In those English lodges which have adopted the "Union System" established by the Grand Lodge of England in 1815, and where the dedication is "to God and his service," the lines parallel represent Moses and Solomon. See *Dedication.*

PASCHALIS, MARTINEZ. The founder of a new rite or modification of masonry, called by him, *the rite of Elected Cohens or Priests.* It was divided into two classes, in the first of which was represented the fall of man from virtue and happiness, and in the second, his final restoration. It consisted of nine degrees,

namely: 1, Apprentice; 2, Fellow-Craft; 3, Master; 4, Grand
Elect; 5, Apprentice Cohen; 6, Fellow Craft Cohen; 7, Master
Cohen; 8, Grand Architect; 9, Knight Commander. Paschalis
first introduced this rite into some of the lodges of Marseilles,
Toulouse, and Bordeaux, and afterwards, in 1767, he extended
it to Paris, where, for a short time, it was rather popular, ranking some of the Parisian literateurs among its disciples. It has
now ceased to exist.

PASSED. A candidate, on receiving the second degree, is
said to be "passed as a Fellow-Craft." It alludes to his having
passed through the porch to the middle chamber of the temple,
the place in which Fellow-Crafts received their wages.

PAST MASTER. An honorary degree conferred on the
W.·. Master, at his installation into office. In this degree, the
necessary instructions are conferred respecting the various ceremonies of the order, such as installations, processions, the laying
of corner stones, etc. The ceremonies of the degree, when properly conferred, inculcate a lesson of diffidence in assuming the
responsibilities of an office without a due preparation for the performance of its duties.

When a brother who has never before presided, has been
elected the Master of a lodge, an emergent lodge of Past
Masters, consisting of not less than three, is convened, and all
but Past Masters retiring, the degree is conferred upon the newly
elected officer.

But the degree is also conferred in Royal Arch Chapters
where it succeeds the Mark Master's degree. The conferring of
this degree, which has no historical connection with the rest of
the degrees, in a chapter, arises from the following circumstance.
Originally, when chapters of Royal Arch Masonry were under
the government of lodges, in which the degree was then always
conferred, it was a part of the regulations that no one could receive the Royal Arch degree, unless he had previously presided

in the lodge as Master. When the chapters became independent, the regulation could not be abolished, for that would have been an innovation; the difficulty has, therefore, been obviated, by making every candidate for the degree of Royal Arch, a Past Master before his exaltation.

For several years past the question has been agitated in some of the Grand Lodges of the United States, whether this degree is within the jurisdiction of Symbolic or of Royal Arch masonry. The explanation of its introduction into chapters, just given, manifestly demonstrates that the jurisdiction over it by chapters is altogether an assumed one. The Past Master of a chapter is only a *quasi* Past Master; the true and legitimate Past Master is the one who has presided over a symbolic lodge.

Past Masters are admitted to membership in many Grand Lodges, and by some the inherent right has been claimed to sit in those bodies. But the most eminent masonic authorities have made a contrary decision, and the general, and, indeed, almost universal opinion now is, that Past Masters obtain their seats in Grand Lodges by courtesy, and in consequence of local regulations, and not by inherent right.

The jewel of a Past Master in the United States is a pair of compasses extended to sixty degrees on the fourth part of a circle, with a sun in the centre. In England it was formerly the square on a quadrant, but is at present the square with the forty-seventh problem of Euclid engraved on a silver plate suspended within it.

PASTOS. (Greek πασrος, *a couch.*) The pastos was a chest or. close cell, in the pagan mysteries, (among the Druids, an excavated stone,) in which the aspirant was for some time placed, to commemorate the mystical death of the god. This constituted the symbolic death, which was common to all the mysteries. In the Arkite rites, the pastos represented the ark in which Noah was confined. We may refer it to the coffin among masonic emblems.

PECTORAL. Belonging to the breast, from the Latin *pectus*, the breast. The heart has always been considered the seat of fortitude and courage, and hence by this word is suggested to the Mason certain symbolic instructions in relation to the virtue of fortitude.

PEDAL. Belonging to the feet, from the Latin *pes*, a foot. The just man is he who, firmly planting his feet on the principles of right, is as immovable as a rock, and can be thrust from his upright position neither by the allurements of flattery, nor the frowns of arbitrary power. And hence by this word is suggested to the Mason certain symbolic instructions in relation to the virtue of justice.

PEDESTAL. The pedestal is the lowest part or base of a column on which the shaft is placed. In a lodge, there are supposed to be three columns, the column of Wisdom in the east, the column of Strength in the west, and the column of Beauty in the south. These columns are not generally erected in the lodge, but their pedestals always are, and at each pedestal sits one of the three superior officers of the lodge. Hence we often hear such expressions as these, *advancing to the pedestal*, or *standing before the pedestal*, to signify advancing to or standing before the seat of the Worshipful Master.*

PELICAN. The pelican is one of the symbols of the Rose Croix degree, and is intended as an allusion to the Redeemer, who shed his blood for the good of man.

Ragon says that in the hieroglyphic monuments the eagle was the symbol of a wise man, and the pelican of a benevolent one, and therefore he thinks that the eagle and pelican of the Rose

---

* The custom in some lodges of placing tables or desks before the three principal officers, is, of course, incorrect. They should, for the reason above assigned, be representations of the pedestals of column, and should be painted to represent marble or stone.

Croix are intended to symbolize perfect wisdom and perfect charity.*

PENALTY. The ceremony of entering into a covenant among the ancient Hebrews, is alluded to in Jeremiah xxxiv. 18. It was usual for the parties covenanting, to cut a beast in twain, and pass between the parts thereof. Jeremiah also relates the penalties to be inflicted upon the people for a breach of their covenant. An English writer, Brother Goodacre, (quoted by Dr. Oliver,) thus fully explains the whole ceremony of making the covenant. The allusion will not escape the attentive Mason.

"After an animal had been selected, his throat was cut across with one single blow, so as to divide the windpipe, arteries, and veins, without touching any bone. The next ceremony was to tear the breast open and pluck out the heart, and if there were the least imperfection, the body would be considered unclean. The animal was then divided into two parts, and placed north and south, that the parties to the covenant might pass between them from east to west; and the carcass was then left as a prey to voracious animals."

PENNY. The penny a day referred to in the Mark degree as the wages of a workman, was the Roman *denarius*, equal to about seven pence three farthings sterling, or twelve cents and a half federal currency.

PENTALPHA. A geometrical figure representing an endless triangle with five points, thus :

---

* Cours des Initiations, p. 320.

It was used by the Pythagoreans as an emblem of health.
(See *Five*.) The Pentalpha of Pythagoras is also called the
pentangle of Solomon, and is said to have constituted the seal or
signet of our Ancient Grand Master, and to have been inscribed
on the foundation stone of Masonry.

PERFECTION. *Grand écossais de la voûte sacrée du Jacques
VI.* The 14th degree in the Ancient Scotch rite, the 20th in
the rite of Misraim. In the Scotch rite, as practised in this
country, the degree receives the name we have given it, as well
as that of " Grand Elect, Perfect and Sublime Mason," but in
France it is called " Grand Scotch Mason of the sacred vault of
James VI." This is one of the evidences of the influence exerted by the Pretender and his adherent, Ramsay, over the organization of this rite. This degree is called by its possessors
the ultimate degree of ancient masonry, and it is indeed the last
of the ineffable degrees that refer to the first temple. Its officers
are a Most Perfect Master, representing Solomon, two Grand
Wardens, a Grand Treasurer, and Grand Secretary. The following history is connected with this degree.

When the temple was finished, the Masons who had been employed in constructing it, acquired immortal honour. Their
order became more uniformly established and regulated than it
had been before. Their caution and reserve in admitting new
members, produced respect, and merit alone was required of the
candidate. With these principles instilled into their minds,
many of the Grand Elect left the Temple after its dedication,
and dispersing themselves among the neighbouring nations, instructed all who applied and were found worthy in the sublime
degrees of ancient craft masonry.

The temple was completed in the year of the world, 3000.
Thus far, the wise King of Israel had behaved worthy of himself, and gained universal admiration; but in process of time,
when he had advanced in years, his understanding became im-
paired; he grew deaf to the voice of the Lord, and was strangely

irregular in his conduct. Proud of having erected an edifice to
his Maker, and intoxicated with his great power, he plunged into
all manner of licentiousness and debauchery, and profaned the
temple, by offering to the idol Moloch, that incense which should
have been offered only to the living God.

The Grand Elect and Perfect Masons saw this, and were sorely
grieved, afraid that his apostacy would end in some dreadful con-
sequences, and bring upon them those enemies whom Solomon
had vain-gloriously and wantonly defied. The people, copying
the vices and follies of their king, became proud and idolatrous,
and neglected the worship of the true God, for that of idols.

As an adequate punishment for this defection, God inspired
the heart of Nebuchadnezzar, King of Babylon, to take vengeance on the kingdom of Israel. This prince sent an army
with Nebuzaradan, Captain of the Guards, who entered Judah
with fire and sword, took and sacked the city of Jerusalem,
razed its walls, and destroyed the temple. The people were carried captive to Babylon, and the conquerors took with them all
the vessels of silver and gold. This happened four hundred and
seventy years, six months and ten days after its dedication.

When, in after times, the princes of Christendom entered into
a league to free the Holy Land from the oppression of the infidels, the good and virtuous Masons, anxious for the success of so
pious an undertaking, voluntarily offered their services to the
confederates, on condition that they should be permitted a chief
of their own election, which was granted; they accordingly ral-
lied under their standard and departed.

The valour and fortitude of these elected knights was such,
that they were admired by, and took the lead of, all the princes
of Jerusalem; who, believing that their mysteries inspired them
with courage and fidelity in the cause of virtue and religion, became desirous of being initiated. Upon being found worthy,
their desires were complied with, and thus, the royal art, meeting the approbation of great and good men, became popular and
honourable, was diffused through their various dominions, and

has continued to spread through a succession of ages to the present day.

The symbolic order of this degree is red, emblematic of fervour, constancy, and assiduity.

The jewel of the degree is a pair of compasses extended on an arc of 90 degrees, surmounted by a crown, and with a sun in the centre.

The apron is white with red flames, bordered with blue, and having the jewel painted on the flap.

PERFECTION, RITE OF. In 1754, the Chevalier de Bonneville established a chapter of the high degrees, which he called the chapter of Clermont, in honour of Louis of Bourbon, Prince of Clermont, at that time Grand Master of the fraternity in France. The system of masonry he there practised received the name of the rite of Perfection, or rite of Heredom. It consists of twenty-five degrees, most of which are the same as those of the Ancient Scotch rite. The degrees are as follows:—1, Apprentice; 2, Fellow Craft; 3, Master; 4, Secret Master; 5, Perfect Master; 6, Intimate Secretary; 7, Intendant of the Buildings; 8, Provost and Judge; 9, Elect of nine; 10, Elect of fifteen; 11, Illustrious elect, Chief of the twelve tribes; 12, Grand Master Architect; 13, Royal Arch; 14, Grand, Elect, Ancient, Perfect Master; 15, Knight of the Sword; 16, Prince of Jerusalem; 17, Knight of the East and West; 18, Rose Croix Knight; 19, Grand Pontiff; 20, Grand Patriarch; 21, Grand Master of the Key of Masonry; 22, Prince of Libanus; 23, Sovereign Prince Adept, Chief of the Grand Consistory; 24, Illustrious Knight, Commander of the Black and White Eagle; 25, Most Illustrious Sovereign Prince of Masonry, Grand Knight, Sublime Commander of the Royal Secret.

The distinguishing principle of this rite is, that Freemasonry was derived from Templarism, and that consequently every Freemason was a Knight Templar. It is still practised, or was a few years since, in a single lodge in Paris.

PERFECT MASTER. *Maître Parfait.* The fifth degree in the Ancient Scotch rite. The ceremonies of this degree were originally established as a grateful tribute of respect to a worthy departed brother. The officers of the lodge are a Right Worshipful Master, who represents the Noble Adoniram, the inspector of the works at Mount Libanus, and a Warden, who is called Inspector. The conductor represents Zerbal, the Captain of the Guards. The symbolic colour of the degree is green, to remind the Perfect Master that, being dead in vice, he must hope to revive in virtue. His jewel is a compass extended 60 degrees, to teach him that he should act within measure, and ever pay due regard to justice and equity.

The apron is white, with a green flap, and in the middle of the apron must be embroidered or painted, within three circles, a square stone, in the centre of which the letter J is inscribed.

PERFECT UNION, LODGE OF. A lodge at Rennes in France, which, in the last century, created a new modification of masonry, under the name of the rite of the Elect of Truth. It consisted of fourteen degrees, divided into three classes, taken with slight alterations from the rite of perfection. The degrees were as follows:

I. *Class.*—1, Entered Apprentice; 2, Fellow-Craft; 3, Master; 4, Perfect Master.

II. *Class.*—5, Elect of nine; 6, Elect of fifteen; 7, Master Elect; 8, Minor Architect; 9, Second Architect; 10, Grand Architect; 11, Knight of the East; 12, Rose Croix.

III. *Class.*—13, Knight Adept; 14, Elect of Truth.

This rite, at one time, had several lodges in various parts of France.

PERPENDICULAR. In a geometrical sense, that which is upright and erect, leaning neither one way nor another. In a figurative and symbolic sense, it conveys the signification of Justice, Fortitude, Prudence, and Temperance. Justice, that leans to no side but that of Truth; Fortitude, that yields to no adverse attack; Prudence, that ever pursues the straight path of integrity; and Temperance, that swerves not for appetite nor passion. See *Plumb.*

PERSECUTIONS. I enter on the history of the persecutions to which our order has been subjected, with a reluctance that I have not felt in the other portions of this work. The record of the follies and the crimes of his race, furnish no pleasant theme to the historian. But truth summons me to the task, odious though it be, of showing that masonry, virtuous as are its principles, charitable as are its objects, and instructive as are its ceremonies, has, nevertheless, been repeatedly exposed to the blinded rage of political hostility, or of religious bigotry.

One of the first persecutions to which masonry, in its present organization, was subjected, occurred in the year 1735, in Holland. On the 16th of October, of that year, a crowd of ignorant fanatics whose zeal had been enkindled by the denunciations of some of the clergy, broke into a house in Amsterdam, where a lodge was accustomed to be held, and destroyed all the furniture and ornaments of the lodge. The States General, yielding to the popular excitement, or rather desirous of giving no occasion for its action, prohibited the future meetings of the lodges. One, however, continuing, regardless of the edict, to meet at a private house, the members were arrested and brought before the Court of Justice. Here, in the presence of the whole city, the Masters and Wardens defended themselves with great dexterity; and while acknowledging their inability to prove the innocence of their institution by a public exposure of their secret doctrines, they freely offered to receive and initiate any person in the confidence of the magistrates, and who could then give them information upon which they might depend, relative to the true designs of the institution. The proposal was acceded to, and the town clerk was chosen. He was immediately initiated, and his report so pleased his superiors, that all the magistrates and principal persons of the city became members and zealous patrons of the order.

In France, the fear of the authorities that the Freemasons concealed, within the recesses of their lodges, designs hostile to the government, gave occasion to an attempt, in 1737, on the part of the police, to prohibit the meeting of the lodges. But this unfavourable disposition did not long continue, and the last instance of the interference of the government with the proceedings of the masonic body, was in June 1745, when the members of a lodge, meeting at the Hotel de Soissons, were dispersed, their furniture and jewels seized, and the landlord amerced in a penalty of three thousand livres.

The persecutions in Germany were owing to a singular cause. The malice of a few females had been excited by their disappointed curiosity. A portion of this disposition they succeeded in communicating to the Empress, Maria Theresa, who issued an order for apprehending all the Masons in Vienna, when assembled in their lodges. The measure was, however, frustrated by the good sense of the Emperor, Joseph I., who was himself a Mason, and exerted his power in protecting his brethren.

The persecutions of the church in Italy, and other Catholic countries, have been the most extensive and most permanent. On the 28th of April, 1738, Pope Clement XII. issued the famous bull against Freemasons, whose authority is still in existence. In this bull, the Roman Pontiff says, " We have learned, and public rumor does not permit us to doubt the truth of the report, that a certain society has been formed, under the name of Freemasons, into which persons of all religions and all sects are indiscriminately admitted, and whose members have established certain laws which bind themselves to each other, and which, in particular, compel their members, under the severest penalties, by virtue of an oath taken on the Holy Scriptures, to preserve an inviolable secrecy in relation to every thing that passes in their meetings." The bull goes on to declare, that these societies have become suspected by the faithful, and that they are hurtful to the tranquillity of the state and to the safety of the soul; and after making use of the now thread-bare argument, that if the actions of Freemasons were irreproachable, they would not so carefully conceal them from the light, it proceeds to enjoin all bishops, superiors, and ordinaries, to punish the Freemasons " with the penalties which they deserve, as people greatly suspected of heresy, having recourse, if necessary, to the secular arm."*

What this delivery to the secular arm means, we are at no loss to discover, from the interpretation given to the bull by Cardinal Firrao, in his edict of publication in the beginning of the following year; namely, " that no person shall dare to assemble at any lodge of the said society, nor be present at any of their meetings, under *pain of death*, and confiscation of goods, the said penalty to be without hope of pardon."†

The bull of Clement met in France with no congenial spirits to obey it.. On the contrary, it was the subject of universal condemnation as arbitrary and unjust, and the parliament of Paris positively refused to enrol it. But in other Catholic countries it was better respected. In Tuscany the persecutions were unremitting. A man named Crudeli, was arrested at Florence, thrown into the dungeons of the inquisition, subjected to torture, and finally sentenced to a long imprisonment on the charge of having furnished an asylum to a masonic lodge. The Grand Lodge of England, upon learning the circumstances, obtained his enlargement and sent him pecuniary assistance. Francis de

---

* As late as 1802, in Austria, and the Ecclesiastical States, all public functionaries were compelled, before their installation, to declare upon oath that they were not members of the order of Freemasons.

† Clavel gives the original of this most merciful interpretation. I quote it, lest the severity of the penalty should throw a doubt upon the correctness of my translation, which my Italian readers may easily verify. "Che nessuno ardisca di radunarsi e congregarsi e di aggregarsi, in luogo alcuno, sotto le sudette società, nè di trovarsi presente a tali radunanze, sotta *pena della morte* e confiscazione do beni, da incorrersi irremisibilmente, senza speranza di grazia.

Lorraine, who had been initiated at the Hague, in 1731, soon after ascended the grand ducal throne, and one of the first acts of his reign was to liberate all the Masons who had been incarcerated by the inquisition, and still further to evince his respect for the order, he personally assisted in the constitution of several lodges at Florence, and in other cities of his dominions.

The other sovereigns of Italy were, however, more obedient to the behests of the holy father, and persecutions continued to rage throughout the peninsula. Nevertheless, masonry continued to flourish, and in 1751, thirteen years after the emission of the bull of prohibition, lodges were openly in existence in Tuscany, at Naples, and even in the "eternal city" itself.

The priesthood, whose vigilance had abated under the influence of time, became once more alarmed, and an edict was issued in 1751, by Benedict XIV., who then occupied the papal chair, renewing and enforcing the bull which had been fulminated by Clement.

This, of course, renewed the spirit of persecution. In Spain, one Tournon, a Frenchman, was convicted of practising the rites of masonry, and after a tedious confinement in the dungeons of the inquisition, he was finally banished from the kingdom.

In Portugal, at Lisbon, John Coustos, a native of Switzerland, was still more severely treated. He was subjected to the torture, and suffered so much that he was unable to move his limbs for three months. Coustos, with two companions of his reputed crime, was sentenced to the galleys, but was finally released by the interposition of the English ambassador. The work of Coustos, in which he recounts the circumstances of his imprisonment and trial, is now before me, and the details of the tortures to which he was subjected, in the hope of extorting the secrets of masonry from him, inspire the most tender pity for his sufferings, and the most unqualified admiration of his fortitude and fidelity.

But the persecutions of the order were not confined to Catholic countries. In 1745, the Council of Berne, in Switzerland,

30

issued a decree prohibiting under the severest penalties, the as
semblages of Freemasons. In 1757, in Scotland, the Synod of
Sterling adopted a resolution debarring all adhering Freemasons
from the ordinances of religion. And, as if to prove that fanaticism is everywhere the same, in 1748 the Divan at Constantinople caused a masonic lodge to be demolished, its jewels and
furniture seized, and its members arrested. They were discharged upon the interposition of the English minister, but the
government prohibited the introduction of the order into Turkey.

Our own country has not been free from the blighting influence of this demon of fanaticism. But the exciting scenes of
anti-masonry are too recent to be treated by the historian with
coolness or impartiality. The political party to which this spirit
of persecution gave birth, was the most abject in its principles, and
the most unsuccessful in its efforts, of any that our times have
seen. It has passed away; the clouds of anti-masonry have been,
we trust, forever dispersed, and the bright sun of masonry, once
more emerging from its temporary eclipse, is beginning to bless
our land with the invigorating heat and light of its meridian rays.

PERSIAN PHILOSOPHIC RITE. A rite attempted to be
established in France about the year 1819. It consisted of seven
degrees, as follows:—1, Listening Apprentice; 2, Fellow-Craft
Adept, Esquire of Benevolence; 3, Master, Knight of the Sun;
4, Architect of all rites, Knight of the philosophy of the heart;
5, Knight of eclecticism and of truth; 6, Master Good Shepherd;
7, Venerable Grand Elect. This rite never contained many members, and is now abolished.

PETITION. When a new lodge is about to be formed, application to the Grand Lodge, within whose jurisdiction it is
situated, must be made in the form of petition. The petition must
be signed by at least seven Master Masons, and the masonic and
moral character of the petitioners certified by one or more well
known brethren. Petitions to a Grand Chapter for the formation

of Chapters of Royal Arch Masons, require the signature of nine companions; and for Encampments of Knights Templars and the appendant orders, the application to the Grand Encampment must be made by nine knights.

PHALLUS. (Greek φαλλος.) The phallus was the wooden image of the *membrum virile*, which being affixed to a pole, formed a part of most of the pagan mysteries, and was worshipped as the emblem of the male generative principle. The phallic worship was first established in Egypt. The origin of its institution was this. After the murder of Osiris, and the mutilation of the body by Typhon, Isis was enabled to recover all the parts of his body except the privities. To this part, therefore, in commemoration of its loss, she paid particular honour. The phallus, its representation, was made of wood, and carried during the sacred festivals in the mysteries of Osiris, as the emblem of fecundity. It was held by the people in the greatest veneration, and the sight or mention of it produced in the minds of the ancients no impure or lascivious thoughts. From Egypt it was introduced into Greece, and its exhibition formed a part of the Dionysian mysteries. In the Indian mysteries, it was called the *lingam*, and was always found in the most holy place of the temple. It was adopted by the idolatrous Israelites, who took it from the Moabites when in the wilderness of Sin, under the name of Baalpeor.* In short, the veneration of the phallus, under different names, was common to all the nations of antiquity. We shall again have occasion to refer to it, in the article on the Point within a Circle, with which masonic emblem the phallus has been identified by Dr. Oliver in an elaborate chapter in his "Signs and Symbols." The masonic explanation, however, it will hereafter be perceived, bears no longer any allusion to the solar orb, or great principle of fecundity, except in its form ⊙, a figure still

---

* Cumberland says Baal-pehor in the Chaldaic signifies the naked god, and is equivalent to the Roman deity Priapus.

retained by astronomers as the representation of the sun. See
Point within a Circle.

PHILALETHES, RITE OF THE. The rite of the Philalethes or Searchers after Truth, was invented in the lodge of Amis
Reunis at Paris, in 1775, by Savalette de Langes, Keeper of the
Royal Treasury. It was compounded of the masonic reveries of
Swedenburg and Paschalis, and was distributed into twelve classes
or chambers of instruction. The names of these classes or degrees
were as follows :—1, Apprentice; 2, Fellow Craft; 3, Master; 4,
Elect; 5, Scotch Master; 6, Knight of the East; 7, Rose Croix;
8, Knight of the Temple; 9, Unknown Philosopher; 10, Sublime
Philosopher ; 11, Initiate ; 12, Philalethes or Searcher after
Truth. The first six degrees were called Petty, and the last six
High Masonry. The rite existed only during the life of de
Langes; at his death in 1788, it ceased to exist, and the lodge
of Amis Reunis was dissolved.

PHILOSOPHICAL DEGREES. All the degrees above the
Rose Croix obtain this appellation. They are so called because
they are particularly directed to the philosophical explanation of
the system of masonry, which, in the inferior degrees, receives a
moral signification. They are not to be confounded with the
philosophical orders which arose on the continent of Europe about
the close of the eighteenth century, and whose tendency, in many
instances, was towards natural religion or deism. Barruel and
Robinson, however, have confounded them, and on this error have
based many, if not all, of their false charges against Freemasonry.

PHILOSOPHIC LODGE. The degree of Knights of the
Sun is sometimes thus styled.

PHILOSOPHIC SCOTCH RITE.—*Rite écossais philosophique.* In the year 1770, one Pernetti founded a rite of Freemasonry, which he called the "Hermetic rite," but which was

rather an alchemical than a masonic society, for its object was, by symbolic lessons, to instruct its disciples in the art of transmuting metals, and preparing the elixir of life. One of Pernetti's most ingenious disciples was a physician of Paris, named Boileau. He modified the system of the Hermetic rite, gave it a more purely masonic character and established its practice in one of the lodges of Paris, under the name of the "Philosophic Scotch Rite." The two rites were subsequently united, and the Grand Lodge was established in 1776, at Paris. It consists of twelve degrees, as follows : 1, 2, 3, Knight of the Black Eagle, or Rose Croix, divided into three parts ; 4, Knight of the Phœnix; 5, Knight of the Sun ; 6, Knight of Iris ; 7, Freemason ; 8, Knight of the Argonauts ; 9, Knight of the Golden Fleece ; 10, Grand Inspector, Perfect Initiate ; 11, Grand Inspector, Grand Scotch Mason ; 12, Sublime Master of the Luminous Ring. The three degrees of ancient Craft Masonry are necessary pre-requisites, though they do not form a part of the rite. It is still practised in France, but to a very limited extent.

We may form some notion of the masonic doctrine taught in this rite, from the name of the degree which is at its summit. The "Luminous Ring" is a Pythagorean degree. In 1780 an Academy of the Sublime Masters of the Luminous Ring was established in France, in which the doctrine was taught that Freemasonry was originally founded by Pythagoras, and in which the most important portion of the lectures consisted of an explanation of the peculiar doctrines of the sage of Samos. We may, therefore, presume that the same doctrines were taught in the rite under examination.

PICKAXE. One of the working tools of a Royal Arch Mason. For its emblematic signification see *Shovel.*

PILGRIM'S SHELL. The shell was an Ancient symbol of the Syrian Goddess Astarte, who was the same as the Venus Pelagia, or Venus rising from the sea, of the western mythology.
30*

The escalop or scollop shell (the *Pecten* of Linnæus) is found in great abundance on the shores of the Mediterranean, and was worn in the time of the Crusades by pilgrims to the Holy Land, as a Memorial of the pious pilgrimage they were then perform ing or had already accomplished. Thus Shakspeare makes Ophelia sing :

> " And how should I thy true love know,
>   From any other one ?
>   O ! by his scollop shell and staff,
>   And by his sandal shoon."

Hence the scollop shell, staff and sandals, form a part of the costume of a candidate in the ceremonies of the Templar's degree.

PILLAR.   In the earliest times it was customary to perpetu ate remarkable events, or exhibit gratitude for providential favours, by the erection of pillars, which by the idolatrous races were dedicated to their spurious gods.   Thus Sanconiatho tells us that Hypsourianos and Ousous, who lived before the flood, dedi cated two pillars to the elements, fire and air.   Among the Egyptians the pillars were, in general, in the form of obelisks, from 50 to 100 feet high, and exceedingly slender in proportion. Upon their four sides, hieroglyphics were often engraved.   According to Herodotus, they were first raised in honour of the sun, and their pointed form was intended to represent his rays. Many of these monuments still remain.

In the antediluvian ages, the posterity of Seth erected pillars ; " for," says the Jewish historian, " that their inventions might not be lost before they were sufficiently known, upon Adam's prediction, that the world was to be destroyed at one time by the force of fire, and at another time by the violence of water, they made two pillars, the one of brick, the other of stone; they in scribed their discoveries on them both, that in case the pillar of brick should be destroyed by the flood, the pillar of stone might remain, and exhibit those discoveries to mankind, and also inform

them that there was another pillar of brick erected by them."[*]
Jacob erected a pillar at Bethel, to commemorate his remarkable
vision of the ladder, and afterwards another one at Galeed as a
memorial of his alliance with Laban. Joshua erected one at
Gilgal to perpetuate the remembrance of his miraculous crossing
of the Jordan. Samuel set up a pillar between Mizpeh and
Shen, on account of a defeat of the Philistines, and Absalom
erected another in honour of himself.

PILLARS OF THE PORCH. The pillars most remarkable
in Scripture history, were the two erected by Solomon at the
porch of the Temple, and which Josephus thus describes:
"Moreover, this Hiram made two hollow pillars, whose outsides
were of brass, and the thickness of the brass was four fingers
breadth, and the height of the pillars was eighteen cubits, (27
feet,) and the circumference twelve cubits, (18 feet;) but there
was cast with each of their chapiters, lily work, that stood upon
the pillar, and it was elevated five cubits, (7½ feet,) round about
which there was net work interwoven with small palms made of
brass, and covered the lily work. To this also were hung two
hundred pomegranates, in two rows. The one of these pillars
he set at the entrance of the porch on the right hand, (*or south*,)
and called it Jachin, and the other at the left hand, (*or north*,)
and called it Boaz."

It has been supposed that Solomon, in erecting these pillars,
had reference to the pillar of cloud and the pillar of fire which
went before the Israelites in the wilderness, and that the right
hand or south pillar represented the pillar of cloud, and the left
hand or north pillar represented that of fire. Solomon did not
simply erect them as ornaments to the temple, but as memorials
of God's repeated promises of support to his people of Israel.

---

[*] Joseph. Antiq. lib. 1. c. ii. Josephus says this pillar in his time was still
remaining in the land of Siriad; but Whiston supposes the pillar thus referred
to, to have been erected by Sesostris, King of Egypt.

For the pillar יכין (*Jachin,*) derived from the words יה (*Jah,*) "Jehovah," and הכין (*achin*) "to establish," signifies that "God will establish his house of Israel;" while the pillar בעז (*Boaz*) compounded of ב (*b,*) "in" and עז (*oaz,*) "strength," signifies, that "in strength shall it be established." And thus were the Jews, in passing through the porch to the temple, daily reminded of the abundant promises of God, and inspired with confidence in his protection and gratitude for his many acts of kindness to his chosen people.

The construction of these pillars.—There is no part of the architecture of the ancient temple which is so difficult to be understood in its details, as the Scriptural account of these memorable pillars. Freemasons, in general, intimately as their symbolical signification is connected with some of the most beautiful portions of their ritual, appear to have but a confused notion of their construction and of the true disposition of the various parts of which they are composed. With a view to relieve this subject from some of the difficulties which surround it, I, some time since, published an essay on these pillars in Moore's Magazine; and as that essay contained all the results of a rather laborious investigation, I shall transfer so much of it as is appropriate to the present article.

The situation of these pillars, according to Lightfoot,* was *within* the porch, at its very entrance and on each side of the gate. They were therefore seen, one on the right, and the other on the left, as soon as the visitor stepped within the porch.† And this, it will be remembered, in confirmation, is the very spot in which Ezekiel places the pillars that he saw in his vision of the Temple. "The length of the porch was twenty cubits,

---

* See his treatise entitled "a Prospect of the Temple."

† If this position be the correct one, and Lightfoot supports the hypothesis by strong arguments, then Oliver, as well as most of our lecturers, is wrong in the statement that the pillars were placed before the porch of the temple, and must have been passed before entering it. See Oliver's Landmarks, vol. 1., p. 451.

and the breadth eleven cubits; and he brought me by the steps whereby they went up to it, and there were pillars by the posts, one on this side, and another on that side."*

These pillars, we are told, were of brass, as well as the chapiters that surmounted them, and were cast hollow. The thickness of the brass of each pillar was "four fingers, or a hand's breadth," which is equal to three inches. According to the accounts in 1 Kings viii. 15, and in Jeremiah lii. 21, the circumference of each pillar was twelve cubits. Now, according to the Jewish computation, the cubit used in the measurement of the temple buildings was six hands' breadth, or eighteen inches. According to the tables of Bishop Cumberland, the cubit was rather more, he making it about twenty-two inches; but I adhere to the measure laid down by the Jewish writers, as probably more correct, and certainly more simple for calculation. The circumference of each pillar, reduced by this scale to English measure, would be eighteen feet, and its diameter about six.

The reader of the Scriptural accounts of these pillars will be not a little puzzled with the apparent discrepancies that are found in the estimates of their height as given in the Books of Kings and Chronicles. In the former book, it is said that their height was eighteen cubits, and in the latter it was thirty-five.† But the discrepancy is easily reconciled by supposing, which, indeed, must have been the case, that in the Book of Kings the pillars are spoken of separately, and that, in Chronicles, their aggregate height is calculated; and the reason why, in this latter book, their united height is placed at thirty-five cubits instead of thirty-six, which would be the double of eighteen, is because they are there measured as they appeared with the chapiters upon them. Now half a cubit of each pillar was concealed in, what Lightfoot calls "the hole of the chapiter," that is, half a

* Ezekiel, xi. 49.

† Whiston observes that the latter height would be contrary to all the rules of architecture.

cubits's depth of the lower edge of the chapiter covered the top
of the pillar, making each pillar, apparently, only seventeen and
a half cubits high, or the two thirty-five cubits, as laid down in
the Book of Chronicles.

This is a much better method of reconciling the discrepancy
than that adopted by Calcott,* who supposes that the pedestals
of the pillars were seventeen cubits high—a violation of every
rule of architectural proportion with which we would be reluc-
tant to charge the memory of so "cunning a workman" as
Hiram the Builder. The account in Jeremiah agrees with that
in the Book of Kings. The height, therefore, of each of these
pillars was, in English measure, twenty-seven feet. The chapiter
or pomel was five cubits, or seven and a half feet more; but as
half a cubit, or nine inches, was common to both pillar and
chapiter, the whole height from the ground to the top of the
chapiter was twenty-two cubits and a half, or thirty-three feet
and nine inches.

Each of these pillars was surmounted by a chapiter, which
was five cubits or seven and a half feet in height. The shape
and construction of this chapiter requires some consideration.
The Hebrew word which is used in this place is כותרת, (kote-
ret.) Its root is to be found in the word כתר, (keter,) which
signified "a crown," and is so used in Esther vi. 8., to designate the royal diadem of the King of Persia. The Chaldaic version expressly calls the chapiter "a crown," but Rabbi Solomon,
in his commentary, uses the word פומיל, (pomel,) signifying
"a globe or spherical body," and Rabbi Gershom describes it as
"like two crowns joined together." Lightfoot says, "it was a
huge, great, oval, five cubits high, and did not only sit upon the
head of the pillars, but also flowered or spread them, being
larger about, a great deal, than the pillars themselves." The
Jewish commentators say that the two lower cubits of its surface

---

* Calcott's Masonry, p. 151.

were entirely plain, but that the three upper were richly ornamented. To this ornamental part we now arrive.

In the first Book of Kings, ch. vii. verses 17, 20, 22, the
ornaments of the chapiters are thus described :

"And nets of checker-work and wreaths of chain work, for the
chapiters which were upon the tops of the pillars ; seven for the
one chapiter, and seven for the other chapiter.

"And he made the pillars, and two rows round about upon
the one net-work, to cover the chapiters that were upon the top,
with pomegranates ; and so did he for the other chapiter.

"And the chapiters that were upon the tops of the pillars were
of lily work in the porch, four cubits.

"And the chapiters upon the two pillars had pomegranates
also above, over against the belly, which was by the net work ;
and the pomegranates were two hundreds in rows, round about
upon the other chapiter.

"And upon the top of the pillars was lily work ; so was the
work of the pillars finished."

Let us endeavour to render this description, which appears
somewhat confused and unintelligible, plainer and more compre-
hensible.

The "nets of checker-work," is the first ornament mentioned.
The words thus translated are in the original שבכים מעשה
שבכה, which Lightfoot prefers rendering "thickets of branch
work ;" and he thinks that the true meaning of the passage is,
that "the chapiters were curiously wrought with branch work,
seven goodly branches standing up from the belly of the oval,
and their boughs and leaves curiously and lovelily intermingled
and interwoven one with another." He derives his reason for
this version, from the fact that the same word, שבכה, is translated, "thicket" in the passage in Genesis (xxii. 13,) where the
ram is described as being "caught in a thicket by his horns,"
and in various other passages the word is to be similarly translated. But, on the other hand, we find it used in the Book of
Job, where it evidently signifies a net made of meshes : " For

he is cast into a *net* by his own feet and he walketh upon a
snare." Job xvii. 8. In 2 Kings i. 2, the same word is used,
where our translators have rendered it a *lattice;* "Ahaziah fell
down through a lattice in his upper chamber." I am, therefore,
not inclined to adopt the emendation of Lightfoot, but rather
coincide with the received version as well as the masonic tradition that this ornament was a simple net-work or fabric consisting
of reticulated lines.

The "wreaths of chain work" that are next spoken of, are less
difficult to be understood. The word here translated "wreath,"
is גְּדִלִים, and is to be found in Deuteronomy xxii. 12, where it
distinctly means *fringes:* "Thou shalt make thee fringes upon
the four quarters of thy vesture." *Fringes*, it should also be
translated here. "The fringes of chain work," I suppose, were,
therefore, attached to, and hung down from, the net-work spoken
of above, and were probably in this case, as when used upon the
garments of the Jewish high priest, intended as a "memorial of
the law."

The "lily work," is the last ornament that demands our attention. And here the description of Lightfoot is so clear and
evidently correct, that I shall not hesitate to quote it at length.
"At the head of the pillar, even at the setting on of the chapiter, there was a curious and a large border or circle of lily work,
which stood out four cubits under the chapiter, and then turned
down, every lily or long tongue of brass, with a neat bending,
and so seemed as a flowered crown to the head of the pillar, and
as a curious garland whereon the chapiter had its seat."

There is a very common error among Masons, which has been
fostered by the plates in our "Monitors," that there were on the
pillars, chapiters, and that these chapiters were again surmounted
by globes. The truth, however, is that the chapiters themselves
were "the pomels or globes" to which our lecture, in the Fellow
Craft's degree, alludes. This is evident from what has already
been said in the first part of the preceding description. The

maps of the earth and the charts of the celestial, constellations which are sometimes said to have been engraved upon these globes, must be referred to the pillars where, according to Oliver, a masonic tradition places them—an ancient custom, instances of which we find in profane history. This is, however, by no means of any importance, as the symbolic allusion is perfectly well preserved in the shapes of the chapiters, without the necessity of any such geographical or astronomical engraving upon them. For being globular, or nearly so, they may be justly said to have represented the celestial and terrestrial spheres.

The true description, then, of these memorable pillars, is simply this. Immediately within the porch of the temple, and on each side of the door, were placed two hollow brazen pillars. The height of each was twenty-seven feet, the diameter about six feet, and the thickness of the brass three inches. Above the pillar, and covering its upper part to the depth of nine inches, was an oval body or chapiter, seven feet and a half in height. Springing out from the pillar, at the junction of the chapiter with it, was a row of lily petals, which, first spreading around the chapiter, afterwards gently curved downwards towards the pillar, something like the Acanthus leaves on the capital of a Corinthian column. About two-fifths of the distance from the bottom of the chapiter, or just below its most bulging part, a tissue of net-work was carved, which extended over its whole upper surface. To the bottom of this net-work was suspended a series of fringes, and on these again were carved two rows of pomegranates, one hundred being in each row.

This description, it seems to me, is the only one that can be reconciled with the various passages in the Books of Kings, Chronicles and Jeremiah, which relate to these pillars, and the only one that can give the masonic student a correct conception of the architecture of these important symbols.

PLATONIC ACADEMY. A society instituted at Florence, in 1480. The hall in which its meetings were held still exists,

and is said to be ornamented with masonic emblems. Clavel
supposes it to have been a society founded by some of the honorary members and patrons of the fraternity of Freemasons who
existed in the Middle Ages, and who, having abandoned the material design of the institution, confined themselves to its mystic
character. If his suggestion be correct, this is one of the
earliest instances of the separation of speculative from operative
masonry.

PLENTY. The ear of corn is the masonic symbol of plenty,
and was derived, as nearly all the masonic symbols have been,
from the ancient system of symbolism. According to Montfau-
con, ears of corn always accompanied the images of the goddess
Plenty in the ancient gems and medals, of which he gives
several examples. The Hebrew word *Shibboleth* signifies an ear
of corn.

PLUMB. An instrument made use of, by operative masons,
for the purpose of erecting perpendicular lines, and which, in
speculative masonry, constitutes one of the working tools of the
Fellow-Craft. As the building which is not erected on a perpendicular line, but leans either one way or the other, becomes inse-
cure, and must eventually fall, by the force of gravity, to the
ground, so he, whose life is not supported by an upright course
of conduct, but whose principles are swayed by the uncertain
dictates of interest or passion, cannot long sustain a worthy reputation, and must soon sink beneath the estimation of every good
and virtuous citizen. But the just, the upright, the unwavering
man, who bends not beneath the attacks of adversity, nor yields
to the temptations of prosperity, but still pursues the "even
tenor of his way," will stand erect amid the fiercest tempests of
fortune, and, like a tall column, lift his head above the frowns of
envy and the slanders of malignity. To the man thus just and
upright, the sacred Scriptures attribute as necessary parts of his
character, kindness and liberality, temperance and moderation,

truth and wisdom; and the heathen poet, Horace, pays, in one
of his most admired odes, an eloquent tribute to his stern immu-
tability.

> The man in conscious virtue bold,
> Who dares his secret purpose bold,
> Unshaken hears the crowd's tumultuous cries
> And the impetuous tyrant's angry brow defies.
> Let the loud winds that rule the seas,
> Their wild tempestuous horrors raise;
> Let Jove's dread arm with thunders rend the spheres,
> Beneath the crush of worlds undaunted he appears.*

[*Francis.*

The plumb is also the jewel of the Junior Warden, and it
seems here symbolically to instruct us, as the authority of this
officer is exercised only in time of refreshment, when the brethren
having ceased to labour, are no longer within the sacred precincts
of the lodge room, that then more particularly, when the eyes of
a censorious world are upon him, should the Mason walk up-
rightly and eschew evil.†

POINTS OF FELLOWSHIP. The pentalpha, or triple tri-

> * Justum et tenacem propositi virum
> Non civium ardor prava jubentium,
> Non vultus instantis tyranni
> Mente quatit solido, neque Auster
> Dux inquieti turbidus Adriæ :
> Nec fulminantis magna Jovis manus.
> Si fractus illabatur orbis
> Impavidum ferient ruinæ.

[*Hor.* lib. iii. od. 3.

† It is worthy of notice that, in most languages, the word which is used in
a direct sense to indicate straightness of course or perpendicularity of position,
is also employed in a figurative sense to express uprightness of conduct.
Such are the Latin "*rectum*," which signifies at the same time a *right line* and
honesty or *integrity* ; the Greek 'ορθός which means *straight, standing upright*,
and also *equitable, just, true* ; and the Hebrew *tsedek*, which in a physical
sense denotes *rightness, straightness*, and in a moral, *what is right and just.*
Our own word RIGHT, partakes of this peculiarity, *right* being *not wrong*, as
well as *not crooked*.

angle, was among the Pythagoreans the emblem of health, because it constituted a figure of five lines and five points; among Masons, in the form of a five-pointed star, it has been adopted as the symbol of the most sacred principles of their profession. See *Five Points of Fellowship*, and *Star*.

POINTS, TWELVE GRAND.   See *Twelve Grand Points.*

POINT WITHIN A CIRCLE.   This emblem is to be found in every well regulated lodge, and is explained as representing— the *point*, the individual brother, and the *circle*, the boundary line of his duty.   But that this was not always its symbolic signification, we may collect from the true history of its connection with the phallus of the ancient mysteries.   The phallus, as I have already shown, under the word, was among the Egyptians the symbol of fecundity, expressed by the male generative principle.   It was communicated from the rites of Osiris to the religious festivals of Greece.   Among the Asiatics the same emblem, under the name of lingam, was, in connection with the female principle, worshipped as the symbols of the Great Father and Mother, or producing causes of the human race, after their destruction by the deluge.   On this subject, Captain Wilford remarks "that it was believed in India, that, at the general deluge, every thing was involved in the common destruction, except the male and female principles, or organs of generation, which were destined to produce a new race, and to re-people the earth when the waters had subsided from its surface.   The female principle, symbolized by the moon, assumed the form of a lunette or crescent; while the male principle, symbolized by the sun, assuming the form of the lingam, placed himself erect in the centre of the lunette, like the mast of a ship.   The two principles, in this united form, floated on the surface of the waters during the period of their prevalence on the earth; and thus became the progenitors of a new race of men."[*]   Here, then, was the first

* Asiat. Researches, cit. apud Oliver, Signs and Symbols, 180.

outline of the point within a circle, representing the principle of fecundity, and doubtless the symbol, connected with a different history, that, namely, of Osiris, was transmitted by the Indian philosophers to Egypt, and to the other nations, who derived, as we have elsewhere shown, all their rites from the East.

As an evidence of this, we find the same symbol in the Druidical and Scandinavian rites. The temples of the Druids were circular, with a single stone erected in the centre. A Druidical monument in Prembrokeshire, called Y Cromlech, is described as consisting of several rude stones pitched on end in a circular order, and in the midst of the circle a vast stone placed on several pillars. Near Keswick, in Cumberland, says Oliver, is another specimen of this Druidical symbol. On a hill stands a circle of forty stones placed perpendicularly, of about five feet and a half in height, and one stone in the centre of greater altitude.*

Among the Scandinavians, the hall of Odin contained twelve seats, disposed in the form of a circle for the principal gods, with an elevated seat in the centre for Odin. Scandinavian monuments of this form are still to be found in Scania, Zealand, and Jutland.†

But it is useless to multiply examples of the prevalence of this symbol among the ancients. And now let us apply this knowledge to the masonic symbol.

We have seen that the phallus, and the point within a circle, come from the same source, and must have been identical in signification. But the phallus was the symbol of fecundity, or the male generative principle, which by the ancients was supposed to be the sun, (they looking to the creature and not to the Creator,) because by the sun's heat and light, the earth is made prolific, and its productions are brought to maturity. The point within the circle was then originally the symbol of the sun, and as the lingam of India stood in the centre of the lunette, so it stands within the centre of the Universe, typified by the circle impreg-

---

* Signs and Symbols, 174.　　† Mallet's Northern Antiquities.

nating and vivifying it with its heat.   And thus the astronomers
have been led to adopt the same figure ⊙, as their symbol of that
luminary.*

The present signification of the point, within the circle, among
Masons, is doubtless comparatively modern, and has superseded
the original meaning of this symbol.

POMEGRANATE.   The pomegranate, as an emblem, was
known to and highly esteemed by the nations of antiquity.   In
the description of the pillars which stood at the porch of the temple, (see 1 Kings vii. 15,) it is said that the artificer "made two
chapiters of molten brass to set upon the tops of the pillars."
Now the Hebrew word *caphtorim*, which has been translated
"chapiters," and for which in Amos ix. 1, the word "lintel"
has been incorrectly substituted, (though the marginal reading
corrects the error,) signifies an *artificial large pomegranate*, or
globe.†   It was customary to place such ornaments upon the tops
or heads of columns, and in other situations.   The skirt of Aaron's
robe was ordered to be decorated with golden bells and pomegranates, and they were among the ornaments fixed upon the
golden candelabra.   There seems, therefore, to have been attached
to this fruit some mystic signification, to which it is indebted for
the veneration thus paid to it.   If so, this mystic meaning should
be traced into spurious Freemasonry; for there, after all, if there
be any antiquity in our order, we shall find the parallel of all its
rites and ceremonies.

1. The Syrians at Damascus worshipped an idol which they

---

* Fellowes, giving an ancient astronomical signification to this symbol, says
that the point was Deity, the circle the path of the sun, and the two parallels
the solstices, beyond which the sun cannot pass.

† Vid. Cumberland Origines Gent. Antiq. tract. II § ii. p. 54.   The original
meaning is not preserved in the Septuagint, which has σφαιρωτηρ, nor in the
Vulgate which uses "sphærula," both meaning simply "a round ball."   But
Josephus, in his Antiquities, has kept to the literal Hebrew.

called Rimmon. This was the same idol that was worshipped by
Naaman before his conversion, as recorded in the second book of
Kings. The learned have not been able to agree as to the nature
of this idol, whether he was a representation of Helios or the Sun,
the god of the Phenicians, or of Venus, or according to Grotius,
in his commentary on the passage in Kings, of Saturn, or what,
according to Statius, seems more probable, of Jupiter Cassius.
But it is sufficient for our present purpose to know that *Rimmon*
is the Hebrew and Syriac for *pomegranate*.

2. Cumberland, the learned Bishop of Peterborough, quotes
Achilles Statius, a converted pagan and Bishop of Alexandria,
as saying that on Mount Cassius, (which Bochart places between
Canaan and Egypt,) there was a temple wherein Jupiter's image
held a pomegranate in his hand, which Statius goes on to say,
"had a mystical meaning."* Sanconiatho thinks this temple
was built by the descendants of the Cabiri. Cumberland attempts
to explain this mystery thus : "Agreeably hereunto I guess that
the pomegranate in the hand of Jupiter or Juno, (because when
it is opened, it discloses a great number of seeds) signified only,
that those deities were, being long-lived, the parents of a great
many children, and families that soon grew into nations which
they planted in large possessions, when the world was newly
begun to be peopled, by giving them laws and other useful inventions to make their lives comfortable."

3. Pausanias (Corinthiaca, p. 59) says, he saw not far from
the ruins of Mycenæ, an image of Juno holding in one hand a
sceptre, and in the other a pomegranate; but he likewise declines
assigning any explanation of the emblem, merely declaring that
it was απορρητοτερος λογος—"a forbidden mystery." That is, one
which was forbidden by the Cabiri to be divulged.

4. In the festival of the Thesmophoria, observed in honour of the
goddess Ceres, it was held unlawful for the celebrants (who were
women) to eat the pomegranate. Clemens Alexandrinus assigns

* Cumberland Orig. Gent. Ant. p. 60.

as a reason, that it was supposed that this fruit sprang from the blood of Bacchus.

The coincidences in the pagan mysteries with respect to this emblem, might, doubtless, be extended still further, but I have neither time nor opportunity to pursue the research. I am, however, content, if by these few illustrations I have added another to the many already existing proofs of the antiquity as well as the beauty, of our beloved order.

POMEL. A round knob; a term applied to the globes or balls on the top of the pillars which stood at the porch of Solomon's Temple.

PONTIFES. The *Frères Pontifes* were a religious and operative community established at Avignon, in Italy, in 1178. They devoted themselves to the construction of stone bridges. They existed in the Duchy of Lucca as late as 1590. Their presiding officer was styled Magister or Master. John de Medicis was Master of the order in 1560.

POT OF INCENSE. The "sweet smelling savour" of fragrant herbs, has, among all nations and modes of worship, been considered an acceptable offering, in sacrifice to the Deity, as an evidence of the desire of the worshipper to honour and please the object of his adoration. Masonry, however, like Christianity, instructs us, that the most pleasing incense that can be offered to the great I AM, is the incense of a grateful and pious heart. Hence, the pot of incense, with a view to remind us of this truth, has been adopted as an emblem in the third degree.

POURSUIVANT. In former times, a messenger who attended upon the king in the army; among Masons, an officer in some Grand Lodges, whose principal duty is to announce the names of visitors.

PRAYER. All the ceremonies of our order are prefaced and terminated with prayer, because masonry is a religious institution, and because we thereby show our dependence on, and our faith and trust in God.

PRECEDENCY OF LODGES. The precedency of lodges is always derived from the date of their Warrants of Constitution, the oldest lodge ranking as No. 1.

PRELATE. The fourth officer in an encampment of Knight Templars in this country. His duties are important, and well known to all knights. He is seated on the right of the Generalissimo in the East. His jewel is a triple triangle, as the emblem of Jehovah, and his title is " Most Excellent."

PRIEST HIGH. See *High Priest.*

PRIMITIVE RITE OF NARBONNE. A rite established at Narbonne, in France, in 1780. Most of its degrees were taken from the other rites. The rite was philosophical, and assumed, as its object, the reformation of intellectual man and his restoration to his primitive rank and privileges.

PRIMITIVE SCOTCH RITE. *Rite écossais primitif.* A rite founded on the rite of Perfection, and established at Namur, in Belgium, by a brother Marchot, an advocate at Nivelles. It never extended far beyond the walls of the city in which it was organized. It is still practised in Belgium, and its principal seat is at Namur, in the lodge of "Bonne Amitie." It consists of thirty-three degrees, as follows: 1, Apprentice; 2, Fellow-Craft; 3, Master; 4, Perfect Master; 5, Irish Master; 6, Elect of Nine; 7, Elect of the Unknown; 8, Elect of Fifteen; 9, Illustrious Master; 10, Perfect Elect; 11, Minor Architect; 12, Grand Architect; 13, Sublime Architect; 14, Master in Perfect Architecture; 15, Royal Arch; 16, Prussian knight; 17, Knight of

the East; 18, Prince of Jerusalem, 19, Master of All Lodges;
20, Knight of the West; 21, Knight of Palestine; 22, Sovereign
Prince of Rose Croix; 23, Sublime Scotch Mason; 24, Knight
of the Sun; 25, Grand Scotch Mason of St. Andrew; 26, Master
of the Secret; 27, Knight of the Black Eagle; 28, Knight of
K——H; 29, Grand Elect of Truth; 30, Novice of the Interior; 31, Knight of the Interior; 32, Prefect of the Interior; 33,
Commander of the Interior.

PRINCE OF JERUSALEM. *Prince de Jérusalem.* The
16th degree in the Ancient Scotch rite. The legend of this
degree is founded on certain incidents which took place during
the re-building of the second temple, when the Jews were so
much incommoded by the attacks of the Samaritans and other
neighbouring nations, that an embassy was sent to King Darius
to implore his favour and protection, which was accordingly
obtained.

The meetings of this degree are called councils. The officers of
a council of Princes of Jerusalem are, a Most Equitable, representing Zerubbabel, a Senior and Junior Most Enlightened, a
Grand Treasurer, and Grand Secretary.

In the Scotch rite, councils of this degree are invested with
important privileges. They are styled " Chiefs in Freemasonry,"
and have the control of all the subordinate degrees as far as
the 15th, or Knights of the East, and all charters for the constitution of lodges, chapters, or councils of any of these degrees,
must emanate from a council of these princes. Yellow is the
emblematic colour of the degree, and the jewel is a gold medal,
on which are inscribed a balance, a two-edged sword, five stars,
and the letters D and Z. The apron is white, lined and bordered
with yellow, with a yellow flap, on which is inscribed a balance
with the same letters that are on the jewel.*

---

* The first Grand Council of Princes of Jerusalem, in the United States,
was formed at Charleston, S. C., by three Inspectors, on the 20th February
1788.

PRINCE OF LIBANUS. See *Knight of the Royal Axe.*

PRINCE OF MERCY. *Prince du Merci.* The 26th degree of the Ancient Scotch rite, sometimes called "Scotch Trinitarian." This is a philosophical degree, whose ceremonies are very impressive. Its meeting is styled a chapter; the chief prince, whose title is "Most Excellent," represents Moses. The Senior Warden represents Aaron, the Junior, Eleazar, and the candidate, Joshua. The jewel is a gold equilateral triangle, within which is a heart of gold, inscribed with the Hebrew letter ה, one of the symbols of the tetragrammaton. It is suspended from a tri-coloured ribbon of green, white and red. The apron is red, bordered with white fringe, and with a blue flap. On the flap is painted the jewel.

It is a Christian degree, and speaks, in the course of its construction, of the triple covenant which the Eternal made first with Abraham by circumcision; next, with the Israelites in the wilderness, by the intermediation of Moses; and lastly, with all mankind, by the death and sufferings of Jesus Christ. It is in allusion to these three acts of mercy, that the degree derives its two names of Scotch Trinitarian and Prince of Mercy, and not, as Ragon supposes, from any reference to the Fathers of Mercy, a religious society formerly engaged in the ransoming of Christian captives at Algiers.

PRINCE OF ROSE CROIX. *Souverain Prince Rose Croix.* The degree of Rose Croix is one of the most important and generally diffused of the higher degrees of masonry. It is to be found in several of the principal rites, and even in those in which it does not exist by name, its place is, for the most part, supplied by some other whose symbolic allusions do not differ materially from it. Thus, although it is not known in the York rite, an excellent substitute for it is found in the Royal Arch, while it constitutes the 18th degree of the Ancient and Accepted, or Scotch rite, the 7th and last of the French rite, and the 17th of the rite of Misraim. Among European Masons, where all these rites are practised, the degree of Rose Croix is consequently well known; and even in this country, although its possession is circumscribed to those brethren who have made some advancement in the Scotch rite, it is so often spoken of, that its name, at least, is familiar to almost every Mason of any intelligence, and much curiosity is often expressed in relation to its history and character.

The degree is known by various names; sometimes its possessors are called "Sovereign Princes of Rose Croix;" sometimes "Princes of Rose Croix de Heroden;" and sometimes "Knights of the Eagle and Pelican." In relation to its origin, masonic writers have made many conflicting statements; some giving it a much higher antiquity than others, but all agreeing in supposing it to be one of the earliest, if not the very earliest, of the higher degrees. The name has, undoubtedly, been the cause of much of this confusion in relation to its history, and the masonic degree of "Rose Croix" has, perhaps, often been confounded with the cabalistical and alchemical sect of "Rosicrucians," or "Brothers of the Rosy Cross," among whose adepts the names of such men as Roger Bacon, Paracelsus, and Elias Ashmole, the celebrated antiquary, are to be found. Notwithstanding the invidious attempts of Baruell, and other foes of masonry, to confound the two orders, there is a great distinction between them. Even their names, although somewhat similar in sound, are totally different in signification. The Rosicrucians, who were alchemists, did not derive their name, like the Rose Croix Masons, from the emblems of the rose and cross, for they had nothing to do with the rose, but from the Latin ros, signifying dew, which was supposed to be of all natural bodies the most powerful solvent of gold, and crux, the cross, a chemical hieroglyphic of light.

Baron Westerode, who wrote in 1784, in the "Acta Latomorum," gives the earliest origin of any masonic writer to the degree of Rose Croix. He supposes that it was instituted among the

Knights Templar in Palestine, in the year 1188, and he adds that Prince Edward, the son of Henry III., of England, was admitted into the order by Raymond Lulle, in 1196. Westerode names Ormesius, an Egyptian priest, who had been converted to Christianity, as its founder.

Others have attributed the origin of this degree to a learned and pious monk, John Valentine Andreæ, Abbot of Adelberg, who died in 1564, and among whose writings are to be found several treatises which relate to this subject.* Ragon says of Andreæ, that, profoundly grieved at seeing the principles of the Christian religion forgotten in vain disputes, and science made subservient to the pride of man, instead of contributing to his happiness, he passed his days in devising what he supposed to be the most appropriate means of restoring each to its legitimate moral and benevolent tendency. It may be that with this view the eminently Christian degree of Rose Croix was invented by him. But notwithstanding the authority of Ragôn, sustained as it is by that of Nicolai in his work on the "Crimes imputed to the Templars," we are inclined to suspect that the labours and the writings of the Abbot of Adelberg referred rather to the Rosicrucian alchemists, than to the Rose Croix Masons.

Other authors have supposed that they could find the origin of the Rose Croix, or at least of its emblems, in a book published in 1601, by Jacobus Typotus, the historiographer to Rhodolph the Second. The book of Typotus, on which rests any claims which may be made to his paternity of the Rose Croix degree, is entitled " *Symbola divina et humana pontificum, imperatorum, regum,*" and it is in that part of it which is devoted to the "symbol of the holy cross," that the allusions are found which seem to indicate the author's knowledge of this degree. Ragon, however, who appears to have seen the work, utterly refutes the idea of any connection between the emblems of Typotus and those of the Rose Croix.

* Two especially, one entitled " *Judicorum de fraternitate R. C. Chaos,*" and the other " *Noces chemiques de Rosen-Crutz.*"

Clavel, with his usual boldness of assertion, which is too often independent of facts, declares that the degree was invented by the Jesuits for the purpose of countermining the insidious attacks of the free-thinkers upon the Roman Catholic religion, but that the philosophers parried the attempt by seizing upon the degree and giving to all its symbols an astronomical signification. Clavel's opinion is probably derived from one of those sweeping charges of Professor Robison, in which that systematic enemy of our institution declares, that about the beginning of the eighteenth century, the Jesuits interfered considerably with masonry, " insinuating themselves into the lodges, and contributing to increase that religious mysticism that is to be observed in all the ceremonies of the order."* But there is no better evidence than these mere vague assertions, of the connection of the Jesuits with the Rose Croix degree.

Oliver says that the earliest notice that he finds of this degree, is in a publication of 1613, entitled "La Reformation universelle du monde entier avec la fama fraternitatis de l' Ordre respectable de la Rose Croix." But he adds, that "it was known much sooner, although not probably as a degree in masonry; for it existed as a cabalistic science from the earliest times in Egypt, Greece, and Rome, as well as among the Jews and Moors in times more recent."†

Oliver, however, undoubtedly, in the latter part of this paragraph, confounds the masonic Rose Croix with the alchemical Rosicrucians, and the former is singularly inconsistent with the details that he gives in another part of his writings respecting an order to which we are now about to allude, and which it seems probable to us had as much as any other, to do with the institution of the degree in question.

There is a tradition among the Masons of Scotland, that after the dissolution of the Templars, many of the knights repaired to

---

* Proofs of a Conspiracy, p. 21.
† Oliver's Landmarks, vol. ii. p. 81, n. 35.

Scotland, and placed themselves under the protection of Robert
Bruce; and that, after the battle of Bannockburn, which took
place on St. John the Baptist's day, in the year 1314, this
monarch instituted the Royal Order of Herodom and Knight of
the Rosy Cross, and established the chief seat of the order at
Kilwinning. From that order, it seems to us by no means im-
probable that the present degree of Rose Croix de Heroden may
have taken its origin. In two respects, at least, there seems to
be a very close connection between the two systems : they both
claim the kingdom of Scotland and the Abbey of Kilwinning as
having been at one time their chief seat of government, and
they both seem to have been instituted to give a Christian explanation to Ancient Craft Masonry. There is, besides, a similarity
in the names of the degrees of "Rose Croix de Heroden," and
"Herodom and Rosy Cross," amounting almost to an identity,
which appears to indicate a very intimate relation of one to the
other.

The subject, however, is in a state of inextricable confusion;
and I confess that, after all my researches, I am still unable distinctly to point to the period when, and to the place where, the
present degree of Rose Croix received its organization as a masonic grade.

No matter, however, where precisely it received its origin, nor
who has the honour of having been its inventor, it is at least
certain that the degree of Rose Croix is to be placed among the
most ancient of the higher degrees of masonry; and that this
antiquity, in connection with the importance of its design and
the solemnity of its ritual, has given to it a universality in the
masonic world, inferior only to the degrees of Ancient Craft
Masonry. It is to be found, as I have already said, in nearly all
the rites, under some name and in some modification, and in
many of them it is placed at the summit of the ritual.

In the Ancient and Accepted Scotch rite, whence nearly all
the Rose Croix Masons of this country have derived the degree,
it is placed as the eighteenth on the list. Some idea of the im-

portance of the degree may be obtained from a brief detail of the
preparatory ceremonies which are necessary to be performed by
all candidates who make application for it.

The ceremonies and history of a chapter of Rose Croix, are
of such a nature as to render it impossible to give any account of
them here. The presiding officer is called "Ever Most Perfect
Sovereign," and the two Wardens are styled "Most Excellent
and Perfect Brothers." The annual feast of the order is on
Shrove Tuesday, and must be celebrated by every member.
There are five other obligatory days of meeting, viz. Ascension
day; St. John the Baptist's day, Pentecost; St. John the Evangelist's day; Tuesday after Easter; and All Saints' day.

The degree is conferred in a body called a "Chapter of the
Sovereign Princes of Rose Croix," which derives its authority
immediately from the Supreme Council of the Thirty-third, and
which confers with it, only one other and inferior degree, that
of "Knights of the East and West." The aspirant for the degree of Rose Croix, who must, of course, have received all the
preparatory degrees, applies at the door of the chapter with a
petition for admission; and if his prayer be granted, the time
and place of his reception are made known to him, when he retires to return on the appointed day.

On his second application, before admission, he is called upon
to make the following engagements: 1, That he will never reveal
the place where he was received, nor the names of those who
were present at his reception; 2, That he will conform to all the
ordinances of the chapter, and keep himself uniformly clothed
as far as he is able; 3, That he will acknowledge his master at
all times and in all places, and never confer this degree without
permission from proper authority, as well as answer for the pro-
bity and respectability of those whom he may thereafter propose;
4, That he will be extremely cautious in granting the degree, so
that it may not be unnecessarily multiplied.

There are two kinds of aprons. The first, or mourning apron,
is white bordered with black; on the flap are a skull and cross-

bones between three red roses; on the apron is a globe surrounded by a serpent, and above the letter J. The second apron, used on festive occasions, is red, lined and bordered with the same; on it a triple triangle of gold, with three squares within three circles, and a J in the centre; above these the compasses extended, one point resting on the triangle, the other on the circles. This is the apron of the Scotch rite. The first apron in the French rite is black with a red cross. The second is white, bordered with red, and inscribed with the jewel of the degree. The collar is red, with the eagle of the degree embroidered on it.

The jewel of the Rose Croix is a golden compass, extended on an arc to the sixteenth part of a circle or twenty-two and a half degrees. The head of the compass is surmounted by a triple crown, consisting of three series of points, arranged by three, five, and seven. Between the legs of the compass is a cross resting on the arc of the circle; its centre is occupied by a full blown rose, whose stem twines around the lower limb of the cross; at the foot of the cross, on the same side on which the rose is exhibited, is the figure of a pelican wounding its breast to feed its young, which are in a nest surrounding it, while on the other side of the jewel is the figure of an eagle with wings displayed. On the arc of the circle, the P∴ W∴ of the degree is engraved in the cipher of the order.

In this jewel are included the most important symbols of the degree. The cross, the rose, the pelican, and the eagle, are all important symbols, the explanation of which will go far to a comprehension of what is the true design of the Rose Croix order.

Of these emblems the *eagle* is perhaps the least important, and its application the most difficult to explain. The symbol, however, is of great antiquity. In Egypt, Greece, and Persia, this bird was sacred to the sun. Among the pagans it was an emblem of Jupiter, and with the Druids it was a symbol of their supreme God. In the Scriptures a distinguished reference is in many instances made to the eagle; especially do we find Moses

representing Jehovah as saying, in allusion to the belief that this
bird assists its feeble young in their flight, by bearing them upon
its own pinions,—"Ye have seen what I did to the Egyptians,
and how I bore you on eagles' wings and brought you unto myself."[*] Hence the eagle in the Rose Croix is very appositely
selected as a symbol of Christ in his divine character, bearing
the children of his adoption on his wings, teaching them with
unequalled love and tenderness to poise their unfledged wings
and soar from the dull corruptions of earth to a higher and holier
sphere.   And for this reason the eagle in the jewel is very significantly represented as having the wings displayed as if in the
very act of flight.

The same allusion to Christ, but still more significantly, is
found in the *pelican* feeding its young, which occupies the other
side of the jewel.   As this bird was formerly supposed to wound
its own breast that it might with its blood feed its young, so has
it been adopted as an emblem of the Saviour who shed his blood
for the salvation of the human race.   The pelican, therefore, on
the jewel of the Rose Croix, is a fitting symbol of Christ in his
mediatorial character.   Ragon[†] says that in the hieroglyphic
monuments the eagle was the symbol of a wise man, and the
pelican of a benevolent one; and, therefore, he thinks that the
eagle and pelican of the Rose Croix are intended to symbolize
perfect wisdom and perfect charity.   But this explanation applying these attributes to Christ, is not at all inconsistent with the
one we have advanced.

It is scarcely necessary to speak of the *cross* as a Christian
emblem.   Although it is an ancient symbol of eternal life, and
is to be found in use even among the Egyptians with that signification, long before the days of Moses, yet since the crucifixion
it has been peculiarly adopted as an emblem of Him who suffered
on it.   In this restricted sense, then, and not in that more general one of immortality, in which it is used in other parts of ma-

---

[*] Exodus xix. 4.   [†] Cours des Initiations.

sonry, is the cross adopted as one of the emblems of the Rose Croix degree.

The *rose*, in ancient mythology, was consecrated to Harpocrates, the god of silence; and in the mysteries the hierophant wore a crown of roses. Hence this flower was considered as the emblem of silence and secrecy; and when any thing was intended to be kept secret, it was said to be delivered *sub rosa*, or "under the rose."

Ragon, in explaining the jewel of the Rose Croix, says that as the cross was in Egypt an emblem of immortality, and the rose of secrecy, the rose followed by the cross was the simplest mode of writing "the secret of immortality." But he subsequently gives a different explanation, namely, that, as the rose was the emblem of the female principle, and the cross or triple phallus of the male, the two together, like the Indian lingam, symbolized universal generation. But Ragon, who has adopted the theory of the astronomical origin of Freemasonry, like all theorists, often carries his speculations on this subject to an extreme point. A simpler allusion will better suit the character of the degree, and be more in accordance with what we have already said of its other symbols.

The rose is, in many places of Scripture, applied as a figurative appellation of Christ. This is familiar to all readers; thus in the Book of Canticles he is called "the rose of Sharon." The cross, of course, alludes, as we have already shown, to his death; the rose on the cross, is therefore an emblem of the death of the Saviour for the sins of mankind.

From this brief review of the symbols of the Rose Croix, it will be evident that it is, in the strictest sense, a Christian degree.* This must, of course, mark it as one of comparatively

---

* The documents of this degree always commence with these words : " In the name of the Holy and Undivided Trinity," and end with the salutation, " In the peaceful union of the sacred numbers." The members place R∴ † at the end of their names.

modern origin, because all the ancient degrees are of universal application as to religion. The Rose Croix is, indeed, an attempt to christianize Freemasonry; to apply the rites, and symbols, and traditions of Ancient Craft Masonry to the last and greatest dispensation; to add to the first temple of Solomon and the second of Zerubbabel, a third, that to which Christ alluded when he said, "Destroy this temple, and in three days will I raise it up." The great discovery which was made in the Royal Arch, ceases to be of value in this degree; for it, another is substituted of more christian application; the Wisdom, Strength, and Beauty, which supported the ancient temple, are replaced by the Christian pillars of Faith, Hope, and Charity; the great lights, of course, remain, because they are of the very essence of masonry; but the three lesser give way to the thirty-three, which allude to the years of the Messiah's sojourning on earth. Every thing, in short, about the degree, is Christian.

Viewed, then, in this light, as a modern invention, and as forming no part of Ancient Freemasonry, we cannot fail to admire it as an ingenious and beautiful adaptation of a universal system to a more contracted principle—and as a pardonable, if not indeed a praiseworthy attempt to apply the sublime principles of our all-tolerant order to the illustration of that last and most perfect dispensation under which we are now living.

PRINCE OF THE ROYAL SECRET. See *Sublime Prince of the Royal Secret.*

PRINCE OF THE TABERNACLE. *Prince du Tabernacle.* The 24th degree of the Ancient Scotch rite. This degree is intended to illustrate the directions given for the building of the tabernacle, the particulars of which are recorded in the twenty-fifth chapter of Exodus. The lodge is called a Hierarchy, and its officers are a Most Powerful Chief Prince, representing Moses, and three Wardens, whose style is Powerful, and who respectively represent Aaron, Bezaleel, the son of Uri, and Aholiab, the son of Abisamach.*

The jewel is the letter A, in gold, suspended from a broad crimson ribbon. The apron is white, lined with scarlet and bordered with green. The flap is sky blue. On the apron is depicted a representation of the tabernacle.

PRINCIPAL OFFICERS. The Worshipful Master and the two Wardens are styled the three principal officers of the lodge.

PRINCIPALS. The officers of a Royal Arch Chapter, known in America as the High Priest, King, and Scribe, are in English Chapters called First, Second, and Third Principals.

PRINCIPAL SOJOURNER. An officer in a Royal Arch Chapter, whose duties are similar to those of a Senior Deacon in a symbolic lodge.

The Hebrew word גֵּר, *ger*, which we translate a sojourner, signifies a man living out of his own country, and is used in this sense throughout the Old Testament. The children of Israel were, therefore, during the captivity, sojourners in Babylon, and the person who is represented by this officer, performed, as the incidents of the degree relate, an important part in the restoration of the Israelites to Jerusalem. He was the spokesman and leader of a party of three sojourners, and is, therefore, emphatically called the chief, or principa sojourner.

PRIORY. The body of Knights Templar which, in this country, is called an Encampment, in Scotland, under the revised statues of the order, is styled a Priory. The presiding officer of a Priory is called a Prior; he is, therefore, equivalent to our Grand Commander. The organization of the Templars in

---

* Levit. xxv. 23; 1 Chron. xxix. 15; Ps. xxxix. 12.

Scotland, is very different from that which exists in America. For a brief account of it, see *Scotland, Knights Templar of.*

PROCESSIONS. Processions, in masonry, are entirely under the charge of the Grand Lodge. No subordinate lodge has a right to appear in public, on any occasion, without the consent and approbation of the Grand Lodge, or of its representative, the Grand Master.* The object of this salutary regulation is, that the reputation of the order shall not suffer by the ill-timed or injudicious appearance of the brethren, when any small number of them, inspired by a love of display or other unworthy or unwise motives, might choose to exhibit themselves, and the jewels and ornaments of the order, to the public gaze. For, on such an occasion, not the lodge alone, but the whole fraternity suffers; for the world is unable to make the distinction, and they often heedlessly and unjustly condemn the craft, in general, for the errors or transgressions of an individual brother, or of a single lodge. To avoid, therefore, any occasion of giving scandal, the Grand Lodge, which is composed of experienced Past Masters, has wisely reserved to itself the right of appointing the time when, the place where, and the manner in which, public displays of the order may take place.

When, however, this consent has been obtained, if a single lodge walks in procession, the Master occupies the place of precedence, and may have the Bible, Square and Compasses, carried on a blue velvet cushion, borne before him. If two or more lodges are present, the Master of the oldest lodge presides. If a past or present Grand Master, or Deputy Grand Master, or the Grand Wardens, join the procession of a subordinate lodge, proper attention is to be paid to them. Their place in the procession is immediately after the Master of the lodge. A Grand

* This rule is, however, dispensed with, in the case of masonic funerals, in places distant from the seat of the Grand Lodge, or residence of the Grand Master.

Warden must be supplied with two Deacons. When a Grand
Master or Deputy Grand Master is present, the Book of Constitutions must be borne before him. But unless the Grand or
Deputy Grand Master is present, the Book of Constitutions can
never be carried in a procession of a private lodge.

The brethren in a Masonic procession always walk two and
two. They should be dressed in proper masonic costume, which
is a suit of black, with shoes and white stockings, white gloves,
and white *leather* aprons. Silk or satin aprons constitute no
part of a Mason's dress. The apron must be of lamb's skin.

PROFICIENCY. One of the requisite qualifications for advancement to a higher degree is, suitable proficiency in the preceding. Unfortunately, this qualification is not always sufficiently
insisted on. Formerly there was a regulation, requiring that the
candidate who desired to be passed or raised, should be examined
in open lodge on his proficiency in the preceding degree. This
salutary regulation is even now adhered to, by some lodges who
look rather to the quality than to the quantity of their members,
and who think that a lodge had better consist of a few skilful,
than many ignorant members. Some Grand Lodges, viewing
the necessity of due proficiency in its proper light, have strength-
ened the ancient regulation by express rules.

The proficiency of officers is also an important requisite. No
brother should accept office in a lodge, unless fully qualified to
perform its duties. An ignorant Master, and unskilful Wardens,
reflect discredit not only on their own lodge, but by their incapa-
city to explain the peculiar tenets of the order, on the whole fraternity. In February, 1844, the Grand Lodge of Ireland
adopted, on this subject, resolutions declaring, that no brother
should be considered eligible for or admissible to the office of
Junior or Senior Deacon, until by strict examination in open
lodge, he shall have proved himself able to administer the mysteries of initiation to a candidate in the first degree; nor for the
office of Junior or Senior Warden, until, by a like examination,

he has proved that he is able to pass a candidate to the second degree; nor for the office of Master, until he has proven his ability to enter, pass and raise, a candidate through the three degrees.

A regulation of this kind ought to be adopted by every Grand Lodge in the universe.

PROVINCIAL GRAND MASTER. An officer under the Grand Lodge of England, the appointment of whom is invested in the Grand Master. He presides over a province as its Grand Master, and is empowered to constitute lodges within its jurisdiction. He is, however, enjoined to correspond with the Grand Lodge, and to transmit, at least yearly, an account of his proceedings. The office was first established in 1726, " when the increase of the craftsmen, and their travelling into distant parts, and concerning themselves in lodges, required an immediate head, to whom they might apply in all cases where it was not possible to wait the decision of the Grand Lodge."*

PROVOST AND JUDGE. *Prévôt et Juge.* The 7th degree of the Ancient Scotch rite. The history of the degree relates, that it was founded by Solomon K. of I. for the purpose of strengthening his means of preserving order among the vast number of craftsmen engaged in the construction of the temple. Tito, Prince Harodim, Adoniram, and Abda his father, were first created Provosts and Judges, who were afterwards directed by Solomon to initiate his favourite and intimate secretary, Joabert, and to give him the keys of all the building. The Master of a Lodge of Provosts and Judges represents Tito, Prince Harodim, the first Grand Warden and Inspector of the three hundred architects. The number of lights is six, and the symbolic colour is red.

The jewel is a golden key, having the letter A within a tri-

---

* Anderson. Const. p. 340.

angle, engraved on the ward. The collar is red. The apron is white, lined with red, and is furnished with a pocket.

PROXY. The representative of a lodge in the Grand Lodge. Every lodge is entitled to be represented by its Master and Wardens. But when a lodge is too far distant from the seat of the Grand Lodge for those officers conveniently to attend, it may depute one or more Past Masters, under the seal of the lodge and the signature of the Worshipful Master and Secretary, to represent it in the Grand Lodge. A proxy has all the power that the Master and Wardens would have, if present. He may vote to the best of his judgment for the interest of the lodge, and the honour of the craft, unless instructed by the lodge, in which case he is bound to obey the expressed will of the lodge which he represents. It is not necessary that a proxy should be a member of the lodge which has appointed him. On the contrary, he generally is not.

PRUDENCE. One of the four cardinal virtues, the practice of which is inculcated upon the Entered Apprentice. Prudence, which, in all men, is a virtue highly to be commended, as teaching them to live agreeably to the dictates of reason, and preserving to them by its cautious precepts the realities of temporal welfare, and the hopes of eternal happiness, is to the Mason absolutely necessary, that being governed by it, he may carefully avoid the least occasion, by sign or word, of communicating to the profane those important secrets which should be carefully locked up only in the repository of faithful breasts. Hence is this virtue, in the lecture of the first degree, intimately connected with, and pointedly referred to, a most important part of our ceremonies of initiation.

PURPLE. The colour of one of the veils in the tabernacle, and the emblematic colour of the three intermediate degrees between the Master Mason and the Royal Arch. Purple, in Royal

33

Arch Masonry, is the emblem of union, because it is produced
by the combination of *blue*, which is the characteristic colour of
the symbolic degrees, and *scarlet*, which is that of the Royal Arch
degree.   It reminds the wearer, therefore, to cultivate between
these different members of the masonic family, a spirit of union
and harmony.

PYTHAGORAS.   Masons, looking to the purity of the principles inculcated in the school of this Grecian sage, to the peculiar
character of the ceremonies with which he clothed and concealed
his doctrines, and to the great respect which he paid to the science of geometry, have delighted to hail him as an "ancient
brother;" and there is no doubt that his mysteries, improved by
his long experience, chastened by his own virtuous character, and
enlarged by his extensive researches into the systems of other
countries, "were the most perfect approximation to the original
science of Freemasonry which could be accomplished by a heathen
philosopher, bereft of the aid of revelation."[*]

Pythagoras was born at Samos, about five hundred and sixty-
eight years before the Christian era.   Having at an early age
distinguished himself in the Olympic games, and obtained the
prize for wrestling, he began his travels in pursuit of knowledge;
retiring into the East, he visited Chaldea and Egypt, the seats
of learning and philosophy, and gaining the confidence of the
priests, he obtained from them a knowledge of their mysteries
and their symbolic writings.   He is said to have been instructed
in the sacred things of the Hebrews by the prophet Ezekiel.[†]

Upon his return to Europe, he settled at the town of Crotona,
in Magna Grecia, where he established the school which afterwards rendered him so illustrious as a teacher of philosophy.

---

[*] Oliver, Init. 123.

[†] Some say by Daniel.   He met the Jews at Babylon, where he visited during
the captivity, and Oliver says, "was initiated into the Jewish system of Freemasonry."   *Landmarks*, vol. ii. p. 412.

His instruction, like that of all the ancient philosophers, was of two kinds, exoteric or public, and esoteric or private. To the former, all persons, indiscriminately, were admitted, but none but pupils, selected by himself for their virtue and capacity, were permitted to enjoy the benefits of the latter.

To be received as a novice in the school of Pythagoras, was no easy task. The most rigid examination was made into the character of the candidate. If he was accepted, he deposited his property in the common fund of the society, and commenced his probation, which was of an exceedingly severe description. The novitiate lasted five years, during which period the aspirant was enjoined to be abstinent in food, and to preserve an uninterrupted silence. If he succeeded in obeying these instructions, he was permitted to aspire to the degrees, which were three in number, the Acousmatici, the Mathematici, and the Pythagoreans, in the last of which he was clothed in a white garment and fully instructed in the secret doctrine.

Pythagoras was, perhaps, the most virtuous, and taught the purest doctrines of all the heathen philosophers. The school which he established was distinguished for the piety as well as the attainments of his disciples. They were animated only by a reverence for the deity, and a love for their fellow-beings. Their respect for the Divine Being was such, that they never pronounced his name in their oaths,* and their brotherly love was such, that they were accustomed to adopt the noble sentiment "my friend is my other self."†

Silence and secrecy were the first lessons taught by Pythagoras to his disciples. The five years novitiate of the candidate was passed in total silence, during which he learned to repress his curiosity; and to employ his thoughts on God. When admitted to the fellowship of the society, an oath of secrecy was propounded to him on the sacred tetractys.

---

* Jamblichus, Vit. Pythag. c. 33.
† Porph. Vit. Pythag.

Implicit obedience was another lesson prescribed to the Pythagoreans. Αυτος εφη, "he, the master, has said it," was considered as the most sufficient of reasons in all questions of propriety.

The institutions of Pythagoras resembled the masonic in other respects besides its principles. His assemblies were arranged due-east and west, because, he said, that motion began in the east and proceeded to the west. He had adopted a system of signs, whereby his disciples, dispersed though various countries, made themselves known to each other at first sight, and became as familiar at the first interview, as if they had been acquainted from their birth. And so closely, says Jamblichus, were their interests united, that many of them passed over seas and risked their fortune to re-establish that of one of their brethren who had fallen into distress.

Jamblichus relates the following incident, which is in evidence both of their brotherly love and of their means of mutual recognition. A Pythagorean travelling in a distant country, fell sick and died at a public inn. Previous, however, to his death, being unable to compensate the landlord for the kindness and attention with which he had been treated, he directed a tablet, on which he had traced some enigmatical characters, to be exposed on the public road. Some time after, another disciple of Pythagoras passed that way, perceived the tablet, and being informed by its enigmatical characters that a brother had been there sick and in distress, and that he had been treated with kindness, he stopped and reimbursed the inn-keeper for his trouble and expense.*

The symbols adopted by Pythagoras in his secret instruction, were principally derived from geometry. A notice of a few of them may be interesting.

The *right angle* was an emblem of morality and justice.

The *equilateral triangle*, was a symbol of God, the essence of Light and Truth. The *square*, like the tetractys, referred to the

---

* Jamblichus, *ut supra*.

Divine mind. The *cube* was the symbol of the mind of man, after it had been purified by piety and acts of devotion, and thus prepared for mingling with the celestial gods. The *point within a circle*, and the *dodecahedron* or figure of twelve sides, were symbols of the universe. The *triple triangle* was an emblem of health, and the letter Y a representation of the course of human life, in which there are two diverging paths, the one of virtue, leading to happiness, and the other of vice, conducting to misery.

Among the doctrines peculiar to the school of Pythagoras, was that of the metempsychosis, or the transmigration of souls, which he derived during his travels from the Brahmins of India He forbade the eating of flesh, and the offering of animals in sacrifice. He taught that the universe was created out of the passive principle of matter, by the Divine Being, who was its mover and source, and out of whose substance the souls of men were formed. He believed in the universal influence of numbers, which he supposed to be the controlling principle of all things. He perceived in the human mind, not only propensities to vice and passion, but the better seeds of virtue. These he sought to cultivate and cherish by labour, study, and abstinence of life. In short, he appears to have extracted from the various sects of heathen philosophy, all that was good, and to have rejected all that was bad, forming thereby an eclectic system which approached nearer to light and truth, than any that had ever, before his day, emanated from the unassisted wisdom of man.

Q.

QUALIFICATIONS OF CANDIDATES. The pre-requisite qualification of candidates for admission into the mysteries of Freemasonry, are of three kinds—mental, moral, and physical.

33⁎

The mental qualifications are, that the candidate shall be a man of sane mind; that is, neither a fool, an idiot, nor a madman; but one responsible for his actions, and competent to understand the obligations, to comprehend the instructions, and to perform the duties of a Mason. The mental qualifications refer to the *security* of the order.

The moral qualifications are, that he shall be no "irreligious libertine," but an obeyer of the moral law. That is, he must be virtuous in his conduct and reputable in his character, lest the dignity and honour of the institution suffer by the admission of unworthy persons. Neither must he be an atheist, but an humble believer in the wisdom, power, and goodness of God, a belief which constitutes the religious creed of Freemasonry, and which is essentially necessary to a Mason as a check upon vice and a stimulus to virtue. Another important moral qualification is, that the candidate must come of his "own free will and accord." Masonry does not delight in proselytism. Though our portals are open to all who are worthy, yet we are unwilling that any should unite with us, except they be persuaded to the act by their uninfluenced convictions of the beauty and utility of our institution. The moral qualifications refer to the *respectability* of the order.

The physical qualifications are, that the candidate shall be twenty-one years old or more, free born and no bondsman, of able body, and "of limbs whole as a man ought to be."

This is one of the oldest regulations of our ancient craft. It arises from the originally operative nature of our institution. Whatever objections some ultra liberal brethren may make to the uncharitable nature of a law which excludes a virtuous man from our fellowship, because he has been unfortunate enough to lose a leg or an arm, we have no right to discuss the question. The regulation constitutes one of the many peculiarities that distinguish our society from all others; its existence continues to connect the present speculative with the former operative character of the institution; it is an important part of our history;

and is, in short, by universal consent, one of the landmarks of
the order. It can never, therefore, be changed. The physical
qualifications refer to the *utility* of the order.

The most ancient charges in which these regulations are to be
found, are those which were collected from the old records, and
ordered to be printed by the Grand Lodge of England, 1722,
and the manuscript charges in the possession of the Lodge of
Antiquity, London. As they are brief, but important, I may be
excused for inserting them here.

"A Mason is obliged, by his tenure, to obey the moral law;
and if he rightly understands the art, he will never be a stupid
atheist nor an irreligious libertine."*

"No master should take an apprentice, unless he has sufficient employment for him, and unless he be a perfect youth,
having no maim or defect in his body, that may render him incapable of learning the art, of serving his master's lord, and of
being made a brother, and then a Fellow-Craft in due time, even
after he has served such a term of years as the custom of the
country directs: and that he should be descended of honest parents; that so, when otherwise qualified, he may arrive to the
honour of being the Warden, and then the Master of the lodge,
the Grand Warden, and, at length, the Grand Master of all the
lodges, according to his merit."†

"Thirdly, that he that be made, be able in all degrees; that
is, free born, of good kindred, true, and no bondsman, and that
he have his right limbs as a man ought to have."‡

In the Constitution, published under the sanction of the
Grand Lodge of Maryland, by Brother Samuel Cole, the physical
disabilities are set forth still more minutely, with an assignment
of what is probably the true reason for their existence. They
say, "no person is capable of becoming a member, unless he is

---

* Old Charges, Sect. 1.—See Anderson, Constitutions.
† Ibm. Sect. 4.
‡ MS. in Lodge of Antiq. See Preston, 273. Note.

free born, of mature and discreet age; of good report; of suffi
cient natural endowments, and the senses of a *man*; with an es
tate, office, trade, occupation, or some visible way of acquiring
an honest livelihood, and of working in his craft, as becomes the
members of this most ancient and honourable fraternity, who
ought not only to earn what is sufficient for themselves and families, but likewise something to spare for works of charity, and
supporting the true dignity of the royal craft. Every person
desiring admission, must also be *upright in body*, not *deformed*
or *dismembered* at the time of making; but of *hale* and *entire*
limbs, as a man ought to be."*

In an able report made by Bro. W. S. Rockwell, Deputy
Grand Master, to the Grand Lodge of Georgia, he traces the existence of the law prohibiting the initiation of maimed candidates, to that early period of Egyptian history, in which a personal defect would exclude from the priesthood—a law which is
again to be found in the Mosaic ritual, from which the masonic
institution is more immediately derived. Looking to the symbolic character of speculative masonry as referring to the material temple for its architype, he explains the present existence of
the law in the following language, with the sentiments of which
I cordially concur.

"It was eminently proper that a temple erected for the worship
of the GOD OF TRUTH, the unchangeable I AM, should be constructed of white stones, perfect stones, the universally recognised symbols of this, his great and constant attribute. The
symbolic relation of each member of his order to its mystic
temple forbids the idea that its constituent portions, its living
stones, should be less perfect, or less a type of their great original, than the inanimate material which formed the earthly
dwelling place of the God of their adoration."

QUESTIONS OF HENRY VI. This is a document which

---

* See Cole, Freemas. Lib. p. 69. Constitutions, Ch. 1, Sect. 4.

has been so often printed in various masonic publications as to
have become familiar to the fraternity. Its full title is, "Cer-
tayne questions with answeres to the same, concernynge the mystery of maconrye; wryttene by the hande of Kynge Henry the
Sixthe of the name, and faythfullye copied by me, Johan Ley-
lande Antiquarius, by the commaunde of His Highnesse." It
first appeared in the Gentleman's Magazine for 1753, where it
purports to be a reprint of the pamphlet published five years before, at Frankfort.* It is there stated to have been copied by
one John Collins, from a MS. in the Bodleian library, and to
have been enclosed in a letter from the celebrated John Locke,
the author of the Essay on Human Understanding, to Thomas,
Earl of Pembroke, and bearing date May 6th, 1696. Preston
afterward incorporated these questions into his work, and appended to them a section of remarks on the manuscript, as well
as on the annotations of Mr. Locke. This work has always been
received as genuine among the craft, and in the life of Leland
its authenticity is positively asserted. But this has lately been
denied by Mr. Halliwell, in a small work entitled, "The Early
History of Freemasonry in England," published at London, in
1840. The document purporting to come from the Bodleian library, is so well known to most Masons, that I should have
passed it over without notice in this work, were it not that I
deemed it necessary to bring the doubts of Mr. Halliwell before
my readers, many of whom may have no opportunity of seeing
the original work in which the subject is discussed. The views
of Mr. Halliwell will, perhaps, be best conveyed in the words of
the doubter himself.

"It is singular," says Mr. Halliwell, "that the circumstances
attending its publication should have led no one to suspect its

---

* The title of the paper, as found in the Gentleman's Magazine for 1753,
page 417, is as follows: "Copy of a small pamphlet consisting of 12 pages,
in 8vo., printed in Germany in 1748, entitled: 'Ein Brief von dem berüchmten
herrn heron Johann Locke betreffend die Frey-Maurreren. So aufeinem
Schrieb-Jisch eines verstrorbnen Bruders ist gefunden worden.'"

authenticity. I was at the pains of making a long search in the Bodleian library last summer, in the hopes of finding the original, but without success. In fact, there can be but little doubt, that this celebrated and well-known document is a forgery!

"In the first place, why should such a document have been printed abroad? Was it likely, that it should have found its way to Frankfort, nearly half a century afterwards, and been published without any explanation of the source whence it was obtained? Again, the orthography is most grotesque, and too gross ever to have been penned either by Henry the Sixth, or Leland, or both combined. For instance, we have Peter Gowere, a Grecian, explained in a note by the fabricator—for who else could have solved it?—to be Pythagoras! As a whole, it is but a clumsy attempt at deception, and is quite a parallel to the recently discovered one of the *first Englishe Mercurie.*"*

Such are the objections of Mr. Halliwell to the authenticity of this celebrated antiquarian document. Let each estimate their value for himself. Fortunately, the dignity of masonry is not at all connected with the dispute. The questions throw but little light upon the history of the order, and its antiquity depends not on them alone for proof.

QUESTIONS TO CANDIDATES. Every candidate, before being admitted to participate in our mysteries, is bound to answer certain questions, respecting the motives that have influenced his application. These questions are generally proposed in the following form:

"Do you seriously declare upon your honour, that, unbiassed by friends against your own inclination, and uninfluenced by mercenary motives, you freely and voluntarily offer yourself as a candidate for the mysteries of Freemasonry?

"Do you seriously declare upon your honour, that you are solely prompted to solicit the privileges of masonry, by a favour-

---

* Halliwell, Hist. of Freemasonry, p. 40.

able opinion conceived of the institution, a desire of knowledge, and a sincere wish of being serviceable to your fellow creatures?

"Do you sincerely declare upon your honour, that you will cheerfully conform to all the ancient established usages and customs of the fraternity?"

These questions should be propounded to the candidate by the Senior Deacon, in the preparation room, before initiation, and in the presence of the stewards or preparers.

R.

RABBONI. This word may be translated as signifying "a most excellent master or teacher." Jahn tells us, (in his Biblical Archæology, § 106,) that the Jews, in imitation of the Greeks, had their seven wise men who were called Rabboni, רבין. Gamaliel, the preceptor of St. Paul, was one of these. They styled themselves the children of wisdom, which is an expression very nearly corresponding to the Greek φιλοσοφοι The word occurs once as applied to Christ, in the New Testament, (John xx. 16.) "Jesus said unto her, Mary. She turned herself, and saith unto him, Rabboni, which is to say, master."

RAISED. This term is used to designate the reception of a candidate into the third degree of masonry. It conveys an allusion to a particular part of the ceremonies, as well as to the fact of his being *elevated* or *raised* to that degree, which is universally acknowledged to be the summit of ancient craft masonry.

RAMSAY. The name of the Chevalier Ramsay is conspicuous

in the masonic history of the last century. He was born at Ayr, in Scotland, in 1686, and died at Germain-en-Laye, in France, in 1743. He was a man of extensive erudition and the friend of the great and good Fenelon. One of the most faithful followers of the Pretender, he sought to identify the progress of Freemasonry with the house of Stuart. For this purpose he endeavoured to obviate the objections of the French nobility to the mechanical origin of the institution, at which their pride revolted, by asserting that it arose in the Holy Land, during the Crusades, as an order of chivalry. His theory was, that the first Freemasons were a society of knights, whose business it was to rebuild the churches which had been destroyed by the Saracens; that the Saracens, with the view of preventing the execution of this pious design, sent emissaries among them, who, disguised as Christians, became confounded with the builders and paralyzed their efforts; that the knights having discovered the existence of these spies, became in future more careful, and instituted signs and words for the purpose of detection; and that as many of their workmen were newly converted Christians, they adopted symbolic ceremonies with the view of instructing their proselytes more readily in their new religion. Finally, the Saracens becoming more powerful, the Knights Masons were compelled to abandon their original occupation; but being invited by a king of England to remove into his dominions, they had accepted the invitation, and there devoted themselves to the cultivation and encouragement of architecture, sculpture, painting and music. Ramsay attempted to support his system by the fact of the building of the College of Templars in London, which was actually constructed in the twelfth century by the fraternity of masons who had been in the holy wars.*

In 1728, Ramsay attempted to lay the foundation of a masonic reform, according to this system. He, therefore, proposed to the Grand Lodge of England to substitute, in the place of the three

---

* Robison, Proofs of a Conspiracy, p. 33.

degrees of Apprentice, Fellow-Craft, and Master, three others of his own invention, those of Scotch Mason, Novice and Knight of the Temple, which he pretended were the only true and ancient ones, and had their administrative centre, from time immemorial, in the Lodge of Saint Andrew, at Edinburgh. His views were at once rejected by the Grand Lodge of England, which has always been the guardian of the purity of Ancient Craft Masonry. But he carried them to Paris, where they met with amazing success, and gave rise to those higher degrees which have since been known by the name of the Ancient Scotch rite.* See a further account of Ramsay under the title *Innovations.*

RECEIVED. After the completion and dedication of the Temple, those brethren who consented to remain and keep that magnificent structure in repair, were, according to masonic tradition, as a reward for their attachment, received and acknowledged as Most Excellent Masters. Hence, the terms are used to express the reception of a candidate into the 6th or Most Excellent Master's degree of the Ancient York rite.

RECOMMENDATION. The letter of every applicant for initiation must be recommended by at least one well-known brother, who should be, if possible, a member of the lodge, and vouched for by another. See *Vouching.*

RECORDER. An officer in an Encampment of Knights

---

* Clavel, p. 165. I find the following paragraph in the Gentleman's Magazine for the year 1738.

"There was lately burnt at Rome, with great solemnity, by order of the Inquisition, a piece in French, written by the Chevalier Ramsay, (author of the Travels of Cyrus,) entitled 'An Apologetical and Historical Relation of the Secrets of Freemasonry, printed at Dublin by Patric Odinoko.' This was published at Paris in answer to a pretended catechism printed there by order of the Lieutenant de Police."

Templar, and a Council of Royal and Select Masters equivalent to
a Secretary in a blue lodge.

RED CROSS KNIGHT.   See *Knight of the Red Cross.*

RED CROSS OF ROME AND CONSTANTINE.   A de-
gree founded on the circumstances of the vision of a cross, with
the inscription *EN TΩ NIKA*, which appeared in the heavens to
Constantine, while on a march.

REFLECTION, CHAMBER OF.   *Cabinet des Reflexions.*
In French lodges the preparation room in which the candidate
remains, until he is introduced.   It is thus called, because the
gloomy furniture, and the moral inscriptions on the walls, are calculated to produce, in his bosom, reflections of the most serious
nature.

A similiar apartment is used in the ceremonies of the degree
of Knight Templar.

REFORMED RITE.   This rite was established in 1782, by a
convention of Masons, who assembled at Wilhelmsbad, under the
presidency of Ferdinand, Duke of Brunswick, who was elected its
Grand Master.   The members of this rite assumed the title of
"Order of Charitable Knights of the Holy City."   It was a reformation of the rite of Strict Observance, which had been established in 1754, and differed from it, principally, in rejecting all
connection with the Knights Templar, of whom, the members of
the rite of Strict Observance had declared that Freemasons were
the successors.   The rite of Martinism was merged in this rite,
whose system the lodges of Martinists universally adopted; and
thus constituted, it spread with astonishing rapidity over France,
Switzerland, and Italy, but met with inconsiderable success in
Germany, where the Templar system appears to have been, for a
long time, the favourite.

The Reformed rite consisted of five degrees: 1, Apprentice; 2,

Fellow-Craft; 3, Master; 4, Scotch Master; 5, Charitable Knight of the Holy City. The last degree was subdivided into three sections, namely: Novice, Professed Brother, and Knight, which actually gives seven degrees in all.

It is still practised in France by one lodge, and in Switzerland by five. Its supreme body is situated at Zurich, in the latter country, under the title of the "Directory of Switzerland."

REFORMED HELVETIC RITE. The rite described in the preceding article was introduced into Poland in 1784, by brother Glayre, of Lausanne, the minister of King Stanislaus, and who was also the Provincial Grand Master of this rite in the French part of Switzerland. But, in introducing it into Poland, he subjected it to several modifications, and called it the Reformed Helvetic rite. The system was adopted by the Grand Orient of Poland.

REFRESHMENT. When a lodge is temporarily adjourned, the adjournment is performed in a manner peculiar to Masons, and the lodge is then said to be "called from labour to refreshment." During refreshment, the column of the W∴ should also be down, and that of the S∴ be up, to indicate that the Junior Warden, not the Senior, now superintends the craft. *Calling from labour to refreshment*, differs from closing, in this, that in the former mode the lodge is still open, nor when the labour is resumed, is there any ceremony of opening. Neither does the re-assembling of the brethren require any other summons or notification than the simple command of the J∴ W∴

High twelve or noon was the hour at the temple when our ancient brethren were regularly called from labour to refreshment. The tradition is that they worked twelve hours a day, and six days in the week.

REINSTATEMENT. When a Mason, who had been expelled or suspended by a lodge, is reinstated by the lodge, which had expelled or suspended him, he is at once restored to all his masonic rights and privileges, just as if no such sentence had ever been passed upon him. But no lodge has the power of reinstating, except the one which inflicted the original punishment. This rule, however, does not apply to the Grand Lodge, which, as the supreme masonic tribunal, may re-instate any expelled or susended Mason within its jurisdiction, whenever the circumstances of the case may seem to warrant such an exercise of prerogative.

REJECTION. One black ball, with a good reason assigned, of the sufficiency of which the Master shall be a competent judge, or two black balls,* without any reason at all being assigned, will reject a candidate for initiation. If a candidate be rejected, he can apply in no other lodge for admission. If admitted at all, in must be in the lodge where he first applied. But the time for a new application has never been specified, so that it is held that a rejected candidate may apply for a reconsideration of his case at any time. The unfavourable report of the committee to whom the letter was referred, or the withdrawal of the letter by the candidate or his friends, is considered equivalent to a rejection

RELIEF. Of the philanthropic tendency of masonry, abundant evidence is afforded in every country in which a lodge exists. Its charities are extended to the poor and destitute, to the widow and the orphan, with a liberal hand; and its numerous institutions for improving the physical and moral condition of the human race, prove that "Brotherly Love, Relief, and Truth," are not the mere idle and unmeaning language of a boastful motto, but the true and guiding principles of our association. In our own land, several of the Grand Lodges have established colleges and schools for the education of the children of Masons.

---

* Most of the Grand Lodges in the United States require unanimity in the ballot. But the Old Constitutions permitted as many as three black balls, if the lodge desired it.

Some of these have been but lately organized, yet are they all in a prosperous condition. In Europe, where the order has been longer in operation, the means of bestowing aid upon the destitute are still more perfect. Among these, the "Royal Freemasons' School for Female Children," in London, is worthy of all commendation. It was instituted in 1788, and the present building erected, at an expense of more than £3000, in the year 1793. The object of the charity is to maintain, clothe, and educate an unlimited number of female children and orphans of reduced Freemasons. It now extends its bounty to sixty-five children, who are received into the school between the ages of eight and eleven, and are wholly supported until they attain their fifteenth year.

The "Asylum for worthy aged and decayed Freemasons," in the same city, is another institution reflecting high honour on the society which gave it birth. It was founded in 1835, and its praiseworthy objects are sufficiently designated by its title.

In Germany, we find "A Lying-in Hospital" for the wives of indigent Freemasons, established at Schleswig; an almshouse and orphan-house at Prague; a public school at Berlin; an institute for the blind at Amsterdam; and a multitude of libraries, schools and hospitals, scattered throughout the German cities.

In Sweden there is an orphan-house, established in 1753, at Stockholm, by the private contributions of the Swedish lodges. Ireland has also an orphan-house. But one of the most philanthropic institutions of our order, is the "Society for patronizing poor children," established at Lyons, in France. Its object is to diminish the primary causes of pauperism. For this purpose, it commences with the child at birth; it selects for him a patron from its members, whose duty it is to advise with and assist the parents in the government and education of the child. He sees that the child is well fed, comfortably clothed, and properly educated. When ready for a trade, he directs him in its selection, and binds him as an apprentice. And when the period of apprenticeship has expired, he furnishes him with his outfit in life.

Of the private relief afforded in individual cases, where the sole claim to sympathy or assistance was the possession of the name of brother, it is unnecessary here to speak. The annals of masonry are crowded with such instances of masonic relief. TRUTH, may be said to be the column of wisdom, whose rays penetrate and enlighten the inmost recesses of our lodge; BROTHERLY LOVE, the column of strength, which binds us as one family, in the indissoluble bond of fraternal affection; and RELIEF, the column of beauty, whose ornaments, more precious than the lilies and pomegranates that adorned the pillars of the porch, are the widow's tear of joy, and the orphan's prayer of gratitude.

RELIGION. Freemasonry does not profess to interfere with the religious opinions of its members. It asks only for a declaration of that simple and universal faith, in which men of all nations and all sects agree,—the belief in a God and in his superintending providence. Beyond this, it does not venture, but leaves the minds of its disciples, on other and sectarian points, perfectly untrammelled. This is the only religious qualification required of a candidate, but this is most strictly demanded. The religion, then, of Masonry, is pure theism, on which its different members engraft their own peculiar opinions; but they are not permitted to introduce them into the lodge, or to connect their truth or falsehood with the truth of masonry.

On this subject, the present Constitution of the Grand Lodge of England, holds the following language:

"A Mason is obliged, by his tenure, to obey the moral law, and if he rightly understand the art, he will never be a stupid atheist nor an irreligious libertine. He, of all men, should best understand that God seeth not as man seeth; for man looketh at the outward appearance, but God looketh to the heart. A Mason is, therefore, particularly bound, never to act against the dictates of his conscience. Let a man's religion, or mode of worship, be what it may, he is not excluded from the order, provided

he believe in the glorious Architect of heaven and earth, and
practise the sacred duties of morality. Masons unite with the
virtuous of every persuasion, in the firm and pleasing bond of
fraternal love; they are taught to view the errors of mankind
with compassion, and to strive, by the purity of their own conduct, to demonstrate the superior excellence of the faith they
may possess. Thus masonry is the centre of union between
good men and true, and the happy means of conciliating friendship amongst those who must otherwise have remained at a perpetual distance."

This tolerant principle is, however, unfortunately not practised
in all masonic lodges. The three Grand Lodges at Berlin, in
Prussia,* and the Grand Lodges of Hanover and Hamburg, refuse not only to initiate Jews, but even to admit as visitors their
Israelitish brethren, who have been made in other countries.
The Grand Lodges of this country have taken this subject into
consideration, and several of them have already passed resolutions, condemning the proceedings of the Prussian and German
Masons, which may possibly have some effect in restoring them
to the purity and liberality of masonic tolerance. The Grand
Lodge of Germany, at Hamburg, which works only in the three
degrees of Ancient Craft Masonry, and derives its Constitutions
from the Grand Lodge of England, is happily actuated by a
more enlightened spirit.

REMOVAL. No lodge can remove from its usual place of
meeting, without the consent of the Grand Lodge thereto. Formerly no proposition could be made, nor vote taken on the question of removal, unless the Worshipful Master was present.
But this regulation appears now to have become obsolete.

REPEAL. A lodge cannot, at an extra communication, re-

---

* The Grand Lodge of the Three Globes, the Royal York Grand Lodge of
Friendship, and the Grand Lodge of Prussia.

peal, annul, or alter a resolution, that has been adopted at a previous regular one.

REPRESENTATIVE SYSTEM. The representative system originated in this country with the Grand Lodge of New-York. Its organization is as follows: It is proposed, that each Grand Lodge in the United States, or, if it can be sufficiently extended, in the world, shall appoint a worthy and intelligent Mason, to reside near and represent it in every other Grand Lodge. These representatives are required to attend regularly the meetings of the Grand Lodges to which they are accredited, to communicate to their constituents an abstract of the proceedings, and such other masonic matter of interest, such as expulsions, rejections, establishment of clandestine lodges, &c., as may occur in the respective jurisdictions in which they reside. Their costume is that of the Grand Lodge which they represent, and they are also entitled to bear a banner with its colours.

This system has not met with universal approbation, and has, as yet, but partially succeeded. Its friends argue, in its favour, the closer union which will thereby be cemented between the various masonic bodies thus represented, and the greater facility of communication.*

But on the other side, its opposers have offered weighty objections against its adoption. Besides the heavy expense which would necessarily attend the universal adoption of the system, there is one, which certainly claims the attentive consideration of every brother. One of the most intelligent of these objectors is Brother Moore, the editor of the Freemason's Monthly Magazine, published at Boston, in whose words, rather than in my own, I desire to present the character of this objection to the reader.

---

* The arduous duty of an extensive correspondence, which had formerly been confided to one officer, the Grand Secretary, being now divided between several.

"Another objection that presents itself to our mind is, that the proceedings of the Grand Lodges would go forth in an unofficial form, and be liable to lead to error and confusion. It is hardly to be presumed that the representatives would all take the same view of every subject that might come under discussion, or that they would understand it alike, in all its bearings. They would undoubtedly faithfully represent the matter to their constituents, as they should respectively understand it. But their understanding it would probably, in many cases, clash with the annual report of the official officer. Their representations would not, therefore, furnish safe grounds of action. The Grand Lodges would still be constrained to wait for the official report. Again, there is danger that the representatives might not always be able to discriminate between what it would be proper to communicate, and what is strictly of a local character. There is not probably a Grand Lodge in the country which has not before it, at every communication, some subject which it would prefer to keep within the limits of its own jurisdiction. And it is one of the errors of human nature, that there should be an ambitious desire on the part of the representatives to communicate every thing which, in their judgment, might tend to raise them in the estimation, or contribute to the interest, of their constituents. They might not always discriminate wisely.*

These objections are certainly important, and seem to have deterred some of the Grand Lodges from appointing representatives. Whether the system will ever become universal is exceedingly problematical. The enthusiasm on the subject, which existed in some parts of the country, when it was first proposed, appears now considerably to have abated.

RESIGNATION. No brother should be allowed to resign, unless he be at the time in good standing. Some lodges, however, from a mistaken feeling of kindness, have permitted a

---

* Moore's Magazine, vol. i. p. 196.

member to resign, rather than resort to the penalty of suspension
or expulsion. This is manifestly wrong. If a Mason be too bad
to belong to a particular lodge, he is too bad to belong to the
order in general. Besides, the acceptation of a letter of resignation is a kind of tacit acknowledgement that the character of the
resigning member is free from reproach. Hence, other lodges
are thus deceived into the admission of one who should originally
have been cured or cut off* by the lodge from which he had
resigned.

The resignation of a member dissolves all connection between
himself and his former lodge, but it does not at all affect his
general relations with the order, or his obligatory duties as a
Mason. See on this subject, the article *Demit*.

RESURRECTION. A resurrection from the grave and a
future immortality were the great lessons which it was the design of the ancient mysteries to inculcate. In like manner by a
symbolic ceremony of great impressiveness, the same sublime
truths are made to constitute the end and object of Freemasonry
in the third degree, or as it has been called by Hutchinson, "the
Master's Order."

RETURNS OF LODGES. Every subordinate lodge must
make an annual return, at some period specified in the local regulations, to the Grand Lodge from which it derives its Warrant,
of the number and names of its members, and of the initiations,
rejections, suspensions, and expulsions which have taken place
during the year. By this means, each Grand Lodge is made
acquainted with the state of its subordinates, and the progress of
the order within its jurisdiction.

RHETORIC. The art of embellishing language with the

---

* Quæ sanari poterunt, quacunque ratione sanabo; quæ resecanda erunt, non
patiar ad perniciem civitatis manare.—*Cicero in Catalin.*

ornaments of construction, so as to enable the speaker to persuade or affect his hearers. It supposes and requires a proper acquaintance with the rest of the liberal arts. For the first step towards adorning a discourse, is for the speaker to become thoroughly acquainted with its subject, and hence, the ancient rule that the orator should be acquainted with all the arts and sciences. Its importance as a branch of liberal education is recommended to the Mason in the Fellow-Craft's degree.

RIGHT ANGLE. A right angle is the meeting of two lines in an angle of ninety degrees, or the fourth part of a circle. Each of its lines is perpendicular to the other, and as the perpendicular line is a symbol of uprightousness of conduct, the right angle has been adopted by Masons as an emblem of virtue. Such was also its signification among the Pythagoreans. The right angle is represented in the lodges by the square, as the horizontal is by the level, and the perpendicular by the plumb.

RIGHT HAND. The right hand has in all ages been deemed an important symbol to represent the virtue of fidelity. Among the ancients, the right hand and fidelity to an obligation, were almost deemed synonymous terms. Thus, among the Romans, the expression "fallere dextram," *to betray the right hand*, also signified *to violate faith*, and "jungere dextras," *to join right hands*, meant *to give a mutual pledge*. Among the Hebrews יָמִין, *iamin*, the right hand, was derived from אָמַן, *aman*, to be faithful.

The practice of the ancients was conformable to these peculiarities of idiom. Among the Jews, to give the right hand, was considered as a mark of friendship and fidelity. Thus St. Paul says, "when James, Cephas, and John, who seemed to be pillars, perceived the grace that was given unto me, they gave to me and Barnabas the *right hand of fellowship*, that we should go unto the heathen and they unto the circumcision." Gal. ii. 6.

The same expression, also, occurs in Maccabees. We meet, indeed, continually in the Scriptures with allusions to the right hand, as an emblem of truth and fidelity. Thus in Psalms (cxliv.) it is said, "their right hand is a right hand of falsehood,"—that is to say, they lift up their right hand to swear to what is not true. This lifting up of the right hand was, in fact, the universal mode adopted among both Jews and Pagans in taking an oath. The custom is certainly as old as the days of Abraham, who said to the King of Sodom, "I have lifted up my hand unto the Lord, the most high God, the possessor of heaven and earth, that I will not take any thing that is thine." Sometimes among the Gentile nations, the right hand, in taking an oath, was laid upon the horns of the altar, and sometimes upon the hand of the person administering the obligation. But in all cases it was deemed necessary to the validity and solemnity of the attestation, that the right hand should be employed.

Since the introduction of Christianity, the use of the right hand in contracting an oath, has been continued, but instead of extending it to heaven, or seizing with it a horn of the altar, it is now directed to be placed upon the Holy Scriptures, which is the universal mode at this day in all Christian countries. The antiquity of this usage may be learned from the fact, that in the code of the Emperor Theodosius, adopted about the year 438, the placing of the right hand on the Gospels is alluded to, and in the code of Justinian, whose date is the year 529, the ceremony is distinctly laid down as a necessary part of the formality of the oath.*

This constant use of the right hand in the most sacred attestations and solemn compacts, was either the cause or the consequence of its being deemed an emblem of fidelity. Dr. Potter† thinks it was the cause, and he supposes that the right hand was

---

* The words of Justinian are, "tactis sacrosanctis Evangeliis"—the Holy Gospels being touched.—Lib. ii. tit. 53. lex. 1.

† Archæologia Græca, p. 229.

naturally used instead of the left, because it was more honourable, as being the instrument by which superiors give commands to those below them. Be this as it may, it is well known that the custom existed universally, and that there are abundant allusions, in the most ancient writers, to the junction of right hands in making compacts.

The Romans had a goddess whose name was *Fides*, or Fidelity,* whose temple was first consecrated by Numa. Her symbol was two right hands joined, or sometimes two female figures holding each other by the right hands, whence in all agreements among the Greeks and Romans, it was usual for the parties to take each other by the right hand, in token of their intention to adhere to the compact.

The joining of the right hands was esteemed among the Persians and Parthians, as conveying a most inviolable obligation of fidelity. Hence, when King Artabanus desired to hold a conference with his revolted subject, Asineus, who was in arms against him, he despatched a messenger to him with the request, who said to Asineus, "the king hath sent me to give you his right hand and security,"—that is, a promise of safety in going and coming. And when Asineus sent his brother Asileus to the proposed conference, the king met him and gave him his right hand, upon which Josephus remarks: "This is of the greatest force there with all these barbarians, and affords a firm security to those who hold intercourse with them; for none of them will deceive, when once they have given you their right hands, nor will any one doubt of their fidelity, when that is once given, even though they were before suspected of injustice."†

It is thus apparent that the use of the right hand, as a token

---

* By a strange error for so learned a man, Oliver mistakes the name of this goddess, and calls her Faith. "The spurious Freemasonry," he remarks, "had a goddess called Faith." No such thing. *Fides*, or, as Horace calls her, "incorrupta Fides," incorruptible Fidelity, is very different from the theological virtue of faith.

† Joseph. Ant. Jud. lib. xviii. cap. ix.
35

of sincerity and a pledge of fidelity, is as ancient as it is universal, a fact which will account for the important station which it occupies among the symbols of Freemasonry.

RIGHT SIDE AND LEFT SIDE. Among the Hebrews, as well as the Greeks and Romans, the right side was considered superior to the left; and as the right was the side of good, so was the left of bad omen. *Dexter*, or right, signified also propitious, and *sinister*, or left, unlucky. In the Scriptures, we find frequent allusions to this superiority of the right. Jacob, for instance, called his youngest and favourite child, *Ben-ja-min*, the son of his right hand, and Bathsheba, as the king's mother, was placed at the right hand of Solomon.

RING, LUMINOUS. The Academy of Sublime Masters of the Luminous Ring, was a pseudo-masonic society founded in France, in 1780. Its ritual was divided into three degrees. The first two were occupied with the history of Freemasonry, and the last with the peculiar dogmas of the institution which were essentially Pythagorean.

RITE. A modification of masonry, in which the three ancient degrees and their essentials being preserved, there are varieties in the ceremonies, and number and names of the additional degrees. A masonic rite is, therefore, in accordance with the general signification of the word, the method, order, and rules, observed in the performance and government of the masonic system.

Anciently, there was but one rite, that of the "Ancient, Free, and Accepted Masons," consisting only of the three primary degrees of Entered Apprentice, Fellow-Craft, and Master Mason, hence called the degrees of Ancient Craft Masonry. But on the Continent of Europe, and especially in France and Germany, the ingenuity of some, and the vanity of others, have added to these an infinite number of high degrees, and of ceremonies unknown to the original character of the institution. Some of these rites lived only with their authors, and died when their paternal energy in fostering them ceased to exert himself. Others have had a more permanent existence, and still continue, nominally, to divide the masonic family. I say, only nominally, for the fact that they are all, no matter what be their unessential difference, based upon the three ancient degrees, enables a brother of any rite to visit the symbolic lodges of all the other rites. A Master Mason is, in all rites and all countries, acknowledged as such, and entitled to all the privileges which that sublime degree confers.

The following are the names of the rites of Freemasonry now practised in Europe and America. The first three are the most important, oldest, and most extensive; and the first, or York rite, approaches nearest in its construction to Ancient Craft Masonry. The degrees conferred by each of these rites, and the places where they exist, will be found under the respective titles in this work.

1. York rite.
2. French, or modern rite.
3. Ancient and Accepted Scotch rite.
4. Philosophic Scotch rite.
5. Primitive Scotch rite.
6. Ancient Reformed rite.
7. Fessler's rite.
8. Rite of the Grand Lodge of the Three Globes at Berlin.
9. Rite of Perfection.
10. Rite of Misriam.
11. Rite or order of the Temple.
12. Swedish rite.
13. Reformed rite.
14. Schroeder's rite.
15. Rite of Swedenborg.
16. Rite of Zinnendrof.

RITUAL. The ritual of Freemasonry comprises the forms of opening and closing a lodge, of initiating candidates, and of conducting the other peculiar ceremonies of the order. The ritual differs in various places, and is not always the same in the same rite. Thus the lodges of England and America practise the same rite, the York, so far as the three symbolic degrees, and yet the rituals of the two countries vary considerably. An intimate acquaintance with the ritual constitutes what is technically called a "bright mason."

ROLL. The roll, or record of members' names, is borne by Secretaries in public processions of the order. At the funeral of a brother, his name, during a portion of the funeral ceremonies, should be inscribed in the roll of the lodge to which he belonged. The rolls, or insignia of office, carried by Secretaries in a funeral procession, are thrown into the grave.

ROMAN COLLEGES OF ARTIFICERS. *Collegia artificum.* Numa collected the various arts and trades which, during his reign, existed at Rome, into separate companies or societies, having their respective halls, courts, and religious exercises. The principal of these *collegia artificum*, was the college of architects, whose members he brought out of Attica, for the purpose of organization. From this time, says Clavel, is to be dated the establishment of the mysteries of Bacchus at Rome.

The eighth of the twelve tables contained laws applicable to the Roman colleges. These associations, which were called *sodalitates*, or *fraternitates*, had the right of making contracts, and of enacting laws for their own government, and a few of the most distinguished, (among which were the college of architects,) were exempted from taxation.

The Roman colleges were, in their character, both civil and religious institutions. Their assemblies were held with closed doors, and the profane were carefully excluded. Their *maceriæ*, or halls, were situated in the neighbourhood of those temples

whose divinities they particularly worshipped, and whose priests
employed them as artificers, in making the necessary repairs.
In their assemblies they deliberated on the works entrusted to
their construction, and initiated candidates into their society by
mysterious ceremonies, and by symbolic instruction, derived from
the working tools of their art. The brothers were divided into
the usual classes of Apprentices, Craftsmen, and Masters. They
contracted an obligation to render each other mutual assistance
when necessary, and were enabled to recognise each other by secret signs. Their presidents, who were elected for five years,
were called *Magistri*, or Masters. Besides these, there were
seniores or elders, treasurers, secretaries, and other necessary
officers.

These colleges became, in time, the depositories of all the
foreign methods of initiation, which were afterwards introduced
into Rome. And it was through them that the most learned
masonic writers have supposed that the Hebrew mysteries were
transmitted, from the Jewish artists who visited Rome in great
numbers during the reign of Augustus, to the travelling Freemasons, by whom all the religious edifices of the Middle Ages
were constructed.

The colleges of artificers, and especially those which professed
architecture, spread from Rome throughout the provinces and
principal cities of the empire. They existed in vigorous activity
until the fall of the Roman Empire, and continued to decline
during the ages which succeeded the invasions of the barbarians,
until they are supposed to have revived in the architectural associations known as the "Travelling Freemasons of the Middle
Ages," an account of which will be found in another part of this
work.*

---

* I have gladly availed myself of the industry of Clavel, who has collected
every thing of importance that has been written on the subject of these associations.

ROSAIC RITE. A rite instituted in Germany by M. Rosa, a Lutheran clergyman, under the patronage of the Baron de Prinzen. It was at first exceedingly popular, but was superseded by the Strict Observance rite of Baron Hunde.

ROSE. For an explanation of the Rose, as a masonic symbol, see the article *Prince of Rose Croix.*

ROSE CROIX. See *Prince of Rose Croix.*

ROSE, KNIGHTS AND NYMPHS OF THE. This was an order of Adoptive or Androgynous Masonry, invented in France towards the close of the eighteenth century. M. de Chaumont, the masonic secretary of the Duc de Chartres, was its author. The principal seat of the order was at Paris. The hall of meeting was called the Temple of Love. It was ornamented with garlands of flowers, and hung round with escutcheons on which were painted various devices and emblems of gallantry. There were two presiding officers, a male and female, who were styled the Hierophant and the High Priestess. The former initiated men, and the latter women. In the initiations the Hierophant was assisted by a conductor or deacon, called Sentiment, and the High Priestess by a conductress or deaconess, called Discretion. The members received the title of Knights and Nymphs. The Knights wore a crown of myrtle, the Nymphs a crown of Roses. The Hierophant and High Priestess wore, in addition, a rose-coloured scarf, on which were embroidered two doves within a wreath of myrtle. During the time of initiation, the hall was lit with a single dull taper, but afterwards it was brilliantly illuminated by numerous wax candles.

When a candidate was to be initiated, he or she was taken in charge, according to the sex, by the conductor or conductress, divested of all weapons, jewels, or money, hoodwinked, loaded with chains, and in this condition conducted to the door of the Temple of Love, where admission was demanded by two knocks.

Brother Sentiment then introduced the candidate by order of
the Hierophant or High Priestess, and he or she was asked his
or her name, country, condition of life, and, lastly, what he or she
was seeking. To this the answer was, "Happiness."

The next question proposed was, "What is your age?" The
candidate, if a male, replied, "The age to love;" if a female,
"The age to please and to be loved."

The candidates were then interrogated concerning their private
opinions and conduct in relation to matters of gallantry. The
chains were then taken from them, and they were invested with
garlands of flowers which were called "the chains of love." In
this condition they were made to traverse the apartment from one
extremity to another, and then back in a contrary direction, over
a path inscribed with love-knots. The following obligation was
then administered :

"I promise and swear by the Grand Master of the Universe
never to reveal the secrets of the order of the Rose, and should
I fail in this my vow, may the mysteries I shall receive add nothing
to my pleasures, and instead of the roses of happiness may I find
nothing but the thorns of repentance."

The candidates were then conducted to the mysterious groves
in the neighbourhood of the Temple of Love, where the knights
received a crown of myrtle, and the nymphs a simple rose.
During this time a soft melodious march was played by the or-
chestra. After this the candidates were conducted to the altar
of mystery, placed at the foot of the Hierophant's throne, and
there incense was offered up to Venus and her son. If it was a
knight who had been initiated, he now exchanged his crown of
myrtle for the rose of the last initiated nymph, and if a nymph,
she exchanged her rose for the myrtle crown of Brother Sentiment. The Hierophant now read a copy of verses in honour of
the God of Mystery, and the bandage was at length taken from
the eyes of the candidate. Delicious music and brilliant lights
now added to the charms of this enchanting scene, in the midst

of which the Hierophant communicated to the candidate the modes of recognition peculiar to the order.*

ROSICRUCIANS. Of the secret society of the Rosicrucians or Brothers of the Rosy Cross, Bailey gives the following account:

"Their chief was a German gentleman, educated in a monastery, where, having learned the languages, he travelled to the Holy Land, anno 1378, and being at Damascus and falling sick, he had heard the conversation of some Arabs, and other Oriental philosophers, by whom he is supposed to have been initiated into this mysterious art. At his return into Germany he formed a society, and communicated to them the secrets he had brought with him out of the East, and died in 1484.

"They were a sect or cabal of hermetical philosophers; who bound themselves together by a solemn secret, which they swore inviolably to observe; and obliged themselves, at their admission into the order, to a strict observance of certain established rules.

"They pretended to know all sciences, and especially medicine, of which they published themselves the restorers; they also pretended to be masters of abundance of important secrets, and among others, that of the philosopher's stone; all which they affirmed they had received by tradition from the Ancient Egyptians, Chaldeans, the Magi and Gymnosophists.

"They pretended to protract the period of human life by means of certain nostrums, and even to restore youth. They pretended to know all things; they are also called the Invisible Brothers, because they have made no appearance, but have kept themselves *incog.* for several years."†

The society of the Rosicrucians or Brothers of the Rosy Cross, thus engaged in the wild studies of alchemy, protracted their

---

* I have given the above details in compliance with a promise made in the article on "Androgynous Masonry," and for the gratification of the curious. I am indebted for them to the industry of Clavel.

† Bailey, Dict. in voce.

existence until the middle of the eighteenth century, when they at length ceased to meet, in consequence of the death of Brun, their chief. Their association was well organized, being divided like the society of Jesuits into bodies, having each its particular chief, with a general chief at the head of all. Their system of initiation was divided into nine degrees, as follows : 1, Zelator; 2, Thericus; 3, Practicus; 4, Philosophus; 5, Adeptus Junior; 6, Adeptus Major; 7, Adeptus Exemptus; 8, Magister; 9, Magus.

Out of this society was formed, in 1777, an association calling itself "The Brothers of the Golden Rosy Cross," whose system was divided only into three degrees. This society was very numerous in Germany, and even extended into other countries, especially into Sweden. A second schism from the Rosicrucians was the society of the "Initiated Brothers of Asia," which was organized in 1780, and whose pursuits, like those of the parent institution, were alchemy and the natural sciences. In 1785, it attracted the attention of the police, and two years later, received a fatal blow, in the revelation of all its secrets by one Rolling, a treacherous member of the association.

The Rosicrucians, as this brief history indicates, had no connection whatever with the masonic fraternity. Notwithstanding this fact, Barruel,* the most malignant of our revilers, with a characteristic spirit of misrepresentation, attempted to identify the two institutions. This is an error, into which others might unwittingly fall from confounding them with the Princes of Rose Croix, a masonic degree, somewhat similar in name, but entirely different in character. To correct this error where it may have been committed, is the object of this article, which otherwise would not have been entitled to a place in a masonic lexicon.†

* Memoirs of Jacobinism.

† The Rosicrucians do not derive their name, like Rose Croix Masons, from the Rose and Cross, for they have nothing to do with the rose, but from the Latin *ros*, dew, and *crux*, the cross, as a hieroglyphic of light, which Mosheim explains as follows : " Of all natural bodies, dew was esteemed the most pow-

ROYAL ARCH. More properly called the Holy Royal Arch. It is the seventh degree in the York rite, as practised in this country, and by some styled the summit of ancient masonry. Dermot says of it, "this I firmly believe to be the root, heart and marrow of masonry." And Hutchinson, speaking of it, uses the following remarkable language : "As Moses was commanded to pull his shoes from off his feet, on Mount Horeb, because the ground whereon he trod was sanctified by the presence of the Divinity, so the Mason who would prepare himself for this exalted stage of masonry, should advance in the naked paths of truth, be divested of every degree of arrogance, and approach with steps of innocence, humility and virtue, to challenge the ensigns of an order, whose institutions arise on the most solemn and sacred principles of religion."

This degree brings to light many essentials of the craft which were for the space of 470 years buried in darkness, and at the same time impresses on the mind of the possessor the belief in a Supreme Being and the reverence due to his holy name.

This is the proper place to introduce a brief account of the Temple from its dedication by Nebuchadnezzar, and its re-erection seventy years afterwards by Zerubbabel.

After the death of Solomon, ten of the twelve tribes revolted from his son Rehoboam. The tribes of Judah and Benjamin, however, continued faithful to the house of David, and were ruled by the descendants of Solomon, until, in the eleventh year of the reign of Zedekiah, the city was taken after a siege of eighteen months, by Nebuchadnezzar, King of Babylon, who destroyed the city, set fire to the Temple, and carried away most of the inhabitants as captives to Babylon, 416 years after the Temple had been dedicated to Jehovah, by King Solomon.

---

erful solvent of gold ; and the cross, in chemical language, is equivalent to light, because the figure of a cross + exhibits at the same time three letters, of which the words LVX, or light, is compounded. Hence a Rosicrucian philosopher is one who, by the assistance of the dew, seeks for light, or the philosopher's stone.

The tribes of Judah and Benjamin remained in captivity seventy years at Babylon, until Cyrus, in the first year of his reign, commiserating the calamity of the Jews, issued an edict, permitting them to return to Jerusalem and rebuild the house of the Lord. This they did under the care of Zerubbabel, Prince of Judah, and Joshua, the High Priest who superintended the work, while Higgai, the Scribe, instigated his countrymen, by his eloquence, to zeal and diligence in the pious labour.

Until the year 1797, as no grand chapters were in existence, a competent number of companions, possessed of sufficient abilities, proceeded, under the sanction of a Master's warrant, to confer the degree of the Royal Arch with the preparatory degrees. But in that year, a convention of delegates from the several chapters in Pennsylvania met, and after mature deliberation, resolved to organize a Grand Chapter, which was accordingly done. Since that period, the jurisdiction of Royal Arch Masonry has been separated from that of the symbolic degrees.

The officers in a chapter of this degree, are a Most Excellent High Priest, King, Scribe, Captain of the Host, Principal Sojourner, Royal Arch Captain, three Grand Masters of the Vails, Secretary, Treasurer, and Sentinel.

The true origin of the Royal Arch is an important question, that has lately engaged the attention of masonic writers. Some have asserted that it was brought by the Templars from the Holy Land; others say that it was established as a part of Templar masonry in the sixteenth century, and others again assert that it was unknown before the year 1780. Dr. Oliver, in a work of profound research on this subject, says that " there exists sufficient evidence to disprove all their conjectures, and to fix the era of its introduction to a period which is coeval with the memorable schism amongst the English Masons about the middle of the last century."*

---

* Some account of the schism which took place during the last century amongst the Free and Accepted Masons in England, showing the presumed origin of the Royal Arch degree, &c., p. 4.

It seems to me, as the result of a careful examination of the evidence adduced, that before the year 1740, the essential element of the Royal Arch constituted a part of the third degree, and that about that year it was severed from that degree and transferred to another, by the schismatic body calling itself "the Grand Lodge of England according to the old Constitutions."

The Royal Arch in England is at present practised as a fourth degree, and the possession of the Past Mastership is not, as in this country, considered as a necessary qualification for exaltation. Any worthy Master Mason is now considered as eligible for the honours of the Royal Arch. The Royal Arch, in that country, is not considered as "essentially a degree, but the perfection of the third."[*] The time and circumstances of the degree as conferred in England coincide with the ritual in this country in the most important particulars. There is, however, an anomaly in the introduction of Ezra and Nehemiah as the companions of the three principal officers.

The Royal Arch, as conferred in Ireland, differs very materially from the degree in England and America. The Irish system consists of three degrees; the Excellent, Super Excellent and Royal Arch, and the Past Master's degree is indispensable as a qualification for exaltation. The Excellent and Super Excellent degrees refer to events connected with the legation of Moses. The events commemorated in the Royal Arch of Ireland refer to 2 Chronicles, chap. xxxiv., and expressly to the 14th verse of that chapter. "And when they brought out the money that was brought into the house of the Lord, Hilkiah, the priest, found a book of the law of the Lord given by Moses." The date of their degree is, therefore, 624 B.C., or ninety years earlier than ours.

In Scotland the era of the legend of the Royal Arch is the same as in England and America, but the organization of the system is very different. The Mark and Past Master, which are

---

* Freemason's Quart. Rev. 1843, p. 464.

called "Chair Master degrees," are indispensable qualifications, and candidates having had these degrees conferred receive two others, Excellent and Super Excellent, as preparatory to the Arch. Chapters in Scotland also confer on Royal Arch Masons the degrees of Royal Ark Mariner and Red Cross Knight, the latter degree receiving from them the name of "Babylonish Pass." The Scotch Masons contend that the Royal Arch, with its subsidiary degrees, constitutes a part of Templar Masonry.*

Badge of the Royal Arch. The badge of a Royal Arch Mason is the apron and sash. In America the apron is a white lambskin, bordered with scarlet edging. The sash is of scarlet silk or velvet, on which are inscribed the words "Holiness to the Lord." The colour is emblematic of fervency and zeal; the words are those which were worn in front of the High Priest's mitre. In England the apron and sash are of purple radiated with crimson,† the former implying awe and reverence, and the latter, justice tempered with mercy. The triple tau ⊥ is delineated on the apron.

Jewel of the Royal Arch. In this country we have lost sight of the jewel, though I hope to see it yet restored. The English Royal Arch jewel is a double triangle within a circle of gold. In the centre of the two triangles, a sun with diverging rays, and underneath, or suspended to this, the triple tau. The intersecting triangles denote the elements of fire and water, the circle, infinity and eternity, and the sun is an emblem of Deity. So important is the triple tau considered that it is called "the emblem of all emblems, and the Grand Emblem of Royal Arch Masonry."

ROYAL ARCH, ANCIENT. See *Knight of the Ninth Arch.*

ROYAL ARCH CAPTAIN. The sixth officer in a chapter

---

* General Regulations for the government of the order of Royal Arch Masons in Scotland. Edinburg, 1845.

† Finch says the colours are purple, red and blue, the blue implying truth and constancy. This agrees better with the colours of our Royal Arch.

of the Royal Arch degree, whose duties and station are, in some respects, similar to those of a Junior Deacon in a symbolic lodge.

ROYAL ARCH OF ENOCH. This is more usually known as the degree of Knights of the Ninth Arch, which see.

ROYAL ART. Masonry is called a Royal Art, not only because it received its present form from the royal hands of Solomon, King of Israel, and Hiram, King of Tyre, and has since enrolled among its members the proudest and most powerful potentates of the earth, but more especially, because of the dignity and majesty of the principles which it inculcates and which elevate it above all other arts, as a king is elevated above his subjects.

ROYAL MASTER. A degree by no means of ancient origin, intimately connected with the degree of Select Master, and with it, as explanatory of the Royal Arch degree, sometimes given in chapters preparatory to that degree,* and sometimes conferred on Royal Arch Masons by a distinct and independent body, called "A Council of Royal and Select Masters." The legend of the degree is brief, but interesting.

RULE. An instrument with which straight lines are drawn, and, therefore, used in the Past Master's degree as an emblem, admonishing the Master punctually to observe his duty, to press forward in the path of virtue, and neither inclining to the right nor the left, in all his actions to have eternity in view. The twenty-four inch guage is often used in giving the instruction as a substitute for this working tool. But they are entirely differ-

---

* Such is the case in the Chapters of R. A. Masons in Virginia; but the Grand Council of R. and S. Masters in Alabama have taken exception to this course and declared all R. and S. Masters, thus made, clandestine, and ineligible to admission into their Councils.

ent; the twenty-four inch gauge is one of the working tools of
an Entered Apprentice, and requires to have the twenty-four
inches marked upon its surface; the rule is one of the working
tools of a Past Master, and is without the twenty-four divisions.
The rule is appropriated to the Past or Present Master, because,
by its assistance, he is enabled to lay down on the trestle board
the designs for the craft to work by.

S.

SABBATH. God having created the world in six days,
rested on the seventh and proclaimed it holy. It is the type of
that time of refreshment which he only should expect who has well
and faithfully fulfilled the days of his labour. Hence, with the
virtuous Mason, the Sabbath day has ever been esteemed as an
occasion on which he might contemplate the works of creation
and humbly adore the great Creator.

SAINT ANDREW, GRAND SCOTCH KNIGHT OF.
Grand Ecossais de Saint André. The 29th degree of the Ancient and Accepted Scotch rite, and may be considered as preparatory to the Kadosh. It is founded on the legend which we
have recorded in the sketch of the Chevalier Ramsay, given in
this work. It is the first of the three degrees which he undertook to substitute in the place of the ancient symbolic degrees.
This degree is sometimes called "Patriarch of the Crusades," in
allusion to its supposed origin during those wars, and sometimes
"Grand Master of Light," on account of the masonic instructions it contains.

The officers are a Master and two Wardens. The lodge is
hung with red, and illuminated with eighty-one lights disposed
by nines.

The jewel proper is the square and compasses with a poignard in the centre, within a triple triangle, the whole surrounded by a sun. There is another jewel, which is a cross of St. Andrew, having a Y within a triangle, surrounded by a circle in the centre of the cross, and one of these letters B. J. M. N. on each of its extremities.

SAINT JOHN OF JERUSALEM. The primitive, or mother lodge, was held at Jerusalem, and dedicated to St. John, and hence was called "The lodge of the holy St. John of Jerusalem." Of this first lodge all other lodges are but branches, and they therefore receive the same general name, accompanied by another local and distinctive one. In all masonic documents the words ran formerly as follows: "From the lodge of the holy St. John of Jerusalem, under the distinctive appellation of Soloman's lodge, No, 1." or whatever might be the local name. In this style foreign documents still run; and it is but a few years since it has been at all disused in this country.* Hence we say that every Mason hails from such a lodge, that is to say, from a just and legally constituted lodge.†

SAINT JOHN'S MASONRY. A term used like "Ancient Craft Masonry," to designate the three primitive degrees. They are so styled by the Grand Lodge of Scotland. "The Grand Lodge of Scotland practises no degrees of masonry but those of Apprentice, Fellow-Craft, and Master Mason, denominated St. John's Masonry."‡

---

* I would certainly recommend the renewal of this masonic style, especially in diplomas.

† In the degree of Grand Master of all Symbolic Lodges, the reason assigned is, "because in the time of the Crusades the Perfect Masons communicated a knowledge of their mysteries to the Knights of St. John of Jerusalem, whereupon it was determined to celebrate their festival annually on St. John's day, as they were both under the same law."

‡ Constitutions of the Grand Lodge of Scotland, c. i, art. 4.

SAINT JOHN THE ALMONER. The saint to whom Encampments of Knights Templar are dedicated. He was the son
of the King of Cyprus, and was born in that island in the sixth
century. He was elected Patriarch of Alexandria, and has been
canonized by both the Greek and Roman churches, his festival
among the former occurring on the 11th of November, and
among the latter on the 23d of January. Bazot, who published
a Manual of Freemasonry, in 1811, at Paris, thinks that it is
this saint, and not St. John the Evangelist, or St. John the
Baptist, who is meant as the true patron of our order. "He
quitted his country and the hope of a throne," says this author,
"to go to Jerusalem, that he might generously aid and assist the
knights and pilgrims. He founded a hospital and organized a
fraternity to attend upon sick and wounded Christians, and to
bestow pecuniary aid upon the pilgrims who visited the Holy
Sepulchre. St. John, who was worthy to become the patron of
a society, whose only object is charity, exposed his life a thousand times in the cause of virtue. Neither war, nor pestilence,
nor the fury of the infidels, could deter him from pursuits of benevolence. But death, at length, arrested him in the midst of his
labours. Yet he left the example of his virtues to the brethren,
who have made it their duty to endeavour to imitate them.
Rome canonized him under the name of St. John the Almoner,
or St. John of Jerusalem; and the Masons, whose temples, over-
thrown by the barbarians, he had caused to be rebuilt, selected
him with one accord as their patron."*

SAINTS JOHN. St. John the Baptist, whose festival falls
on the 24th of June, and St. John the Evangelist, whose festival
occurs on the 27th of December, have been selected by Christian
Masons as the patrons of their order; and to them, under the
appellation of the "Holy Saints John," all Christian lodges

---

† Manual du Franc-Maçon, p. 144.

should be dedicated. See, for the author's theory on the subject of this dedication, the article *Dedication* in this work.

SAMARITAN, GOOD. The Good Samaritan is a side degree given to Royal Arch Masons and their wives. Of all the side degrees it is decidedly the most beautiful and impressive. It is founded on the tenth chapter of St. Luke, 30–35 verses. A Good Samaritan is bound, when duly summoned, to nurse a companion in sickness.

SANCTUARY. That part of the temple, being two-thirds of its length, which was in front of the Holy of Holies, and between it and the porch. See *Temple.*

SANCTUM SANCTORUM. *Holy of Holies.* The innermost part of the temple, into which, after its dedication, none entered but the High Priest. It was twenty cubits square, and was separated from the sanctuary by a door of cedar and four curtains of blue, purple, scarlet, and fine linen. It contained the ark of the covenant, with its mercy seat and overshadowing cherubim. See *Temple.*

SASH. The old regulation on the subject of wearing sashes in a procession, is in the following words: " None but officers, who must always be Master Masons, are permitted to wear sashes; and this decoration is only for particular officers." In this country the wearing of the sash appears, very properly, to be confined to the W∴ Master, as a distinctive badge of his office.

The sash is worn by all the companions of the Royal Arch degree, and is of a scarlet colour, with the words, " Holiness to the Lord," inscribed upon it. These were the words placed upon the mitre of the High Priest of the Jews.

The sash, or scarf, seems to have been derived from the Zennar, or sacred cord, placed upon the candidate in the initiation into the mysteries of India, and which every Brahmin was compelled to wear. This cord was woven with great solemnity, and being put upon the left shoulder passed over to the right side, and hung down as low as the fingers could reach.

SCANDINAVIAN MYSTERIES. The rites of initiation practised in Scandinavia, were introduced there from Scythia, by Sigge, a Cymrian warrior, who afterwards assumed the name of Odin, with whom we are all familiar as the Gothic representative of Mercury or Hermes. This origin of these rites accounts for their general resemblance in legend and ceremonies to the Eastern mysteries. In them was celebrated the death of Balder, who was killed by Loke, who fatally wounded him with a branch of mistletoe. Balder was the sun, Loke the principle of winter, to which season the mistletoe belongs. The ceremonies of initiation represented the wailings of the gods for the death of Balder, the search for his body, in which the candidate was made to engage, and its final discovery, and his restoration to life and vigour. The ceremonies were accompanied by all the paraphernalia of dismal noises and hideous sights, which was calculated to inspire the aspirant with terror and confusion, and were terminated by the administration to the initiate of a solemn oath, in which he swore to pay due submission to the chief officers of state, to practise devotion to the gods, and to protect and defend his initiated companions, at the hazard of his life from all their enemies, and if slain to avenge their death.

The legend of the death of Balder, which we can scarcely doubt was the subject of initiation, is thus related. Balder was invulnerable; for Odin and Friga, (the Gothic Venus,) had exacted, in his favour, an oath of safety from every thing in nature except the mistletoe, whose promise of immunity, in contempt of its ignoble qualities, they had neglected to obtain. Loke, the principle of evil, had discovered this exception, and on a day when Balder, was sportively offering himself as a mark to the skill and dexterity of the gods, Loke presented Hoder, who was blind, with a branch of mistletoe, with which he pierced the body of Balder, who instantly fell dead. His body was then placed in a boat, and set afloat on the waters, while all the gods mourned for his decease.[*] The reader who is familiar with the other mysteries of paganism, will readily detect in this legend, an obvious relation to the murder of Adonis by the boar, of Osiris by Typhon, and of Bacchus by the Titans.

The ceremonies of initiation were very similar to those which have already been described in this work, as appertaining to the other rites. The candidate having been previously prepared by the necessary purifications, was conducted into the sacred cavern of initiation, his feet being naked, and led by a winding descent amid the howling of dogs, and appearance of phantoms, to the tomb of the prophetess Volva. Here, having been properly instructed, he inquires of her respecting the fate of Balder. The prophetess now foretells the circumstances which have already been related in the legend above cited. The candidate presses onward, and soon hears the bewailings for the death of Balder. He is now confined in the Pastos[†] until a term of penance is completed, when he is directed to search for the body of Balder, and to use his utmost endeavours to raise him from death to life. He now descends through *nine* subterranean passages, where sights and sounds of the most terrific character conspire to excite his imagination. He finally enters the sacellum, or holy place, and finds Balder enthroned in a distinguished seat. The aspirant was now received, as in the mysteries of Egypt, with acclamations of joy and welcome, and the Scalds, or sacred bards, like the priests of Isis, chanted hymns descriptive of the generation of the gods and the creation of the world. The initiation was then terminated by the administration of the oath of fidelity already described.[‡]

SCARLET.· The emblematic colour of the Royal Arch degree. It is significant of the zeal and ardour which should inspire the

---

[*] Oliver, Hist. Initiat. p. 256.   [†] See the article *Coffin*.
[‡] Oliver, Hist. of Initiat., lect. x.

possessors of that august summit of our ritual. It was also the colour of one the vails in the sacred tabernacle. The Hebrew words *carmil, shani,* and *tolahht,* are indifferently rendered by our translators, as crimson, or scarlet. The words appear to have been synonymous among the Jews, and to have signified a bright red colour. The colour was much worn by great men.

SCHROEDER'S RITE. This is a rite consisting of the three degrees of Ancient Craft Masonry, and several higher ones, containing a mixture of magic, theosophy, and alchemy. It was invented by an impostor, of the name of Schroeder; who, having founded at Marburgh, in 1766, a chapter of "True and Ancient Rose Croix Masons," afterwards established, in 1779, in a lodge of Sarreburg, a school of the above named pseudo-sciences. Clavel calls Schroeder the Cagliostro of Germany. The rite is still practised by two lodges under the Constitution of the Grand Lodge of Hamburg.

SCIENCES LIBERAL. See *Arts Liberal.*

SCOTCH MASON. *Ecossais.* The 5th degree of the French rite. In this degree is related the manner in which the sacred word was preserved through the skill and wisdom of our ancient brethren. The American degree of "Select Master" appears to be little more than a modification of this interesting degree. See *Ecossais.*

A tradition contained in this degree may be interesting to the Master Mason. We there learn that HAB engraved the W.∴ upon a triangle of pure metal, and fearing that it might be lost, he always bore it about his person, suspended from his neck, with the engraved side next to his breast. In a time of great peril to himself, he cast it into an old dry well, which was in the south-east corner of the temple,* where it was afterwards found by three

---

* The Ineffable degrees of the Ancient Scotch rite say in the north side of the temple, which is more consistent with probability.

Masters. They were passing near the well at the hour of meridian, and were attracted by its brilliant appearance; whereupon, one of them descending by the assistance of his comrades, obtained it, and carried it to King Solomon. What was his disposition of it is known to the Royal Arch Mason.

SCOTCH RITE, ANCIENT AND ACCEPTED. This rite, which was organized in its present form in France, early in the eighteenth century, derives its title from the claim made by those who established it in that country, that it was originally instituted in Scotland, a claim whose validity is now generally disputed. It is, next to the York rite, perhaps the most extensively diffused throughout the masonic world. Supreme Councils, or lodges of this rite, exist in England, Scotland, Ireland, France, Belgium, the United States, and many other countries. The administrative power of the rite is deposited in Supreme Councils of Sovereign Grand Inspectors General, one of which Councils only can exist in a nation, except in the United States of America, where there are two, one at Charleston, in South-Carolina, for the South, and one at Boston, for the North.*

The Scotch rite, or as it is now more usually designated, the Ancient and Accepted rite, consists of thirty-three degrees, divided as follows:

1. Entered Apprentice.
2. Fellow-Craft.
3. Master Mason.

These degrees are conferred in a symbolic lodge, and differ only in a few points from the same degrees as conferred in a lodge of the York rite.

4. Secret Master.
5. Perfect Master.
6. Intimate Secretary.
7. Provost and Judge.

---

* See *Supreme Council*.

8. Intendant of the Buildings.
9. Elected Knights of Nine.
10. Illustrious Elect of Fifteen.
11. Sublime Knights Elected.
12. Grand Master Architect.
13. Knight of the Ninth Arch.
14. Grand Elect, Perfect and Sublime Mason.

These degrees are conferred in a body called a Lodge of Perfection, the presiding officer of which must be in possession of the 16th degree.

15. Knight of the East.
16. Prince of Jerusalem.

These two degrees are conferred in a body called a Council of Princes of Jerusalem.

17. Knight of the East and West.
18. Sovereign Prince of Rose Croix.

These two degrees are conferred in a body called a Chapter of Princes of Rose Croix.

19. Grand Pontiff.
20. Grand Master of all Symbolic lodges.
21. Noachite, or Prussian Knight.
22. Knight of the Royal Axe, or Prince of Libanus.
23. Chief of the Tabernacle.
24. Prince of the Tabernacle.
25. Knight of the Brazen Serpent.
26. Prince of Mercy, or Scotch Trinitarian.
27. Sovereign Commander of the Temple.
28. Knight of the Sun.
29. Grand Scotch Knight of St. Andrew.
30. Grand Elect Knight Kadosh.
31. Grand Enquiring Commander.
32. Sublime Prince of the Royal Secret.

These degrees, from the 19th inclusive, are conferred in a body designated as a Consistory of Princes of the Royal Secret, but they confer the 30th, 31st, and 32d, only as the proxies of the Supreme Councils.

33. Sovereign Grand Inspector Generals.

This degree is given in a body called the Supreme Council, which is the administrative head of the rite.

For further details, see the article *Supreme Council*.

SCOTCH TRINITARIAN. See *Prince of Mercy*.

SCRIBE. The Scribe is the third officer in a Royal Arch Chapter, and is the representative of Haggai. The *Sophar*, or Scribe, in the earlier Scriptures, was a kind of military secretary, but in the latter he was a learned man, and doctor of the laws, who expounded them to the people. Thus Artaxerxes calls Ezra the priest, "a Scribe of the law of the God of heaven." Horne* says that the Scribe was the King's Secretary of State, who registered all acts and decrees. It is in this sense that Haggai is called the Scribe in Royal Arch Masonry.

SCYTHE. This is one of the melancholy emblems in the Master's degree, reminding us of the rapid flight of time, and that death, with inexorable haste, will visit alike the prince's palace and the peasant's hut.

SEAL. No masonic document is valid beyond the jurisdiction in which the lodge from which it emanates, resides, unless it have appended to it the seal of the Grand Lodge. Foreign Grand Lodges never recognise the transactions of subordinate lodges out of their jurisdiction, unless the good standing of the said lodges is guaranteed by the seal of their Grand Lodge, and the signatures of the proper officers.

SEAL OF SOLOMON. This is supposed to have been either

---

* Introduction to Scriptures, iii. 93.

a pentangle, or, as the archæologists more generally think, a double triangle. Richardson, in his Persian and Arabic Dictionary, says, that the *muchra Salimani*, or Seal of Solomon was two triangles interlaced. The Orientalists attributed many virtues to this seal, and the Talmudists say that it was inscribed on the foundation stone of the Temple.

SECRECY. The objection which has been urged against Freemasonry on the ground of its secret character, is scarcely worthy of serious refutation. It has become threadbare, and always has been the objection only of envious and illiberal minds. Indeed, its force is immediately destroyed, when we reflect that to no worthy man need our mysteries be, for one moment, covered with the veil of concealment, for to all the deserving are our portals open. But the traditions and esoteric doctrines of our order are too valuable and too sacred to be permitted to become the topic of conversation for every idler who may desire to occupy his moments of leisure in speculations upon subjects which require much previous study and preparation to qualify the critic for a ripe and equitable judgment. Hence are they preserved, like the rich jewel in its casket, in the secret recesses of our lodge, to be brought forth only when the ceremonies with which their exhibition is accompanied, have inspired that solemnity of feeling with which alone they should be approached.

SECRETARY. An officer who records the proceedings and conducts the correspondence of the lodge. The office of Grand Secretary, in the Grand Lodge, was created in the year 1722, under the Grand Mastership of the Duke of Wharton, the duties having been previously performed by the Grand Wardens.*

SECRET MASTER. The fourth degree of the Ancient Scotch rite, and the first of what are called the "Ineffable or

---

* See Anderson's Constitutions, p. 205.

Sublime degrees." In it is explained the mystic meaning of those things which are contained in the Sanctum Sanctorum. The Master represents Solomon coming to the temple to elect seven experts to replace the loss of an illustrious character. He is styled Most Powerful. There is one Warden who represents the noble Adoniram, who had the inspection of the workmen on Mount Libanus, and who was the first Secret Master. The lodge is clothed with black, and enlightened by eighty-one lights, *arranged by nine times nine.*

The jewel of this degree is an ivory key, on which is engraved the letter Z, suspended from a white ribbon edged with black.

The apron is white, edged with black; the flap blue, and an All-Seeing Eye engraved thereon. The white is emblematic of candour and innocence, the black of grief.

SECRET MONITOR. A side degree very extensively known in the United States, and which is intended to strengthen the bonds of fraternal affection which should exist among all Masons. During its ceremonies, which are very simple, the beautiful and affecting history of the friendship between David and Jonathan, which is contained in the twentieth chapter of the first book of Samuel, is recited.

SEEING. One of the five human senses, whose importance is treated of in the Fellow-Craft's degree. By sight, things at a distance are, as it were, brought near, and the obstacles of space overcome. So in Freemasonry, by a judicious use of this sense, in modes which none but Masons comprehend, men distant from each other in language, in religion and in politics, are brought near, and the impediments of birth and prejudice are overthrown. But, in the natural world, sight cannot be exercised without the necessary assistance of light, for in darkness we are unable to see. So in the Mason, the peculiar advantages of *masonic sight* require, for their enjoyment, the blessing of *masonic light.* Illu-

minated by its divine rays, the Mason sees where others are
blind; and that which to the profane is but the darkness of ignorance, is to the initiated filled with the light of knowledge and
understanding.

SELECT MASTER. The same observations that have been
made in relation to the degree of Royal Master, are applicable
to this, as they are both intimately connected. It records the
traditions connected with the concealment of important mysteries
at the building of the first temple, and furnishes an important
link in the great chain of history which connects the incidents
of Ancient Craft Masonry with those that constitute the essence
of the Royal Arch.

In the United States, the Royal Arch is considered as the
seventh degree, those of Mark Past and Most Excellent Master
being interposed between it and the third. In one or two of the
States, however, the Royal and Select Masters have been inserted
after the Past and before the Most Excellent, and within a few
years an attempt has been made to make this innovation general.

This has arisen from a recent controversy on the subject of
jurisdiction. The Royal and Select degrees belonged originally
to the Supreme Councils of the Ancient and Accepted Rite, and
were conferred under their authority, and by their deputies.
This authority and jurisdiction the Supreme Councils still claim;
but, for many years past, through their negligence, the Councils
of Royal and Select Masters, in some of the States, have been
placed under the control of independent jurisdictions called
Grand Councils. Like all usurped authority, however, this claim
of the State Grand Councils does not seem to have ever been
universally admitted, or to have been very firmly established.
Repeated attempts have been made to take the degrees out of the
hands of the Councils, and to place them in the chapters, there
to be conferred as preparatory to the Royal Arch. The General
Grand Chapter, in the triennial session of 1847, adopted a resolution, granting this permission to all chapters in States where

no Grand Councils exist. But, seeing the manifest injustice and inexpediency of such a measure, at the following session of 1850, it refused to take any action on the subject of these degrees. In 1853 it disclaimed all control over them, and forbade the chapters under its jurisdiction to confer them.

There is no doubt in my own mind that the true jurisdiction of these degrees is vested in the Supreme Councils of the Ancient and Accepted Rite, and that they should be conferred rather as illustrations of, than as preparatory to, the Royal Arch. The Royal Arch degree itself contains the most essential parts of the legends of these degrees, and can be understood without them, although they furnish many additional particulars which it would be interesting to the masonic student to know.

SENIOR WARDEN. See *Wardens*.

SENSES. The five human senses are Seeing, Hearing, Feeling, Smelling, and Tasting; of which the first three are, for certain well known reasons, held in great estimation among Masons. Their nature and uses form a part of the instruction of the degree of Fellow-Craft. See them under their respective titles.

SENTINEL. An officer in a Royal Arch Chapter, in a Council of Knights of the Red Cross, and in an Encampment of Knights Templar, whose duties are similar to those of a Tiler in a symbolic lodge.

SERPENT. The serpent obtained a prominent place among the symbols of the Spurious Freemasonry of the earliest ages. Among the Egyptians, it was the symbol of Divine Wisdom, when extended at length, and the serpent with his tail in his mouth was an emblem of eternity. The winged globe and serpent symbolized their triune deity. In the ritual of Zoroaster, the serpent was a symbol of the universe. In China, the ring between two serpents was the symbol of the world governed by the power and wisdom of the Creator. The same device with, it is presumed, the same signification, is several times repeated on the Isiac table, which shows the universality of the symbol. In fact, serpent worship was one of the earliest deviations from the true system, and in almost all the ancient rites we find same allusion to this reptile. At the orgies of Bacchus,* the serpents were carried in the hands, or crowned the heads of the Bacchanalians, while frequent cries of "Eva, Eva," were frantically uttered. One of the ceremonies in the rites of Jupiter Sabasius was to let a serpent slip down the back of the person to be initiated. According to Plutarch, the women of Mount Hæmus, in Thrace, practised similar rites. According to Bryant, the worship of the serpent began in Chaldea, and thence passed into Egypt, where the serpent-god was called Can-oph, Can-eph, and C'neph. The Ethiopians introduced it into Greece. And so long did the serpent worship continue, that it is mentioned by Tertullian, and other fathers, as one of the early heresies of the Church, and practised by a sect called Ophites. Oliver says, that in Christian masonry the serpent is an emblem of the fall and subsequent redemption of man. I do not, however, myself, deem it as a pure masonic symbol. When used, I suppose it to be with its ancient signification of Divine Wisdom and Eternity; accordingly as it is exhibited in a lengthened form, or convoluted with its tail in its mouth

SEVEN. The number seven, among all nations, has been considered as a sacred number, and in every system of antiquity we find a frequent reference to it. The Pythagoreans called it a

---

* The Greek name of Bacchus is Dionysus, an account of whose mysteries is to be found in this volume. Wilford (Essay on Egypt, in the Asiatic Researches) supposes this deity to have been identical with the Hindoo god, Deva-Nahusha, popularly called Deo-Naush. Now Faber (Horæ Mosnicæ) derives Dionysus from this Deo-Naush, and Naush fram the Hebrew word נֶחָשׁ, or Naash, a *serpent*, making Dionysus, or Deo-Naash, equivalent, therefore, to the god Naash, or the serpent-god.

venerable number, because it referred to the creation, and because it was made up of the two perfect figures, the triangle and the square. Among the Hebrews, the etymology of the word shows its sacred import; for, from the word שֶׁבַע (shebang,) *seven*, is derived the verb שָׁבַע (shabang,) *to swear*, because oaths were confirmed either by seven witnesses, or by seven victims offered in sacrifice, as we read in the covenant of Abraham and Abimelech.* (Gen. 21-28.) Hence, there is a frequent recurrence to this number in the Scriptural history. The Sabbath was the *seventh* day; Noah received *seven* days' notice of the commencement of the deluge, and was commanded to select clean beasts and fowls by *sevens; seven* persons accompanied him into the ark; the ark rested on Mount Ararat in the *seventh* month; the intervals between despatching the dove, were, each time, *seven* days; the walls of Jericho were encompassed *seven* days, by *seven* priests, bearing *seven* rams' horns; Solomon was *seven* years building the temple, which was dedicated in the *seventh* month, and the festival lasted *seven* days; the candlestick in the tabernacle consisted of *seven* branches, and finally, the tower of Babel was said to have been elevated *seven* stories before the dispersion.

Among the heathens, this number was equally sacred.† A few instances of their reference to it, may be interesting. There were *seven* ancient planets, *seven* Pleiades, and *seven* Hyades; *seven* altars burnt continually before the god Mithras; the Arabians had *seven* holy temples; the Hindoos supposed the world to be enclosed within the compass of *seven* peninsulas; the Goths

---

* The radical meaning of שָׁבַע, is *sufficiency* or *fulness*, and the number seven was thus denominated, because it was on the seventh day that God completed his work of creation; and "hence," says Parkhurst, "seven was both among believers and heathens the number of sufficiency or completion."— *Lexic. N. T. in voc. בָרא.*

† Cicero, in his Dream of Scipio, calls it the *binding knot of all things:* "qui numerus rerum omnium ferĕ nodus est." *Som. Scrip.* 5. And Plato, in his Timæus, taught that the soul of the world, "anima mundana," was generated out of the number seven.

had *seven* deities, viz.: the Sun, the Moon, Tuisco, Woden, Thor, Friga, and Seatur, from whose names are derived our days of the week; in the Persian mysteries were *seven* spacious caverns, through which the aspirant had to pass; in the Gothic mysteries, the candidate met with *seven* obstructions, which were called the "road of the seven stages; and finally, sacrifices were always considered as most efficacious when the victims were *seven* in number.*

---

* An anonymous writer adds the following to the list above cited, of the consecrations of the number seven:

"In six days earth's creation was perfected—the seventh was consecrated to rest. If Cain be avenged sevenfold, Lamech seventy and sevenfold. Abraham pleaded seven times for Sodom; he gave seven ewe lambs to Abimelech for a well of water. Jacob served seven years for Rachel, and also another seven years. Joseph mourned seven days for Jacob. Laban pursued after Jacob seven days' journey. The seven years of plenty, and the seven years of famine, were foretold in Pharaoh's dream by the seven fat and lean beasts, and the seven ears of blasted corn. The children of Israel were to eat unleavened bread seven days. The young of animals were to remain with the dam seven days, and at the close of the seventh to be taken away. By the old law, man was commanded to forgive his offending brother seven times, but the meekness of the Saviour extended his forbearance to seventy times seven. On the seventh month a holy observance was commanded to the children of Israel, who fasted seven days, and remained seven days in tents. Every seventh year was directed to be a year of rest for all things, and at the end of seven times seven years commenced the jubilee; they were to observe a feast seven days, after they had gathered in their corn and wine; seven days they were to keep a solemn feast, as they had been blessed in the work of their hands. Every seventh year the land lay fallow. Every seventh year there was a general release from all debts, and bondsmen were set free. Every seventh year the law was directed to be read to the people. If they were obedient, their enemies should flee before them seven ways; if disobedient, their enemies should chase them seven ways. Hannah, the mother of Samuel, in her thanks says, that the barren hath brought forth seven, as some Jewish writers say that his name answers to the value of the letters in the Hebrew word, which signify seven. Seven of Saul's sons were hanged to stay a famine. Jesse had seven sons, the youngest of whom ascended the throne of Israel. The number of animals in sundry of their oblations, were limited to seven. Seven days were appointed for an atonement on the altar, and the priest's son was appointed to wear his father's garment seven days."

Were it necessary, the list might be still further enlarged.

In Freemasonry, seven is an essential and important number, and throughout the whole system the septenary influence extends itself in a thousand different ways.

SHEKEL. A weight among the Hebrews, of which there were two kinds, the king's shekel, and that of the sanctuary; the latter being double the value of the former. The common or king's shekel, which is the one alluded to, in the Mark degree, was worth about half a dollar. The shekel was not a coin, but a definite weight of gold or silver, which, being weighed out, passed as current money among the Hebrews. The half shekel has been adopted as the value of a mark, because it was the amount paid by each Israelite after he arrived at manhood, towards the support of the Temple, and was hence, called tribute money.

SHEKINAH. The Divine presence manifested by a visible cloud resting over the mercy seat in the holy of holies. It first appeared over the ark when Moses consecrated the Tabernacle; and was afterwards, upon the consecration of the Temple by Solomon, translated thither, where it remained until the destruction of that building.

SHIBBOLETH. The word שכלת, in Hebrew, has two significations; 1, An ear of corn; and 2, A stream of water. This is the word which the Gileadites, by the order of Jeptha, required the Ephraimites to pronounce. As the latter were desirous of crossing the river Jordan, and as the word signifies a stream of water, it is probable that this meaning suggested it as an appropriate test word on that occasion. The proper sound of the first letter of this word is *sh*, a harsh breathing which is exceedingly difficult to be pronounced by persons whose vocal organs have not been accustomed to it. Such was the case with the Ephraimites, who substituted for the aspiration the hissing sound of *s*. Their organs of voice were incapable of the aspiration and, therefore, as

the record has it, they "could not frame to pronounce it right."
The learned Burder remarks that in Arabia the difference of pronunciation among persons of various districts is much greater than
in most other places, and such as easily accounts for the circumstance mentioned in the passage of Judges.* Hutchinson, speaking of this word, rather fancifully derives it from the Greek σιβω,
I revere, and λιθος, *a stone,* and therefore, he says "Σιβολιθον,
Sibbolithon, *Colo Lapidem,* implies that they (the Masons) retain and keep inviolate their obligations, as the *Juramentùm
per Jovem Lapidem,* the most obligatory oath held among the
heathen." †

SHOE. Among the Ancient Israelites, the shoe was made
use of in several significant ways. *To put off the shoes,* imported
reverence, and was done in the presence of God, or on entering
the dwelling of a superior. *To unloose one's shoe and give it to
another,* was the way of confirming a contract. Thus we read in
the book of Ruth, that Boaz having proposed to the nearest kins-
men of Ruth, to exercise his legal right, by redeeming the land
of Naomi which was offered for sale, and marrying her daughter-
in-law, the kinsman being unable to do so, resigned his right of
purchase to Boaz; and the narrative goes on to say, "Now this
was the manner in former time in Israel concerning redeeming
and concerning changing, for to confirm all things; a man plucked
off his shoe, and gave it to his neighbour: and this was a testimony
in Israel. Therefore the kinsman said unto Boaz, Buy it for thee.
So he drew off his shoe." Ruth iv. 7, 8.

As to the ancient custom of taking off the shoes as a mark of
reverence, the reader is referred to the article *Discalceation.*

SHOVEL. One of the working tools of a Royal Arch Mason.

* Burder's Oriental Customs, vol. ii. numb. 782.
† Hutchinson, Spirit of Masonry, p. 113.

The working tools of this degree are the Crow, Pickaxe and Shovel, which may be thus explained.

The crow is an implement used to raise heavy stones, the pickaxe to loosen the soil and prepare it for digging, and the shovel to remove rubbish. But the Royal Arch Mason is speculatively taught to use them for a more glorious and exalted purpose. By them he is admonished to raise his thoughts above the corrupting influence of wordly-mindedness, loosening from his heart the hold of evil habits, and removing the rubbish of passions and prejudices that he may be fitted, when he thus escapes from the captivity of sin, for the search and the reception of Eternal Truth and Wisdom.

SIDE DEGREES. These are degrees, which have generally been the invention of Grand Lectures, but which have no connection with the ritual of masonry, and whose legality is not acknowledged by Grand Lodges. Some of them are very interesting, with an evident moral tendency, while others again, are trifling, and with no definite nor virtuous object in view. The worst of them, however, can only be considered, in the language of Preston, as "innocent and inoffensive amusements."

SIGNATURE. A Mason receiving from a lodge a certificate, is required to affix in the margin his signature in his usual handwriting, as a means of identifying the true owner from a false pretender, in case the certificate should be lost, and thus come into the possession of any one not legally entitled to it. See *No Varietur*.

SIGNET. A private seal set in a ring. The ancient Orientalists engraved names and sentences on their seals, a custom which the modern Mohammedans continue to follow. Many of these signet rings have, within a few years past, been dug up in Egypt, having the letters of a name cut in cameo on one side, and a figure of the sacred beetle on the other. A signet was often given by the owner to another person, and served in such a case as a pass, investing the receiver with all the authority possessed by the giver.

Signets were originally engraved altogether upon stone, and, according to Pliny, metal ones did not come into use until the time of Claudius Cæsar. The signet of Zerubbabel was, therefore, most probably of stone. The signet of Solomon is said to have been a pentalpha or endless triangle within a circle, and having the name of God engraved thereon.

SITUATION OF THE LODGE. See *East*.

SIX PERIODS, THE GRAND ARCHITECT'S. "The Grand Architect's six periods" is an expression used by Masons to designate the six days of the Creation. Our masonic books dilate upon them as a proper means of stimulating the Mason to industrious labour during the week, that he may be enabled to rest upon the Sabbath, to contemplate the glorious works of Creation and adore their great Creator.

SMELLING. One of the five human senses, and as the recipient of the numerous fragrant odours that arise from the flowers of the field and other objects of nature and art, a source of enjoyment to man.

SOLOMON. King of Israel and First Grand Master of Freemasonry. His history is full of interest to the fraternity. He was the son of David and Bathsheba, and was born in the year of the world 2871. Of him it had been prophecied to his father, " Behold a son shall be born to thee, who shall be a man of rest; and I will give him rest from all his enemies round about; for his name shall be Solomon, and I will give peace and quietness unto Israel in his day. He shall build a house for my name, he shall be my son, and I will be his father; and I

will establish the throne of his kingdom over Israel' forever."
1 Chron. xxii. 9, 10.

Solomon had scarcely commenced his reign, when he began
to prepare for the fulfilment of his father's last solemn injunc-
tions to build a temple to the Most High. With this view he
applied for help to the most powerful of his allies, Hiram, King
of Tyre, a prince of a liberal disposition, who, far from envying
Solomon's wealth and fame, cordially assisted him, and supplied
him, not only with the proper materials, but also with labourers,
and above all with an architect of surpassing skill in every kind
of cunning workmanship. Solomon now appointed a tribute to
be laid on all the people, of 30,000 labourers, whom he divided
into three classes of 10,000 in each. Each of these classes
worked one month in cutting timber on Mount Lebanon, and
then rested two. Over these he placed Adoniram as Junior
Grand Warden. There were also 80,000 masons, and 70,000
labourers or men of burden, the remains of the old Canaanites,
who are not reckoned among the masons, and 3300 overseers,
with 300 rulers, making in all 183,600 persons engaged upon
the Temple, of whom 113,600 were masons.

The Temple was begun on Monday, the 2d day of the month
Zif, corresponding to the 21st of April, in the year of the world
2992, and 1012 years before the Christian era, and was completed in a little more than seven years, on the 8th day of the
month Bul, or the 23d of October, in the year of the world
2999, during which period no sound of axe, hammer, or other
metallic tool was heard, every thing having been cut and framed
in the quarries or on Mount Lebanon and brought properly prepared to Jerusalem, where they were fitted up by means of
wooden mauls.

"The Old Constitutions aver," (I here quote from Anderson,)
"that some short time before the consecration of the Temple,
King Hiram came from Tyre, to take a view of that mighty edifice, and to inspect the different parts thereof, in which he was
accompanied by King Solomon and the Deputy Grand Master,

Hiram Abif; and after his view thereof declared the Temple to
be the utmost stretch of human art. Solomon here again renewed the league with Hiram, and made him a present of the
Sacred Scriptures translated into the Syriac tongue, which, it is
said, is still extant among the Maronites and other Eastern Christians, under the name of the old Syriac version."

Solomon next employed the craft in the construction of other
works, such as his two palaces at Jerusalem, and his house of the
forest of Lebanon, besides several cities, the most magnificent of
which was Tadmor or Palmyra.

But although Solomon had now become the most renowned of
all the princes of his time, exceeding in riches and wisdom all
who had gone before him, he, at length, forsook the law of his
fathers, and began to worship the false gods of his strange wives.
During his idolatry, he built temples to Chemosh, Moloch, and
Ashtaroth. But repenting of his grievous sin, about three years
before his death, he exclaimed, "Vanity of Vanities, all is Vanity!" He died at the age of fifty-eight, in the year of the world
3029, and before Christ 975.

Solomon is supposed to preside, or rather the Master is his
representative, in Lodges of Fellow-Crafts, Master Masons, Mark,
Past and Most Excellent Masters, and in Councils of Select
Masters, and also in several of the Ineffable degrees. See more
on this subject under the title *Temple, Organization at the.*

SORROW LODGES. It is the custom among Masons on
the continent of Europe to hold special lodges at stated periods,
for the purpose of commemorating the virtues and deploring the
loss of their departed members and other distinguished worthies
of the fraternity who have died. These are called Funeral or
Sorrow lodges. In Germany they are held annually; in France
at longer intervals. A French lodge in New York, "L'Union
Francaise," holds them decennially. Sorrow lodges have also,
but not lately, been held by a French lodge in Charleston, S. C.,
"La Candeur." The custom has been pursued by two lodges in

New York, "Pythagoras, No. 86," and "St. John's, No. 6," but
I know of no other instances of Sorrow lodges being held in the
United States. The custom is, however, a good one, eminently
consistent with the principles of Freemasonry, and which I
should rejoice to see universally adopted by American lodges.
On these occasions the lodge is clothed in the habiliments of
mourning and decorated with the emblems of death, solemn
music is played, funeral dirges are chanted, and eulogies on the
life, character and masonic virtues of the dead are delivered.

SOUTH. When the sun is at his meridian height, his invigorating rays are darted from the south. When he rises in the
east, we are called to labour; when he sets in the west, our daily
toil is over; but when he reaches the south, the hour is high
twelve, and we are summoned to refreshment.

SOVEREIGN COMMANDER OF THE TEMPLE. *Souverain Commandeur du Temple.* The 27th degree of the Ancient Scotch rite. The presiding officer is styled "Most Illustrious and Most Valiant," the Wardens are called "Most Sovereign Commanders," and the Knights "Sovereign Commanders."
The place of meeting is called a "Court." The apron is flesh-
coloured, lined and edged with black, with a Teutonic cross en-
circled by a wreath of laurel and a key beneath, all inscribed in
black upon the flap. The scarf is red bordered with black,
hanging from the right shoulder to the left hip, and suspending
a Teutonic cross in enamelled gold. The jewel is a triangle of
gold, on which is engraved the ineffable name in Hebrew. It is
suspended from a white collar bound with red and embroidered
with four Teutonic crosses.

Vassal, Ragon, and Clavel are all wrong in connecting this degree with the Knights Templar, with which order its own ritual
declares that it is not to be confounded. It is without a lecture.
Vassal expresses the following opinion of this degree:

"The 27th degree does not deserve to be classed in the Scotch rite as a degree, since it contains neither symbols nor allegories that connect it with initiation. It deserves still less to be ranked among the philosophic degrees. I imagine that it has been intercalated only to supply an hiatus, and as a memorial of an order once justly celebrated."*

SOVEREIGN GRAND INSPECTOR GENERAL. The 33d and last degree of the Ancient and Accepted Scotch rite. Its members constitute a Supreme Council, which is the chief tribunal of masonry in that rite. This degree was instituted in the year 1786, under the following circumstances. By the constitutions of the Scotch rite, which were ratified on the 25th of October, 1762, the King of Prussia was proclaimed as its chief, with the title of Sovereign Grand Inspector General and Grand Commander. The higher councils and chapters could not be opened without his presence, or that of a substitute appointed by him. All the transactions of the Consistory of the 32d degree, then the highest, required his sanction, or that of his substitute, and various other masonic prerogatives were attached to his office. No provision had, however, been made in the constitutions for his successor; and, as it was absolutely necessary that some arrangement should be made by which the supreme power should not become extinct on his death, the king established the 33d degree, out of the possessors of which the Supreme Council is formed, a body possessing all the masonic rights and prerogatives formerly exercised by the King of Prussia. See *Supreme Council.*

The order or badge of the degree is a white sash, four inches broad, edged with gold fringe, and suspended from the right shoulder to the left hip. At the bottom is a red and white rose, and on the part that crosses the breast must be a triangle of gold surrounded by a sun, and within the triangle the figures 33. On each side of this emblem, at the distance of two inches, must be a drawn dagger.

---

* Vassal, Cours Maçonique, p. 507.

The jewel is a black-double headed eagle of Prussia, with golden beaks and crowned with an imperial crown of gold, holding a naked sword in his claws.

There is no apron worn in this degree.

The motto of the order is *Deus meumque Jus*, "God and my right."

SOVEREIGN MASTER. The presiding officer in a Council of Knights of the Red Cross. He represents Darius, King of Persia.

SPECULATIVE MASONRY. Freemasonry is called speculative masonry, to distinguish it from operative masonry, which is engaged in the construction of edifices of stone. Speculative masonry is a science, which, borrowing from the operative art its working tools and implements, sanctifies them, by symbolic instruction, to the holiest of purposes—the veneration of God, and the purification of the soul.

The operative mason constructs his edifice of material substances; the speculative mason is taught to erect a spiritual building, pure, and spotless, and fit for the residence of him who dwelleth only with the good. The operative mason works according to the designs laid down for him on the trestle board by the architect; the speculative is guided by the great trestle board, on which is inscribed the revealed will of God, the Supreme Architect of heaven and earth; the operative mason tries each stone and part of the building by the square, level and plumb; the speculative mason examines every action of his life by the square of morality, seeing that no presumption nor vain glory has caused him to transcend the level of his allotted destiny, and 'no vicious propensity has led him to swerve from the plumb line of rectitude. And lastly, as it is the business of the operative mason, when his work is done, to prove every thing "true and trusty," so is it the object of the speculative mason, by a uniform tenor of virtuous conduct, to receive, when his allotted course of life has passed, the inappreciable reward, from his Celestial Grand Master, of "Well done, thou good and faithful servant."

SPHINX. A fabulous monster, to which the ancients give the face of woman and the body of a lion. It is found in great abundance on Egyptian monuments, and Plutarch says that it was always placed before the temples of the Egyptians to indicate that their religion was enigmatical. As a symbol of mystery it has been adopted as a masonic emblem.

SPURIOUS FREEMASONRY. Dr. Oliver, one of the most learned and philosophic Masons of this or perhaps any other time, contends that "the science which we now denominate Speculative Masonry was coeval, at least, with the creation of our globe, and that the far-famed mysteries of idolatry were a subsequent institution, founded on similiar principles, with the design of conveying unity and permanence to the false worship, which it otherwise could never have acquired." This schism from the pure and original source has been designated by the name of the Spurious Freemasonry of Paganism, to distinguish it from the purer system, which this theory supposes to have descended in a direct and uninterrupted line to the Freemasons of the present day.

In a later work, Dr. Oliver still further explains his idea of the spurious Freemasonry. The legends and truths which were transmitted pure through the race of Seth, were altered and corrupted by that of Cain, and much confusion arose in consequence of the frequent intercommunications of these two races before the Deluge, though the truth would still be understood by the faithful. Of these was Noah, who, out of all these deviations of the antediluvians, was enabled to distinguish truth from falsehood, and to transmit the former in a direct line, according to Rosenberg, through Shem, Abraham, Isaac, Jacob, Levi, Kelhoth, Amram, Moses, Joshua, the Elders, the Prophets and the wisemen to Solomon. Hence Freemasons are sometimes called Noachidæ, the descendants and disciples of Noah.

38*

But Ham had been long familiar with the corruptions of the system of Cain and with the gradual deviations from truth which had crept into the system of Seth, and after the deluge he propagated the worst features of both systems among his descendants, out of which he or his immediate posterity formed the institution known, by way of distinction, as the Spurious Freemasonry.*

Such is the theory advanced on this subject which is now very generally admitted by masonic writers. The doctrine is, however, imperfect, unless we advance one step further.

The spurious Freemasonry had descended through the Gymnosophists of India to Egypt, and thence into Greece, and perhaps by a different route to Scandinavia and the northern nations of Europe. Among all these it appeared in the form of initiations and mysteries whose legends bore just so much of the remains of truth as to evince their divine origin, and yet so much of falsehood as to demonstrate their human corruption.

There was, in after times, a communication between one branch of this spurious Freemasonry and the true system. This took place at the Temple of Solomon, between the Jewish Masons and the Dionysian Artificers, when true Freemasonry borrowed its present organization from the greater practical wisdom of the Dionysian, without, however, surrendering any of its truth. And the bond of this union between the two bodies which had so long divided the world, was Hiram Abif, who was himself a member of both systems—of the true system by birth, as the son of Jewish parents—and of the spurious by profession and residence, as an artificer of Tyre.

SQUARE. The square is an angle of ninety degrees, or the fourth part of a circle. It is one of the working tools of a Fellow Craft, and the distinctive jewel of the Master of a lodge. The square is an important implement to operative masons, for

---

* Oliver's Histor. Landmarks, 1. 60.

by it they are enabled to correct the errors of the eye, and to adjust with precision the edges, sides, and angles of their work. The nicest joints are thus constructed, and stones are fitted with accuracy, to fill their destined positions. Not less useful is this instrument to speculative masons, as a significant emblem of morality. As, by the application of the square, the stone is tried and proved, so, by the application of the principles of morality, each action of human life is judged, and approved or condemned, as it coincides with, or deviates from, those eternal and immutable principles. And as the stone, that on inspection with the square does not prove "true and trusty," is rejected or its defects amended, so each action that is not consistent with the dictates and rules of morality is carefully avoided by him who wishes to erect a mental structure of virtue, that shall afford him honour in life and repose in death.

And hence, as it is the duty of the Master of the lodge to preserve among its members a strict attention to moral deportment, and to mark and instantly correct the slightest deviation from the rules of propriety and good conduct, the square is appropriately conferred upon him as the distinctive jewel of his office.

Masons are said to part on the square, because having met together, their conduct should be such that, when they part, no unkind expression or unfriendly action shall have deranged that nice adjustment of the feelings, which alone unites them in a band of brothers; an adjustment which can only be preserved by a constant application of the square of morality.

STANDARD BEARER. An officer in an Encampment of Knights Templar, whose duty is sufficiently explained by his title. A similar officer exists in a Council of Knights of the Red Cross.

STAR. The star with five points, which is found among the

emblems of the Master's degree, is an allusion to the five points of Fellowship, or summary of a Mason's duty to his brother.*

The *blazing star* in the centre of the Mosaic pavement, is an emblem of that Divine Being, whose beneficence has chequered the dark field of human life with brighter spots of happiness. Those brethren who delight to trace our astronomical symbols to the cradle of that science, Egypt, and to the Egyptian priests, its earliest cultivators, find in the seven stars depicted on the Master's carpet, a representation of the Pleiades, and in the blazing star an allusion to the dog-star, which the Egyptians called Anubis or the *barker*, because its rising warned them of the inundation of the Nile, which always quickly followed its appearance, and thus admonished them to retire from the lower grounds, just as the barking of a dog admonishes his master of approaching danger.

---

* It is dangerous to differ in opinion, on a masonic subject, from Brother Moore, the Editor of the Magazine published at Boston (a work, my numerous obligations to which, I may as well take this opportunity of acknowledging); but in his opinion of the five-pointed star, I cannot, unfortunately, agree with him. In his Magazine, (vol. iv. no. 5,) he remarks, that "it has no explanation in the degree, and is not a masonic emblem as genuine masonry is practised in this country." The star of five points, so far as my opportunities reach, has been adopted in all our lodges, and if no explanation of it is given in our lectures, its manifest allusion is well understood. It is, therefore, as much a masonic emblem, as the equilateral triangle, which has the same universal acceptation among the fraternity, without receiving any notice in our lectures.

While on the subject of the star with five points, I cannot refrain from recording an interesting historical document, for which, by the bye, I am indebted to the work in which this emblem is denounced as unmasonic. At a celebration of the Festival of St. John the Baptist, in 1844, at Portland, Maine, R∴ W∴ Brother Teulon, a member of the Grand Lodge of Texas, in reply to a toast complimentary to the Masons of that republic, observed, "Texas is emphatically a masonic country; *all* our Presidents and Vice-Presidents, and four-fifths of our State officers, were and are Masons : our national emblem, the '*Lone Star,—was chosen from among the emblems selected by Freemasonry, to illustrate the moral virtues—it is a five-pointed star, and alludes to the five points of fellowship.*"—See *Moore's Freemason's Mag. vol. iii.,* p. 309.

In the English ritual, and formerly in our own, the star is said to be commemorative of that star which appeared to guide the wise men of the East to the place of our Saviour's birth.

In the Spurious Freemasonry of the Egyptians, the blazing star was the symbol of Horus the son of Isis—the sun—the primordial principle of existence.

STATISTICS OF MASONRY. The universality of masonry is not more honourable to the order, than it is advantageous to the brethren. From East to West, and from North to South, over the whole habitable globe, are our lodges disseminated. Wherever the wandering steps of civilized men have left their foot-prints, there have our temples been established. The lessons of masonic love have penetrated into the wilderness of the West, and the red man of our soil has shared with his more enlightened brother the mysteries of our science; while the arid sands of the African desert have more than once been the scene of a masonic greeting. The Mason, indigent and destitute, may find in every clime a brother, and in every land a home.

The evidence of these assertions will be found in the following table of the countries in which Freemasonry is openly and avowedly practised, by the permission of the public authorities. Such places as Italy, where, owing to the suspicious intolerance of the government, the lodges are obliged to be holden in private, are not mentioned.

I. EUROPE.

Anhalt-Bernburg,	Malta,
Anhalt-Dessau,	Mecklenburg-Schwerin,
Bavaria,	Norway,
Belgium,	Portugal,
Bremen,	Posen, Duchy of
Brunswick,	Prussia,
Denmark,	Prussian-Poland,

England,
France,
Frankfort-on-Maine,
Guernsey, Isle of
Hamburg,
Hanover,
Hesse-Darmstadt,
Holland,
Holstein Oldenburg,
Ionian Islands,
Ireland,
Jersey, Isle of
Lubeck,
Luxemburg,

Saxe,
Saxe-Coburg,
Saxe-Gotha,
Saxe-Hilberghausen,
Saxe-Meningen,
Saxe-Weimer,
Saxony,
Schwartzenberg-Rudolstadt,
Scotland,
Spain,
Sweden,
Switzerland,
Wurtemburg.

II. ASIA.

Ceylon,
China, (Canton,)
India,

Persia,
Pondicherry,
Prince of Wales' Island.

III. OCEANICA.

New South Wales,
Java,

Sumatra.
Sandwich Islands.

IV. AFRICA.

Algeria,
Bourbon, Isle of
Canary Islands,
Cape of Good Hope,
Goa,

Guinea,
Mauritius,
Mozambique,
Senegambia,
St. Helena.

V. AMERICA.

Antigua,
Barbadoes,
Bermudas,

Martinico,
New Brunswick,
Nova Scotia,

Brazil,	Panama,
Canada,	Peru,
Colombia,	Rio de la Plata,
Curacoa,	St. Bartholomew's,
Dominica,	St. Christopher's,
Dutch Guiana,	St. Croix,
English Guiana,	St. Eustatia,
French Guiana,	St. Martin,
Grenada,	St. Thomas,
Guadeloupe,	St. Vincent,
Hayti,	Trinidad,
Jamaica,	United States,
Labrador,	Venezuela.

STEWARDS. Officers in a symbolic lodge, whose appointment is generally vested in the Junior Warden. Their duties are, to assist in the collection of dues and subscriptions; to provide the necessary refreshments, and make a regular report to the Treasurer; and generally to aid the Deacons and other officers in the performance of their duties. The jewel of the office is a cornucopia.

STEWARDS' LODGE. The Stewards' or Grand Stewards' lodge, which still exists in some jurisdictions under peculiar local regulations, as a Standing Committee on Grievances, Charity, &c., was originally instituted on the 24th of June, 1735. In that year, says Anderson, upon an address from those that had been Stewards, the Grand Lodge, in consideration of their past services and future usefulness, ordained that they should be constituted a lodge of Masters, to be called the Stewards' lodge; to be registered as such in the Grand Lodge book and printed lists, with the times and place of their meetings, and that they should have the privilege of sending twelve representatives to the Grand Lodge, namely, a Master, two Wardens, and nine more.

STONE OF FOUNDATION. Masonry contains a legend of a cubical stone, on which was inscribed the sacred name within a mystical diagram. This stone is known as the "stone of foundation." For its history, see *Cubical Stone.*

STRENGTH. One of the three principal supports of masonry. It is represented by the Doric column and the S∴ W∴, because the Doric is the strongest and most massy of the orders, and because it is the duty of the S∴ W∴, by an attentive superintendence of the craft, to aid the W∴ M∴ in the performance of his duties, and to strengthen and support his authority. Hiram, King of Tyre, is also considered as the representative of the column of strength which supported the temple.

SUBLIME. In York masonry, this is the epithet applied to the Master's degree. It alludes to the sublime nature of the doctrines taught in that degree, which are the resurrection of the body and the immortality of the soul.

SUBLIME GRAND LODGE. Sometimes called the Ineffable Lodge, or Lodge of Perfection. It is, in the Ancient Scotch rite, the lodge which confers the degrees from the fourth to the fourteenth inclusive. It must derive its Warrant of Constitution from a Grand Council of the Princes of Jerusalem, or from a higher council, or Sovereign Grand Inspector General.

SUBLIME KNIGHT ELECTED. *Sublime Chevalier élu.* The 11th degree in the Ancient Scotch rite, sometimes called "Twelve Illustrious Knights." After vengeance had been taken upon the traitors already mentioned in the decrees of Elected Knights of Nine and Illustrious Elected of Fifteen, Solomon, to reward those who had exhibited their zeal and fidelity in inflicting the required punishment, as well as to make room for the exaltation of others to the degree of Illustrious Elected of Fifteen, appointed twelve of these latter, chosen by ballot to constitute a new degree, on which he bestowed the name of Sublime

SUB457

Knights Elected, and gave them the command over the twelve tribes of Israel. The Sublime Knights rendered an account each day to Solomon of the work that was done in the temple by their respective tribes, and received their pay. The lodge is called a Grand Chapter. Solomon presides, with the title of Thrice Púissant, and instead of Wardens, there are a Grand Inspector and a Master of Ceremonies. The room is hung with black, sprinkled with white and red tears.

The apron is white, lined and bordered with black, with black strings; on the flap, a flaming heart.

The sash is black, with a flaming heart on the breast, suspended from the right shoulder to the left hip.

The jewel is a sword of justice.

This is the last of the three Elus which are found in the Ancient Scotch rite. In the French rite they have been condensed into one, and make the fourth degree of that ritual, but not, as Ragon admits, with the happiest effect.

SUBLIME PRINCE OF THE ROYAL SECRET. *Souverain Prince du Royal Secret.* The 32d degree, and until the year 1786, when the 33d was instituted by Frederick, King of Prussia, the summit of the Ancient Scotch rite. The members are styled the Guardians of the Treasure of the Temple. Its meetings are called Consistories. The 32d degree can only be conferred by authority of the Supreme Council of the 33d. This degree furnishes a history peculiar to itself, of the origin of masonry, and an explanation of the symbolic meaning of the preceding degrees.

Its officers are numerous. The principal ones are a Thrice Illustrious Grand Commander, two Thrice Illustrious Lieutenant Grand Commanders, a Minister of State, Grand Chancellor, Grand Treasurer, and Grand Secretary.

The hangings of a Consistory are black, strewed with tears.

The jewel is a Teutonic cross. The apron is white, bordered

39

with black, and on it is inscribed the tracing-board of the degree.
On the flap of the apron is a double-headed eagle.

SUBSTITUTE WORD. The true English translation of
this most important word has been most miserably distorted and
corrupted by illiterate lecturers. A moderate acquaintance with
the Hebrew language would have shown its correct meaning, and
that when first used it was but a natural expression of horror
and astonishment uttered by King Solomon. Its signification
may be discovered by a reference to the separate syllables of
which it is composed, and which are to be found in their alphabetical order in the present work. The intelligent mason by
putting them together in their proper order will obtain the whole
sentence. On such a subject I cannot, of course, be more explicit. It may, however, be observed, in conclusion, that there
can be no doubt that the word originally consisted of four syllables, by which an equal, alternate division was made, and that in
its present form it has been subjected to much corruption, the
fourth or last syllable being now altogether omitted in pronunciation.

SUCCOTH. A town of Judea, 34 miles north-east of Jerusalem, near which Hiram Abif cast the sacred vessels of the Temple. See *Clay Grounds*.

SUN AND MOON. The sun and the moon, with the Master
of the lodge, are depicted in the lodge by the three lesser lights,
whose presence are to instruct the last that he should exercise
the same regularity and precision in the superintendence of his
lodge, as the two others exhibit in their government of the day
and night.

In all the Pagan initiations, we find traces of these symbols
which, as in masonry, were represented by the three superior
officers of the mysteries. In Greece, the Hierophant, or revealer
of sacred things, the Daduchus or torch-bearer, and Ho epi bo-

mos, or altar-server, were the representatives of the Creator, the
sun and moon, while the Ceryx or herald, as a Deacon, represented Mercury, who was the messenger of the gods. In the
mysteries of India, the chief officers were placed in the east, the
west, and the south, respectively to represent Brahma, or the
rising; Vishnu, or the setting; and Siva, or the meridian sun.
In the Druidical rites, the Arch-druid, seated in the east, was
assisted by two other officers, the one in the west representing
the moon, and the other in the south, representing the meridian
sun.*

The sun and the moon are preserved in our lodges, as emblems
of the wisdom, and power, and goodness of God, who made the
one to rule the day, and the other to govern the night; but the
heathens, in departing from the true light, which masonry has
preserved, confounded the creature with the Creator, and gave
that adoration to the instruments which should only have been
paid to the First Great Cause.

Hence the origin of sun-worship, which was one of the first
deviations from pure and patriarchal religion, and the evidence
of which is to be found in the earliest mysteries of Osiris in
Egypt, of Adonis in Phenicia, and of Mithras in Persia.

SUPER EXCELLENT MASTER. A degree which was
formerly conferred in Councils of Select Masters. It is founded
on circumstances that occurred at the destruction of the Temple
by Nebuchadnezzar, King of Babylon. Its presiding officer is
called "Most Excellent King," and represents Zedekiah, the
last King of Judah. The historical incidents of this degree,
but less in detail, are to be found in the first part of the Royal
Arch.

I have the ritual of another degree of Super Excellent, given
in Ireland, preparatory to the Royal Arch. But it is, or seems

* Oliver, Signs and Symbols, p. 203.

to be, a modification of the Most Excellent Master of the York rite, and the Perfect Master of the Ancient Scotch rite.

SUPPORTS OF THE LODGE. The institution of masonry, venerable for its antiquity, and its virtuous character, is said to be supported by *Wisdom, Strength,* and *Beauty;* for the wisdom of its eminent founders was engaged in its first design; the strength of its organization has enabled it to survive the fall of empires, and the changes of languages, religions, and manners which have taken place since its formation; and the beauty of holiness is exhibited in the purity and virtue that it inculcates, and in the morality of life which it demands of all its children.

Our lodges, thus supported, will find in these columns another analogy to their great prototype, the Temple of Jerusalem. For that mighty fabric was designed by the *wisdom* of Solomon, King of Israel, who found *strength* to carry on the great undertaking in the assistance and friendship of Hiram, King of Tyre; and *beauty* to adorn the structure in the architectural skill and taste of Hiram, the widow's son.

SUPREME COUNCIL OF GRAND INSPECTORS GENERAL. The supreme masonic authority of the Ancient Scotch rite. It was established in 1786, by Frederick II., King of Prussia, for the purpose of exercising, after his death, the masonic prerogatives which he personally possessed as the acknowledged head of the rite. Not more than one Supreme Council can exist in each nation,* and it must be composed of nine members, called Sovereign Grand Inspectors General, five of whom, at least, must profess the Christian religion. Not less than three constitute a quorum for the transaction of business. Its officers are as follows, all of whom are elected for life :—

A Most Puissant Grand Commander, who is the representative of Frederick II., King of Prussia.

---

* Two are permitted in the United States.

A Most Illustrious Lieutenant Grand Commander, representing Louis of Bourbon.

An Illustrious Treasurer General of the Holy Empire.

An Illustrious Secretary General of the Holy Empire.

An Illustrious Grand Master of Ceremonies.

An Illustrious Captain of the Guards.

The following account of the institution of the Supreme Council I have condensed from Dalcho,* and other authorities.

In 1761, the lodges and councils of the superior degrees, being extended throughout the continent of Europe, Frederick II., King of Prussia, as Grand Commander of the order of Prince of the Royal Secret, was acknowledged as the head of the Scotch rite. The Duke of Sudermania was his deputy in Sweden, and Louis of Bourbon in France.

On the 25th of October, 1762, the Grand Masonic Constitutions were finally ratified in Berlin, and proclaimed for the government of all masonic bodies working in the Scotch rite over the two hemispheres.

In the same year, they were transmitted to Stephen Morin, who had been appointed in August, 1761, Inspector General for the New World, by the Grand Consistory of Princes of the Royal Secret, convened at Paris, under the presidency of Chaillon de Joinville, Substitute General of the order.

When Morin arrived in the West Indies, he, agreeably to his patent, appointed a Deputy Inspector General. This honour was conferred on M. Hayes, with the power of appointing others where necessary.

Hayes appointed Isaac Da Costa, Deputy Inspector General for the State of South Carolina, who, in 1783, established a Sublime Grand Lodge of Perfection in Charleston. After Da Costa's death, Joseph Myers was appointed to succeed him by Hayes, who also appointed Solomon Bush, Deputy Inspector General for Pennsylvania, and Barend M. Spitzer for Georgia ;

* Orations, p. 68.
39*

which appointments were confirmed by a Council of Inspectors that convened in Philadelphia on the 15th of June, 1781.

On the 1st of May, 1786, the Grand Constitutions of the Supreme Council of the 33d degree were ratified by the King of Prussia, by which the masonic prerogatives of Inspectors were deposited in a council consisting of nine brethren in each nation.

On the 20th of February, 1788, a Grand Council of Princes of Jerusalem was opened in Charleston, by Myers, Spitzer, and A. Forst, Deputy Inspector General for Virginia.

In 1795, Col. John Mitchell was appointed by Spitzer a Deputy Inspector General, in the place of Myers, who had removed, but he was restricted from acting until after Myers' death, which took place in the following year.

On the 31st of May, 1801, the Supreme Council of the 33d degree was opened in Charleston with the grand honours of masonry, by John Mitchell and Frederick Dalcho, Sovereign Grand Inspectors General, and in the course of the succeeding two years, the whole number of Inspectors General was completed.

On the 5th day of August, 1813, a similar Supreme Council was, in accordance with the Secret Constitutions, duly and lawfully established and constituted at the city of New York,* by Emanuel De La Motta, as the representative, and under the sanction and authority of the council at Charleston. The masonic jurisdiction of the New York council is distributed over the northern, north-western, and north-eastern parts of the United States. And this, with the council at Charleston, are the *only* recognised councils which exist, or *can exist*, according to the Secret Constitutions in the United States.

This was the origin of the Scotch rite in the United States, of which there now exist two Supreme Councils; one at Charleston, S. C., and the other in the city of Boston, both bodies being in active operation.

---

* The seat of this Council has lately been removed to Boston.

SUSPENSION. A masonic punishment by which a party is temporarily deprived of his rights and privileges as a mason. Suspension may be definite or indefinite in the period of its duration. A mason who has been indefinately suspended can be restored only by a vote of the body which suspended him. One who has been suspended for a definite period is restored by the termination of that period, without any special action of the lodge.

SWEDENBORG, RITE OF. — We have seen in the article "Illuminati of Avignon," that the religious dogmas of Swedenborg were brought, in the middle of the eighteenth century, (the great season of rite-making,) to the aid of masonry for the purpose of manufacturing a new rite. In 1783, the Marquis de Thomé modified the system which has been adopted in the lodge of Avignon, to suit his peculiar views, and thus instituted what is properly known as the rite of Swedenborg. It consists of six grades, namely: 1, Apprentice; 2, Fellow-Craft; 3, Master Theosophite; 4, Illuminated Theosophite; 5, Blue Brother; 6, Red Brother.

It is still practised in some lodges in the north of Europe.

SWEDISH RITE. The rite practised by the Grand Lodge of Sweden consists of twelve degrees, the fifth of which gives the possessor the rank of civil nobility in the state. The degrees are as follows:

1, Apprentice; 2, Fellow-Craft; 3, Master; 4, Apprentice and Fellow-Craft of St. Andrew; 5, Master of St. Andrew; 6, Brother Stuart; 7, Favourite Brother of Solomon; 8, Favourite Brother of St. John, or White Ribbon; 9, Favourite Brother of St. Andrew, or Violet Ribbon; 10, Member of the Chapter; 11, Dignitary of the Chapter; 12, Reigning Grand Master.

SWORD BEARER. An officer in a council of Knights of the Red Cross, and in an encampment of Knights Templar, whose

station is in the west, on the right of the Standard Bearer, and
when the knights are in line, on the right of the second division.
His duty is, to receive all orders and signals from the Grand
Commander, and see them promptly obeyed. He is, also, to
assist in the protection of the banners of his order. His jewel
is a triangle and cross swords.

The Grand Sword Bearer is also an officer of a Grand Lodge,
whose duty it is to carry the Sword of State in public processions. In some Grand Lodges he receives the title of Grand
Pursuivant.

SWORD POINTING TO THE NAKED HEART. A
symbol of that Divine justice which must, sooner or later, over-
take all who have sinned; for, though man looketh to the outward appearance, God looketh to the heart alone, which, concealing its inmost passions from the world, is naked and open to his
ALL-SEEING EYE.

It is an emblem of the Master's degree.

SYMBOL. A sensible image used to express an occult but
analogical signification. Almost all the instruction given in masonry is by symbols. Such was also the case in the ancient
mysteries. "The first learning in the world," says Stukely,
"consisted chiefly in symbols. The wisdom of the Chaldeans,
Phenicians, Egyptians, Jews, of Zoroaster, Sanchoniathon, Phe-
recydes, Syrus, Pythagoras, Socrates, Plato, of all the ancients
that is come to our hand, is symbolical. It was the mode, says
Serranus, on Plato's Symposium, of the ancient philosophers to
represent truth by certain symbols and hidden images."

Symbols were first adopted by the Egyptian priests for the
purpose of secrecy; they concealing, by their use, those profound speculations which constituted the *apporeta* of their mysteries, and which they were unwilling to divulge to the unpre-
pared and uninitiated vulgar. From the Egyptians, Pythagoras
received a knowledge of this symbolical mode of instruction, and

communicated it to the sect of philosophy which he afterwards instituted.

According to Porphyry, there was this distinction between the *hieroglyphic* and *symbolic* method of writing among the Egyptians : that the former expressed the meaning by an imitation of the thing represented, as when the picture of smoke ascending upwards denoted fire; and the latter allegorizing the subject by an enigma, as when a hawk was used to signify the sun, or a fly to express the quality of impudence.* The former of these methods was open to all who chose to learn it; the latter was reserved by the priests for the purpose of mystic instruction, and was, as I have already said, communicated only to the initiated.

The symbols, says Warburton,† were of two kinds, *tropical* and *enigmatical*. The tropical, which were the more natural, were made by employing the more unusual properties of things to express subjects. Thus, a cat signified the moon, because the pupil of her eye was observed to be dilated at the full and contracted at the decrease of that satellite.‡ The tropical were constituted by the mystical assemblage of two or more things whose combined properties expressed a particular quality. Thus, a beetle, with a round ball in its claws, denoted the sun, because this insect makes a ball of dung, which he rolls in a circular direction, and with his face looking towards the sun.§

But the priests, in adopting the symbol, as a depository of their secret doctrines, were not contented with the use of it to designate only substances; their mystic instruction was of too elaborate a nature, to be satisfied with so circumscribed an alpha-

---

* τῶν μὲν (γραμμάτων ἱερογλυφικῶν) χοινολογουμένων χατὰ μίμησιν, τῶν δὲ (συμβολικῶν) ἀλλεγορυμένων χατὰ τινὰς αἰνιγμους.—*De Vit. Pythag.* xi. 15.

† Divine Legation, vol. iii. 141.

‡ Such is Plutarch's account of this symbol; but I am not aware that modern zoologists support this theory of lunar influence. *N'importe,* the Egyptians believed it, and that is all that the argument requires.

§ Clem. Alexand. Stromats.

bet; they next, therefore, had recourse to sensible objects, as a
means of expressing mental and moral qualities; thus, destruction was expressed by the mouse, impurity by the goat, aversion
by the wolf, knowledge by the ant; and the reason of the signification, as well as the thing signified, formed a part of their
apporeta, or secrets.

This is the highest and most intellectual method of applying
symbols, and it is the method adopted in Freemasonry, which, in
its use of symbolic instruction, is an exact counterpart of the
ancient mysteries.

SYMBOLIC DEGREES. The first three degrees of Freemasonry, the Entered Apprentice, Fellow Craft, and Master
Mason, are called in the York rite, symbolic degrees, because
they abound in symbolic instruction, not to be found in the
remaining degrees, which are principally historical in their
character.

SYMBOLIC LODGE. A lodge in which the symbolic degrees are conferred; that is, a lodge of Entered Apprentices,
Fellow Crafts, or Master Masons.

T.

TABERNACLE. The tabernacle was the place of worship,
representing a temple, which God commanded Moses to construct
in the wilderness for the religious service of the Jews, and in
which the ark of the covenant and sacred vessels were kept until
Solomon removed them into the temple. The tabernacle was so
contrived as to be taken to pieces and put together again at pleasure. The tabernacle was in shape a parallelogram fronting
the East, thirty cubits or forty-five feet in length, and ten cubits

or fifteen feet in height and breadth. The inside was divided by a richly embroidered vail of fine linen into two parts, the holy place and the holy of holies, in the latter of which was placed the ark of the covenant. Besides this vail of fine linen which separated the most holy place, the tabernacle was furnished with other vails of divers colors: namely, of blue and purple, and scarlet and fine twined linen, from which are derived the emblematic colours of the several degrees of masonry.*

The room in which a Chapter of Royal Arch Masons meets, is called the tabernacle, and is a representation of that temporary tabernacle which was erected by Zerubbabel near the ruins of old temple while the Jews, under his direction, were constructing the new one.

TABERNACLE, CHIEF OF THE. See *Chief of the Tabernacle*.

TABERNACLE, PRINCE OF THE. See *Prince of the Tabernacle*.

TALMUD. As many of the traditions of masonry are to be found in the Talmud, some acquaintance with the character of that work is essential to the masonic student.

The Talmud, which is a Hebrew word, תלמוד, signifying *doctrine*, is a collection of treatises written by the rabbins and wise men and embodying the civil and canonical law of the Jews. Moses is believed to have received two kinds of law on Mount Sinai, the

---

* According to Josephus (*Antiq. Jud. lib. iii. c.* 7.) the tabernacle was a symbol of the universe. The 12 loaves placed on the table were emblematic of the 12 months of the year; the 70 branches of the candlesticks represented the 70 *decani* or divisions of the planets; and the 7 lamps, the 7 planets. The vails of the tabernacle composed of four different colours, were emblematic of the four elements; the fine linen, made of flax, the produce of the earth, represented the earth; the purple represented the sea, because it was stained by the blood of a marine shell-fish, the murex; the blue represented the air, it being the colour of the sky; and the scarlet represented fire.

one *written* and the other *oral*. The written law is to be found
in the Pentateuch. The oral law was first communicated by
Moses to Aaron, then by them to the seventy elders, and finally
by these to the people, and thus transmitted, by memory, from
generation to generation. This oral law was never committed to
writing until about the beginning of the 3rd century,* when Rabbi
Jehuda the Holy, finding that there was a possibility of its being
lost from the decrease of students of the law, collected all the
traditionary laws into one book, which is called the " Mishna,"
a word signifying *repetition*, because it is, as it were, a repetition
of the written law.

The Mishna was at once received with great veneration, and
many wise men among the Jews devoted themselves to its study.
Towards the end of the 4th century, Rabbi Jochanan, the president of a school at Tiberias in Palestine collected their several
opinions on the Mishna, into one book of commentaries which he
called the " Gemara," a word signifying *completion*, because the
the Gemara completes the work. The Mishna and the Gemara
united constitute the Talmud.

The Jews in Chaldea, not being satisfied with the interpreta-
tions in the work of Rabbi Jochanan, composed others, which
were collected together by Rabbi Asche into another Gémara.
The work of R. Jochanan has since been known as the " Jerusalem Talmud" and that of R. Asche as the "Babylonian Talmud," from the places in which they were respectively compiled.
In both works, the Mishna or Law is the same; it is only the
Gemara or commentary that is different.

The Jewish scholars place so high a value on the Talmud, as
to compare the Bible to water, the Mishna to wine, and the Gemara to spiced wine; or the first to salt, the second to pepper, and
the third to spices. This work, although it contains many puc-

---

* Morin, however, in his "Exercitationes Biblicæ," assigns the 6th century
as the date of the composition. There is much controversy on this subject
among scholars. I have, in this article, given the dates agreed upon by the
greater number.

rilities, is, however, extremely serviceable as an elaborate compendium of Jewish customs, and has therefore been much used in the criticism of the Old and New Testaments. It furnishes also many curious illustrations of the masonic system; and several of the traditions and legends, especially of the higher degrees, are either found in or corroborated by the Talmud. The treatise entitled "Middoth," for instance, gives us the best description extant of the Temple of Solomon.

TASSELS. The Tracing-board of the Entered Apprentice's degree, when properly constructed, has a border or skirting around it, and at each corner a tassel attached to a cord or cable tow. These refer to the *four perfect points* and to the four cardinal virtues, and are called the guttural, pectoral, manual, and pedal tassels. They are also said in the English ritual to refer to the four rivers of Paradise.

TASTING. One of the five human senses, of but little importance in masonry, except as one of the sources of our enjoyment and protection, by enabling us to distinguish food which is pleasant and wholesome, from that which is disagreeable and unhealthy. Hence, for this as well as for every blessing of life, are we taught to be thankful to Him who is the "author of every good and perfect gift."

TATNAI AND SHETHAR-BOZNAI. The names of two Persian governors who opposed the attempts of the Jews to rebuild the temple. When, by the command of Artaxerxes, Zerubbabel and his followers had discontinued the rebuilding of the temple, which they had commenced by permission of Cyrus, his predecessor, they remained quiet until the reign of Darius, who succeeded Artaxerxes. They then recommenced the work, but Tatnai, the Persian governor on the Jewish side of the Euphrates, accompanied by Shethar-Boznai and his companions, not being aware of the previous edict of Cyrus permitting the Jews to

40

rebuild, proceeded to Jerusalem, and demanded by what right they were rebuilding the temple; and when the Jews informed them that they were working under the authority of a former decree of Cyrus, the Persian governors wrote to Darius, giving an account of these circumstances, and inquiring if such a decree was in existence, and if it was the king's pleasure that it should still be obeyed.   Darius, influenced by his friendship for Zerubbabel, who visited him on the occasion of this interference, gave orders not only that the Jews should not be molested, but that they should receive every assistance from the Persian officers in their pious undertaking of rebuilding the house of the Lord.

TAU CROSS.   The Tau Cross or Cross of St. Antony,* is a cross in the form of a Greek T.   It was among the ancients a hieroglyphic of eternal life.   It was the form of the Nilometer, or measure of the Nile, used to ascertain the height of the inundation, upon which the prosperity of the country and the life of the inhabitants depended, and was, in consequence, used among the Egyptians as an amulet, capable of averting evil.   Hence it was a favourite symbol of the Egyptians, and under the form of the "Crux ansata" was to be seen in all their temples, very often held in the hands of their deities or suspended from their necks. Jablonski† says it is the Egyptian representation of the Phallus, considered by some as the symbol of the deity, and by others as that of eternal life.   Kircher thinks that the Crux ansata was a monogram denoting Mercury or Phtha, who was the conductor of the souls of the dead; and Dr. Clarke‡ says that the tau cross was a monogram of Thoth, "the symbolical or mystical name of hidden wisdom among the ancient Egyptians; the $\Theta E O \Sigma$ of the Greeks."   In the initiation in Hindostan the tau cross, under the name of "tiluk," was marked upon the body of the candidate, as a sign that he was set apart for the sacred mysteries.   The

---

* So called because it is said to have been the cross on which that saint suffered martyrdom.

† Panth. Ægypt. i. 282.   ‡ Travels, vol. v. p. 311.

same mark was familiar to the ancient Hebrews, for, in the vision of Ezekiel, it is thus alluded to : " Go through the midst of the city, and set a mark, (in the original נ.ת, tau,) upon the foreheads of the men that sigh, and that cry, for all the abominations that be done in the midst thereof."* This mark was to distinguish them as persons to be saved on account of their sorrow for sin, from those who, as idolators, were to be slain, and its form was that of the Hebrew letter tau, which, in the ancient Phenician alphabet, and on the coins of the Maccabees, has the shape of a cross.

Among the Druids it was the custom to consecrate a tree by cutting the form of a tau across upon its bark. In ancient times it was set as a mark on those who had been acquitted by their judges, and by military commanders on such of their soldiers as had escaped unhurt from battle, and hence it was considered as an emblem of life.† Finally, observe that the tau is the last letter of the Hebrew alphabet, as the Aleph is the first, and that the tau assumes in the Ancient Phenician and Samaritan alphabets the form of a cross, and we see another consecration of this symbol in the expression, " I am the Alpha and the Omega, the beginning and the end," which, spoken in the Hebrew language, would be, " I am the Aleph and the Tau."‡

We are not, therefore, to be surprised that the Tau Cross has been adopted as one of the symbols of Freemasonry, and that in the form of the Triple Tau it constitutes the most sacred emblem of the Royal Arch, symbolizing the fact that the possessors of that degree are consecrated and separated, or set apart, as the recipients of a sublime but hidden wisdom. See *Triple Tau.*

TEMPERANCE. One of the four cardinal virtues, the

---

* Ezekiel, ix. 4. The Septuagint has το σημειον, *the mark,* which Lowth suggests should read ταυ σημειον, *the mark tau.*

† Oliver, Landmarks, ii. p. 621.

‡ My esteemed friend, George R. Gliddon, Esq., the celebrated Egyptian Archæologist, first called my attention to this illustration, which he extended still further, but on a subject irrelevant to the present occasion.

practice of which is inculcated in the first degree. The mason who properly appreciates the secrets, which he has solemnly promised never to reveal, will not, by yielding to the unrestrained call of appetite, permit reason and judgment to lose their seats; and subject himself, by the indulgence in habits of success, to discover that which should be concealed, and thus merit and receive the scorn and detestation of his brethren. And lest any brother should forget the danger to which he is exposed in the unguarded hours of dissipation, the virtue of Temperance is wisely impressed upon his memory, by its reference to the most solemn portion of the initiatory ceremony.

TEMPLARS.   See *Knights Templar.*

TEMPLARS OF SCOTLAND.   By the "Revised Statutes of the Grand Conclave of the Knights of the Temple,"* of Edinburgh, Scotland, the Knights Templars have an organization very different from that existing in any part of the world where this ancient and honourable order is to be found.   Some account of it may, therefore, not be uninteresting.

"The religious and military order of the Temple," in Scotland, consists of two classes : 1. Novice and Esquire; 2. Knight Templar.   The Knights consist of three grades, 1. Knights created by Priories; 2. Knights Commanders, elected from the Knights, on memorial to the Grand Master and Council, supported by the recommendation of the Priories to which they belong.   3. Knights Grand Crosses, to be nominated by the Grand Master.

---

* According to the organization of the order in Scotland, it is not a prerequisite qualification towards becoming a Knight Templar, that the candidate should possess the preparatory masonic degrees.   The Knight Templar of Scotland is not, therefore, necessarily a mason.   I give this strange, and I cannot help thinking, illegal regulation, on the authority of Brother C. W. Moore.   (Mag. vol. iv. p. 138.)   It must have been a late enactment, for in the Statutes, adopted April 13th, 1843, (ch. vi. 1,) it is declared " to be imperative that all candidates be Royal Arch Masons."

The supreme legislative authority of the order is the Grand
Conclave, which consists of the Grand Officers, the Knights
Grand Crosses, the Knights Commanders, and the Prior of each
Priory. .Four Chapters are held annually, at which times the
Grand Master, if present, acts as President. At the quarterly
meeting in March, the Grand Officers are elected.

During the intervals of the meetings of the Grand Conclave,
tne affairs of the order, with the exception of altering the Statutes, is entrusted to the Grand Council, which consists of the
Grand Officers elected by the Conclave, the Grand Priors of
Foreign Langues, and the Knights Grand Crosses.

The Grand Officers, with the exception of the Past Grand
Masters, who remain so for life, the Grand Master, who is elected
triennially, and the Grand Aides-de-Camp, who are appointed by
him and removed at his pleasure, are elected annually. They
are as follows :

Grand Master,
Past Grand Masters,
Grand Seneschal,
Preceptor and Grand Prior of Scotland,
Grand Constable and Mareschal,
Grand Admiral,
Grand Almoner or Hospitaller,
Grand Chancellor,
Grand Treasurer,
Grand Secretary and Registrar,
Primate or Grand Prelate,
Grand Provost or Governor-General,
Grand Standard-Bearer or Beaucennifer,
Grand Bearer of the Vexillum Belli,
Grand Chamberlain,
Grand Steward,
Two Grand Aides-de-Camp.

A Grand Priory may be instituted by the Grand Conclave, in
any nation, colony or langue, to be placed under the authority

of a Grand Prior who is elected for life, unless superseded by
the Grand Conclave.

A Priory, which is equivalent to our Encampments, consists
of the following officers:

Prior,
Sub-Prior,
Mareschal or Master of Ceremonies,
Hospitaller or Almoner,
Chancellor,
Treasurer,
Secretary,
Chaplain and Instructor,
Beaucennifer, or Bearer of the Beauseant,
Bearer of the Red Cross Banner, or Vexillum Belli,
Chamberlain,
Two Aides-de-Camp,
Band, Guards, etc.

The Grand Conclave may unite two or more Priories into a
Commandery, to be governed by a Provincial Commander, who
is elected by the Grand Conclave.

The costume of the Knights, with the exception of a few
slight variations to designate difference of rank, is the same as
that described as the ancient costume in page 270, of this work.

TEMPLE OF SOLOMON. The Temple of the Lord,* at
Jerusalem, was commenced by Solomon, King of Israel, in the
year of the world 2992, and being finished in seven years and
six months, was dedicated to the service of the Most High, in
the year 3000. It stood on Mount Moriah, one of the eminences
of the ridge, called in Scripture Mount Zion, and was originally
the property of Ornan the Jebusite, who used it as a threshing-

---

* It is called in Scripture, *hekal adonai*, " the palace of Jehovah," to intimate that its splendour and magnificence were not intended to reflect honour
on those who constructed it, but only to prepare it as a fit dwelling for Him,
who is the " King of kings and Lord of lords."

floor, and from whom it was purchased by King David, for the purpose of erecting an altar.* It retained its original splendour only thirty-four years, when Shishak, King of Egypt, took away its richest treasures ;† it was afterwards, in the eleventh year of the reign of Zedekiah, plundered and burnt by the Chaldeans, under Nebuchadnezzar.‡ After the captivity, the temple was rebuilt by Zerubbabel, with greater extent, but inferior glory.

The temple was originally built on a very hard rock, encompassed with frightful precipices. The foundations were laid very deep, with immense labour and expense. It was surrounded with a wall of great height, exceeding in the lowest part four hundred and fifty feet, constructed entirely of white marble.

The temple itself, which consisted of the porch, the sanctuary, and the holy of holies, was but a small part of the edifice on Mount Moriah. It was surrounded with spacious courts, and the whole structure occupied at least half a mile in circumference. Upon passing through the outer wall, you came to the first court, called the court of the Gentiles, because the Gentiles were admitted into it, but were prohibited from passing farther. It was surrounded by a range of porticos or cloisters, above which were galleries or apartments, supported by pillars of white marble.

Passing through the court of the Gentiles you entered the court of the children of Israel, which was separated by a low stone wall, and an ascent of fifteen steps, into two divisions, the outer one being occupied by the women, and the inner by the men. Here the Jews were in the habit of resorting daily for the purposes of prayer.

Within the court of the Israelites, and separated from it by a wall one cubit in height, was the court of the priests. In the centre of this court was the altar of burnt offerings, to which the people brought their oblations and sacrifices, but none but the priests were permitted to enter it.

From this court, twelve steps ascended to the temple, strictly

* See 2 Sam. xxiv. 23, 24; 1 Chron. xxi. 25.   † 2 Chron. xii. 9.
‡ See *Captivity*.

so called, which, as I have already said, was divided into three parts, the porch, the sanctuary, and the holy of holies.

The PORCH of the temple was twenty cubits in length, and the same in breadth. At its entrance was a gate made entirely of Corinthian brass, the most precious metal known to the ancients. Beside this gate there were the two pillars Jachin and Boaz, which had been constructed by the architect whom the King of Tyre had sent to Solomon, and which are thus described by Josephus: "Moreover this Hiram made two hollow pillars, whose outsides were of brass, and the thickness of the brass was four fingers' breadth, and the height of the pillars was eighteen cubits, and their circumference twelve cubits; but there was cast with each of their chapiters, lily work that stood upon the pillar, and it was elevated five cubits, round about which there was net-work, interwoven with small palms made of brass, and covering the lily work. To this also, were hung two hundred pomegranates in two rows."*

From the porch you entered the SANCTUARY by a portal, which, instead of folding doors, was furnished with a magnificent vail of many colours, which mystically represented the universe. The breadth of the sanctuary was twenty cubits, and its length forty, or just twice that of the porch and holy of holies. It occupied, therefore, one half of the body of the temple. In the sanctuary were placed the various utensils necessary for the daily worship of the temple, such as the altar of incense, on which incense was daily burnt by the officiating priest; the ten golden candlesticks; and the ten tables on which the offerings were laid previous to the sacrifice.

The HOLY OF HOLIES, or innermost chamber, was separated from the sanctuary by doors of olive, richly sculptured and inlaid with gold, and covered with vails of blue, purple, scarlet, and the finest linen. The size of the holy of holies was the same as that of the porch, namely, twenty cubits square. It contained

---

* Antiq. lib. viii. c. 3.

the ark of the covenant, which had been transferred into it from
the Tabernacle, with its overshadowing cherubim and its mercy-
seat. Into the most sacred place, the High Priest alone could
enter, and that only once a year, on the day of atonement.

The temple, thus constructed, must have been one of the most
magnificent structures of the ancient world. For its erection,
David had collected more than four thousand millions of dollars,*
and one hundred and eighty-four thousand six hundred men
were engaged in building it for more than seven years; and
after its completion it was dedicated by Solomon, with solemn
prayer, and seven days of feasting; during which, a peace-offer-
ing of twenty thousand oxen and six times that number of
sheep, was made, to consume which the holy fire came down
from heaven.

Thirty-three years after its completion this beautiful edifice
was despoiled, in the reign of Jeroboam, by Shishak, King of
Egypt, and finally burnt to the ground by Nebuchadnezzar, King
of Babylon, and the inhabitants of Jerusalem carried as captives
to that city in the year 588, B. C., during the reign of Zedekiah.

TEMPLE, CLASSIFICATION OF THE WORKMEN
AT THE. In 2 Chronicles, chap. ii. verses 17 and 18, we read
as follows:

"And Solomon numbered all the strangers that were in the
land of Israel, after the numbering wherewith David his father
had numbered them; and they were found an hundred and fifty
thousand and three thousand and six hundred.

"And he set threescore and ten thousand of them to be
bearers of burdens, and fourscore thousand to be hewers in the
mountain, and three thousand and six hundred overseers to set
the people a-work."

The same numerical details are given in the 2d verse of the same
chapter. Again, in 1 Kings, chap. v., verses 13 and 14, it is said:

---

* One hundred and eight thousand talents of gold, and one million seventeen thousand talents of silver.

"And King Solomon raised a levy out of all Israel; and the levy was thirty thousand men.

"And he sent them to Lebanon, ten thousand a month by courses: a month they were in Lebanon, and two months at home: and Adoniram was over the levy."

The succeeding verses make the same enumeration of workmen as that contained in Chronicles quoted above, with the exception that by omitting the three hundred Harodim, or rulers over all, the number of overseers is stated in the book of Kings to be only three thousand three hundred.

With these authorities, and the assistance of masonic traditions, Anderson constructs the following table of the craftsmen at the temple.

Harodim, Princes, Rulers, or Provosts,	300
Menatzchim, Overseers or Master Masons,	3,300
Ghiblim, Stone Squarers, *Ischotzeb*, Hewers, *Benai*, Builders, } all Fellow Crafts,	80,000
All the Freemasons employed in the work of the Temple, exclusive of the two Grand Wardens, }	113,600

Besides the *Ish Sabbal*, or men of burden, the remains of the old Canaanites, amounting to 70,000, who are not numbered among masons.

In relation to the classification of these workmen, Anderson says, "Solomon partitioned the Fellow-Crafts into certain lodges, with a Master and Wardens in each; that they might receive commands in a regular manner, might take care of their tools and jewels, might be regularly paid every week, and be duly fed and clothed; and the Fellow-Crafts took care of their succession by educating Entered Apprentices."*

Josephus makes a different estimate. He includes the 3,300 overseers in the 80,000 Fellow-Crafts, and makes the number of masons, exclusive of the 70,000 bearers of burdens, only 110,000.

A work published in 1764, entitled the "Masonic Pocket

* Constitutions, p. 22, ed. 1769.

Book," gives a still different classification. The number, according to this work, was as follows:

Harodim,	-	-	-	-	300
Menatzchim,	-	-	-	-	3,300
Ghiblim,	-	-	-	-	83,000
Adoniram,	-	-	-	-	30,000

Total, - - - - 116,000 Masons, which, with the 70,000 Ish Sabbal or labourers, will make a grand total of 186,600 workmen.

According to the authority of Webb, there were three Grand Masters, 3,300 Overseers, 80,000 Fellow-Crafts, and 70,000 Entered Apprentices. This account makes no allusion to the 300 Harodim, nor to the levy of 30,000. It is, therefore, manifestly incorrect. Indeed, I doubt whether we have any certain authority for the complete classification of the workmen, as neither the Bible nor Josephus gives any account of the number of Tyrians employed. Oliver,* however, has collected from the masonic traditions an account of the classifications of the workmen, which I shall insert, with a few additional facts, taken from authorities in my possession.

According to these traditions, the following was the classification of the Masons who wrought in the quarries of Tyre

6	Super-Excellent Masons,
48	Excellent Masons,
8	Grand Architects,
16	Architects,
2,376	Master Masons,
700	Mark Masters,
1,400	Markmen,
53,900	Fellow-Crafts.

58,454 Total.

* See the whole subject treated at length in the 15th lecture of his " Historical Landmarks."

These were arranged as follows : The Super-Excellent Masons
were divided into two Grand Lodges, with three brethren in
each to superintend the work. The Excellent Masons were divided into six lodges, of nine each, including one of the Super-
Excellent Masons, who acted as Master. The eight Grand Architects constituted one lodge, and the sixteen Architects another.
The Grand Architects were the Masters, and the Architects the
Wardens of the lodges of Master Masons, which were eight in
number, and consisted, with the officers, of three hundred each.
The Mark Masters were divided into fourteen lodges of fifty in
each, and the Markmen into fourteen lodges, also of one hundred
in each. The Mark Masters were the Masters, and the Markmen
the Wardens of the lodges of Fellow-Crafts, which were seven
hundred in number, and with these officers consisted of eighty in
each.

The classification in the forest of Lebanon, was as follows :

    3 Super-Excellent Masons,
   24 Excellent Masons,
    4 Grand Architects,
    8 Architects,
  1,188 Master Masons,
   300 Mark Masons,
   600 Markmen,
 23,100 Fellow-Crafts,
 10,000 Entered Apprentices.
     ———————
 35,227 Total.

These were arranged as follows : The three Super-Excellent Masons formed one lodge. The Excellent Masons were divided into
three lodges of nine each, including one of the Super-Excellent Masons as Master. The four Grand Architects constituted one lodge,
and the eight Architects another, the former acting as Masters and
the latter as Wardens of the lodges of Master Masons, which

were four in number, and consisted with these officers of three hundred in each. The Mark Masters were divided into six lodges of fifty in each, and the Markmen into six lodges of one hundred in each. These two classes presided, the former as Masters and the latter as Wardens in the lodges of Fellow-Crafts, which were three hundred in number, and were composed of eighty each, including these officers.

After three years had been occupied in "hewing, squaring, and numbering," the stones, and "felling and preparing" the timbers, these two bodies of Masons united for the purpose of properly arranging the materials, so that no metallic tool might be required in putting them up, and they were then carried up to Jerusalem. Here the whole body was congregated under the superintending care of HAB, and to them were added four hundred and twenty lodges of Tyrian and Sidonian Fellow-Crafts, having eighty in each, and the twenty thousand Entered Apprentices of the levy from Israel, who had been therefore at rest, and who were added to the lodges of Entered Apprentices, making three hundred in each, so that the whole number engaged at Jerusalem amounted to two hundred and seventeen thousand two hundred and eighty-one, who were arranged as follows:

Nine lodges of Excellent Masons, nine in each, are	81
Twelve lodges of Master Masons, three hundred in each, are	3,600
One thousand lodges of Fellow-Crafts, eighty in each, are	80,000
Four hundred and twenty lodges of Tyrian Fellow-Crafts, eighty in each, are	33,600
One hundred lodges of Entered Apprentices, three hundred in each, are	30,000
Seventy thousand Ish Sabbal, or labourers, are	70,000
Total	217,281

41

Such is the system adopted by our English brethren; the American ritual has greatly simplified the arrangement. According to the system now generally taught, the workmen at the building of the temple were classed as follows :

Three Grand Masters.

Three hundred Harodim, or chief superintendents, who may be called Past Masters.*

Three thousand three hundred Master Masons, divided into lodges of three each.

Eighty thousand Fellow-Crafts, who were also divided into lodges of five each.

Seventy thousand Entered Apprentices, divided into lodges of seven each.

According to this account, there must have been—

One thousand one hundred lodges of Master Masons.

Sixteen thousand lodges of Fellow-Crafts.

Ten thousand lodges of Entered Apprentices.

No account is here taken of the levy of thirty thousand, who are supposed not to have been Masons, nor of the builders of Hiram, whom the English ritual places at thirty-three thousand six hundred, and most of whom were, as I suppose, members of the Dionysiac fraternity. On the whole, the American system seems too defective to meet all the demands of the student, an objection to which the English is not so obnoxious. I should be rejoiced, therefore, to see this latter system, with some modifications, generally adopted by our Grand Lecturers.

TEMPLE OF ZERUBBABEL. Cyrus, King of Persia, having liberated the Jews, seventy years from the commencement of their captivity, in the reign of Jehoiakim, and fifty-two years after the destruction of the Temple, forty-two thousand

---

* They cannot according to our ritual, be Most Excellent Masters, because, according to the legend of that degree, it was not established until the Temple was completed.

three hundred and sixty of the liberated captives, by permission
of the king, returned to Jerusalem under the guidance of Joshua
the High Priest, Zerubbabel the Prince or Governor, and Haggai
the Scribe, and two years after, that is, 535 years B. C., they
laid the foundations of the second temple. They were, however,
much disturbed in their labours by the Samaritans, whose offer
to unite with them in the building they had rejected. Artaxerxes,
known in profane history as Cambyses, having succeeded Cyrus
on the throne of Persia, he forbade the Jews to proceed with the
work, and the Temple remained in an unfinished state until the
death of Artaxerxes and the succession of Darius to the throne.
As in early life there had been a great intimacy between this
sovereign and Zerubbabel, the latter proceeded to Babylon, and
obtained permission from the monarch to resume the labour.
Zerubbabel returned to Jerusalem, and notwithstanding some
further delays consequent upon the enmity of the neighbouring
nations, the second Temple, or as it may be called by way of distinction from the first, the Temple of Zerubbabel, was completed
in the sixth year of the reign of Darius, 515 years B. C., and
just twenty years after its commencement. It was then dedicated with all the solemnities that accompanied the dedication of
the first.

This second Temple did not equal the first in the glory and
splendour of its decorations—the ark of the covenant was lost,
although, by the precautions of our ancient Grand Masters, an
exact copy of it had been preserved amid the ruin and desolation
of Jerusalem. Both the Shekinah, the glory of God, and the
Bathkol, or oracle, were departed forever.* Still, there is much
to interest the people in this second house of the Lord. The
masonic stone of foundation, which had been safely deposited by
the wisdom of the first Masons, was found and made the chief

---

* The Jews say that there were five things wanting in the second temple,
which had been in the first, namely: the Ark, the Urim and Thummin, the
fire from heaven, the divine presence, or cloud of glory, and the spirit of prophecy and power of miracles.

corner-stone, and all the holy vessels were returned by order of the King of Persia; the Tyrians again furnished timbers from the forest of Lebanon, and at length the cope-stone, on which seven eyes had been engraved by the express command of God, was celebrated with sacrifices and rejoicings.

TEMPLE, ORDER OF THE. A masonic institution in France, whose members claim to be the lineal descendants of the Knights Templar. It appears, however, that this claim is unfounded, and that the society is only a masonic rite, in which something that they call a continuation of the order of the Templars, is engrafted on degrees borrowed from the Ancient Scotch rite. Originally the order of the Temple consisted of the following six degrees: 1, Apprentice; 2, Fellow-Craft; 3, Master; 4, Master of the East; 5, Master of the Black Eagle of St. John; 6, Perfect Master of the Pelican. But in 1808, to disguise this evident masonic origin, the degrees received the following names: 1, Initiate, (this is the degree of the Entered Apprentice;) 2, Initiate of the Interior, (this is the degree of Fellow-Craft;) 3, Adept, (this is the Master;) 4, Adept of the East, (the Illustrious Elected of Fifteen of the Scotch rite;) 5, Grand Adept of the Black Eagle of St. John, (the Elected Knights of Nine;) these constitute the House of Initiation; 6, Postulant of the order, (Perfect Adept of the Pelican;) this is called the House of Postulance, and is nothing but the Rose Croix of the Scotch rite; 7, Esquire; 8, Knight or Levite of the Interior Guard. These last degrees are called the Covenant, and are the same as the Scotch degree of the Knight of K–H.*

TESSELATED BORDER. The skirting which surrounds the mosaic pavement. A late masonic writer suggests that the proper term is "tasselled border;" the word *tasselled* alluding, he thinks, to the four tassels that are placed at the corners of the

---

* Clavel Hist. Pittoresq., pp. 66, 214–219.

tracing-board. The suggestion is ingenious, but not correct. *Tesselated* means inlaid with various kinds of colours, or variegated with flowers, &c., and the word alludes to the variegated ornaments of the border. See *Mosaic Pavement*.

TETRACTYS. (*Greek*, τετραχτυς, *four*. The tetractys was a sacred symbol of the Pythagoreans, which was expressed by ten jods disposed in the form of a triangle, each side containing four as in the annexed figure. This they explained as follows :—

The one point represented the Monad, or active principle.
The two points, the Duad, or passive principle.
The three, the Triad, or world arising from their union.
The four, the Quarternary, or the liberal sciences.
On this figure, the oath was propounded to the aspirant in the esoteric school of Pythagoras. Jamblichus gives this oath in his life of Pythagoras :

Ου μα αμετερη γενεη, παραδοντα τετραχτυν
Παγαν αεναου φυσεως, ριζωμα' τ'εχουσαν.

By that pure quadrilit'ral name on high,
Nature's eternal fountain and supply,
The parent of all souls that living be,—
By it, with faithful oath, I swear to thee.

The tetractys was undoubtedly borrowed by Pythagoras from the tetragrammaton of the Jews,[*] when he visited Babylon, and was instructed by Ezekiel in the Jewish mysteries.

TETRAGRAMMATON. (*Greek*.) The word of four letters. The incommunicable name of God in Hebrew, יהוה, which, as consisting of four letters, was thus called. See *Jehovah*.

---

[*] Cudworth (Intellectual system, p. 376) thinks there is no doubt of this, and the most learned writers have generally agreed with him in the opinion.

T∴ G∴ A∴ O∴ T∴ U∴   *The Grand Architect of the Uni-verse.*   A very common abbreviation of the name of God, used by masonic writers.

THEOLOGICAL VIRTUES. These are Faith, Hope, and Charity, which, as forming the principal rounds of the masonic ladder, constitute a part of the instruction of the Entered Apprentice. Of these, Faith may be explained to be the first round, because faith in God is the first requisite qualification of a candidate for masonry; Hope is the second, because hope in immortality, is a necessary consequence of faith in a divine being; and Charity is the third, because the mind that is elevated by such a faith, and the heart that is warmed by such a hope, cannot fail to be stimulated by that universal love of the human race, which is but another name for Charity.

Again. Charity is the highest round, because Charity is the greatest of these virtues. Our faith may be lost in sight; "faith is the evidence of things not seen;" he that believes only on the evidence of his senses, believes from demonstration, and not from faith, and faith in him is dead. Hope ends in fruition; we hope only for that which we desire, but do not possess; and the attainment of the object is the termination of our hope. But Charity extends beyond the grave, through the boundless realms of eternity; for there, even there, the mercy of God, the richest of all charities, throws a veil over our transgressions, and extends to the repentant sinner the boon of that forgiveness which divine justice must have denied.

THIRTY-THIRD DEGREE. See *Supreme Council.*

THREE. One of the sacred numbers of Freemasonry. Three was considered among all the Pagan nations as the chief of the mystical numbers, because, as Aristotle remarks, it contains within itself a beginning, a middle, and an end. Hence we find it designating some of the attributes of almost all the gods. The thunder-bolt of Jove was three-forked; the sceptre of Neptune was a trident; Cerberus, the dog of Pluto, was three-headed; there were three Fates and three Furies; the sun had three names, Apollo, Sol, and Liber; and the moon three also, Diana, Luna, and Hecate. In all incantations, three was a favourite number, and hence, the poet says, *numero Deus impari gaudet*. A triple cord was used, each cord of three different colours, white, red, and black, and a small image of the subject of the charm was carried thrice around the altar, as we see in Virgil's eighth eclogue :

> "Terna tibi hæc primum triplici diversa colore
> Licia circumdo, terque hæc altaria circum
> Effigiem duco."

The Druids paid no less respect to this sacred number. Throughout their whole system, a reference is constantly made to its influence; and so far did their veneration for it extend, that even their sacred poetry was composed in triads.

In all the mysteries, from Egypt to Scandinavia, we find a sacred regard for the number three. In the rites of Mithras, the Empyrean was said to be supported by three intelligences, Ormuzd, Mithra, and Mithras. In the rites of Hindostan, there was the trinity of Brahma, Vishnu, and Siva. It was, in short, a general character of the mysteries to have three principal officers and three grades of initiation.

In Freemasonry, the number three is the most important and universal in its application of all the mystic numbers. Thus we find it pervading the whole ritual. There are three degrees of Ancient Craft Masonry—three principal officers of a lodge—three supports—three ornaments—three greater and three lesser lights—three movable and three immovable jewels—three principal tenets—three rounds of Jacob's ladder—three working tools of a Fellow-Craft—three principal orders of architecture—three important human senses—three ancient Grand Masters—three recreant F∴ C∴;—and indeed so many instances of the consecration of the number that it would exceed the limits of this volume to record them.

THREE GLOBES, RITE OF THE GRAND LODGE OF. The lodge of "Three Globes" was established at Berlin in 1746, and in 1765 was constituted as a Grand Lodge. It, for a long time, practised only the three primitive degrees of Ancient Craft Masonry; but afterwards adopted seven others, borrowed from France. The three ancient degrees are under the control of the Grand Lodge, but the seven higher ones are governed by an Internal Supreme Orient, whose members are, however, elected by the Grand Lodge. The rite of the Grand Lodge of the Three Globes is practised by one hundred and seventy-seven lodges in Germany.

THREE STEPS. The three steps on the Master's carpet are emblematic of the three stages of human life—youth, manhood, and old age, and allude to the three degrees which are respectively representations of these three stages.

THRESHING-FLOOR. The threshing-floor of Araunah, or Ornan the Jebusite, was on Mount Moriah. It was purchased by David for a place of sacrifice, for six hundred shekels of gold, and on it the temple was afterwards built. See *Ornan the Jebusite.*

THUMMIN. See *Urim and Thummim.*

TILER. An officer in a symbolic lodge, whose duty it is to guard the lodge against the intrusion of the profane. As in operative masonry, the tiler, when the edifice is erected, finishes and covers it with the roof, so in speculative Masonry, when the lodge is duly organized, the Tiler closes the door and covers the sacred precincts from all intrusion. The Tiler is not necessarily a member of the lodge, but should always be a worthy Mason and skilful in the craft. He generally receives a moderate compensation for his services.

TITO. Tito Prince Harodim was one of the especial favourites of King Solomon. He presided over the lodge of Intendants of the Building, and was one of the twelve Illustrious Knights who were set over the twelve tribes, that of Napthali being placed under his care.

TOKEN. This word, in Hebrew, אות, *oth*, is frequently used in Scripture to signify a sign or memorial of something past, some covenant made or promise given. Thus God says to Noah, of the rainbow "it shall be for a *token* of a covenant between me and the earth;" and to Abraham, he says of circumcision, "it shall be a *token* of the covenant betwixt me and you." In masonry, the grip of recognition is called a token, because it is an outward sign of the covenant of friendship and fellowship entered into between the members of the fraternity, and is to be considered as a memorial of that covenant which was made, when it was first received by the candidate, between him and the order into which he was then initiated.

TRACING-BOARD. A painting representing the emblems peculiar to a degree, arranged for the convenience of the lecturer. Each degree of symbolic masonry has its tracing-board, which are distinguished as tracing-boards the first, second, and third. It is, therefore, the same as the flooring or carpet.

TRADITIONS. The legends or traditions of Freemasonry constitute a very considerable and important part of its ritual. In many instances these traditions have been corrupted by anachronisms and other errors, which have naturally crept into them during a long series of oral transmission. No one, therefore, can for a moment contend that all the legends and traditions of the order are, to the very letter, historical facts. All that can be claimed for them is, that in some there is a great deal of truthful narrative, more or less overlaid with fiction; in others, simply a mere substratum of history; and in others, nothing more than an idea, to which the legend or myth is indebted for its existence, and of which it is, as a symbol, the exponent.

The intelligent Mason will always, however, be able, after a little consideration, to separate the substratum of truth from the superstructure of fiction which has been imposed upon it. And then, what is presented as a tradition will often be found to be a mere myth or allegory, whose symbolic teaching is of great beauty and importance. It is a part of the science of Freemasonry to elaborate out of these traditions the truth, symbolic or historical, which they are intended to convey, and to distinguish a tradition founded in fact from one which is based upon a myth, so as to assign to the annals and the poetry of the order their respective portions.

TRANSIENT BRETHREN. Transient brethren, when they visit a lodge, are to be cordially welcomed and properly clothed. But on no occasion are they admitted until, after the proper precautions, they have proved themselves to be " true and trusty." See *Visit, Right of.*

TRANSIENT CANDIDATE. A transient candidate is one not living in the place where he applies for admission. If well recommended by two or more members of the lodge, a ballot may take place on the same night that he applies; whereas, in the case of a permanent resident, the letter must be referred to a committee, and lie over for at least a month.

TRAVELLING FREEMASONS. There is no portion of our annals so worthy of investigation as that which is embraced by the middle ages of Christendom, when the whole of Europe was perambulated by our brethren in associations of travelling artisans, under the name of "Free and Accepted Masons," for the purpose of erecting religious edifices. There is not a country of Europe which does not at this day contain honourable evidences of the skill and industry of our masonic ancestors. I therefore propose, in the present article, to give a brief sketch of the origin, the progress and the character of these travelling architects.

Clavel, in his "Histoire Pittoresque de la Franc-Maçonnerie," has traced the organization of these associations to the "collegia artificum," or colleges of artisans,* which were instituted at Rome by Numa, in the year B. C. 714, and whose members were originally Greeks, imported by this lawgiver for the purpose of embellishing the city over which he reigned.

These associations existed in Rome in the time of the emperors. They were endowed with certain privileges peculiar to themselves, such as a government by their own statutes, the power of making contracts as a corporation, and an immunity from taxation. Their meetings were held in private, like the esoteric schools of the philosophers. Their presiding officers were called "magistri." They were divided into three classes, corresponding with the three degrees of Freemasonry, and they admitted into their ranks, as honorary members, persons who were not, by profession, operative masons. Finally, they used a symbolic language drawn from the implements of masonry, and they were in possession of a secret mode of recognition.

In time, the "collegia artificum" became the repository of all the rites which were brought to Rome from foreign countries, and thus we may suppose the Hebrew mysteries, or Temple Masonry, to have been introduced into that country. This supposition may derive some support from the fact, that in the time of Julius Cæsar the Jews were first permitted to open their synagogues and worship the God of their fathers, without restraint, at Rome,—a toleration for which they were probably indebted to their fraternization with the members of the colleges of artificers;

---

* See *Roman Colleges*, in this work.

and in the reign of Augustus, many of the Roman knights embraced Judaism, and publicly observed the Sabbath.

These "sodalitates," or fraternities, began upon the invasion of the barbarians to decline in numbers, in respectability, and in power. But on the conversion of the whole empire, they or others of a similar character began again to flourish. The priests of the Christian church became their patrons, and under their guidance they devoted themselves to the building of churches and monasteries. In the tenth century, they were established as a free guild or corporation in Lombardy. The most celebrated of these corporations in Italy was that of Como, and the name of "Magistri Comacini," or Masters of Como, became at length, says Muratori, the generic name for all these associations of architects.

From Lombardy, which they soon filled with religious edifices, they passed beyond the Alps, into all the countries where Christianity, but recently established, required the erection of churches. The popes encouraged their designs, and more than one bull was despatched, conferring on them privileges of the most extensive character. A monopoly was granted to them for the erection of all religious edifices; they were declared independent of the sovereigns in whose dominions they might be temporarily residing, and subject only to their own private laws; they were permitted to regulate the amount of their wages; were exempted from all kinds of taxation; and no Mason, not belonging to their association, was permitted to compete with or oppose them in the pursuit of employment. And in one of the papal decrees on the subject of these artisans, the supreme pontiff declares that these regulations have been made "after the example of Hiram, King of Tyre, when he sent artisans to King Solomon for the purpose of building the Temple of Jerusalem."

After filling the continent with cathedrals, parochial churches, and monasteries, and increasing their own numbers by accessions of new members from all the countries in which they had been labouring, they passed over into England, and there introduced their peculiar style of building. Thence they travelled to Scotland, and there have rendered their existence ever memorable by establishing, in the parish of Kilwinning, where they were erecting an abbey, the germ of Scottish Freemasonry, which has regularly descended through the Grand Lodge of Scotland to the present day.

The government of these fraternities, wherever they might be for the time located, was very regular and uniform. When about to commence the erection of a religious edifice, they first built huts, or, as they were termed, lodges in the vicinity, in which they resided for the sake of economy as well as convenience. It is from these that the present name of our places of meeting is derived. Over every ten men was placed a warden, who paid them wages, and took care that there should be no needless expenditure of materials, and no careless loss of implements. Over the whole, a surveyor or master, called in their old documents, "magister," presided, and directed the general labour.

The Abbé Grandidier, in a letter at the end of the Marquis Luchet's "Essai sur les Illuminés," has quoted from the ancient register of the Masons at Strasburg, the regulations of the association which built the splendid cathedral of that city. I have not been successful in my efforts to obtain a sight of the original work, but the elaborate treatise of Clavel furnishes us with the most prominent details of all that Grandidier has preserved. The Cathedral of Strasburg was commenced in the year 1277, under the direction of Hervin de Steinbach. The Masons who, under his directions, were engaged in the construction of this noblest specimen of the Gothic style of architecture, were divided into the separate ranks of Masters, Craftsmen, and Apprentices. The place where they assembled was called a "hutte," a German word equivalent to our English term, lodge. They employed the implements of masonry as emblems, and wore them as insignia. They had certain signs and words of recognition, and received their new members with peculiar and secret ceremonies,

42

admitting into their ranks many eminent persons who were not operative Masons by profession.*

The fraternity of Strasburg became celebrated throughout Germany; their superiority was acknowledged by the kindred associations, and they in time received the appellation of the "haupt hutte," or Grand Lodge, and exercised supremacy over the *hutten* of Suabia, Hesse, Bavaria, Franconia, Saxony, Thuringia, and the countries bordering on the river Moselle. The Masters of these several lodges assembled at Ratisbon in 1459,

---

* The correspondent of the Boston Atlas gave, in 1847, the following details of the Cathedral at Cologne, another labour of the Travelling Freemasons of the Middle Ages:

"There stood the huge mass, a proud monument to Gerhard, Master of the Cologne Lodge of Freemasons, and resisting, as it does, the attacks of nature and the labour of man, a symbol of that mystic brotherhood which, to use the words of Lafayette, 'owes a double lustre to those who have cherished, and to those who have persecuted it.'

* * * * * * *

"During the interval between 1248 and 1323, there were not only fifty Masters, and three times as many Fellow-Craft, daily employed, but a large number of Entered Apprentices, from all parts of Christendom, who had come to study both the operative and speculative branches of the art, and carried home with them the principles which directed the erection of almost every Gothic monument of the age; others, which prepared the way for the light of the Reformation:

    'They dreamt not of a perishable home,
    Who could thus build.'

"After the secession of the Freemasons from the church, the works were suspended, leaving only the choir, with its side aisles, completed. Saxatile creepers covered the other foundations, and after remaining untouched, except by the iron hand of Time, for nearly five centuries, it could but remind one of a 'broken promise to God.' In 1829, the attention of the King of Prussia was directed to it, and the work recommenced with such skill, that an association was formed in 1842 for the purpose of continuing it vigorously. * * * * The original plans, which were taken from the lodge by the French in 1794, have been recovered, and are strictly adhered to by the architect, M. Zmerner, who has even adopted the ancient and accepted division of the workmen. The first class receives 57 cents per diem, the second, 48 cents, and the third, 41 cents, those in the two latter receiving promotion when their industry and ability merit it."

and on the 25th of April contracted an act of union, declaring the chief of the Strasburg Cathedral the only and perpetual Grand Master of the General Fraternity of Freemasons of Germany.

Similar institutions existed in France and in Switzerland. In the latter country the Grand Lodge was established originally at Berne, about the middle of the fifteenth century, during the construction of the cathedral at that place, but in 1502 it was transferred to Zurich.

The details of the proceedings of the travelling Freemasons in England are more familiar, as well as more interesting, to us. They entered that kingdom at an early period. We have already seen that their organization in Italy, as a free guild, took place early in the tenth century; and we know, from undoubted documents, that Prince Edwin assembled the English Masons at York in 926, when the first English Grand Lodge was constituted. It is from this general assembly of our ancestors at York, that all the existing constitutions of our English and American lodges derive their authority. From that period the fraternity, with various intermissions, continued to pursue their labours, and constructed many edifices which still remain as monuments of their skill as workmen, and their taste as architects. Kings, in many instances, became their patrons, and their labours were superintended by powerful noblemen and eminent prelates, who, for this purpose, were admitted as members of the fraternity. Many of the old charges, for the better government of their lodges, have been preserved, and are still to be found in our books of Constitutions, every line of which indicates that they were originally drawn up for associations strictly and exclusively operative in their character.

In glancing over the history of this singular body of architects, we are struck with several important peculiarities.

In the first place, they were strictly ecclesiastical in their constitution. The Pope, the supreme Pontiff of the Church, was their patron and protector. They were supported and encouraged by bishops and abbots, and hence their chief employment appears to have been in the construction of religious edifices. Like their ancestors, who were engaged in the erection of the magnificent Temple of Jerusalem, they devoted themselves to labour for the "House of the Lord." Masonry was then, as it had been before, and has ever been since, intimately connected with religion.

They were originally all operatives. But the artisans of that period were not educated men, and they were compelled to seek among the clergy, the only men of learning, for those whose wisdom might contrive, and whose cultivated taste might adorn, the plans which they by their practical skill were to carry into effect. Hence the germ of that speculative masonry, which once dividing the character of the fraternity with the operative, now completely occupies it, to the entire exclusion of the latter.

But, lastly, from the circumstance of their union and concert, arose a uniformity of design in all the public buildings of that period—a uniformity so remarkable as to find its explanation only in the fact, that their construction was committed throughout the whole of Europe, if not always to the same individuals, at least to members of the same association. The remarks of Mr. Hope on this subject, in his "History of Architecture," (p. 239,) are well worthy of perusal. "The architects of all the sacred edifices of the Latin church, wherever such arose,—north, south, east, or west,—thus derived their science from the same central school; obeyed in their designs the same hierarchy; were directed in their constructions by the same principles of propriety and taste; kept up with each other, in the most distant parts to which they might be sent, the most constant correspondence; and rendered every minute improvement, the property of the whole body and a new conquest of the art. The result of this unanimity was, that at each successive period of the monastic dynasty, on whatever point a new church or new monastery might be erected, it resembled all those raised at the same period in every other place, however distant from it, as if both had been built in the same place by the same artist. For instance, we find, at particular epochs, churches as far distant from each other as the north of Scotland and the south of Italy, to be minutely similar in all the essential characteristics."

In conclusion, we may remark, with some pride as their descendants, that the world is indebted to this association for the introduction of the Gothic, or, as it has lately been denominated, the pointed style of architecture. This style—so different from the Greek or Roman orders—whose pointed arches and minute tracery distinguish the solemn temples of the olden time, and whose ruins arrest the attention and claim the admiration of the spectator, has been universally acknowledged to be the invention of the travelling Freemasons of the Middle Ages.

TRAVELLING WARRANTS. These are Warrants of Constitution granted to lodges, empowering the members to remove their lodge at pleasure, and to open it and transact lodge business in any part of the world in which they may be stationed. Such Warrants are granted generally to lodges in the army. In 1779, the Massachusetts Grand Lodge granted a warrant to Gen. Patterson and others, to hold a travelling lodge in the American army, to be called "Washington Lodge." In 1756, *R. W.* Richard Gridley was authorized "to congregate all Free and Accepted Masons, in the expedition against Crown Point, and form them into one or more lodges." In 1738, St. John's Grand Lodge, at Boston, granted a travelling warrant to a lodge to be holden in His Majesty's 28th regiment, then stationed at Louisburg.* Lodges of this character are still very common in the British army.†

In the London Review, 1834, two interesting anecdotes are recorded of lodge No. 227, attached to the 46th regiment of the

---

* Moore's Magazine, vol. i, p. 15.

† During the late war between the United States and Mexico, travelling warrants were granted to some of the regiments of volunteers in the American army.

British army, and working under a travelling warrant from the
Grand Lodge of Ireland. During the Revolution, "the masonic
chest of the 46th, by the chance of war, fell into the hands of
the Americans: the captors reported the circumstance to Gen.
Washington, who embraced the opportunity of testifying his admiration of masonry in the most marked and gratifying manner,
by directing that a guard of honour, under the command of a
distinguished officer, should take charge of the chest, with many
articles of value belonging to the 46th, and returned them to the
regiment. In 1805, the chest was captured again in Dominica,
by the French, who carried it on board their fleet without knowing its contents. Three years afterward, the chest, at the request of the officers who had commanded the expedition, was
returned by the French government with several complimentary
presents."

TREASURER. The fourth officer of a symbolic lodge, whose
duty it is to receive all money from the hands of the Secretary,
or otherwise, and pay it out again by the order of the Worshipful Master, and with the consent of the lodge. He is a responsible officer, and is generally required to give security for the
faithful performance of his duties.

TRESTLE-BOARD. A trestle-board, from the French tres-
teau, is a board placed on a wooden frame of three legs. Masonically, it means the board on which the master workman lays
his designs to direct the craft in their labours. In speculative
Freemasonry, it is symbolical of the books of nature and revelation, in which the Supreme Architect of the Universe has developed his will, for the guidance and direction of his creatures,
in the great labour of their lives, the erection of a temple of
holiness in the heart.

TRIANGLE, DOUBLE. The double triangle is described
by some writers as identical with the pentalpha of Pythagoras,

or pentangle of Solomon. This, however, is not the case. The pentalpha has five lines and five angles, and the double triangle has six lines and six angles. The former, was among the Pythagoreans, an emblem of health, and among Masons it is the outline or origin of the five-pointed star, the emblem of fellowship; the latter is a symbol of Deity. In Christian churches the double triangle is used as a symbol of the twofold nature of Christ.

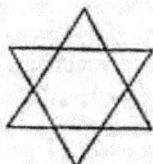

TRIANGLE, EQUILATERAL. This, as the most perfect of figures, was adopted by all the ancient nations as a symbol of the Deity. It still retains that allusion as an emblem of Freemasonry. Among the Hebrews, a jod in the centre of an equilateral triangle, was one of the emblems of Jehovah. In the system of Pythagoras, the obligation was administered to the candidate on the Tetractys, which was expressed by ten jods arrayed in the form of a triangle, which, with them, was the symbol of Deity, as embracing in himself the three stages of time, past, present, and future; he *was*, he *is*, and he *shall be*. Among the Hebrews, a jod in the centre of a triangle was one of the modes of expressing the incommunicable name of Jehovah, and was supposed, by some authors, to refer to the triune God. This allusion to Deity it still preserves in the masonic ritual.

TRIANGLE, TRIPLE. This is another of the numerous forms in which the triangle is arranged, and like all the others, it is used as a symbol of Deity, though perhaps it is here made to assume a still more sacred character from its triple form. As such, it has been adopted as the most appropriate jewel of the Illustrious Prelate in an Encampment of Knights Templar.

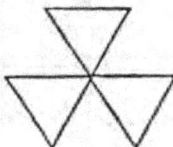

TRIPLE TAU. The Tau Cross, or Cross of St. Anthony, is
a cross in the form of a Greek T. The triple tau is a figure
formed by three of these crosses meeting in a point, and therefore resembling a letter T resting on the traverse beam of an H.
This emblem is not adopted in American Freemasonry, but placed
in the centre of a triangle and circle—both emblems of the
Deity; it constitutes the jewel of the Royal Arch as practised
in England, where it is so highly esteemed as to be called the
"emblem of all emblems," and "the grand emblem of Royal
Arch Masonry." The original signification of this emblem has
been variously explained. Some suppose it to include the initials
of the Temple of Jerusalem, T. H., *Templum Hierosolymæ;*
others, that is a symbol of the mystical union of the Father and
Son, H signifying Jehovah, and T, or the cross, the Son. A
writer in Moore's Magazine ingeniously supposes it to be a representation of three T squares, and that it alludes to the three
jewels of the three ancient Grand Masters. It has also been
said that it is the monogram of Hiram of Tyre, and others assert
that it is only a modification of the Hebrew letter *shin*, ?, which
was one of the Jewish abbreviations of the sacred name. Oliver
thinks, from its connection with the circle and triangle in the
Royal Arch jewel, that it was intended to typify the sacred name
as the author of eternal life. The English Royal Arch lectures
say that "by its intersection it forms a given number of angles
that may be taken in five several combinations; and, reduced, their
amount in right angles will be found equal to the five Platonic
bodies which represent the four elements and the sphere of the
Universe." Amid so many speculations, I need not hesitate to
offer one of my own. I have already stated under the article
Tau Cross, that the Prophet Ezekiel speaks of the *tau* or tau
cross as the mark distinguishing those who were to be saved, on
account of their sorrow for their sins, from those who, as idolaters,
were to be slain. It was a mark or sign of favourable distinction, and with this allusion we may, therefore, suppose the triple
tau to be used in the Royal Arch degree as a mark designating

and separating those who know and worship the true name of God, from those who are ignorant of that august mystery.

TROWEL. An implement of operative masonry, which has been adapted by speculative Masons as the peculiar working tool of the Master's degree. By this implement, and its use in operative masonry to spread the cement which binds all the parts of the building into one common mass, we are taught to spread the cement of affection and kindness, which unites all the members of the masonic family, wheresoever dispersed over the globe, into one companionship of Brotherly Love, Relief, and Truth.

This implement is also very appropriately devoted to the Master's degree, because, as Master Masons only, do we constitute the recognised members of the great brotherhood of masonry. The Entered Apprentice and Fellow-Craft are not considered as members of the masonic family.

Again is this implement considered the appropriate working tool of a Master Mason, because, in operative masonry, while the Apprentice is engaged in preparing the rude materials, which require only the guage and gavel to give them their proper shape, the Fellow-Craft places them in their proper position by means of the plumb, level, and square; but the Master Mason alone, having examined their correctness, and proved them true and trusty, secures them permanently in their place by spreading, with the trowel, the cement that irrevocably binds them together.

The trowel has also been adopted as the jewel of the Select Master. But its uses in this degree are not symbolical. They are simply connected with the historical legend of the degree.

TROWEL AND SWORD. In the degree of Knights of the East we are told that at the building of the second temple, Zerubbabel ordered the workmen to carry a sword in one hand and a trowel in the other, so that while they worked with one hand they might be enabled to defend themselves with the other from the attacks of their envious neighbors, the Samaritans. To commemorate the valour of these worthy craftsmen, the sword and trowel *en saltire* have been place upon the English Royal Arch Tracing-board. In the American ritual this expressive symbol of valour and piety has been omitted.

TROWEL, COMPANY OF THE. A society composed of learned and eminent persons, instituted at Florence in 1512. Its emblems were the trowel, the gavel and the square, and its patron was St. Andrew. Clavel thinks the institution was derived from the society of Travelling Freemasons, and was organized by persons of quality, who had been admitted as honorary members of that operative association.

TRUE MASONS, ORDER OF THE. A branch of the Hermetic rite of Pernetti, under the name of the order of True Masons, was established at Montpelier, in 1778, by Boileau, who subsequently introduced the Philosophic Scotch rite. It consisted of six degrees. 1, the True Mason; 2, the True Mason in the right way; 3, Knight of the Golden Key; 4, Knight of the Rainbow; 5, Knight of the Argonauts; 6, Knight of Golden Fleece.

TRUTH. Truth is one of the three principal tenets of our order, Brotherly Love and Relief being the other two. To be "true and trusty" is one of the first lessons in which the aspirant is instructed. All other things are mortal and transitory, but truth alone is immutable and eternal; it is the attribute of Him in whom there is no variableness nor shadow of changing.

TUBAL CAIN. The son of Lamech; the first who wrought in iron and brass. He was the inventor of edge-tools, and introduced many arts into society which tended towards its improvement and civilization. Tubal Cain is the Vulcan of the pagans, and is thought to have been closely connected with Ancient Freemasonry. Faber says that "all the most remarkable ancient buildings of Greece, Egypt and Asia Minor, were ascribed to Cabirean or Cyclopean Masons," the descendants of Vulcan, Dhu Balcan, the god Balcan, or Tubal Cain. Oliver says "in after times Tubal Cain, under the name of Vulcan and his Cyclops, figured as workers in metals and inventors of the mysteries; and hence it is probable that he was the hierophant of a similar institution in his day, copied from the previous system of Seth, and applied to the improvement of schemes more adapted to the physical pursuits of the race to which he belonged."[*] For these reasons Tubal Cain has been consecrated, among masons of the present day, as an ancient brother. His introduction of the arts of civilization having given the first value to property, Tubal Cain has been considered among masons as a symbol of *worldly possessions*.

TUSCAN ORDER. One of the five orders of architecture, and of comparatively modern date, having been invented by the Italians. It so much resembles the Doric, that it has been considered by most writers as merely a variety of that order. Its want of antiquity causes it to be held in but little esteem among Freemasons.

TWELVE ILLUSTRIOUS KNIGHTS. See *Sublime Knight Elected*.

TWELVE GRAND POINTS OF MASONRY. The old English lectures contain the following passage : "There are in Freemasonry twelve original points, which form the basis of the system, and comprehend the whole ceremony of initiation. Without the existence of these points, no man ever was or can be legally and essentially received into the order. Every person who is made a mason must go through all these twelve forms and ceremonies, not only in the first degree, but in every subsequent one."

[*] Oliver, Landmarks, ii. p. 213.

Important as our ancient brethren deemed the explanation of these points, the Grand Lodge of England thought proper, in 1813, to strike them from its ritual, and as they never were introduced into this country, a synopsis of them may not be uninteresting or unacceptable.

These twelve points refer the twelve parts of the ceremony of initiation to the twelve tribes of Israel, in the following manner:

1. To Reuben was referred the *opening of the lodge*, because he was the first-born of his father.

2. To Simeon was referred the *preparation* of the candidate, because he prepared the instruments of destruction for the slaughter of the Shechemites.

3. To Levi was referred the *report*, because he gave a signal or report to his brothers when they assailed the men of Shechen.

4. To Judah was referred the *entrance*, of the candidate, because this tribe first entered the promised land.

5. To Zebulun was referred the *prayer*, because the prayer and blessing of his father was conferred on him in preference to his brother, Issachar.

6. To Issachar was referred the *circumambulation*, because, as an indolent and thriftless tribe, they required a leader to advance them to an equal elevation with the other tribes.

7. To Dan was referred the ceremony of *advancing* to the altar, as a contrast with the rapid advance of that tribe to idolatry.

8. To Gad was referred the *obligation*, because of the vow of Jephtha, a member of that tribe.

9. To Asher was referred the time when the candidate was *intrusted*, because Asher, by the fertile soil of its district, was represented by fatness and royal dainties, which were compared to the riches of masonic wisdom which the candidate then received.

10. To Naphthali was referred the *investment*, when the candidate, having received his apron, was declared free, because the

tribe of Naphthali had a peculiar freedom attached to them in conformity with the blessing pronounced by Moses.

11. To Joseph was referred the *north-east corner*, because, as this reminds us of the most superficial part of masonry, so the two half tribes of Ephraim and Manasseh, of which the tribe of Joseph was composed, were accounted more superficial than the rest, inasmuch us they were only the grandsons of the patriarch Jacob.

12. To Benjamin was referred the *closing of the lodge*, because he was the last son of Jacob.

These points, as I have already observed, are now obsolete, but they afford instruction, and will be found worthy of attention.

TWENTY-FOUR INCH GUAGE. An instrument made use of in operative masonry, for the purpose of measuring and laying out work, and which, in speculative masonry, constitutes one of the working tools of the Entered Apprentice. The twenty-four inches which are marked upon its surface, are emblematical of the twenty-four hours of the day, which, being divided into three parts, instruct the mason to give eight hours to labour, eight hours to the service of God and a worthy, distressed brother, and eight to refreshment and sleep. William of Malmsbury tells us, that this method of dividing the day is the same that was adopted by King Alfred. Why the twenty-four inch guage has been adopted as the working tool of an Entered Apprentice, may be seen by a reference to the word *Implements*.

TYLER. See *Tiler*.

TYRE. A city of Phenicia, on the coast of the Mediterranean sea, ninety-three miles north of Jerusalem. It is distinguished in masonic history for the part taken by Hiram, its king, in supplying workmen and materials for the building of the Temple. This magnificent place, once the richest and most powerful of the cities

of the coast, has long since been demolished, and on a part of
its ruins the insignificant village of Sur has been founded by the
Metoualies.

U.

UNANIMITY. Unanimity in the choice of candidates is considered so essential to the welfare of the fraternity, that the old
regulations of the Grand Lodge of England, have expressly provided for its preservation in the following words :

"But no man can be entered a brother in any particular lodge,
or admitted a member thereof, without the unanimous consent of
all the members of the lodge then present, when the candidate
is proposed, and when their consent is formally asked by the Master. They are to give their consent it their own prudent way,
either virtually or in form, but with unanimity. Nor is this inherent privilege subject to a dispensation ; because the member
of a particular lodge are the best judges of it ; and because, if a
turbulent member should be imposed upon them, it might spoil
their harmony, or hinder the freedom of their communication, or
even break and disperse the lodges, which ought to be avoided by
all true and faithful."* See *Ballot*.

UNFAVOURABLE REPORT. The unfavourable report of
a committee on the application of a candidate is equivalent to a
rejection, and precludes the necessity of a ballot. For the reason,
see *Election*.

UNIVERSI TERRARUM ORBIS ARCHITECTONIS
PER GLORIAM INGENTIS. *By the Glory of the Grand*

---

* Revised Regulations, anno 1767.

Architect of the Universe.—This is the caption to all balustres or documents emanating from a Sovereign Inspector or Supreme Council of the 33d degree of the Ancient Scotch rite.

UPRIGHT POSTURE. To man alone, of all the inhabitants of the earth, has his Creator given an upright and erect posture, to elevate his mind by the continual sight of the heavenly host, and by the noble thoughts that his natural attitude inspires, to draw him from the grovelling cares of earth, to a contemplation of the divine sources from whence he sprang. In the human race this erect stature is the foundation of their dominion and superiority over all the rest of the animal world.*

> "Thus while the mute creation downward bend
> Their sight, and to their earthly mother tend,
> Man looks aloft, and with eternal eyes
> Beholds his own hereditary skies."†

The man who has planted his feet upon the immutable square of morality, and whose body is erect in the proud consciousness of virtue, is, indeed, worthy of the dominion which has been given him over the beasts of the field and the fowls of the air. And the mason, remembering that "God hath made man upright,"‡ should constantly endeavour to preserve that upright posture of his body and his mind.

URIM AND THUMMIM. Two Hebrew words, אורים and תמים, Aurim and Thummim, signifying, as they have been translated in the Septuagint, "Light and Truth."§ They were sacred lots worn in the breast-plate of the High Priest, and to be consulted by him alone for the purpose of obtaining a revelation

---

* Turner, Sac. His. World. I. lett. 21, p. 426.

† Pronaque cum spectent animalia cætera terram
  Os homini sublime dedit: cœlumque tueri
  Jussit, et erectos ad sidera tollere vultus.
  Ovid. Met. B. i. 84.

‡ Ecclesiastes, vii. 29.   § δήλωσις και αλήθεια.

of the will of God in matters of great moment. What they
were, authors on Jewish antiquities have not been able to agree.
Some suppose, that the augury consisted in a more splendid appearance of certain letters of the names of the tribes inscribed
upon the stones of the breast-plate ; others, that it was received
by voice from two small images which were placed beyond the folds
of the breast-plate. A variety of other conjectures have been
hazarded, but as Godwyn observes, "he spoke best, who ingeniously confessed that he knew not what Urim and Thummim was."[*]

But the researches of Egyptian Archæologists have thrown
much light upon this intricate subject, and relieved it of many
of its difficulties. It is now known that the Egyptian judges
wore breast-plates having inscribed on them two figures, the one
of the Sun *Ra*, in a double sense, that of physical and intellectual light, and the other, that of the goddess *Thme* in her twofold capacity of truth and justice.

Now in Hebrew the double capacity of any thing is expressed
by the plural form of the noun. But the Egyptian *Ra*, the sun
or light, is in Hebrew *Aur* and *Thme*, truth is *Thme*. *Aur*, in
the plural, is *Aurim*. *Thme*, in the plural, is *Thmim*. Now it
seems to me, and I have the high authority of the Egyptian
archæologists with me, that the Aurim and Thummim of the
Hebrew breast-plate were borrowed from the breast-plates of the
Egyptian judges. Moses, we know, was versed in all the learning of the Egyptians, and these very breast-plates had already
been consecrated in the eyes of the Jews by their seeing them
worn as tokens of official dignity by the ministers of justice,
who were also High Priests in that Egypt which had formerly
been the land of their task-masters.

URN. The urn has been adopted as a memorial of death ;
because formerly it was the custom, instead of burying corpses,
to burn them upon a funeral pyre, and deposit the ashes in an

---

* Moses and Aaron, B. iv. ch. 8.

urn. This custom was sometimes adopted by the Jews, as in the case of Saul, whose body was burnt by the men of Jabesh, though their usual method was that of inhumation.

V.

VEILS. The veils of the tabernacle were of four colours, blue, purple, scarlet, and white or fine linen. These colours have been adopted as the symbolic colours of masonry. White is the emblem of innocence, and is found in the gloves and apron; blue is the emblem of universal friendship, and is appropriated to the symbolic degrees; scarlet is the emblem of zeal and fervency, and is appropriated to the Royal Arch; purple, which is the union of blue and scarlet, is thence the emblem of unity and concord, and has been adopted as the colour of the intermediate degrees between the symbolic and the Royal Arch. The Jews, according to Josephus, gave to these veils an astronomical signification, and supposed them to represent the four elements. Fine white linen was a symbol of the earth, because it was made out of flax, a production of the earth: the blue, as the colour of the sky, was a symbol of the air; the purple, of the sea, because it derived its colour from the murex, a shell-fish that inhabits the sea; and the scarlet was the natural symbol of fire.*

VEILS, MASTERS OF THE. Three officers of a Royal Arch Chapter, who, being armed with a sword, and bearing a banner of the appropriate colour, are stationed at the blue, purple, and scarlet veils. The white veil is guarded by the Royal Arch Captain.

* Josephus, Antiq. Judaic. lib. iii. c. 7.

43*

VERGER. An officer in a Council of Knights of the Holy Sepulchre, corresponding to the Senior Deacon in a symbolic lodge.

VISITATION. The official visit of the Grand Master and his officers to a subordinate lodge, for the purpose of inspecting its books and mode of work, is called a visitation. On this occasion, the lodge should be opened in the Master's degree; the Grand Officers should be received with all the honours of masonry, and the seats of the officers of the lodge should be surrendered to the corresponding Grand Officers. This last is done as an acknowledgment of the authority from which the lodge derives its Warrant of Constitution.

The Grand Master and the Deputy Grand Master are entitled, in all their visits to subordinate lodges, to certain privileges, which are thus laid down in the English Constitutions:

"The Grand Master has full authority to preside in any lodge, and to order any of his Grand Officers to attend him; his Deputy is to be placed on his right hand, and the Master of the lodge on his left hand. His Wardens are also to act as Wardens of that particular lodge during his presence." P. 30.

"The Deputy Grand Master has full authority, unless the Grand Master, or Pro-Grand Master, be present, to preside in every lodge which he may visit, with the Master of the lodge on his right hand. The Grand Wardens, if present, are to act as Wardens." P. 33.

But this power of presiding, in an informal visit, does not seem to have been extended to the Grand Wardens; though, of course, if the visit be official, and the Grand and Deputy Grand Masters be absent, the Senior Grand Warden will preside as Deputy Grand Master, and the Master of the lodge will, in that case, sit on the right.

VISIT, RIGHT OF. Every mason who is a *working brother*, that is to say, who is a subscribing member of a lodge, has a right to visit any other lodge as often us it may suit his convenience or his pleasure.*

This right is guaranteed to every mason by the most ancient regulations. In the "Ancient Charges at the Constitution of a Lodge," contained in a MS. of the Lodge of Antiquity in London, it is directed, "That every mason receive and cherish strange fellowes when they come over the countrie, and sett them on worke, if they will worke, as the manner is; that is to say, if the mason have any mould stone in his place, he shall give him a mould stone, and sett him on worke; and if he have none, the mason shall refresh him with money unto the next lodge."

This regulation is explicit. It not only infers the right of visit, but it declares that the strange brother shall be welcomed. It refers, however, only to the case of "strange fellowes," whom we now denominate transient brethren. But in the case of brethren who reside in the place where the lodge is situated, to which they demand admittance, other and subsequent regulations have been created. In this case it seems to be necessary that the visiting brother shall be a member of some other lodge. This doctrine is expressed in the following sections of the Constitution of the Grand Lodge of England: "A brother, who is not a subscribing member to some lodge, shall not be permitted to visit any one lodge in the town or place where he resides, more than once during his secession from the craft." P. 89.

A non-subscribing brother is permitted to visit each lodge once, because it is supposed that this visit is made for the purpose of enabling him to make a selection of the one in which he may prefer working. But afterwards he is excluded, in order to discountenance those brethren who wish to continue members of the order, and to partake of its benefits, without contributing to its support.

---

* I shall not enter upon the question that has been mooted by Brother Moore, [*Freemason's Mag.* vol. iii. 225,] whether this is an inherent right. It will be sufficient, as seen above, that the right is secured by the oldest regulations.

Another regulation on this subject is, that no visitor can be admitted into a lodge, unless he is personally vouched for by a brother present, or has submitted to a due examination.

A fourth regulation, and one that has lately given occasion to considerable discussion, is, that a strange brother shall furnish the lodge he desires to visit with a certificate of his good standing in the order. The regulation requiring certificates has been said by some to be an innovation. That it is not so, but, on the contrary, was in force at an early period, will appear from the following extract, from the "Regulations made in General Assembly, Dec. 27, 1663," under the Grand Mastership of the Earl of St. Albans: "3. That no person hereafter who shall be accepted a Freemason, shall be admitted into any lodge or assembly, until he has brought a certificate of the time and place of his acceptation, from the lodge that accepted him, unto the Master of that limit or division where such a lodge is kept." This regulation has since been reiterated on several occasions; by the Grand Lodge of England in 1772, and at subsequent periods by several of the Grand Lodges of this and other countries.

The right of visit is, therefore, regulated by the following principles : Transient brethren may visit lodges, provided they prove themselves qualified by a voucher or by examination, and by the possession of a certificate; and resident brethren after the first visit, only while they are contributing members to the order.

VOTING. Voting in lodges *viva voce* is an innovation. The ancient method was by holding up one of the hands. In the regulations of the Grand Lodge of England, revised in 1767, it is said, "The opinions or votes of the members are always to be signified by each holding up one of his hands; which uplifted hands the Grand Wardens are to count, unless the number of hands be so unequal as to render the counting useless. Nor should any other kind of division be ever admitted on such occasions."

VOUCHING. To vouch is to bear witness; vouching for a brother is, therefore, bearing witness that he is a true and trusty mason. And no one can, of course, give this testimony of a stranger's character, unless he has personally satisfied himself of his qualifications.

A candidate's letter must be signed by two brethren, one of whom vouches for his possessing the necessary qualifications, moral, mental, and physical, and is, hence, called the voucher; and the other, upon this vouching, recommends him to the lodge; and no candidate, unless thus properly vouched for, can be suffered to enter upon the ceremonies of initiation.

W. -

WAGES. There are various masonic traditions respecting the wages paid to the workmen at the building of the temple. The whole is stated to have been equal to six hundred and seventy-two millions of dollars, but the authorities differ as to the proportion in which it was distributed. Of course, the higher the degree, the higher must have been the amount of wages. A Master must have received more than a Fellow-Craft.

There was an old tradition among the English masons, that the men were paid in their lodges by shekels—a silver coin of about the value of fifty cents—and that the amount was regulated by the square of the number of the degree that the workman had attained. Thus, the Entered Apprentice received one shekel per day; the Fellow-Craft, who had advanced to the second degree, received the square of 2, or $2 \times 2 = 4$ shekels; and the Markman, or third degree, received the square of 3, or $3 \times 3 = 9$ shekels; whilst the ninth degree, or Super-Excellent Mason, received the square of 9, or $9 \times 9 = 81$ shekels.

According to this tradition, the pay-roll would be as follows:

An Entered Apprentice received 1 shekel or			. .	$00 50 cts.
A Fellow-Craft,	"	4	"	. .	2 50
A Mark Man,	"	9	"	. .	4 50
A Mark Master,	"	16	"	. .	8 00
A Master Mason,	"	25	"	. .	12 50
An Architect,	"	36	"	. .	18 00
A Grand Architect,	"	49	"	. .	24 50
An Excellent Mason,	"	64	"	. .	32 00
A Super-Excellent Mason,		81	"	. .	40 50

But this calculation seems to have been only a fanciful speculation of some of our ancient brethren.

The traditions preserved among us relate only to the pay of the Fellow-Crafts, and carry with them a much greater air of probability.

According to these, such of the Fellow-Crafts as worked in the quarries, and had been made the possessors of a mark, received their wages in specie, at the rate of a half shekel a day, and were paid on the sixth day of the week, at the office of the Senior Grand Warden of their lodge. But all the other Fellow-Crafts received theirs in the middle chamber, and were paid in corn, wine, and oil, according to the stipulation of King Solomon with Hiram, King of Tyre: "And, behold, I will give to thy servants, the hewers that cut timber, twenty thousand measures of beaten wheat, and twenty thousand measures of barley, twenty thousand measures of wine, and twenty thousand baths of oil." 2 Chron. ii. 10.

WARDENS. Two officers in a symbolic lodge, whose duty it is to assist the Worshipful Master in the government of the craft. The first of these officers is called the Senior, and the second the Junior, Warden.

Senior Warden. The duties of a Senior Warden are highly

important He is, under the Master, to superintend the craft during labour, and, in his absence, to preside over the lodge. With the Worshipful Master and the Junior Warden, he represents the lodge in the Grand Lodge. The Senior Warden has the privilege of appointing the Junior Deacon; and to him, when the Master is otherwise engaged, are all reports to be made by that officer. His jewel is a level—an emblem of the equality and harmony which should exist among Masons in the lodge while at work. Before the Senior Warden is placed, and he carries in all processions, a column, which is a representation of the right-hand pillar that stood at the porch of King Solomon's Temple.

In case of the death, removal from the State, or expulsion of the Master, the Senior Warden presides over the lodge for the remainder of his term of office. During the temporary absence the Master, the Senior Warden will, sometimes, through courtesy, resign the chair to a former Past Master; yet, in this case, the latter officer derives his authority from the Warden, and cannot act until this officer has congregated the lodge. The same thing is applicable to the Junior Warden, in case of the absence both of the Master and the Senior Warden. This rule arises from the fact that the Warrant of Constitution is granted to the Master, Wardens, and their successors in office, and not to the members of the lodge. A lodge, therefore, cannot be legally congregated without the presence of at least one of these officers, or a Past Master.

Junior Warden. The Junior Warden presides over the craft during refreshment, and in the absence of the Worshipful Master and Senior Warden, he performs the duties of presiding officer. The jewel of the Junior Warden is a plumb, emblematic of the rectitude of conduct which should distinguish the brethren, when, during the hours of refreshment, they are beyond the precincts of the lodge. His seat is in the S.·., and he represents the Pillar of Beauty. He has placed before him, and carries in procession, a column, which is the representative of the left-hand pillar which stood at the porch of Solomon's Temple.*

One other regulation in relation to these officers, requires to be mentioned. When the lodge, by death or otherwise, is deprived of the services of any of the other officers, an election may be immediately held, under the dispensation of the Grand Master, to supply the vacancy. But no election can be had to supply the place *ad interim*, of either the Master or Wardens, while one of the three remains. If two of them, as, for example, the Master and Senior Warden, have died or been deposed, the Junior Warden must occupy the chair during the remainder of the term, and appoints his Wardens *pro tempore* at each communication, until the regular constitutional night of election. It is only in the case where the whole three have died, or otherwise left the lodge, that a dispensation can be granted for an election to supply their place. Because, by the regulation granting to them only the Warrant of Constitution, without, at least, one of them to preside, and to assume the authority delegated by the Warrant of Constitution, the lodge is virtually extinct.

The situation of the three superior officers in the lodge differs somewhat in the different rites. In the French rite, they are placed in the east, in a triangular form; in the Scotch rite, the Wardens are in the west; in the York rite their respective situations are well known.

The Senior and Junior Wardens are also officers in an Encampment of Knights Templar, whose duties are, in some respects, similar to those of the Senior Deacon in a symbolic lodge.

WARDENS, GRAND. The Grand Wardens, who are the

---

* The two columns which, in the York rite, are small, and placed upon the pedestals of the two Wardens, are much better represented in the French rite. There, two large pillars of bronze, ornamented with net-work, lily-work, and pomegranates, are placed on each side of the entrance of the lodge, in the west, and at their bases are placed two triangular tables, at which the Wardens are seated.

assistants of the Grand Master in the government of the Grand Lodge, must be Past Masters of skill and good report. In the absence of the Grand and Deputy Grand Master, the Senior Grand Warden takes the chair, and in his absence, the Junior. And, in case of the death of the Grand Master, the same order of precedence is to be observed, until a new Grand Master is elected.

In visitations, when the Grand Master and his Deputy are absent, the Senior or Junior Grand Warden may preside, but in this case he acts only as a Deputy, and must be.received with the honours due to his rank, the Master of the lodge sitting on his right hand.

When a Grand Warden attends in the procession of a private lodge, he takes place immediately after the Master of the lodge, and two Deacons, with black rods, are to attend him, but the Book of Constitutions is not borne before him : this can only be carried in a procession where the Grand Master or his Deputy is present.

WARDER. An officer in an Encampment of Knights Templar, whose duties are similar in general to those of the Junior Deacon of a symbolic lodge.

WARRANT OF CONSTITUTION. No assemblage of Masons can be legally congregated for work, as a lodge, except under the authority of a Warrant of Constitution, granted by some Grand Lodge. This regulation has been in existence ever since the present organization of Grand Lodges, though formerly, a sufficient number of brethren meeting together within a certain district, with the consent of the civil authorities of the place, were empowered to make Masons, and to practice the rites of Freemasonry ; and this privilege was inherent in them as individuals : it was, however, on the organization of the order in its present form, resigned into the hands of the Grand Lodges.

The Warrant of Constitution is granted to the Master and

Wardens, and to their successors in office; it continues in force
only during the pleasure of the Grand Lodge, and may, therefore,
at any time be revoked, and the lodge dissolved by a vote of that
body.   This will, however, never be done, unless the lodge has
violated the ancient landmarks, or failed to pay due respect and
obedience to the Grand Lodge.

When a Warrant of Constitution is revoked, or recalled, the
jewels, furniture, and funds of the lodge revert to the Grand
Lodge.

Lastly, as a lodge holds its communications only under the
authority of this Warrant of Constitution, no lodge can be opened,
or proceed to business, unless it be present.   If it be mislaid or
destroyed, it must be recovered, or another obtained; and until
that is done, the communications of the lodge must be suspended;
and if the Warrant of Constitution be taken out of the room, during the session of the lodge, the authority of the Master instantly
ceases.

It is called a " Warrant of Constitution," because it is the in-
trument which authorizes or *warrants* the persons therein named
to open and *constitute* a lodge.

WELCOME.   It is the duty of every lodge to welcome and
clothe every worthy and well-qualified brother who visits it.
That is, to receive him with the honours due to his rank, and to
furnish him, if necessary, with the proper investiture.   And a
particular officer, the Senior Deacon, is directed to see that this
duty is performed.

WEST.   In the early ages of the world, the wisdom of men
was concentrated in the easternmost parts of the earth; and the
nations which had disseminated themselves along the shores of
the Mediterranean, to the west of the plains of Shinar, were obliged
to return towards the East in search of the knowledge of their
forefathers.   The West was then a place of darkness, and he who
sought light was obliged to leave it and travel to the East.   In

astronomy, there is the same peculiarity in relation to the course of light. The earth revolves upon its axis from west to east. But the sun rises in the latter point, and while the eastern hemisphere is enjoying the light of day, the western parts of the globe are enveloped in darkness; until, by the diurnal revolution of the earth, they are brought towards the East, and placed within the influence of the enlightening rays of the solar orb. Masons do not forget these facts in history and science; and they know that he who, being in the darkness of the West, would seek true light, must travel to the East.

WHITE. One of the emblematic colours of masonry, which is preserved in the apron and gloves, with which the initiate is invested. It is a symbol of innocence and purity. The white investiture, as may be seen throughout this work, was a part of the ceremonies of all the ancient mysteries.

WIDOW'S SON. One of the most illustrious personages in masonic history is so called, because he is described in Scripture as having been "the son of a widow of the tribe of Napthali."

WINDING STAIRS. These constitute an important part of the esoteric instruction of masonry. We are told in 1 Kings vi. 8, that "they went up with winding stairs into the middle chamber." Masonic tradition tells that there were fifteen steps, divided into unequal courses. The English Masons formerly said that there were twenty-seven, divided into one, three, five, seven, and eleven, but they have now abandoned the eleven of the last course, and leave but sixteen. The one they refer to the unity of God.

WISDOM. One of the three principal supports of masonry. It is represented by the Ionic column, and the W∴ M∴; because, the Ionic column wisely combines the strength without

the massiveness of the Doric; with the grace, without the exu-
berance of ornament of the Corinthian; and because it is the
duty of the W∴ M∴ to superintend, instruct, and enlighten the
craft by his superior wisdom. Solomon, King of Israel, is also
considered as the column of wisdom that supported the temple.

WOMAN. The objection so often made by the fair sex, that
they are most ungallantly refused an entrance into our order,
and a knowledge of our secrets, is best answered by a reference to
the originally operative character of our institution. That
woman is not admitted to a participation in our rites and ceremonies, is most true. But it is not because we deem her unworthy
or unfaithful, or deny her the mind to understand, or the heart to
appreciate our principles; but simply because, in the very organization of masonry, man alone can fulfil the duties it inculcates, or perform the labours it enjoins. Free and speculative masonry is but an application of the art of operative masonry to moral and intellectual purposes. Our ancestors worked at the construction of the Temple of Jerusalem; while we are engaged in
the erection of a more immortal edifice—the temple of the mind.
They employed their implements for merely mechanical purposes;
we use them symbolically, with more exalted designs.

Thus, in all our emblems, our language, and our rites, there
is a beautiful exemplification and application of the rules of operative masonry, as it was exercised at the building of the temple.
And as King Solomon employed in the construction of that edifice, only hale and hearty men, and cunning workmen, so our
lodges, in imitation of that great exemplar, demand as the indispensable requisite to admission, that the candidate shall be free-
born, of lawful age, and in the possession of all his limbs and
members, that he may be capable of performing such work as the
Master shall assign to him.

Hence, it must be apparent that the admission of women into
our order would be attended with a singular anomaly. As they
worked not at the temple, neither can they work with us. But

we love and cherish them not the less. One of the holiest of our mystic rites inculcates a reverence for the widow, and pity for the widow's son. The wife, the mother, the sister, and the daughter of the Mason, exercise a peculiar claim upon each Mason's heart and affections. And while we know that woman's smile, like the mild beams of an April sun, reflects a brighter splendour on the light of prosperity, and warms with grateful glow the chilliness of adversity, we regret, not the less deeply, because unavailingly, that no ray of that sun can illume the recesses of our lodge, and call our weary workmen from their labours to refreshment.

WORK. See *Labour.*

WORKING TOOLS. See *Implements.*

WORSHIPFUL. The title given to a symbolic lodge, and to its presiding officer, the Master. Past Masters, after leaving the chair, still retain the title of Worshipful. In the French rite, the lodge is called "Respectable," and the Master "le Vénérable." See *Master of a Lodge,* for the duties of this officer.

X.

XEROPHAGISTS. Pope Clement XII. having issued a Bull forbidding the practice of Freemasonry, the Masons of Italy, who continued to meet, for the purpose of avoiding the penalties of the Bull, called themselves Xerophagists. The word means literally *dry livers,* persons who do not drink, and they adopted the title, because they introduced something like the principle of total abstinence from intoxicating drinks into the institution.

44*

Y.

YEAR OF LIGHT. *Anno Lucis.* The date used by symbolic Masons, as being the era of the creation, when LIGHT was called into existence by the fiat of the Almighty, and when the true principles which distinguish our order first received their birth. Masons do not now adopt this era, because they any longer believe that Freemasonry, as it now appears, is to be dated from the creation; but simply, because the great moral and religious system, which masonry has preserved amid ages of darkness, is coeval with the hour when the Supreme Will called light and life into existence.

YORK. A city in the north of England, memorable for being the place where Freemasonry was officially re-established in that kingdom, and the first Grand Lodge formed in 926, by Prince Edwin, the brother of King Athelstane, from whom he purchased a free charter for that purpose.*

YORK RITE. The Ancient York rite is that practised by all English and American lodges, though it has deviated somewhat from its original purity. It derives its name from the city of York, where the first Grand Lodge of England was held.

The Ancient York rite originally consisted of but the three primitive degrees of Ancient Craft Masonry, but in this country four others have been added to it; and its degrees, as it is at present practised, are as follows: 1, Entered Apprentice; 2, Fellow-Craft; 3, Master Mason; 4, Mark Master; 5, Past Master; 6, Most Excellent Master; 7, Holy Royal Arch. In some of the United States, two other degrees are also given, in this rite, those of Royal and Select Master. The order of High Priest-

---

* See this work, p. 168.

hood is also given, as an honorary degree appertaining to the presiding officer of a Royal Arch Chapter.

The York rite is the mother of all the other rites; from it, they have separated as so many schisms : it is the most ancient, the most simple, and most scientific, and so far as my knowledge of the other rites extends, with the principal of which I am sufficiently acquainted, I may be permitted to say, that it is the only one in which the true system of symbolic instruction has been preserved.

Z.

ZEDEKIAH. The last King of Judah, before the captivity of Babylon, in whose reign the Temple was destroyed by Nebuchadnezzar. The eyes of Zedekiah were put out, and being loaded with chains of brass, he was carried a captive to Babylon, where he afterwards died.

ZÆNITH. That point of the heavens situated immediately over the head of the spectator, and which the sun reaches at meridian. The Supreme Councils of the 33d degree of the Ancient Scotch rite, do not date their documents as other Masons do, from the *Orient*, but from the *Zenith.*

ZEREDATHA. A town of Judea, 35 miles north of Jerusalem, in the clay ground near which, Hiram Abif cast the sacred vessels of the Temple. See *Clay Grounds.*

ZERUBBABEL. The grandson, though called by Ezra, the son, of Salathiel, who was the son of Jeconiah, King of Judah. He was, therefore, of the royal race of David. He was born at Babylon, as the Hebrew signification of his name imports, and returned to Jerusalem in the beginning of the reign of Cyrus,

with the sacred vessels of the Temple, which Cyrus had committed to his care, as the chief of the Jews who were in captivity
at Babylon.   He laid the foundations of the second Temple, and
restored the worship of the Lord and the usual sacrifices.   He
is represented by the second officer in the Royal Arch degree.
The incidents of Zerubbabel' life are also referred to in several
other degrees, such as Knight of the Red Cross, Knight of the
East, and Prince of Jerusalem.

ZINNENDORF, RITE OF.   Count Zinnendorf, chief physician of the Emperor Charles VI., invented a new rite, which was
a modification of the Illuminism of Avignon, adding to the mysteries of Swedenborg, of which this latter rite was principally
composed, several things taken from the Scotch, German, and
Swedish degrees, as well as from Templar Masonry.   His system
consisted of seven degrees, divided into three sections, as follows :—

I. *Blue, or St. John's Masonry.*—1, Entered Apprentice; 2,
Fellow-Craft; 3, Master Mason.

II. *Red Masonry.*—4, Scotch Apprentice and Fellow-Craft;
5, Scotch Master.

III. *Capitular Masonry.*—6, Favourite of St. John; 7, Elected
Brother.

Zinnendorf died in the year 1800, having attempted, without
success, to introduce his system into England.

THE END.

New Orleans Scottish Rite College

http://www.youtube.com/c/NewOrleansScottishRiteCollege

Clear, Easy to Watch
Scottish Rite and Craft Lodge
Video Education

www.ingramcontent.com/pod-product-compliance
Lightning Source LLC
Chambersburg PA
CBHW030632270326
41929CB00007B/50